Continental Order?

CRITICAL MEDIA STUDIES
INSTITUTIONS, POLITICS, AND CULTURE

Series Editor
Andrew Calabrese, University of Colorado

Advisory Board

Recent Titles in the Series

Forthcoming in the Series

Continental Order?

Integrating North America for Cybercapitalism

Edited by
Vincent Mosco and Dan Schiller

ROWMAN & LITTLEFIELD PUBLISHERS, INC.
Lanham • *Boulder* • *New York* • *Oxford*

ROWMAN & LITTLEFIELD PUBLISHERS, INC.

Published in the United States of America
by Rowman & Littlefield Publishers, Inc.
4720 Boston Way, Lanham, Maryland 20706
www.rowmanlittlefield.com

12 Hid's Copse Road, Cumnor Hill, Oxford OX2 9JJ, England

British Library Cataloguing in Publication Information Available

Library of Congress Cataloging-in-Publication Data

Continental order? : integrating North America for cybercapitalism / edited by Vincent
Mosco and Dan Schiller.
   p. cm.
   Includes bibliographical references and index.
   ISBN 0-7425-0953-2 (alk. paper) — ISBN 0-7425-0954-0 (pbk. : alk. paper)
   1. North America—Economic integration. 2. Canada. Treaties, etc. 1992 Oct. 7. I.
Mosco, Vincent. II. Schiller, Dan, 1951–

HC95.C665 2001
333.1'7—dc21   2001019014

Printed in the United States of America

∞™ The paper used in this publication meets the minimum requirements of
American National Standard for Information Sciences—Permanence of Paper
for Printed Library Materials, ANSI/NISO Z39.48-1992.

Contents

1

Introduction: Integrating a Continent for a Transnational World

Dan Schiller and Vincent Mosco

South of the United States, April 1999 saw the first season-opening baseball game played in Mexico, as the Colorado Rockies triumphed against the San Diego Padres in Monterrey (regular-season play dates to 1996). To the north, meanwhile, as summer waned, the six major league Canadian hockey teams announced their demand (subsequently denied) for an annual subsidy of $30 million (CD) from the Canadian government to forestall their relocation to more lucrative home bases across the border in the United States.

These are not isolated incidents. Rather, they are points on the main trend-line of contemporary social development: the transnationalization of the capitalist political economy. They are indicative, more specifically, of a dramatic transformation occurring within that political economy's leading sector. The term "cybercapitalism," denoting the market system's rapidly deepening reliance on networked business processes, covers a vast field of active change. On one side, network systems that move information—voices, images, videos, and data—instantly around the globe have become a prime business necessity. On the other side, the process of market development itself has gripped networked communications and information industries, as this sector morphs into a general platform for subsequent capitalist development. *Continental Order? Integrating North America for Cybercapitalism* engages this metamorphosis through a series of linked studies on the converging culture, media, telecommunications, and information industries in North America since the 1989 Canada–U.S. Free Trade Agreement (CUSFTA) and the 1993 North American Free Trade Agreement (NAFTA).

This book assesses the extent of continental integration throughout these industries, within the context of more encompassing processes of transnational social reorganization. In order to do this, it adopts a broadly political economic perspective that starts from the relationships between business, labor, and government, and concentrates on the analysis of corporate decision making and resource deployment.

Following this chapter, which provides an overarching analysis of the processes that are underway, are a series of contributions by experts addressing specific sectors and problems: newspapers and magazines, video and film, telecommunications and new media, sport and leisure, marketing, and education. We also feature an encompassing analytical assessment by an economic historian. Our goal is to generate improved understanding of the emerging phase of transnational cybercapitalist development in culture and communications.

JUSTIFICATION AND FOCUS

Why study the reconstitution of the communications and culture industries in the context of the North American political economy during the post-NAFTA period? What makes North America a salient entry point for examining processes of political-economic reorganization in the communications and cultural industry? Are there ways in which the study of the communications and culture industry throws light on present-day structural changes throughout North America?

The region comprising the United States, Mexico, and Canada is vital in its own right, as this continent comprises a primary component of the global political economy. Canada is the United States' largest trading partner, and Mexico, vaulting over Japan in the wake of the NAFTA accords, has become its second largest; the NAFTA region in itself accounts for a substantial share of the global economy. In addition, it constitutes the largest of the three territorial blocs—the other two span Europe on the one hand, and Japan and Southeast Asia on the other—that together account for the lion's share of world economic activity. Finally, the shifts under way within North America sometimes can claim a portentous weight.

The North American region long has provided a site for experiments in globalization. Just as Green Revolution agricultural policies and practices were first instituted on a large scale in Mexico during the 1940s, today "Mexico has become a testing ground for the products of the imminent biorevolution" (Otero, Scott, and Gilbreth 1997, 257–258). Specific policy levers like the national treatment provisions of CUSFTA and NAFTA, moreover, have functioned as templates for other regional agreements such as the 1994 Colonia Protocol of the Mercado Común del Sur (MERCOSUR) free trade agreement that liberalized cross-border investment among Brazil, Argentina, Paraguay, and Uruguay (Galperin 1999), and the Mexican–European Union Free Trade Agreement of 2000.[1]

CUSFTA and NAFTA also constituted models for global trade negotiations that, complementing and extending the framework supplied by the existing

General Agreement on Tariffs and Trade (GATT; which Mexico endorsed in 1986), resulted in the formation of the World Trade Organization (WTO). Furthermore, NAFTA provisions to protect foreign investors provided a breakthrough in international governance that the WTO continues to try to incorporate in a global framework. Not only did NAFTA provide procedures for resolving disputes between governments and foreign investors through binding arbitration, it also took the further step of establishing a broad definition of expropriation that allows a foreign firm to sue a government for compensation against regulations that negatively affect the firm's investments (Ostry 2000, 48). This has been used primarily to win compensation for environmental regulations, as Virginia-based Ethyl Corporation did when it successfully sued the Canadian government for $19 million Canadian, thereby forcing a reversal of restrictions on the gasoline additive methylaydopentadienyl manganese tricarbonyl (MMT).

Things also work in the other direction; the WTO is being used today as an instrument to extend and harden NAFTA's neoliberal, or market-led, grip on that treaty's signatories. For example, as Catherine McKercher demonstrates in her chapter on the impact of NAFTA on the publishing industry, with a cultural exemption limiting its ability to act against Canada's protectionist policies in regard to magazines, the United States used the WTO to force Canada to end its restrictions on foreign magazine imports. During 2000, the Office of the U.S. Trade Representative also sought to use WTO guidelines to force changes within the telecommunications policies of both Canada and Mexico.

North America has, finally, furnished models for alternatives to continental integration on a neoliberal basis. For example, Canada's long experience with national cultural policies has served as an important standard for such policies in other parts of the world. These include promotional policies to support national cultural institutions like the Canadian Broadcasting Corporation (CBC) and to subsidize private-sector production in film and television, which, as the chapter by Ted Magder and Jonathan Burston documents, create cross-border conflicts within the context of the increasingly transnational film and video industry. They also include restrictive strategies, such as regulations that limit both foreign ownership of its cultural industries and the extent of foreign content of its radio and television broadcasts.

Having said this, we need to clarify the concept of "integration," or "convergence." Regional integration means something other than merely creating a geographic network of North American firms. As we will see, the continent hosts an increasing range of economic actors based outside of North America, but which have become important participants in the process of North American restructuring as well. Improved access to the giant U.S. domestic market has been a chief trigger of this investment. The French audiovisual company Vivendi built on its early activity in the province of Quebec by purchasing the Seagram corporation, a Canadian giant that prior to its purchase diversified itself into the global media industry by acquiring Universal Studios and Polygram Records. Major foreign consumer electronics companies, such as Sony and Thompson, have built extensive manufacturing plants in Mexico. As Richard B. Du Boff underlines in chapter 2, continental integration is a global corporate project, one of whose major foci is the North American region.

Du Boff also stresses that regional integration does not signify the elimination of fundamental economic disparities between and within the three nations. On the contrary. Integration instead builds on the glaring wage differentials between the United States and Canada on one side, and Mexico on the other. In the years following NAFTA, indeed, Mexico has experienced increasing income inequality, including a growing poverty rate (from 36 percent of households in 1992–1994 to 43 percent in 1996), and a 20 percent deterioration in real wages in the period 1994–1998 (Castro Rea 2000, 26–27). Therefore, no overarching convergence toward a shared, continent-wide standard of living may be projected. Absent radical social change, profound inequality of condition will persist—even as economic integration deepens.

Nor does integration portend a unitary North American monoculture. The transnationalization of commercial cultural production and distribution involves differentiation as well as amalgamation. It is characteristic that Spanish-language as well as English-language audiovisual services are both flourishing, as media corporations target populations across the region (and beyond). Likewise in Canada, communications companies aim to reach English, French, and other language groups.

Integration does imply, however, that economic relations between Canada, the United States, and Mexico are entering a new phase of transnational development and consolidation. Within Mexico, a vast border belt of capital-intensive export-oriented industry has been created. As manufacturing investment has relocated, Du Boff shows that corporate supply-chains extend, intrafirm transactions (as well as traditional exports and imports) increase, and transnational corporations (TNCs) continue to reorganize the different phases of the production and distribution process on a world scale. But uneven economic development—and cultural variation—are being reconstituted, rather than eradicated. How then can one make sense of this restructuring process? What are its typifying features and strategies? And what are its major implications?

A careful inventory and analysis of changing patterns of political-economic practice throughout the culture and communications sector speaks to these questions. Developments in manufacturing, energy, and transportation claim much of the limelight in the business press. However, the related transnationalization of cultural and informational production and communications distribution is every bit as vital. In fields as diverse as television networking, telecommunications service provision, advertising and marketing, and education, the global political economy is being redefined. Indeed, developments in communications and culture are in a symbiotic relationship with the more well-remarked changes that are occurring in manufacturing and other seemingly disparate areas—as is illustrated in Lora E. Taub and Dan Schiller's chapter on transnationally networked educational provision.

The region thus comprises a central site for understanding the scope and character of the mutations taking place within capitalism, as the political economy begins to pivot more extensively and intensively around communications and culture. With that said, it is also important to stress at the outset that the process of integrating a continent for cybercapitalism faces numerous challenges, limitations, and roadblocks, including political opposition and movements to create alternatives to the agenda advanced by NAFTA.

CENTRAL ISSUES

This book, which builds on important earlier work in the area (McAnany and Wilkinson 1996), covers a wide range of topics but is unified around two central concerns. First, it examines the history of continental integration by addressing major steps in the run-up to the free trade agreements. It demonstrates how free trade agreements embody both continuities, the extension of the marketplace for example, and discontinuities, such as the establishment of supranational mechanisms for managing the continent.

Second, this book is interested in the different forms of convergence or integration that we can now observe across the North American continent. As we have already said, integration does not entail any fundamental break with historical patterns of uneven development. But the current stage of development unfolds through a process of convergence at several levels, beginning with the technology, which is coming together around a common digital language facilitating the physical integration of networks and devices. It also refers to the convergence of organizations, especially businesses, that use convergent communications and information technologies to build powerful vertically and horizontally integrated structures that increasingly span the continent and beyond. Moreover, convergence draws these organizations and their products into an increasingly integrated electronic services arena. Consequently, traditional economic and policy divisions among a number of sectors that, however linked, were historically treated separately as the print media, electronic media, and telecommunications and information industries are being crosscut. Convergence also takes on a spatial significance as the drawing together of technologies, institutions, and whole sectors of the economy redraws the continental map to create closer connections between cross-border regions, new notions of what constitutes borders, and new means of policing them. Finally, convergence holds powerful implications for labor, including tendencies toward the integration of trade unions once divided by industry or national boundaries.

In addition, though to a lesser extent, this book takes up the tensions, pressure points, and conflicts that accompany this process. These include the relationships of national states to TNCs that span the continent and, often, beyond. Furthermore, it examines the relationship between the North American regime and global organizations like the WTO, which was modeled in part on NAFTA policies and practices but which is struggling to supersede them. Additionally, this book addresses the conflicts between continental integration and organizations and movements opposed to it, including labor and civil society organizations.

The culture and communications industries provide a unique prism through which to view these stress points. These industries have not easily fit into broad policies of economic integration because their influence extends beyond markets to issues like access to information and communications that go to the heart of governance and democracy. As a result, most treaties have conferred special status on the cultural sector, exempting it from the broad strokes of free trade language. But this cultural exceptionalism is increasingly under attack, partly because of another trend to which we give special attention.

The expansion of the industries that occupy this book is led by increasingly dense networks of business-to-business communications. While the growth of mass media and the cultivation of global audiences for all forms of communications, cultural, and informational products takes up considerable attention, it has been the acceleration in business-to-business communications that, we contend, tips the balance by pressuring governments to incorporate all forms of networked communications within the scope of free trade, and thus to eliminate remaining impediments to market expansion (Oppel 2000). As a result, this book emphasizes the development of continental networks of inter- and intracorporate communications and their links to global communications networks.

THE RUN-UP TO NAFTA

National Control and Public Service Principles

The expansion of transnational capital, which encompasses North American integration, confronts two primary political impediments. These are national control[2]—the organization of economic, social, political, and cultural life around the nation-state axis—and public service—the idea that principles of citizenship, equality, and democratic participation count as much as or more than the market and private property in decision making. The major processes behind continent-wide and global trade agreements have been driven by the business-led attempt selectively to reduce national control and generally to eliminate public service principles as alternative standards for reaching decisions about economic, political, and cultural life. Substantiating this point requires some historical elaboration.

The history of economic integration across the NAFTA region does not by any means commence with the treaty instrument that was finalized in 1993, or with the 1989 CUSFTA that preceded it. Far from it. In the nineteenth century, North American development already had long proceeded on a supranational basis, as it was shaped by rival quests for empire by the contending powers of that time: England, France, Spain, and—from the moment of its founding—the United States. As it ousted the established European powers, the United States seized large chunks of Mexican territory by military force. It then turned to make profitable use of its privileged access to Canadian and Mexican staples and raw materials. Where its business interests saw prospective benefits, the United States also found means of harnessing Mexican and Canadian immigrant labor. Early transport and communications networks linking the three countries comprised a needed hinge for these developments.

Exposed by the misfortune of geography, Canada and Mexico were subjected to repeated episodes of U.S. expansionism and to generalized U.S. political-economic dominance. The history of the continent's communications and culture industry, however, both exemplifies and importantly modifies this portrait of unrelieved U.S. domination.

U.S. companies certainly carved out market control across great reaches of Canadian culture. Throughout the first half of the twentieth century, for example, the giant American Telephone and Telegraph (AT&T) corporation managed much of the telecommunications grid throughout both the United States and Canada. Unified control was advantageous, in that it allowed an unusually wide application of cross-border private-line circuits—and the organizational innovations that relied on them—to big businesses (and military agencies). Unified control under AT&T's stewardship was also expressed through the North American Numbering Plan. This was an area-code scheme that accommodated an interoperable telecommunications service within the United States and Canada through a division of the two countries into eighty-three uniquely designated three-digit zones. Developed by AT&T beginning in the early 1940s (and eventually taking in most of the Caribbean as well), this numbering plan did not require callers throughout the two linked nations to employ country codes, while callers elsewhere used the country code "1" to reach locations throughout both the United States and Canada (U.S. Federal Communications Commission [U.S. FCC] 1997, 3).

These developments notwithstanding, Canadian capital eventually supplanted what had been direct U.S. corporate control over the core of Canada's telephone system, when Bell Canada shook off its ties to AT&T—a process that occurred between 1956 and 1975. (Three prairie provinces already had long since assumed direct control over telecommunications within their boundaries.) Nationwide, moreover, as Vanda Rideout and Andrew Reddick's chapter on new media policy explains, public service principles were used by government regulators to promote inclusive access to Canada's telecommunications system, extending service to even remote and rural users.

A similar pattern may be detected on the mass media side. By the 1990s, as McKercher's and Magder and Burston's chapters document, U.S. companies controlled over 60 percent of the Canadian magazine market, 75 percent of Canadians' television viewing, and all but 2 percent of the country's cinema attendance. Nevertheless, the establishment of the CBC meant that first in radio and then in television, Canada expressed vital public service principles including rules protecting a minimum of Canadian content, state support for a national information service, and limitations on advertisements. The French language in Quebec and, to a lesser degree, throughout French-speaking centers in English Canada, historically screened portions of Canada from direct U.S. influence over culture. Canada's educational system, finally, comprised a public service operation par excellence that recognized teachers unions and provided widespread free access.

Mexico's communications and cultural sector exhibits a distinct yet partly comparable dualism. On the one hand, U.S. companies again exerted a powerful early pressure. During the decades spanning the turn of the twentieth century, for example, most Mexican textbooks were written by U.S. authors and published by the New York–based Appleton Publishing Company (Cockcroft 1998, 84). The U.S. company International Telephone and Telegraph Corporation (ITT) obtained one of two major Mexican telephone concessions in the 1920s (the other went to the Swedish company Ericsson). In the 1920s, Mexico lagged behind only Canada in the volume of U.S. radio equipment it imported (Schwoch 1990, 106, 142–143). Through alliances with the Mexican capitalist Emilio Azcárraga Vidaurreta (who would go on to introduce television to Mexico after World War II) during the interwar era, both the National Broadcasting Company (NBC) and the Columbia Broadcasting Systems (CBS) built up important radio network businesses in Mexico and elsewhere in Latin America (Sinclair 1999, 13–15).

On the other hand, however, as explained in Enrique E. Sánchez-Ruiz's and Andrew Paxman and Alex M. Saragoza's chapters, which address NAFTA's impact on Mexico's audiovisual sector, national capital successfully colonized Mexican broadcasting and, after a series of mergers, formed the Televisa Group (1972), with its powerful though informal and sometimes unstable links to the Mexican state. These two chapters provide two different lenses through which to view this important development. Sánchez-Ruiz presents a structuralist perspective on the Mexican state, whereas Paxman and Saragoza offer a more instrumentalist account. Nevertheless, their conclusions are similar. Televisa built itself up into a diversified media corporation, with interests extending into other Latin American countries and, episodically beginning in the early 1960s, into the United States. Its vast programming operation produced the great majority of the shows it aired (Sinclair 1999, 39), which provided an important basis for further expansion. After foreign-owned enterprises in select Mexican industries were nationalized during the middle decades of the twentieth century, moreover, a state-run organization, Teléfonos de México (Telmex), gained operating control (in 1972) of the country's telecommunications network. Although Mexico differs from Canada in that public service principles did not become a significant factor in its media system, Mexican capital historically played—and, as is shown by the Sánchez-Ruiz and Paxman and Saragoza contributions to this volume, continues to play—a critical role in the country's culture and communications sector.

Though the point is often forgotten, the United States itself also developed a nationally controlled communications system. Indeed, the growth of a gigantic U.S. domestic market for cultural commodities provided a necessary foundation for subsequent transnational expansion. Nor were public service principles entirely absent in this, the core of global capitalism. From the New Deal (1932–1945) through the Great Society (1965–1968) periods, social welfare policies put capital throughout electronic communications and information on a (loose) tether. In retrospect, restrictions on media ownership seem particularly noteworthy.

The assertion of national control over communications and culture was not comprehensive in either Canada or Mexico. Various forms of dependence on imports from U.S. suppliers (of capital, of hardware, and of services and programming) signified that the development of the communications sector in both Canada and Mexico "was conditioned by the subordinate position which [the two countries] occup[y] within the world system, especially relative to the U.S." (Sinclair 1999, 33). Nonetheless, together with a variable commitment to some idea of public service, the emergence of national proprietorship, particularly over electronic communications, placed limits—limits that have only recently become apparent—on capital's continued self-expansion.

These limits were most significant where direct government operation prevailed. As long as there existed throughout the world state-run telecommunications systems (as in Mexico), and state-affiliated broadcast systems (as in Canada), the mode of growth of the U.S.–based capitalist communications and culture industry was largely confined to exports of cultural commodities, and traffic hand-offs and other forms of cooperation between national telecommunications carriers. In addition, nationally embedded public service principles obstructed the secular deepening and widening of market relationships and commercial advertising in and around network industries.

These were anything but parochial policy concerns. The greater portion of the transnationalizing corporate political economy had, by the 1980s, acquired a stake in their resolution.

Free Trade Policy and Foreign Direct Investment

The United States has long deployed the enticement of easy access to its domestic market as a policy weapon. Indeed, throughout the Cold War, the promise of such access constituted a vital plank in the United States' wider "containment" strategy against the erstwhile Soviet Union. The reconstruction of the Western European and Japanese economies during the 1950s rested on this selective free trade policy. These states, soon followed by others, were successfully encouraged to build up export-led domestic industries by the U.S. commitment to throw open its own unmatched national market (Greider 1997). In return, Japan, like several Western European countries, granted economic, military, and foreign policy concessions to the United States (Johnson 2000).

Despite an unrelieved emphasis by the United States on a free trade policy, however, during the 1980s and 1990s the seemingly unchanged doctrine accommodated a vitally enlarged agenda. To clear the way for a hoped-for new round of accumulation would require corporate reintegration on an expanded supranational basis. Foreign direct investment (FDI)—the amalgamation and integration of worldwide productive assets by TNCs—accordingly developed a new strategic focus, as capital within communications, culture, and information set itself the task of inventing "means to expand the market output to a global scale" (Schiller 1989, 32).

Systematic attempts to export private capital (FDI) were, of course, already of long standing. Active growth of TNCs based in the United States commenced on a significant scale as far back as the 1880s. A marked acceleration of FDI had occurred during the first two post–World War II decades, and this phase of expansion had been dominated overwhelmingly worldwide by U.S. capital. By the 1970s and 1980s, however, as European and Japanese companies claimed a growing role in several key industries, the picture of world FDI became more complex. On the one hand, flows of foreign investment into factories and offices were no longer so asymmetrical; the United States retained its leadership role, but TNCs based in other countries supplied an increasing proportion of worldwide FDI. Indeed, in a profound structural reversal, the United States became a net importer of capital. More foreign investment began to flow into the giant U.S. market, that is, than was flowing out of the United States toward the rest of the world. Moreover, a growing fraction of FDI—in absolute terms, truly significant quantities—began to move into less-developed countries. On the other hand, crucially, FDI no longer merely encompassed agricultural and extractive and manufacturing industries, but also began to include a growing set of culture and communications and other service industries.

Profound changes within the U.S.–based communications industry helped to catalyze these sweeping shifts in the character of FDI and in the trade policy that sought to sustain it.

The Changing Political Economy of the Communications Industry

Beginning as far back as the late 1950s, the U.S. telecommunications industry began to be systematically liberalized, engendering hothouse innovation in industrial and, secondarily, consumer markets. While business and residential use of the public switched telephone network increased, specialized services sold exclusively to corporate and government users expanded even more. Long-distance private-line services, use of which has been a key prerequisite of corporate networking applications, increased from an $81 million annual business in 1951 (2.2 percent of Bell System revenues) to a $1.4 billion business by 1976 (4.2 percent of Bell System revenues) (Schiller 1982, 15). Well-capitalized service suppliers catering to business users, such as Microwave Communications Incorporated (MCI) and Sprint, were authorized and soon claimed a significant share of the business market. A reorganization of corporate functions around networks commenced, as big businesses redesigned their U.S. (and sometimes Canadian) operations to take maximum advantage of this increasingly capacious and generative infrastructure. Corporations' growing reliance on extended production and sales chains relied on telecommunications networks to link and control multiple factories, warehouses, and sales offices.

Even before the breakup of AT&T in 1984, the U.S. telecommunications industry sought to export this emergent liberalized model. Large business users advanced policies that strengthened and expanded their evolving network platforms, as well as the overall commodification of networked culture and information services. Manufacturers, energy companies, banks and insurance companies, giant retailers, and other large firms relying extensively on telecommunications and information technology pressed for regulatory changes that would favor them with faster, more secure, more comprehensively integrated, and cheaper networks for their businesses. Because these business users were themselves mainly TNCs, their lobbying extended into the international arena (Schiller 1982). In the Canadian market, for example, by the mid-1980s organizations of large users like the Information Technology Association of Canada were promoting liberalized markets harmonized with those of the United States—among other things, to allow corporations to interconnect their own private networks with the public telecommunications network.

A corporate "right" to invest in network technologies and services was rapidly elevated into a new policy orthodoxy and incorporated in NAFTA. As the World Bank, the International Monetary Fund (IMF), and other "aid" agencies began to target telecommunications via a raft of new initiatives, an update of the reigning wisdom about communications and development—that telecommunications investment is a needful prerequisite of economic development (Jussawalla 1986)—burgeoned in the scholarly literature. A worldwide move toward transnationalized telecommunications networks and service offerings had been engendered. The U.S. computer industry, meanwhile, continued to enjoy munificent support from the federal government (principally the military), which supplied research and development funding as well as a large protected market, and worked closely with the liberalized sector of the telecommunications industry to develop and institutionalize new networking technologies. The largely deregulated, supranational Internet would eventually emerge as the outstanding result of this collaboration.

The latter half of the 1980s likewise witnessed the beginning of a globally significant reorganization in the U.S.–based culture industry. This push gained momentum insofar as the U.S. domestic market had been saturated in certain well-established areas, such as radio and television set manufacture. But a more important cause was the rapid development and commercialization of services based on a whole series of new electronic production and distribution technologies.

Between around 1975 and 1990, the traditional media—and analog broadcasting in the ultrahigh frequency and very high frequency bands in particular—were supplemented by cable television systems, home videos, and videocassette recorders; and wireless services and personal computers began to secure a growing market. Satellite direct-to-home (DTH) systems were innovated (though still largely unsuccessful). As this parade of new media rolled onward, existing media owners faced both threats and opportunities. Audiences were all too evidently drifting away from the mass-market model pioneered by radio and television broadcasters through earlier decades. Unless ownership of diversified media platforms could be consolidated, both existing media owners' and their leading advertisers' access to most-needed audiences might be jeopardized. Both direct sales and advertising revenue streams in turn were being placed at risk. Media owners began to clamor that the key to continued profitability was to acquire control over both programming, or content, and media distribution systems.

The U.S. communications industry had, as we have emphasized, long been the preeminent purveyor of movies, television programming, recordings, magazines, books, and other products to the global market. But relentless liberalization of the giant U.S. domestic market, beginning in the 1980s, encouraged media owners to accelerate their transnationalization initiatives, even as they also aggressively pursued cross-media consolidation deals. Acquiescence by the Federal Communications Commission (FCC) to Australian Rupert Murdoch's establishment of Fox Television Stations Incorporated, and the latter's purchase of six prime U.S. television broadcast stations from Metromedia in 1985, comprised a milestone. Although it took an additional decade to finalize, and though the result was accomplished only through a species of legerdemain, the FCC thereby acceded to foreign ownership well in excess of its long-standing 25 percent ownership cap (Sidak 1997, 205–214). This special treatment accorded to Murdoch's News Corporation turned what would once have been considered a foreign company with limited rights in the U.S. market into a de facto U.S. firm. By the time it had been finalized, as we will see, other large foreign companies had also assumed ownership of core U.S. media assets.

Substantial limits continued, to be sure, to obstruct foreign investment in the U.S. electronic media and in telecommunications; the process of market opening remained contentious and selective. Mexico's Televisa, for example, was denied ownership rights to U.S. television stations after a protracted legal struggle culminated in 1986 (soon afterward, however, Televisa did find ways back into U.S.–based satellite communications, television broadcasting, and even, briefly, sports newspapers [Sinclair 1999, 44–57, 97–117, passim]). To this day, no foreign company other than News Corporation has been allowed to acquire outright a major U.S. broadcast network or station group.

Nonetheless, it is indisputable that the world's dominant economic and military power threw open its culture and communications industry to progressively more significant foreign ownership. That the United States embarked on this course during the late 1980s must be seen as a radical policy change aimed at forging a new structural basis for transnational market expansion.

As liberalization proceeded throughout the U.S. communications industry, capital flooded in and the scale and scope of enterprise swiftly increased. The year 1985 furnished three milestones as General Electric acquired NBC, Loew's Corporation assumed control of CBS, and America Broadcasting Corporation (ABC) was taken over by Capital Cities (Auletta 1991). Time Incorporated then paired with Warner Brothers in 1989. Most of these combinations were without real historical precedent. When ITT sought to buy ABC in the mid-1960s, for example, that merger was stopped in its tracks by the federal government (Mazzocco 1994, 45–46). Media industry restructuring throughout the 1980s, in contrast, rapidly produced a handful of giant entertainment conglomerates, whose asset bases had been broadened to encompass film and recording companies, television and radio networks, broadcast station and cable groups, publishers, sports teams, and theme parks.

It should be stressed that these dramatic changes stemmed not only from a series of steps to liberalize the domestic market by corporate executives and government agencies, but also from the related Reagan-era weakening of forces that historically fought for regulations limiting the ability of capital in culture and communications to expand just as it preferred. Through the midcentury decades, in contrast, trade unions, educators, voluntary associations, and public interest organizations had succeeded in constraining at least somewhat the dominant market impulse.

As the policy of throwing open the U.S. market gained ground, and the U.S.–based communications and culture industry liberalized and concentrated, the vertically integrated titans that emerged were well equipped to move into foreign markets on a prospective new basis: that of FDI and the freedom to develop media systems as corporate-commercial enterprises. The continuing growth of FDI in manufacturing and other industries presented additional opportunities for expansion across borders—by suppliers of strategic information and communications technology and services.

Existing national restrictions on foreign investment throughout the world's communications systems and services, therefore, now began to constitute an increasingly visible drag on capital's continued growth—both within the communications sector and more generally. As political-economic frictions heightened, transnational capital turned to the U.S. state and other agencies for assistance.

To advance TNC network services in general, and media services in particular, nationally controlled communications institutions would have to be dissolved or marginalized, and public service principles would have to be sharply curtailed. U.S. corporate and political leaders lobbied ceaselessly during the 1980s and 1990s to foreground these sweeping changes within broader efforts to liberalize rules on investment and trade. Federal initiatives, private economic diplomacy, bilateral negotiations between states, and ostensibly multilateral organizations such as the World Bank, the IMF, the WTO, and the International Telecommunications Union all played roles. CUSFTA and NAFTA comprised prominent initiatives within this larger movement, and each was perceived as a prelude to a more encompassing push for liberalization of global trade and investment within the organizational context of the GATT/WTO. Had the WTO's contemplated Multilateral Agreement on Investment (MAI) initiative not met with fierce global resistance and been temporarily withdrawn, it would have pressed even further in the same direction. Renewed attempts to revive the MAI may yet do so.

Although U.S.–based companies and state agencies functioned as the historical source and center of the liberalization trend, it would be a mistake to view this process simply as a reflex of U.S. corporate or state power. Make no mistake: external pressures bore down hard on the policy options deemed acceptable by national elites in other countries. But so did likemindedness. By the 1980s, policymakers throughout Western Europe and Japan were realizing that traditional policies stressing national control and public service were limiting their own leading enterprises. Many therefore began to open their domestic markets to corporate commercial broadcasters, and a few (notably Britain) began to accede to corporate ownership of telecommunications systems. It would not take long for these entering wedges to split apart existing communications industry structures, and to place policies in this critical sector on a strikingly new basis.

A CULTURAL EXCEPTION?

The effective transnationalization of the communications and culture industry comprised the sine qua non of a new and more comprehensive phase of corporate transnationalization in general. Production chains that link multiple corporate sites across national borders, including those of a single giant business together with those of its needed suppliers and customers, require and rest upon ever more sophisticated network capabilities. Sales by consumer products companies into global markets require and rest upon routine access to commercial media advertising.

In this regard, however, the 1989 CUSFTA itself created a paradoxical obstacle. Even as free foreign trade and investment policies were strengthened, the culture and communications sector was allotted exceptional status. Under great pressure from supporters of Canadian culture, particularly from organizations representing cultural and communications workers, the Canadian government held out for an exemption for the cultural industries. For its part, the United States was under no such pressure. The United States viewed Canada's call for exempting cultural industries as embodying the very national control and public service principles that the United States was committed to eliminating. The United States thus resisted the exclusion of culture from the deal, fearing that the agreement might turn into the wrong model for future regional and international treaties. Negotiators settled on a compromise that indeed exempted culture from the agreement but permitted a party to retaliate against what it perceived to be cultural protectionism by taking action against other industries.[3]

The deal also severely restricted the creation of new government institutions, including state-supported monopolies that might give a party an advantage in any sector, including the cultural.[4] Finally, the agreement's "national treatment" provisions guaranteed that government agencies and regulatory bodies provide the same treatment for foreign firms wishing to do business as they do for nationally based firms. This created a market opening in culture because it meant that the Canadian Radio-Television and Telecommunications Commission (CRTC), Canada's national communications regulatory authority, would be expected to treat non-Canadian firms in culture, communications, and telecommunications just as it treated Canadian companies (Mosco 1990).

When it came time a few years later to extend CUSFTA to include Mexico, the United States pressed to lift the cultural exemption. Mexico barely objected. As Sánchez-Ruiz's and Paxman and Saragoza's chapters explain, Televisa, the world's largest Spanish-language broadcaster, coveted the increasingly lucrative Spanish-language cultural and communications markets in the United States and did not want to face continued restrictions on its activities—as when the United States earlier had banned Televisa's Spanish International Network under its foreign ownership restrictions (Castro Rea 2000, 25–26).

Nevertheless, facing recessionary pressures that many groups linked directly to CUSFTA–induced restructuring, Canada held firm for a cultural exemption in NAFTA. The result was a treaty containing not one cultural policy, but two.

NAFTA continued the cultural exemption that existed between Canada and the United States with Canada additionally retaining the right to review any investment that might relate to its national identity or cultural heritage. The exemption did not, however, apply to Mexico, which accepted limited cultural protection, primarily a 49 percent limit on foreign ownership of its audiovisual industries (Galperin 1999).

In the critical telecommunications field, moreover, NAFTA's article 1302 threw open the doors to far more thoroughgoing TNC integration around networks. NAFTA, declared a report by the Office of the U.S. Trade Representative, "eliminated all investment and cross-border service restrictions in enhanced or value-added telecommunications services and private communications networks" (U.S. Trade Representative 2000, 289). TNCs, we will see, were quick to exploit these new freedoms, especially as policies that aimed to protect culture and communications from the flood tide of capitalist transformation were reciprocally weakened.

THE POST–NAFTA ERA

Throughout the post–NAFTA era, the ongoing trend toward transnational investment in a liberalized communications industry intensified. Industrial practices beyond the traditional reliance on exports and imports proliferated. One such means was to expand reliance on industry partnerships worldwide, especially around new distribution systems such as satellites and Internet systems and services. A second was to offer further grants of access to foreign investors in the U.S.–based culture and communications industry. As they incorporated these new practices, foreign companies throughout the sector acquired additional incentives to join the U.S.–led bandwagon in favor of continued liberalization.

A harbinger was provided by the FCC's approval in 1989 of a 22 percent interest in McCaw Cellular Communications—then the largest cellular service provider in the United States—by British Telecom (Sidak 1997, 197–201). Though McCaw was subsequently acquired by AT&T, the policy itself expanded in range. Reed Hundt, the FCC chairman between 1993 and 1997, sought, as a general matter, "to allow foreign investment in communications companies in the United States." A reciprocal objective, Hundt asserts, was that "every country . . . allow foreign investment in communications" (2000, 99, 203). In 1998 and 1999, foreign investors' spending to acquire or establish U.S. businesses exploded (more than tripling from the $80 billion a year that had been characteristic through 1997), most notably, through the takeovers of companies in the information and communications industries—which comprised fully one-third of the total (U.S. Department of Commerce 2000).

Politically induced liberalization of the U.S. domestic communications market therefore helped transform what had been once considered the threat of foreign takeovers of American firms into breathtaking new opportunities for accumulation. This was because such acquisitions frequently conferred access not only to an unmatched national market, but also to transnational marketing networks and/or new distribution technologies and services, among which the Internet had become far and away the most important by the later 1990s.

We have suggested that liberalization concurrently encouraged the assembly of a handful of U.S.–based megamedia and telecommunications conglomerates. In a deepening of this consolidation trend, Viacom, which had absorbed the Paramount film studio and the Simon and Schuster publishing house, and which had developed the popular cable networks Music Television (MTV) and Nickelodeon, went on to acquire CBS in 1999–2000. Viacom, ironically, had been created in 1971 as a spin-off of CBS, after passage of the Financial Interest and Syndication rules by the FCC had prohibited the major television networks from owning and thereby fully controlling the distribution of programs they aired. These rules were withdrawn in the mid-1990s. As a result, industrial interlocks were free to tighten between Hollywood film studios and broadcast television networks. With bipartisan political support through the 1990s for unprecedented cross-media concentration, the largest recording companies, cable and satellite television systems, book publishers, and other media continued to be merged summarily into just a few great combines. In telecommunications, the whirl of deal making was even more frenzied; hundreds of billions of dollars worth of assets concentrated the market into the hands of four or five huge companies, each offering a bundle of services. The corporate commercial development of the Internet beginning in the mid-1990s fell within, and greatly accentuated, this existing trend.

The emergence of a corporate commercial Internet beginning in the mid-1990s, together with passage in the United States of the Telecommunications Act of 1996 (Aufderheide 1999) and the surge in wireless systems and applications, radically intensified the existing tendency to vertical integration. The Internet impinged more or less immediately on every existing medium, either by threatening to usurp its distribution system, allowing augmentation of existing services, or both. The Internet became a core infrastructure for networked systems and services, moreover, on a transnational scale. Hothouse innovation of wireless technology, above all in northern Europe and Japan but increasingly as well in the United States, also converged progressively on Internet development. For these reasons, major media and telecommunications groups moved with alacrity, though with mixed results, to assimilate Internet and/or wireless systems and services into their established offerings (Schiller 1999). One important result was to increase still further efforts by foreign competitors to buy their way into the unexcelled U.S. communications market.

But consumer media services accounted for just a fraction of the changes that were under way. The transformation of the communications and information sector drew force most centrally from a wider ongoing re-organization of big business in general.

Networked Production Chains

In the wake of NAFTA, U.S. trade with Canada, its single most important commercial partner, continued to thrive, growing to a total of nearly $1 billion each day by 1998—more than U.S. trade with the rest of the Western Hemisphere. FDI between the two nations likewise expanded, with the Canadian investment in the United States constituting fully three-quarters of reciprocal U.S. FDI in Canada in 1998—$74.8 billion versus $103.9 billion (U.S. Trade Representative 2000, 30).

Long-standing and deep disparities in real wages, as already noted, constituted the basis for increasingly comprehensive TNC integration across the U.S.–Mexico border. Hectic growth of low-wage ($5–10 per day) manufacturing for the North American market in turn engendered hundreds of export-platform factories. In the five years after NAFTA was signed, U.S., European, and Asian companies invested more than $50 billion in Mexico (Millman 1999a; UN Conference on Trade and Development 1998, 243–263)—a rate near double that which preceded NAFTA, and one that continued into 1999 and 2000 (Smith 2000, A1, A10). U.S. manufacturers alone hired six hundred thousand Mexican workers during this same five-year interval (Millman 1999b). Mexico was frequently chosen as a site for production over lower-wage locations like China, where it took two weeks to move goods between local manufacturing locations and the United States, because proximity to U.S. markets both lowered transport costs and enhanced the flexibility and speed with which production chains could function. This changing investment pattern in turn ramified across the economic landscape.

Mexico's manufacturing base exhibited disparate features. On the one hand, small shop and household production of textiles, setting superexploited labor to work on individual sewing machines, continued to exist on a vast scale. On the other hand, Mexico also came to boast some of the most sophisticated factories in the world, so that Guadalajara for example became a leading location for ultramodern information technology manufacturing (Friedland 2000). *Maquiladoras* encompassed both low-tech operations reliant on outmoded production plants, and state-of-the-art factories producing automobiles, consumer appliances, and television sets.

Services, including call centers and data processing functions, also migrated to Mexico on an increasing scale; in 1999, fifty thousand Mexican workers were employed in service *maquiladoras*, which conducted over $1 billion in transactions with foreign companies (Millman 2000a). FDI in services businesses (especially finance) in Mexico likewise increased. In 2000, through acquisitions as well as new investment, Wal-Mart de México, with

460 outlets in 43 cities, became the largest Mexican retailer (Rangel 2000). U.S. health maintenance organizations even underwrote cross-border health coverage for selected groups of commuting workers and their families (Millman 2000b).

The development of these high-tech export factories and service providers involved an evolutionary shift in industrial organization. TNCs, as we have already observed, were striving to restructure, upgrade, and harmonize production across every nation in which they were active. The emergence of hundreds of export-platform plants, parts factories, and service centers in Mexico was just one piece of this larger development. It betokened an intensifying, albeit selective, effort to extend modernized production chains both to and from Mexico. As such, the growth of *maquiladoras* was embedded within a wider attempt to bring suppliers and customers and support and repair services into new, transnationally organized production and sales processes. This series of changes, however, did not signify the end, or even the lessening, of corporate reliance upon the most exploited and dependent forms of low-paid wage labor.

Enhanced and reorganized infrastructural services of different kinds constituted an indispensable foundation for this larger process of TNC reintegration. Mexican railroads, to be sure, had always been configured northward, around trade with the giant neighbor to the north (Rico Ferrat 1999, 467–468). With the 1999 merger of the U.S. Illinois Central and the Canadian National railways, however, the continental rail transport network as a whole began to be restructured on a north–south rather than an east–west axis. (A proposed merger of Burlington Northern–Santa Fe and Canadian National, however, was sidelined by U.S. congressional resistance.) Such linkups aimed to ship bulk goods like coal and manufactured goods like automobiles across national borders without having to switch lines.

"Seamless shipping" across every major mode (ocean transport, rail, air, and trucking), and across both of the continent's international borders, remained a distant reality. Reorganizing the continent's transportation grid on such a model necessitated reforms far beyond mere technical change. Privatization of state airlines and airports, authorization of transborder takeovers of what had been national carriers, and loosened operating rules and regulations would be needed—and such radical shifts were not free of controversy and resistance. Nonetheless, seamless shipping across borders and transport modes was undeniably the norm toward which continental policymaking proceeded (Zuckerman 2000; Sowinski 2000).

To a growing extent, a parallel trend gripped the energy sector. For example, the Houston-based natural gas giant Burlington Resources was in a pending $2.7 billion (CD) takeover of Poco Petroleum of Calgary, a move that a business report dubbed "unthinkable in the mid-1980s" but one that, with free trade in both natural gas and crude oil taking hold across the continent, became more likely. As a result of this and the entry of several other heavyweights in the U.S. energy business into the Canadian market, the energy grid was increasingly oriented in a north–south direction. Whether Mexico would be able to denationalize its politically sensitive petroleum industry remained less certain, but power plants being built in Baja and Mexicali—the U.S.–Mexico energy grid's connection point—were slated, in any case, to provide new sources of energy on both sides of the international border (Lindquist 2000, A1, A12).

Recent developments in the continent's telecommunications network infrastructure need to be situated in this same dynamic context. The fact that U.S. companies invested a colossal trillion dollars in information technology in the decade up to 1994, with the rate of investment only peaking in the five years that followed (*Economic Report of the President* 2000, 29, 109), carried far beyond U.S. borders. Overseas private-line service offerings garnered revenues of just $14 million to U.S. carriers in 1978; by 1998, even as the prices charged for long-distance services plummeted, they brought in $912.4 million (U.S FCC 1979, *Statistics of Communications Common Carriers [Statistics]*, table 14; U.S. FCC 1999, *Statistics*, table 3.2). Even more telling, in 1988, there were a total of 4,828 leases by U.S. carriers of international private-line circuits of all grades; in 1998, there were 21,023—more than four times as many (U.S. FCC 1988/89, *Statistics*, table 4.5; U.S. FCC 2000, *Statistics*, table 3.2). However, these figures still dramatically discount the growth of corporate reliance on proprietary networks, as over this one decade the proportion of high-capacity (9.6 thousand to 30 million bits per second and above) circuits in use increased from 12.7 percent to 84.5 percent of the total (U.S. FCC 1988/89, *Statistics*, table 4.5; U.S. FCC 2000, *Statistics*, table 3.2). Between 1992 and 1998, the number of international private-line circuits leased between U.S. and Mexican locations increased from 1,403 (generating revenue of $16.4 million) to 3,709 ($41.6 million) (U.S. FCC 1992/93, *Statistics*, table 4.4; U.S. FCC 2000, *Statistics*, table 3.2).

Modernization of the public telecommunications network likewise occurred. As Gerald Sussman demonstrates in his chapter on Mexico's telecommunications industry in the post–NAFTA era, escalating corporate reliance on networks stimulated an investment-led technical overhaul and expansion of Mexican telecommunications, as around one-third of total FDI in Mexico for 1997—some $5 billion—was channeled into this vital infrastructure (Schiller 1999, 43). At the time NAFTA was negotiated, Canada and Mexico already comprised major export markets for U.S. telecommunications equipment and services. By 1999, however, Canada and Mexico were the two top markets for U.S. high-tech exports overall, with a commanding lead over the next three recipient countries—Japan, the United Kingdom, and South Korea. Together, Canada and Mexico drew nearly 30 percent of all U.S. high-tech exports. Between 1993 and 1999, these exports grew by 170 percent in the case of U.S.–Mexico trade, to $22 billion; in 1999, Canada took $29 billion of high-tech U.S. exports ("New AEA/NASDAQ Report Highlights

World's Top Technology Markets" 2000, 2–3). (Since NAFTA tariff reductions, mainly as a result of FDI, the two nations have also become top exporters of telecommunications equipment to the United States [Cass and Haring 1998, 123].) That the United States' top two trading partners also became the leading hubs for its high-tech exports is anything but coincidental.

The Emerging Order

U.S.–based megamedia companies, tied closely to a base of perhaps a thousand leading corporate advertisers, and U.S.–based telecommunications companies, equally closely linked to a few thousand TNC users of specialized equipment and services, were well positioned to supply business-to-business communications on a transnational scale and advertising across multiple media platforms. Increasingly, they adhered to a new principle in developing strategy and operations: direct TNC supply of communications and cultural services and infrastructures.

FDI in communications and culture industry markets accordingly surged. Efforts likewise increased to pry open markets further, where they were deemed insufficiently supportive of FDI. The watershed event in this process was the 1997 WTO accord on basic telecommunications. This agreement threw open the markets of nearly seventy nations, which together accounted for 94 percent of world telecommunications markets, to liberalized investment on the U.S. model (Schiller 1999, 47–48). Still, the United States continued to press for yet more favorable investment and trade concessions; the Office of the U.S. Trade Representative's annual summaries of "barriers" to U.S. trade and investment focused relentlessly on the culture and communications sector, and heralded additional initiatives. Mexico and Canada, for example, each ran afoul of U.S. ambitions in telecommunications services.

The cultural and communications reservations that had provided some solace to groups opposed to CUSFTA and NAFTA likewise began to be dismantled. For example, CUSFTA and NAFTA permitted continuing Canadian government protection of its magazine industry. But efforts to defend national culture on existing terms received a major blow in 1999 when the WTO ruled in favor of a U.S. complaint that such protections violated global trade rules.

At the same time, major communications corporations lavished increasing attention on non-English-language markets. Mari Castañeda Paredes's chapter shows how, confronted by the prospect of a growing Spanish-speaking populace in the United States, newly extensive Spanish-language marketing and commercial media services have taken root in the United States in the years since NAFTA. Both Mexican (and other Latin American) and major U.S.–based media groups and advertisers participated. Especially if the often-disparate practices of Puerto Rico, Mexico, and other Spanish-speaking societies could be melded into common "Hispanic" musical and televisual currencies, then media conglomerates could move forcefully to engage the attention of hundreds of millions of consumers comprising the worldwide Spanish-speaking market.

The major U.S.–based media groups' moves on non-English-language markets likewise marked a critical departure. In the past, they had been content mainly to export programs, which were dubbed into other languages and aired by national broadcasters in other countries. Now, in contrast, media conglomerates aimed to develop direct commercial access to audiences on a transnational scale. In 1999, for example, Sony created no less than four thousand hours of non-English-language television programming—more than twice its output of English-language programming—both for its own foreign channels and for sale to other groups (Guider 1999). U.S.–based media combines, writes a business insider, "may well maintain their leadership roles, but they will have to adapt to local audiences and include local content. Moreover, foreign content will begin to nudge its way onto the global hit parade" (Wolf 1999, 114).

In the media segment, accordingly, Sony of Japan, Bertelsmann of Germany, Pearson of the United Kingdom, and Seagram of Canada joined Australia's News Corporation in laying claim to prime U.S. assets. Ten of the top twenty U.S. media companies, including three of the top four book publishers, along with three of the top four recording companies, passed into foreign hands. Additional moves in the same direction were manifest. When, in early 2000, Pearson merged its television unit with Bertelsmann's broadcasting subsidiary, the new multi–billion dollar media company immediately announced that it would try to expand into the U.S. market by urging "relaxation of U.S. laws limiting foreign ownership of television stations" (Goldsmith 2000, A26).

Liberalization of foreign ownership restrictions in U.S. telecommunications also widened episodically throughout the 1990s. In telecommunications, important precedents were laid when the FCC authorized Spain's Telefonica to purchase the state-owned Puerto Rican long-distance telephone company (1992) and the U.S. Internet portal Lycos (2000); British Telecom to purchase 20 percent of MCI (1994); and France Telecom and Deutsche Telekom (DT) to acquire a minority (10 percent each) interest in Sprint (1995) (Sidak 1997, 179–197). Meanwhile, Alcatel, based in France, bought ITT's huge international telecommunications equipment manufacturing unit; Nortel, based in Canada, expanded forcefully into the U.S. and Mexican telecommunications equipment markets (DePalma 2000a, C1, C4). The Japanese telecommunications behemoth Nippon Telegraph and Telephone Corporation received clearance from the U.S. executive branch to purchase the large website hosting company Verio. Finally, DT rocked the telecommunications industry with its planned $50.7 billion purchase of the U.S. wireless company VoiceStream.

Continental integration comprised only one important facet of a larger process of building a new order in the global political economy—both in general and in communications, culture, and information in particular. While there were general tendencies, the particular steps in the process of continental integration differed depending on which subsector was involved and the specific power relations that held at each moment. Sometimes it was the United States that took the lead in bringing rivals into the fold with partnerships and access; sometimes it was competitors from outside the region that pushed their way into North American markets.[5] Sometimes, indeed, Canadian and Mexican companies seized the initiative, based on what they perceived to be the inevitability of continental and global integration.

Throughout Anglophone Canada, there continued to exist a tradition of cultural protection, and in some quarters a continuing orientation toward Britain as opposed to the U.S.–Canadian English-language audiovisual space was already dominated in key respects, as we have noted, by U.S.–based interests. Well before NAFTA, however, one major Canadian company, Rogers Communication, already possessed substantial U.S. cable system interests. Northern Telecom had also reoriented its successful business in the liberalized telecommunications equipment market toward its leading corporate customers in the United States, and the Thomson Corporation already held major interests in newspapers across the United States.

Following passage of the 1989 CUSFTA that presaged NAFTA, linkages between U.S. and Canadian media and communications interests tightened swiftly. Seagram, a beverage company with considerable interests in U.S. petrochemicals, shifted into the leading group of U.S. based culture conglomerates by purchasing Universal Studios (in 2000, Seagram sold its entertainment business to the French company Vivendi). Meanwhile, Bell Canada, the nation's dominant telephone service company, in 1999 permitted the U.S. telephone giant Ameritech to acquire a 20 percent stake. Rogers, Canada's largest cable company and diversified holder of numerous media properties, including Canada's leading newsweekly *Maclean's*, struck a deal with Microsoft Corporation to sell a minority stake in the company to the U.S. firm—which would use it to develop high-speed cable Internet access services. Furthermore, in August 1999 Rogers sold a $1 billion stake in its mobile telephone company to AT&T and British Telecom (who had partnered more generally to serve business customers' international telecommunications needs). AT&T itself used the WTO agreement on basic telecommunications to challenge the dominance of Bell Canada and government policies that had kept local telephone rates low to ensure universal access (Baxter 2000).

Even in the newspaper business, which still operated behind a wall of government protection enshrined in the Income Tax Act (which effectively limited foreign ownership of Canadian newspapers to no more than 25 percent), major newspaper companies forged strategic alliances anticipating the end of such restrictions. For example, the *Globe and Mail*, which billed itself as Canada's national newspaper, struck deals with Dow Jones to include a page of news directly from the *Wall Street Journal*, with Time-Warner to include a section of *Sports Illustrated* magazine news, and with the *New York Times* for exclusive rights to home delivery of the Sunday edition of that newspaper across Canada. Blocked by the Canadian government from establishing its own set of retail chains in Canada (partly because of pressure from Canadian business interests), Barnes & Noble, the giant book retailer, took a minority stake in Canada's largest bookseller, Chapters Incorporated.

Structural realignment in telecommunications likewise proceeded on a supranational scale. Nortel Networks purchased the large U.S.–based telecommunications company Bay Networks (for $7.6 billion), which extended the integration of what was once a leading force of Canadian nationalism (as the manufacturing arm of Bell Canada it received substantial government subsidies and protection) into the U.S. economy. Meanwhile, the two major Canadian carriers entered a new phase of competitive struggle as each linked itself with a rival U.S. telecommunications group. Bell Canada, backed by its minority partner Ameritech (itself a unit of parent Southwestern Bell Communications Corporation [SBC]), vied with a newly merged firm—British Columbia Telephone–Telus (BCT.Telus)—representing the telecommunications companies in the provinces of British Columbia and Alberta. BCT.Telus's U.S. partner was General Telephone and Electronics Corporation (GTE; a new subsidiary of Verizon, the name given to merged company that joined GTE to Bell Atlantic), which once owned half of the British Columbia telephone company and which flexed its muscle by forcing the departures of the top senior executives of Telus in order to make way for a GTE–backed management team.

A large and powerful group of Canadian companies thus came to harbor a structural interest in supporting uninterrupted TNC reorganization of the English-language audiovisual space.

Other formidable actors, to be sure, continued to press, contrariwise, for a policy of protection. For example, the Canadian magazine industry strongly resisted an end to the policy of keeping out Canadian editions of U.S.–owned magazines. Some of this protectionist sentiment was frankly a smoke screen for industrial interests, notably those of Canadian media firms Rogers and Telemedia, which controlled two-thirds of the magazine industry.

More important, a general switch in public policy was taking place. The Canadian federal Liberal Party that had held national power since 1993 historically supported strong national regulation of Canadian communications and cultural industries and Canadian controls over American cultural imports. Now, with a few exceptions, it joined the side of ending domestic regulations and import controls. In May 2000, the Ministry of Canadian Heritage, which had been closely identified with nationalist policies, threw in the towel and announced a review of all foreign ownership restrictions on newspapers, radio, and television broadcasting (Scoffield and Craig 2000). Among other reasons was the pressure exerted by Canada's two dominant newspaper publishers, who wanted to sell their newspapers and buy Internet properties, and American newspaper companies eager to expand their advertising revenue base without having to produce much new content. Indeed, it is fair to say that in some areas the Canadian government blazed new ground, as in May 1999 when it fully supported the decision of its chief communications regulatory authority to formally rule against regulation of the Internet (Canadian Radio-television and Telecommunications Commission 1999). Electronic commerce thus achieved unprecedented freedom to develop as a market-led phenomenon in Canada and, indeed, across the continent. The impact of this particular policy change promised to be profound, because the Internet was rapidly beginning to usurp conventional media and telecommunications services.

Protectionism, moreover, changed its character as it no longer attempted to counter the strategy of including the culture and communications sector of the state in the general process of cutbacks in government funding. Canada authorized a substantial decline in public service communications and culture evidenced in budget cuts to the CBC, and government programs that provided subsidies to arts and culture media and their organizations. Even as the Canadian government advanced legislation that would protect its magazine industry, it was cutting off subsidies and thereby killing small-circulation Canadian magazines. In the same week that the WTO was announcing its decision to support Time-Warner's bid to permit a split-run "Canadian" version of *Sports Illustrated* magazine, Atlantic Canada's best-known alternative magazine *New Maritimes* went out of business primarily because it had lost its grant from the Canada Council, a government agency responsible for supporting Canadian arts organizations. Citing budget cuts and the consequent need to narrow its grant mandate, the council also warned the national magazine *Canadian Forum* that its subsidy would be lost unless it shifted focus from politics to the arts (Mosco 1997).

Admittedly, some nationalist concerns reflected a genuine interest in preserving autonomy in the audiovisual space, and this could even crystallize momentarily in high-level government policy proposals—such as the 1999 Canadian government effort to forge a global cultural pact among the world's threatened nations—that would provide stronger protection for national cultural industries. But Canadian capital was increasingly closely wedded to the U.S. market, and state policy could hardly avoid recognizing and, in some measure, reconciling to this reality (Stairs 2000). Reconciliation extended across the cultural industries, including the increasingly significant sport and leisure sectors, which, as Richard Gruneau and David Whitson's chapter explains, led by their commercial sponsors, were integrating national professional leagues into transnational enterprises.

Finally, some companies continued to try to make use of government protection to expand both their continental and domestic links. For example, Bell Canada Enterprises (BCE), the holding company that contained Bell

26 *Chapter 1*

Canada, benefited from limits on foreign ownership, even as it used the capital raised by selling a minority stake in Bell Canada to Ameritech by going on a domestic shopping spree that included a $2.5 billion (CD) bid for Canadian Television Network (CTV), Canada's major private television network. In September 2000, the company built on this by announcing a joint deal with the Thomson Corporation, whose Canadian newspaper holdings remained legally protected from foreign competition. Following on the addition of CTV and Thomson's national newspaper the *Globe and Mail*, BCE announced in February 2001 that it planned to build an integrated home communications system that would bring together its high-speed Internet service and satellite-developed television system to provide homes with fully networked communications and information products that would eventually extend to monitoring and controlling all household utilities (Reuters 2001).

Similarly, in what amounted to the largest media deal in Canadian history, CanWest Global Communications Corporation, one of the country's largest broadcasters, paid $3.5 billion (CD) for many of the major holdings of Hollinger Incorporated, Canada's largest newspaper company. Both of these companies had enjoyed decades of government protection. CanWest operated a national private broadcasting network whose stations primarily rebroadcast American programming. It had not lived up to repeated promises to produce and air Canadian programming, but government regulators had turned a blind eye. With holdings that encompassed over half the circulation of Canadian dailies and one of the country's two national newspapers, Hollinger rose to become the dominant company in the Canadian newspaper business. It achieved this position in no small measure due to the government's effective prohibition on foreign ownership of Canadian newspapers. With no external competition and with its primary internal competitor the Thomson Corporation shedding dailies to enter the dot.com world, Hollinger was able to monopolize almost every major Canadian market.

The merger of these two companies not only accelerated media concentration in Canada, it also expanded the transnationalization of broadcasting, print, and new media. This was primarily because Hollinger International, the company's global holding company, included among its major properties the *Daily Telegraph* of the United Kingdom, the *Chicago Sun-Times*, and the *Jerusalem Post*. In essence, Hollinger transnationalized its Canadian newspaper holdings by making extensive use of these publications. This process stood to be extended to broadcasting as Hollinger joined CanWest. The objective was to do more than build a transnational newspaper and broadcasting empire. One of the primary reasons why Hollinger sold so many properties in the first place was because its institutional shareholders insisted that the company needed to build its share price and specifically to do so by placing greater emphasis on new media. So CanWest was buying not only a newspaper empire with significant international connections, but also the website canada.com, which, along with a national network of city portals, already comprised at the time of purchase the second most popular network of websites in the country.

In Mexico, a comparable process of integration was tied politically to the decline of nationalistic anti-imperialism in public policy, and its replacement by neoliberal doctrines, beginning in the early 1980s. The process originated economically in the ambitions of Mexican-based as well as U.S.–based capital.

For some decades, much of Mexico's culture and communications industry had been centralized in the commercial broadcast empire of the Azcárraga family—Televisa. While the national film industry, a paragon during the 1950s, was brought to ruin during the 1980s and 1990s, Televisa thrived, even to the point of widely exporting its prime time fare of *telenovelas* (Sinclair 1999); Televisa comprised the fourth-largest Mexican firm in 1999. In addition, Telmex, the country's dominant telecommunications carrier, sported a higher market value ($33.3 billion) in 1999 than BCE ($29.5 billion), and comprised the top-ranked "emerging-market company" anywhere.

These Mexican corporations continued to hold high hopes for additional expansion, especially if they or their allies in state agencies could help to steer the process of liberalization. As NAFTA and the WTO threw open the country's telecommunications market to FDI, however, U.S.–based carriers were intent on claiming substantial chunks of the Mexican business and high-end consumer market. MCI and AT&T each partnered with powerful Mexican financial and industrial groups to gain entry, spending more than $2 billion between themselves in building out Mexican networks (Preston 2000, C4). Mexican telecommunications comprised not merely one more market for these two giant transnational carriers, "but also the missing link needed to complete their proprietary networks in Canada and the U.S. With Mexico, both companies will have uniform networks that span all North America— the world's most lucrative call corridor. Some 1,000 multinational corporations in Mexico could use North American network services" (Torres 1996, A1, quoted in Schiller 1999, 64).

In this context, transnational partnerships extended as well into the heartland of Mexico's telecommunications industry. Telmex accorded a 9.6 percent ownership stake to SBC—which also eventually obtained a 20 percent stake in Bell Canada. Telmex then enlarged its alliance with SBC when each company took stakes in Williams Communications, a provider of longdistance services within the United States. As Telmex used its status as Mexico's dominant carrier to forestall incursions by its new rivals, mainly by compelling the two companies to pay generously for interconnection rights with its own network, AT&T and MCI responded by turning to the Office of the U.S. Trade Representative and the FCC for redress. Both duly singled out Telmex for its monopolistic practices and, in July 2000, the U.S. government formally initiated a WTO case against Mexico for allegedly failing to open its telecommunications market.

With the surging growth of Spanish-speaking populations within the United States, Telmex purchased a lackluster U.S. Internet service, Prodigy, in hopes of adapting it as a Spanish-language service on a transborder basis. Telmex likewise joined with Bell Canada International and, again, with SBC, to furnish fixed-line, wireless, and Internet services throughout South America; a deal was also struck with Microsoft to develop a Spanish-language Internet portal (Fritsch 2000).

Parallel efforts by other firms to launch transnational investment vehicles, particularly for Spanish-language Internet services, also boomed (Lynch 2000, B1, B2; Druckerman 1999, A19; 2000a, A23). By participating in Univisión Network, the leading U.S. Spanish-language broadcast network, and through a radio partnership with the giant U.S. broadcaster Clear Channel, Televisa continued to pursue the U.S. market. The company also acceded to a partnership with a U.S.–based consortium in developing the platform of DTH satellite broadcasting in Mexico. To be sure, the ownership of Televisa remained tightly locked in the hands of some of Mexico's leading capitalists. To this extent, Televisa's bid to remain an independent force in determining the fate of the more encompassing Spanish-language audiovisual space— not only in the NAFTA countries, but also throughout Central and South America as well—survived. Whether this stance would prove viable, however, remained to be seen.

Competitors, newly licensed as the liberalization process took hold within Mexican politics, again tended to join up with U.S. partners, as NBC's renewed ties with Televisión Azteca suggested (Druckerman 2000b). With continued growth projected for Spanish-language print-media markets worldwide (Taylor 1999, 16–17), Time-Warner's *Sports Illustrated* forged a licensing agreement with Consorcio Interamericano de Comunicación to publish several of its articles each Saturday in three leading Mexican newspapers (Brockington 1999, 8).

Across the NAFTA countries, therefore, the movement toward a consolidated communications and culture industry, dominated by transnational consortia, gained growing force. What this swift change in industrial organization portended for cultural practice comprises the chief subject of the ensuing chapters. It is a profound question, not least because it remained open to political intervention if the will to intervene arose.

CONCLUSION

Continental integration for cybercapitalism resulted in large measure from the perception among economic elites that significant blockages were preventing the global expansion of the market and eroding opportunities for business. It comprised one piece of an aggressive policy to reintegrate telecommunications and mass media markets on a global basis. The major obstructions to attaining this goal were national control over key institutions and policy levers, and public service principles restricting advertising and emphasizing rights of access irrespective of market power.

The telecommunications and mass media sectors were and are central to the strategy of doing away with these impediments. Global telecommunications networks are critical to permit businesses to restructure along transnational lines, as well as to provide business-to-business and business-to-consumer electronic services. Mass media are equally important because the provision of advertiser-sponsored programs on all media platforms, from print through the Internet, is vital to the development of global markets in every sector. Again, national media policies that limited advertising, foreign content, and corporate control, along with public service objectives imposing limits on commercial programming and asserting non-market-based rights of citizen access, blocked the full development of global commercial systems.

The United States took the lead in eliminating these obstructions. It did so in important part by restructuring its own markets through a series of policy decisions that did away with most regulation of the telecommunications and mass media sectors; privatized much of what remained of government involvement in these sectors; and generally set aside requirements that advanced specifically national and public service objectives where these conflicted with the goal of building global markets. This led to unprecedented foreign entry into the U.S. economy, not least, in the telecommunications and mass media sectors. But it also made it easier for U.S. policymakers to promote the additional opening of regional and global markets to American firms eager to sell telecommunications and mass media products and services. More generally, it enabled U.S.–based companies to spearhead a great range of industrial partnerships, which in turn aimed to build the communications infrastructure necessary to reorganize national enterprises along global lines, both in business and consumer markets.

The transition to a global strategy faced formidable challenges. The transformation of the communications and cultural industries that forms the subject of this book comprised more than just an organizational or economic project. Cultural practices do not always follow the structure of markets and incentives, which, however powerful, often fail to overcome countervailing pressures. Indeed, capital itself is not a thing but a relationship—between wage labor and the owners of capital. Social class relations themselves therefore stood to be reconfigured in some measure, as a result of the same generative processes of reorganization analyzed here. In this context, we might do well to recall what Raymond Williams reminds us is the power of the local, of specific places and experiences, that make up what he called the "militant particularism" of daily life (1989). How, in particular, may changing class relations come to impinge on "imagined communities" (Anderson 1991)—which range from collective images of neighborhood and ethnicity to identification with the national state—and which have previously made considerable room for national controls and public service principles? Even as market-led transnationalization aims to whittle these away, new forms of community and new public service principles, such as the electronic commons, arise to motivate social movements to pursue more democratic agendas. They work on the stress points between community and market, between democratic state and global corporate governance, and, once more, between labor and capital. These stress points are not likely to disappear.

Subsequent chapters provide a status report documenting both progress in realizing continental integration and considerable unfinished work. The project's outcome is far from certain. That outcome will be considerably more significant than one or another trade agreement, one or another approach to opening markets. At stake is the transition to a global economy, the balance of uneven development therein, the fate of national and public service principles, and the possible emergence of new countervailing forces that seek to resist the unfettered self-expansion of transnational capital.

NOTES

Unless noted otherwise, all dollar amounts are in U.S. currency. When reference is made to Canadian dollars, "CD" is used.

1. National treatment requires states to treat businesses from signatory countries as they treat their own businesses. As a result, unless specified in the agreement, a government agency, like a regulatory body or a department responsible for procuring goods and services, cannot discriminate along national lines by providing its own companies with advantages that do not extend to foreign companies.

2. We do not seek to suggest an absolute opposition between nation-state and transnational capital.

3. Specifically, CUSFTA allows measures of "equivalent commercial effect" by which a party acts against another if it concludes that the other party unfairly protects its cultural industries. The cultural "exemption" means that the retaliation cannot take the form of action against the cultural sector of the party perceived to be offending. Instead, it must be directed to a different economic sector. For example, when the United States claimed that Canada was unfairly protecting its magazine industry, in addition to petitioning the WTO, it threatened to restrict imports of Canadian steel to the value of what it perceived the U.S. magazine industry was hurt by Canadian protectionism.

4. This would deter Canada from expanding the role of the CBC or, even more importantly, creating a new version of the CBC for new media that might provide what some have called a "public lane" on the information highway. The U.S. company United Parcel Service (UPS) took advantage of this clause in its April 2000 decision to sue the Canadian government claiming that it wrongly permitted Canada Post Corporation to use the infrastructure built for letter delivery for its courier products, thereby violating CUSFTA's prohibition on the creation of new institutions that might monopolize an industry. UPS sought damages of $160 million for violations it argued began in 1997.

5. Pushes, pulls, and resistances take place from a variety of sides. Companies based in the European Union have sought entry into the U.S. telecommunications market for years and so DT's bid for VoiceStream represented an external push. But there is no doubt that some U.S. interests were pleased, because this bid created opportunities for liberalizing U.S. telecommunications policies to be pressed abroad. Nevertheless, U.S. congressional interests, worried at the large stake the German government held in DT, resisted the merger (DePalma 2000b, C4).

REFERENCES

Anderson, B. 1991. *Imagined Communities*. London: Verso.

Aufderheide, P. 1999. *Communications Policy and the Public Interest: The Telecommunications Act of 1996*. New York: Guilford.

Auletta, K. 1991. *Three Blind Mice: How the TV Networks Lost Their Way*. New York: Random House.

Baxter, J. 2000. "AT&T Complains Telephone Regulation Thwarts Competition." *Ottawa Citizen*, 17 March, D4.

Brockington, L. 1999. "*Sports Illustrated* Takes Brand to Mexico in New Three-Newspaper Deal." *Street and Smith's Sports Business Journal*, 5–11 April, 8.

Canadian Radio-Television and Telecommunications Commission. 1999. *Final Report: New Media, Telecom Public Notice CRTC 99-14* and *Broadcasting Public Notice CRTC 1999-84*, 17 May.

Cass, R. A., and J. Haring. 1998. *International Trade in Telecommunications*. Washington, D.C.: AEI Press.

Castro Rea, J. 2000. "The North American Challenge: A Mexican Perspective." *Canadian Journal of Policy Research* 1 (1): 24–30.

Cockcroft, J. D. 1998. *Mexico's Hope. An Encounter with Politics and History*. New York: Monthly Review.

DePalma, A. 2000a. "Nortel Makes Inroads in Building Wireless World in Latin America." *New York Times*, 19 June, C1, C4.

———. 2000b. "The Response to Deutsche Telekom's Bid for VoiceStream Brings into Focus an Unwritten Tenet of U.S. Trade Policy." *New York Times*, 7 August, C4.

Druckerman, P. 1999. "Investors Rush South of the Cyberborder." *Wall Street Journal*, 26 July, A19.

———. 2000a. "Latin Web Firms Venture out to Markets in Spain, U.S." *Wall Street Journal*, 12 April, A23.

———. 2000b. "NBC and TV Azteca End Feud with a Friendly Pact." *Wall Street Journal*, 3 May, A21.

Economic Report of the President. 2000. Washington, D.C.: U.S. Government Printing Office.

Friedland, J. 2000. "How a Need for Speed Turned Guadalajara into a High Tech Hub." *Wall Street Journal*, 2 March, A1.

Fritsch, P. 2000. "Bell Canada Joins Telmex in Targeting South America." *Wall Street Journal*, 9 June, A15.

Galperin, H. 1999. "Cultural Industries Policy in Regional Trade Agreements: The Cases of NAFTA, the European Union, and MERCOSUR." *Media Culture and Society* 21 (5) (September): 627–648.

Goldsmith, C. 2000. "Pearson-Bertelsmann TV Firm Plans for Its U.S. 'Dream' Market." *Wall Street Journal*, 16 April.

Greider, W. 1997. *One World, Ready or Not: The Manic Logic of Global Capitalism.* New York: Simon and Schuster.

Guider, E. 1999. "Sony Ups Its Local Payoff." *Variety*, 26 July–1 August, 23.

Hundt, R. E. 2000. *You Say You Want a Revolution: A Story of Information Age Politics.* New Haven, Conn.: Yale University Press.

Johnson, C. 2000. *Blowback: The Costs and Consequences of American Empire.* New York: Holt.

Jussawalla, M. 1986. *The Passing of Remoteness: The Information Revolution in the Asia-Pacific.* Singapore: Institute of Southeast Asian Studies.

Lindquist, D. 2000. "An Energy Source Beckons from Baja." *San Diego Union-Tribune*, 12 August.

Lynch, D. J. 2000. "Net Company Terra Aims for Hispanic Connection." *USA Today*, 20 January, B1, B2.

Mazzocco, D. 1994. *Networks of Power.* Boston: South End.

McAnany, E., and K. T. Wilkinson, eds. 1996. *Mass Media and Free Trade: NAFTA and the Cultural Industries.* Austin: University of Texas Press.

Millman, J. 1999a. "U.S. Companies Coach Mexican Partners to Y2K Fitness." *Wall Street Journal*, 22 September, A19.

———. 1999b. "What Southeast Was to U.S. Companies, Mexico Is Becoming." *Wall Street Journal*, 29 October, A1, A6.

———. 2000a. "First Came Assembly; Now, Services Soar." *Wall Street Journal*, 28 February, A1.

———. 2000b. "U.S. HMOs Cross the Mexican Border." *Wall Street Journal*, 27 June, A21, A22.

Mosco, V. 1990. "Toward a Transnational World Information Order: The Canada–U.S. Free Trade Agreement." *Canadian Journal of Communication* 15 (2) (Spring): 46–63.

———. 1997. "Marketable Commodity or Public Good: The Conflict between Domestic and Foreign Communication Policy." In *How Ottawa Spends, 1997–1998*, ed. Gene Swimmer. Ottawa: Carleton University Press.

"New AEA/NASDAQ Report Highlights World's Top Technology Markets." 2000. American Electronics Association press release, 13 March. <http://www.aeanet.org/aeanet/PressRoom/pradet0010_cybernation20_031300.htm> [last accessed: 14 March 2000].

Oppel, R. A., Jr. 2000. "The Higher Stakes of Business-to-Business Trade." *New York Times*, 5 March, B3.

Ostry, S. 2000. "Regional versus Multilateral Trade Strategies." *Canadian Journal of Policy Research* 1 (1) (Spring): 45–56.

Otero, G. S. Scott, and C. Gilbreth. 1997. "New Technologies: Neoliberalism and Social Polarization in Mexico's Agriculture." In *Cutting Edge: Technology, Information Capitalism, and Social Revolution*, ed. J. Davis, T. A. Hirschl, and M. Stack. London: Verso.

Preston, J. 2000. "U.S. Trade Representative May Take Action against Mexico." *New York Times*, 5 April, C4.

Rangel, E. 2000. "Wal-Mart Is Grande." *San Diego Union–Tribune*, 2 June, C1, C3.

Reuters. 2001. "BCE Set to Marry High-Speed Internet, Satellite, TV." *New York Times*, 5 February. On-line edition.

Rico Ferrat, C. 1999. "Mexico, the Latin North American Nation: A Conversation with Carlos Rico Ferrat." *Journal of American History* 86 (2) (September): 467–480.

Schiller, D. 1982. *Telematics and Government*. Norwood, N.J.: Ablex.

———. 1999. *Digital Capitalism: Networking the Global Market System*. Cambridge: Massachusetts Institute of Technology Press.

Schiller, H. 1989. *Culture, Inc*. New York: Oxford University Press.

Schwoch, J. 1990. *The American Radio Industry and Its Latin American Activities, 1900–1939*. Urbana: University of Illinois Press.

Scoffield, H., and S. Craig. 2000. "Review of Media Rules to Be Broad." *Report on Business*, 3 May, B3.

Sidak, J. G. 1997. *Foreign Investment in American Telecommunications*. Chicago: University of Chicago Press.

Sinclair, J. 1999. *Latin American Television: A Global View*. Oxford: Oxford University Press.

Smith, J. F. 2000. "Mexico on a Roll with New Foreign Investment." *Los Angeles Times*, 21 March, A1, A10.

Sowinski. L. 2000. "Moving Goods in and out of Mexico." *World Trade* (April): 67–68.

Stairs, D. 2000. "Liberalism and the Triumph of Efficiency in Canada–US Relations." *Canadian Journal of Policy Research* 1 (1) (Spring): 11–16.

Taylor, S. 1999. "Guadalajara '99: Best Is Yet to Come for the Spanish Market." *Publishers Weekly*, 20 December, 16–17.

Torres, C. 1996. "Taking a Gamble, MCI Plunged into Mexico as AT&T Hesitated." *Wall Street Journal*, 18 November, A1, A7.

UN Conference on Trade and Development. 1998. *World Investment Report 1998: Trends and Determinants*. New York: United Nations.

U.S. Department of Commerce. Bureau of Economic Analysis. 2000. "Foreign Investors' Spending to Acquire or Establish U.S. Businesses Increased Sharply to $283 Billion in 1999." *BEA* 00-14, 7 June. <http://www.bea.doc.gov/bea/articles/internat/fdinvest/2000/0600fdi.pdf> [last accessed: 19 February 2001].

U.S. Federal Communications Commission. 1979. *Statistics of Communications Common Carriers*. Washington, D.C.: U.S. Government Printing Office.

———. 1988/89. *Statistics of Communications Common Carriers*. Washington, D.C.: U.S. Government Printing Office, 1989.

———. 1992/93. *Statistics of Communications Common Carriers*. Washington, D.C.: U.S. Government Printing Office, 1993.

———. 1997. CC Docket 92-237, CC Docket 95-155, "In the Matters of Administration of the North American Numbering Plan [and] Toll Free Service Access Codes," Third Report and Order, Adopted 9 October.

———. 1999. *Statistics of Communications Common Carriers*. Washington, D.C.: U.S. Government Printing Office.

———. 2000. *Statistics of Communications Common Carriers*. Washington, D.C.: U.S. Government Printing Office.

U.S. Trade Representative. 2000. *2000 National Trade Estimate Report on Foreign Trade Barriers*. <http://www.ustr.gov/html/2000_contents.html> [last accessed: 19 February 2001].

Williams, R. 1989. *Resources of Hope*. London: Verso.
Wolf, M. J. 1999. *The Entertainment Economy*. New York: Times Books.
Zuckerman, A. 2000. "NAFTA Signatories Utilizing Technology to Speed Transport." *World Trade* (April): 66.

2

NAFTA and Economic Integration in North America: Regional or Global?

Richard B. Du Boff

In the late 1980s, a wave of economic integration began to roll across North America. After a half century of promises and false starts, including unsuccessful trade talks in 1948, a defense production agreement in 1958, and an automobile trade agreement in 1965, the United States and Canada concluded a comprehensive free trade pact. Approved by both countries in 1988, the Canada–United States Free Trade Agreement (CUSFTA) went into effect on January 1, 1989. Five years later to the day, Mexico was drawn into the U.S.–Canadian economic orbit, as CUSFTA was incorporated into a broader instrument, the North American Free Trade Agreement (NAFTA).

Is NAFTA ushering in a new economic era in North America, with different flows of trade and investment? Is it expanding markets and production possibilities, with benefits for workers and consumers in all three countries? And does continental integration in North America represent a movement toward regional economic blocs like the European Union and the Japan–East Asia sphere, or does it reflect the universal process of globalization of the world economy?

The roots of NAFTA, and of globalization as we see it today, go back to the 1960s. As NAFTA moves toward the end of its first decade, the economic landscape of North America might still look familiar to an observer transported in time from 1980 or 1990; and that observer might not notice any major differences between regional forces unleashed by NAFTA and international economic and financial forces being promoted by global capital.

THE ROAD TO NAFTA: FAST TRACK, BUMPY RIDE

CUSFTA engaged the United States and Canada in a liberalization project— one free trade area encompassing both countries, but without a common external tariff barrier (each would maintain distinct tariffs for goods and services from third countries). Over a ten-year period, CUSFTA was to eliminate all tariffs and most nontariff import restrictions and move both countries toward fully integrated markets for goods, services, and capital. The agreement also established more effective dispute settlement processes, as well as new rules dealing with unfair pricing and subsidization. In the last months of 1988, the "subsidies" question nearly torpedoed the negotiations. The U.S. Congress approved the agreement on September 19 but remained unwilling to discuss its own subsidies, which are less publicly visible (e.g., tax exemptions, low-interest loans, and loan guarantees) than Canada's direct grants and regional assistance programs. After receiving a set of assurances about open access to U.S. markets and submission of trade disputes to judicial review, Canada gave final approval on December 30.

Mexico's road to NAFTA began in the 1960s. As a response to the termination in 1964 of the Bracero Program, created by the U.S. government during World War II to admit Mexican farm workers to allay labor shortages in the United States, Mexico inaugurated its Border Industrialization Program the following year. Under the program, licenses were granted to foreign companies to set up plants in Mexico, soon known as *maquiladoras*, to import raw materials, parts, and components for assembly and reexport. Yet as late as 1979 Mexico rejected membership in the General Agreement on Tariffs and Trade (GATT). During the 1970s, Mexico, like many Third World countries, took out large loans from foreign banks, which found themselves with surplus "petrodollar" deposits and were aggressively pushing loans on Latin American and Asian countries. In Mexico's case, the borrowed funds were to be used to strengthen its longtime development strategy of import substitution, whereby domestic manufacturers, behind high tariff walls, were encouraged to produce goods that would replace imports.

The timing of this increase in external indebtedness could not have been worse. The worldwide recession of 1980–1982 hit Mexico hard, and it was followed by a precipitous drop in world oil prices, weakening Mexico's export earnings on which its borrowing and domestic spending projects were based. In August 1982, Mexico announced that it could not meet its obligations on external debts. Borrowing from abroad plummeted, and the ensuing economic crisis led to a historic departure from the country's longstanding foreign trade and domestic economic policies.[1] The "debt crisis" was resolved by what eventually would be four rounds of negotiations. In late 1982, outstanding loans were restructured, and many were paid off by new loans principally from the United States and the International Monetary Fund (IMF), which established an "extended fund facility" to be disbursed over the next three years.

The cost of debt repayment was high. To help service it, Mexico had to adopt a rigorous "stabilization" policy, with deep reductions in public spending, subsidies, credit, and wages, all aimed at reducing both of Mexico's deficits—its external deficit (imports exceeding exports) and its internal one (government expenditures exceeding tax revenues). The stabilization strategy did produce a surplus in the balance of trade; and in 1983 an ambitious market-oriented plan for the economy was introduced, a first step toward moving the country away from import substitution. At the same time, a series of trade-related agreements were being worked out between Mexico and the United States, culminating in Mexico's entry into GATT in 1986, with Mexico unilaterally setting a 20 percent tariff level on most imports from the United States, less than half the rate it had been applying within GATT. Further U.S.–Mexican agreements followed, covering subsidies, countervailing duties, and certain categories of traded goods.

It was through the framework of CUSFTA that NAFTA was extended to Mexico. The origins of CUSFTA can be traced to the 1965 United States–Canada Automobile Agreement, which allowed duty-free trade in autos and original-equipment parts between the two countries. This pact led to a large increase in trade between the two countries, and it had a dramatic effect on Canada's automobile industry, formerly protected by high tariffs (17.5 percent). Up to 1965, about 3 percent of cars purchased in Canada came from the United States. Canadian exports of cars were constrained by higher production costs, so that even though U.S. tariffs were lower, only 7 percent of Canada's automobile output was exported to the United States. By 1970—five years into the automobile agreement—that figure exceeded 60 percent (Clement et al. 1999, 170–172). The price of cars dropped in Canada, and the wages of its auto workers rose to roughly the American level, as Canadian plants began to specialize in producing certain models and component parts, thereby allowing longer production runs and economies of scale. Canada built more cars, but fewer Canadians drove Canadian-built cars and fewer Americans drove 100 percent American-built cars. The auto pact brought rationalization to the world's sixth largest automobile industry, one that is run by a few non-Canadian producers. General Motors, Ford, and Daimler-Chrysler controlled 79 percent of total output in 1998, Honda, Toyota, and Nissan another 13 percent.[2]

Canada and Mexico concluded ten bilateral accords on trade and nontrade issues in March 1990. It was a sign—the last-ditch one—that President Carlos Salinas de Gortari of Mexico, who had taken office in December 1988, was still shying away from the idea of a free trade area with the United States. Only when it became clear that neither the foreign investment nor the export markets that he sought for his country would be forthcoming from Japan and Europe (let alone Canada) did Salinas finally opt for closer economic integration with the United States. Just three months later, in June 1990, Mexico and the United States announced their intention to form a free trade area. Canada joined the U.S.–Mexican talks in September. The three countries began official negotiations to forge the North American Free Trade Area in June 1991, after the U.S. Congress approved the "fast-track" ratification process requested by

President George Bush in exchange for assurances that labor and environmental standards would be part of any final accord.

Mexico was now reversing a half century of trade protectionism and import substitution and moving toward an open-market, outward-oriented development strategy: Its unilateral trade liberalization policy of 1984 to 1988 put it on a path leading straight to accelerated trade and investment flows with the colossus to the north. The strategy stood out as the most expedient way to attract foreign capital, revive the economy, and deal with some of the problems facing Mexico's ruling party, the Partido Revolucionario Institucional (PRI; Institutional Revolutionary Party), with its virtual one-party monopoly and its long record of corruption and electoral fraud under increasing attack (and ultimately leading to defeat in the July 2000 election). President Salinas needed greater legitimacy in the wake of the 1988 election, widely believed to have been stolen by the PRI from leftist candidate Cuauhtémoc Cárdenas; and he promoted NAFTA as promising growth and "partnership" with the United States. In the PRI, the new generation of Mexican leaders were well trained in the liberal economics of free markets and global capital and identified themselves and the interest of their country with it. Salinas himself has a doctorate in political economy and government from Harvard; his finance minister, Pedro Aspe Armella, has a doctorate in economics from the Massachusetts Institute of Technology and currently sits on the boards of McGraw-Hill Companies (New York), Banco Santander (Madrid), and the Overseas Development Council (Washington, D.C.). The minister in charge of NAFTA negotiations, Jaime Serra Puche, holds an economics doctorate from Yale and runs his own law and economics consulting firm (Serra and Associates International). Salinas would be succeeded in December 1994 by Ernesto Zedillo Ponce de León, another Yale economics Ph.D.

The negotiations that lasted from June 1991 to August 1992 were the easy part compared to ratification, which quickly became a hot political issue in the United States and Canada.[3] The Bush administration found that NAFTA was a "hard sell" to an American public more concerned with downsizings and job losses than with possible future benefits from expanded trade. Once president, Bill Clinton faced rebellion by members of his own party, reopened negotiations with Mexico to add formal environmental and labor standards, and asked Congress for a worker retraining program. As a result of these concerns, "side agreements" were written into the final version of NAFTA.[4] A labor agreement established National Administrative Offices in each of the three countries to deal with complaints regarding violations of domestic labor laws; the environmental agreement set up a similar overseer body. A North American Development Bank was also established to provide low-interest loans for environmental infrastructure projects on the U.S.–Mexican border.

Like President Bush, Prime Minister Brian Mulroney of Canada was already using the anticipated benefits of NAFTA in his own upcoming bid for reelection. But Canadian support was thrown into doubt by the resounding defeat of the Mulroney government in the general election of October 1993. Only after the three countries worked out a nonbinding pledge to codify antidumping measures by the end of 1995 did the new prime minister, Jean Chrétien, agree to reconsider the pact—which he privately favored and worked for once he took office ("My desire was to be able to sign and not lose face," he later stated [MacArthur 2000, 266–269]). Canada also submitted a unilateral statement that NAFTA could not require Canada "to export a given level or proportion of any energy resource to another NAFTA country," with water the resource that most worried Canadians (Swardson 1993; Ferguson 1993). Final approval came on December 2, 1993, only fifteen days later than in the United States. Ratification in Canada had taken sixteen months—two months longer than the official negotiations.

NAFTA went into effect on January 1, 1994. It called for elimination of most tariffs over a ten- to fifteen-year period, including (unlike most trade agreements) those in agriculture. Due to Mexico's determined defense of its own nationalized petroleum industry, energy was among the list of "exceptions" in the final agreement (annex 602.3 and chapter 26, annex III of the NAFTA agreement). Tariff reductions in textiles and automobiles were to be limited by strict "rules of origin" requiring that a product be "North-American made"; one effect was to discourage U.S. car makers, especially Ford and Daimler-Chrysler, from sourcing their components outside of North America. Significantly, NAFTA also liberalized investment and financial services. Investment was more broadly defined in order to cover all financial aspects related to investment in an enterprise (outstanding debts, interest payments, profits, real estate, and other equity holdings), and financial services were to embrace the securities industry, banking, insurance, and other parts of this rapidly growing sector. At the insistence of the United States, all three countries agreed to protect "trade-related intellectual property rights" of individuals and businesses operating in North America (chapter 17 of the NAFTA agreement). This convention prevents anyone else from using or copying a product without permission from the original developer, and it covers patents, copyrights, trademarks, trade secrets, industrial designs, sound recordings, encrypted satellite signals, and other rights related to a range of industries (e.g., computers and software, pharmaceuticals, and films and video recordings). Finally, all trade disputes were to be referred to panels representing the three countries, a system carried over from the binational panels of CUSFTA.

NAFTA was hailed as a pivotal event in the history of the North American economy, one that would create a continental-scale market through trade, investment, and property rights provisions going well beyond the simple removal of trade barriers. It brought together one developing and two developed countries, with characteristics that seemed to cry out for economic convergence and integration. Disparities in economic development, like those between Canada and the United States on the one hand and Mexico on the other, were supposed to lead to reallocation of resources from high-cost to low-cost production, and to widespread productivity increases and income and employment gains in all countries involved.

THE FIRST SIX YEARS: WHAT HATH NAFTA WROUGHT?

With the year 2000, NAFTA began its seventh year of operation. What impact has it had? Has it lived up to expectations, fallen below them, or moved beyond in ways that few foresaw?

It is too soon to give any definitive answer—if such an answer will ever be possible amid similar forces operating at a global level and over much the same period of time. But some effort must be made to look at the structure of the continental economy before NAFTA and after, to see whether any changes appear to be under way. Special attention should be paid to those sectors most likely to be affected by the establishment of a free trade area with NAFTA's characteristics.

One cannot fail to be struck by the unique nature of NAFTA. Mexico's economy is less than one-twentieth the size of the U.S. economy and half the size of the Canadian, although its population is more than triple Canada's (see table 2.1). Its per capita incomes are a quarter those of the (weighted) average of its two neighbors, calculated in purchasing power parity (PPP) for equivalent quantities of goods and services (table 2.1), but less than an eighth in standard terms ($329 billion for a population of 94.8 million yields $3,470 per person). The economic profile of NAFTA shows another large disparity—in foreign trade ratios. This one separates one of the two high-income countries, the United States, from the other two NAFTA countries, which have economies much smaller and more dependent on trade with the outside world.

The foreign trade ratio measures a country's exports of both goods and services plus its imports of them, as a percentage of gross domestic product (GDP). Over the past twenty years, world trade in services has been growing faster than trade in goods (merchandise). Trade in services covers banking and finance, insurance, transportation and communications, law and accounting, engineering, and other business and technical services. For the United States, services trade with Canada and Mexico has grown slowly and is much less important than its merchandise trade with them. Mexico accounts for less than 5 percent of total U.S. exports of services and 6 percent of its imports, Canada, 8 percent to 9 percent of both.[5] This represents less than half their shares of U.S. trade in goods (see table 2.2).

For merchandise trade, the great bulk of it for Mexico and Canada has been taking place with the United States (see tables 2.3 and 2.4). For the United States itself, trade with its two neighbors constitutes around 30 per-

Table 2.1   Economic Profile of NAFTA Countries, 1997–1998 (annual averages)

	Canada	Mexico	United States
Gross Domestic Product (in billions of 1995 U.S. dollars)	$621.9	$329.0	$8,124.6
GDP per capita (PPP basis)	$24,322	$7,772	$30,827
Population (in millions)	30.1	94.8	269.3
Foreign Trade Ratio (to GDP)	79.2%	61.1%	24.1%
Foreign Direct Investment Ratio (to Domestic Fixed Investment)	12.7%	8.4%	8.2%
Percentage of Nonagricultural Labor Force in Manufacturing	16.1%	22.8%	15.1%
Government Spending Ratio (to GDP)	42.5%	16.6%	31.0%
Electricity Production per capita (in kilowatt hours)[a]	20,904	1,754	12,977
Human Development Index[a,b]	.932	.786	.927

[a]For 1997.
[b]Defined as measuring "achievements in the most basic human capabilities—life expectancy, educational attainment, and income."
Sources: Rows 1 and 2, Organization for Economic Cooperation and Development (OECD) (2000). Rows 3, 4, and 6, Canada (2000); Mexico (2000); U.S. President (2000), appendix B. Row 5, UN Conference on Trade and Development (1999), annex table B.5. Row 7, Inter-American Development Bank (2000); OECD (1999), annex table 28. Rows 8 and 9, UN Development Program (1999), tables 1, 17

cent of its total trade in goods (table 2.2), far higher than its services trade with them—but only two-fifths as important as their trade with the United States is to them. The United States and Canada nonetheless have the largest bilateral trading relationship in the world, an economic fact not likely to be relegated to secondary status by U.S. policymakers, as the 1965 auto pact and 1989 CUSFTA demonstrate. Merchandise trade between the two countries totaled $367 billion in 1999, $24 billion larger than U.S. trade with the entire fifteen-country European Union (which excludes Switzerland, Norway, and eastern Europe).[6]

With the advent of NAFTA in 1994, *trends* in these trade flows take on greater significance. U.S. trade with Canada (table 2.2) appears to be unaffected by NAFTA, at least for the time being. Through NAFTA's first five years (1994–1998), U.S. exports to Canada made up 22.6 percent of total U.S. exports, not much higher than before and 10 percent below the 1985–1987 level. Imports from Canada may have crept up slightly, to 19.4 percent of all U.S. imports, but in fact they remain well below their 1974–1976 level of 21.8 percent.[7] U.S. trade with Mexico is another matter. It has risen substantially during the NAFTA years for both exports and imports (table 2.2), but the rise in imports is more striking, from 1 percent of all U.S. merchandise imports in 1979–1981 to

Table 2.2   U.S. Trade in Goods, 1979–1998 (annual averages)

	1979–1981	1985–1987	1991–1993	1996–1998
Exports				
Total (in millions of U.S. dollars) of which, to	$215,244	$229,822	$438,032	$654,006
Canada	19.6%	25.2%	21.2%	22.6%
Mexico	6.7	5.8	8.8	10.5
Europe	31.2	27.9	27.3	24.1
Asia and Pacific	28.4	30.1	32.8	32.0
Latin America and Western Hemisphere (excluding Mexico)	10.3	8.2	7.7	9.1
Other (Africa and Middle East)	3.8	2.8	2.2	1.7
Imports				
Total (in millions of U.S. dollars) of which, from	$242,275	$372,093	$538,960	$865,624
Canada	18.0%	19.1%	19.0%	19.4%
Mexico	1.1	5.1	6.7	9.9
Europe	20.1	24.0	21.1	21.5
Asia and Pacific	35.2	41.6	44.3	41.1
Latin America and Western Hemisphere (excluding Mexico)	9.9	7.0	6.2	5.9
Other (Africa and Middle East)	15.7	3.2	2.7	2.2

Sources: Survey of Current Business, June 1993, table 2, 78, 96; July 1999, table 2, 94, 96.

nearly 10 percent in the late 1990s. Both Canada and Mexico have been sending more of their exports to the United States than anywhere else (tables 2.3 and 2.4), but Mexico's have been heading to *El Norte* at a faster rate (62 percent of them in 1979–1981, and nearly 84 percent by 1995–1997).

Overwhelmingly, Mexico has become an exporter of manufactured goods, which made up 85 percent of Mexico's total merchandise exports in 1998–1999, compared to one-fifth in the early 1980s (Mexico 2000; UN Statistical Office 1999, 626, and earlier editions).[8] This reflects a parallel change in U.S. trade itself. In 1979–1981, manufactured consumer goods, automobile vehicles, engines, and parts, and capital goods (including electric and non-electric machinery, computers, semiconductors, and telecommunications equipment) accounted for 39 percent of U.S. merchandise imports—but 67 percent of them by 1996–1998, a figure that would be higher were it not for the decline in imports of automobiles resulting from the increase in production of Japanese cars inside the United States in recent years.[9] During the 1980s and 1990s, as table 2.2 indicates, U.S. imports from Canada increased

Table 2.3   Canadian Trade in Goods, 1979–1998 (annual averages)

	1979–1981	1985–1987	1991–1993	1996–1998
Exports				
Total (in millions of U.S. dollars)	$62,168	$87,668	$134,630	$197,669
Of which, to United States	65.6%	76.8%	78.0%	82.2%
Mexico	0.7	0.4	0.4	0.5
All other	33.7	22.8	21.6	17.3[a]
Imports				
Total (in millions of U.S. dollars)	$58,409	$80,615	$123,801	$189,632
Of which, from United States	70.2%	68.9%	65.4%	67.8%
Mexico	0.7	1.1	2.0	2.6
All other	29.1	30.0	32.6	29.6[b]

[a]Two largest, 1996–1998: Japan 3.7 percent and United Kingdom 1.4 percent.
[b]Two largest, 1996–1998: Japan 4.6 percent and China 2.3 percent.
Sources: Canada (2000), UN Statistical Office (1999) and earlier editions.

Table 2.4   Mexican Trade in Goods, 1979–1997 (annual averages)

	1979–1981	1985–1987	1991–1993	1995–1997
Exports				
Total (in millions of U.S. dollars)	$14,501	$18,809	$41,733	$95,083
Of which, to United States	62.1%	65.0%	78.9%	83.8%
Canada	2.0	1.5	3.0	2.3
All other	35.9	33.5	18.1	13.9[a]
Imports				
Total (in millions of U.S. dollars)	$18,737	$11,638	$55,106	$91,261
Of which, from United States	63.1%	67.6%	73.0%	74.8%
Canada	1.8	2.1	1.5	1.9
All other	35.1	30.3	25.5	23.3[b]

[a]Two largest, 1995–1997: Japan 1.1 percent and Spain 0.9 percent.
[b]Two largest, 1995–1997: Japan 4.5 percent and Germany 3.6 percent.
Sources: Mexico (2000); UN Statistical Office (1999) and earlier editions.

modestly, with most of the growth occurring before NAFTA. The large increases in U.S. imports—dominated by manufactures—came from Mexico and non-Japan Asia (table 2.2; imports from Japan were falling in relative terms, to less than 14 percent in 1996–1998). From 1970 to 1990, during a period when total imports were increasing as a share of U.S. GDP, the share of U.S. manufacturing imports coming from less-developed countries jumped from 14 percent to 36 percent, probably higher by the late 1990s. Nine countries, Mexico among them, were responsible for 80 percent of the increase (Freeman 1995, 19; Sachs and Shatz 1994, 1).[10] Not only in North America, but also across the world, developing economies are becoming more important suppliers of manufactured producer and consumer goods. Since 1965, these economies have increased their share of aggregate world exports from 26 percent to 33 percent, taking a larger share of a many-times-larger world export market even though the shares of African and most Latin American countries fell (Organization for Economic Cooperation and Development [OECD] 1998, 206–208).

International trade is the oldest and most familiar link between national economies; trade in goods and services has been increasing faster than world output since 1950, and much faster since 1970 (Dicken 1998, 24–26). But foreign direct investment (FDI) has been growing even faster than trade since 1970. FDI occurs when companies invest abroad for purposes of establishing and exercising control over operations. It is done by building production or marketing facilities ("greenfield" FDI) or acquiring them ready-made from their owners. The foreign enterprises acquired—"affiliates" of the parent company—can be owned by the parent or jointly, with foreign partners. At least 10 percent equity ownership is deemed sufficient to constitute FDI. The stake usually runs higher, and an affiliate becomes "majority owned" when foreign ownership of the voting stock exceeds 50 percent.

The accumulated global stock of FDI was valued at $4.1 trillion in 1998, eight times greater than in 1980. Adjusted for inflation, its rate of growth has been triple that of world trade, and more than twice that of world fixed investment (UN Conference on Trade and Development [UNCTAD] 1997, xvi, 3–4; UNCTAD 1999, table I.2 and annex table B.4). Annual flows of new FDI tripled during the 1990s and reached $649 billion in 1998; in real terms, they are estimated to be seven to eight times larger than in the 1970s (UNCTAD 1999, table I.1; UNCTAD 1999, 25). The overriding importance of FDI is that it gives rise to *international production,* a more advanced form of economic integration that goes far beyond traditional trade in goods and services, by allowing multinational corporations (MNCs) to shift production and distribution to wherever it is most profitable to do so.

FDI outflows from all three NAFTA members together averaged around 17 percent of the world's total in the decade leading up to NAFTA, then rose to 27 percent in NAFTA's first five years (1994–1998).[11] The rise occurred because U.S. and Canadian MNCs both increased their aggregate overseas investments faster than their Japanese and European competitors. Companies based in the United States also stepped up investments in Canada and Mexico—but to levels still well below those of the 1980s (see table 2.5). U.S. MNCs also renewed their investment activities in several countries in Africa and the Middle East in the late 1990s (notably Israel, Egypt, Saudi Arabia, Algeria, and Nigeria). Canadian MNCs sharply increased their own FDI outflows to the Pacific Rim and Japan, and at rates considerably higher than

Table 2.5   U.S. Foreign Direct Investments, 1979–1998 (annual averages)

	1979–1981	*1985–1987*	*1991–1993*	*1996–1998*
Outflows				
Total (in billions of U.S. dollars) of which, to	$18.0	$26.2	$57.1	$111.8
Canada	14.1%	14.0%	4.5%	8.2%
Mexico	6.0	1.0	4.0	3.5
Europe	56.5	44.3	55.1	54.5
Asia and Pacific	14.1	10.6	13.6	13.9
Latin America and Western Hemisphere (excluding Mexico)	5.1	30.3	20.0	15.6
Other (Africa and Middle East)	4.2	–0.2	1.8	4.3
Inflows				
Total (in billions of U.S. dollars) of which, from	$18.0	$38.2	$32.4	$130.5
Canada	11.7%	5.1%	8.5%	9.5%
Mexico	0.1	0.6	0.7	0.3
Europe	61.0	75.0	64.7	77.6
Asia and Pacific	11.4	23.8	19.8	10.7
Latin America and Western Hemisphere (excluding Mexico)	10.4	–4.4	4.8	1.4
Other (Africa and Middle East)	5.4	–0.1	1.5	0.5

Sources: Survey of Current Business, November 1984 and August 1985, table 1; August 1990, tables 22 and 42; July 1993; September 1997; September 1999, tables 16 and 17; July 1999, table 1.

their investing in the United States. Two-thirds of all Canadian FDI outflows went to the United States in 1982–1989, but only a third in the 1990s, even after NAFTA went into effect (Industry Canada 1999/2000, 36–38).

Meantime, FDI inflows into the NAFTA area fell, from 36 percent of the world total in the pre–NAFTA years to 28 percent in 1994–1998. Some of the FDI inflows into the three countries come from each other, almost entirely from the United States and Canada. But, as noted, FDI outflows from the United States into Canada and Mexico show no sign of increasing any faster since 1994; and Canadian outflows to the United States have grown less rapidly than they have to the Pacific area and Europe. Total FDI inflows into Canada (about 70 percent of them from the United States) grew more slowly in the 1990s than during the two preceding decades. In 1996, for the first time in its history, Canada became a net exporter of capital: Its stock of outward FDI (held by Canadian MNCs abroad) exceeded that of its inward FDI

(Industry Canada 1999/2000, 23–30). Since NAFTA went into effect, in other words, North America as a whole appears to be attracting foreign capital no faster—in fact somewhat more slowly—than other regions of the world. The flow of FDI into Mexico, however, has accelerated. From 1994 through 1998, it averaged $10.8 billion per year, compared to $4.7 billion annually during 1987–1993, with European and Japanese MNCs increasing their presence in Mexico faster than U.S. MNCs (UNCTAD 1999, annex table B.1).

International production takes place when MNCs produce goods and services outside their country of origin; an affiliate of Toyota makes automobiles in the United States or an affiliate of Hoover assembles vacuum cleaners in Scotland. It gives rise to intrafirm trade (IFT), or transactions between units of a single company—the parent firm and its affiliates abroad. MNCs can "slice up the value chain" by geographically dispersing stages of production, from raw materials to intermediate goods requiring further processing, near-finished goods for wholesale trade, and finished goods for sale to customers. IFT has grown from an estimated 20 percent of total world trade in 1970 to 40 percent or more by the late 1990s.[12] Within North America, IFT has been spreading since the 1960s; a landmark was the 1965 Canada–U.S. auto pact. U.S. exports of goods to foreign affiliates of U.S.–based companies averaged $205 billion per year in 1996–1997; of that sum, 31.9 percent went to Canada, 10.8 percent to Mexico, with both figures, especially Canada's, lower since NAFTA went into effect. The share going to Europe was 26.3 percent (also lower than in 1992–1993), while 24.9 percent went to Pacific Asia (nearly a quarter more than before NAFTA).[13] Imports of goods shipped to the United States by foreign affiliates of U.S. companies totaled $171.7 billion per year in 1996–1997, with IFT imports from Mexico reaching 15.1 percent of the total against 10.7 percent in 1992–1993. Canada supplied 40.5 percent, nearly the same as four years earlier. IFT flows between Canada and Mexico appear to be negligible.

Clearly, the United States is at the center of IFT in the NAFTA area, and its two-way trade with Mexico is rising steeply. Mexico may in effect be taking some of Canada's share, or its future growth, in the international production operations of U.S. MNCs, at least if the automobile industry is any indication. Vehicle and parts imports coming into the United States from Canada peaked in 1968–1970, when they represented 8.7 percent of total U.S. merchandise imports. They slipped to 7.2 percent in 1985 then fell more steeply to 5.6 percent in 1998.[14] By then, U.S. automotive imports from Mexico were 54 percent as large as imports from Canada, compared with 20 percent in 1989 (U.S. Department of Commerce, Office of Automotive Affairs 1999, 1–3).[15] Mexico's road vehicle industry started to expand in the 1980s, with plants inside the country owned by American, German, and Japanese companies. With the latest production technologies supplied by their foreign owners, Mexican automobile facilities are now on a par with those in the high-income countries; and they hire workers educated in Mexico's public universities, technical institutes, and secondary schools, many of whom "are overqualified for the jobs they now can get" (according to the director of Chihuahua's Institute of Technology) (Uchitelle 1993b, F5). These workers receive from a fourth to an eighth the compensation of their U.S. counterparts, depending on whether they work in the parts or vehicle assembly sector, although quality and productivity sometimes exceed U.S. levels (Shaiken 1993, 28; U.S. Department of Commerce, Office of Automotive Affairs 1999, 6). Since 1980, General Motors has built more than fifty parts factories in Mexico with seventy-two thousand workers; its Delphi Automotive Service subsidiary is Mexico's largest private employer. Volkswagen's Beetle, revived in 1998, is made exclusively in Mexico, where wage levels "make line workers cringe from Detroit to Stuttgart" (Millman 1998, A17). In Mexican manufacturing as a whole, hourly compensation for production workers averages one-tenth that in the United States and Canada (U.S. International Trade Commission [USITC] 1999, table B-19).

Through the 1960s and 1970s, greenfield FDI was the dominant mode of market entry and development for multinational enterprise, but mergers and acquisitions (M&As) are being increasingly used to accomplish these goals. Since 1985, M&As establishing a majority-ownership share are running at more than half of all FDI inflows worldwide, higher if cross-border M&As that involve minority-held transactions were included, and they represent one-quarter of all M&As in both value and number of deals (UNCTAD 1999, 94–96; 1998, 19–20). During 1997 and 1998, there were 147 cross-border "megadeals"—that is, M&As with a value exceeding $1 billion. Only eleven of them (7.5 percent) took place within the NAFTA area. Of these, six— including the three largest—involved Canadian firms acquiring U.S. firms: Northern Telecom acquired Bay Networks ($9.0 billion), Teleglobe acquired Excel Communications ($6.9 billion), and Canadian National Railway took over Illinois Central ($2.9 billion). U.S. MNCs carried out 34 of the 147 megadeal acquisitions worldwide, but only 5 of the 34 were within NAFTA; three of the acquired firms were Canadian, and two Mexican (including a merchandise and apparel chain taken over by Wal-Mart) (UNCTAD 1999, annex table A.III.1; 1998, annex table A.1.1).

NAFTA'S IMPACT: PLUS CHANGE . . . ?

NAFTA is less than a decade old. So far, it seems safe to say that it has not brought basic changes in the structure of the North American economy, and that any such future changes would have to represent large departures from historical trend even to restore some of the levels of economic integration that existed in the 1970s and 1980s.

Merchandise trade between the United States and Canada has been stable. The percentage of Canada's exports going to the United States is higher than ever, but it was on the rise well before 1994, and Canada's share of U.S. imports (19.5 percent in 1999) is marginally higher than in the pre–NAFTA years. U.S. exports to Canada are running below their share levels of the late 1980s. International trade in services, growing faster than trade in goods in the world as a whole, is lagging in the NAFTA area. Relatively less U.S. and Canadian FDI is flowing to fellow NAFTA countries since NAFTA went into effect. IFT by U.S.–based MNCs with their affiliates in Canada and Mexico is relatively lower now than it was before NAFTA, except for IFT imports from Mexico; production by affiliates of U.S. MNCs declined as a proportion of Canada's GDP from the 1980s through the 1990s (from 11 percent to 9 percent), while rising in Mexico (2 percent to 3 percent).[16] Within NAFTA, cross-border M&A activity has been disproportionately small, given the size of the combined NAFTA economies in the world economy.

One set of changes does stand out, although at this point in time it appears to be more of the same, rather than a NAFTA–induced break in trend or reallocation of resources across the entire continent. The theme that emerges from trade in goods (tables 2.2, 2.3, and 2.4) is one of increased dependence of the United States, and Canada to a much lesser extent, on Mexico as a source of supply of manufactures.

Since the abrupt turnabout in the mid-1980s toward an open-economy model, Mexico has transformed itself into a poorer North American version of an East Asian "tiger," with exports catering to consumer and industrial goods markets in higher-income nations, especially the United States. Leading Mexico's export growth are telecommunications and sound equipment, office machines and equipment, electrical machinery, general and specialized industrial machines, road vehicles and transport equipment, chemicals and related products, clothing and accessories, and toys and sporting goods, which together comprised 63 percent of Mexico's total exports in the late 1990s (UN Statistical Office 1999, 631–633). Usually, these products originate as imports of intermediate goods (which constitute three-fourths of Mexican imports) that undergo further processing for reexport. Of the FDI on which this export-oriented production is based, only a third is from the United States since NAFTA went into effect (UNCTAD 1999, annex table B.1);[17] two-thirds has come from Japan and Europe, whose MNCs and banks want to establish their own presence inside a growing free trade area, just as U.S. and Canadian (and Japanese) MNCs have done in Europe and elsewhere.

Most of Mexico's export growth has come from the *maquiladoras*, which are clustered along the U.S. border and have turned into export platforms for Mexican manufactures; typically, U.S. firms send U.S.–made components to Mexico for processing and assembly and then reimport the finished products. Under a number of earlier agreements and tariff-preference programs, much of this trade was already duty-free well before NAFTA. In 1963, item 807.00 of the Tariff Schedules of the United States first made it possible for U.S. firms to reimport goods, paying tariff only on the value-added, or the actual wages and related costs incurred in foreign production. Tariff rates on these trade flows were further slashed in 1965 and 1966 (USITC 1999, chapter 1 and appendix A; MacArthur 2000, 36–38). Within five years, imports under item 807.00 were increasing faster from Mexico than any other country, and were concentrated in consumer electronic products and components, toys and dolls, and wearing apparel (U.S. Tariff Commission 1970, 15–17, 70–72). On the Mexican side, the tariff codes governing the *maquiladora* program allowed for the duty-free import of intermediate goods, and they predated Mexico's general policies of liberalized foreign trade and investment by at least two decades (Clement et al. 1999, 80–81; Kamel and Hoffman 1999, 1–4). This meant that tariffs on both sides of the border were favorable to U.S. manufacturing companies looking to relocate to lower-wage areas—and which at home were using large numbers of low- and semiskilled workers who were unionized. Twelve plants were opened when the *maquiladora* program was established in 1965; the number exceeded six hundred in 1980 and three thousand in 1998 (Hufbauer and Schott 1992, 91–92; Kamel and Hoffman 1999, 18). The *maquiladoras* were "rapidly becoming the newest American industrial belt" in the 1990s, with a list of manufacturers that looked like a cross-section of the Fortune 500, including, among others, Ford, Zenith, Whirlpool, AT&T, Bendix, G. D. Searle, Parker Hannifin, and Data General (Uchitelle 1993a).

One aim of NAFTA, for Mexico, was to extend the tariff and tax provisions of the *maquiladora* throughout the whole country to generate more jobs everywhere. But manufacturing remains disproportionately concentrated in the *maquiladora* zone, which accounts for a third of Mexico's manufacturing employment. In the *maquiladora*, employment rose from 120,000 in 1980 to 583,000 in 1994, then to a million by year-end 1998, making it the fastest-growing industrial sector in Latin America over the period 1980–1998 (Larudee 1998, table 2; United Nations 1998, table VII.2). Fifty-six percent of all production workers are women (Kamel and Hoffman 1999, 18). For some key products, the *maquiladoras*' share of U.S. imports coming from Mexico is almost absolute. Of total U.S. imports of motor vehicles and parts from Mexico, 99.8 percent came from the *maquiladoras* in 1998, as did 99.9 percent of television receivers and parts (Mexico is the leading exporter of television sets to the United States) and 95.2 percent of apparel and other textiles (USITC 1999, table C-2). Sixty-four percent of *maquiladora* output is concentrated in three industries—electrical and electronic products, apparel and textile products, and road vehicles and parts, which are also the top three exports to the United States (Kamel and Hoffman 1999, 19; USITC 1999, 2–5). Ownership alone has become more diversified in the *maquiladoras*, as several large Asian electronic and consumer appliance manufacturers and Swedish truck and car makers (e.g., Scania and Volvo) have established plants there to avail themselves of the tariff benefits inside NAFTA (U.S. Department of Commerce, Office of Automotive Affairs 1999, 8–9; USITC 1999, 3–5). The late 1990s' employment boom and the concentration of so much production-for-export in the *maquiladoras* notwithstanding, their major growth phase occurred before NAFTA, not after. Employment in the *maquiladoras* increased nearly four times in the 1980s; it doubled from 1990 through 1998. The value of *maquiladora* industrial exports grew nearly twice as fast during the 1980s even though the Mexican economy as a whole grew twice as fast during the 1990s (Mexico 2000; OECD 1999, annex table 1).

So it cannot be said that NAFTA has caused any takeoff or accelerated growth in the *maquiladora* economy. Nor has it delivered broad-based economic growth for the Mexican people. Instead, the first phase of NAFTA looks very much like the path charted for developing countries in the new era of global capital. In December 1994, the newly elected President Zedillo attempted a long-overdue devaluation of the peso by 14 percent ($3.50 to $4). The market expected more and unleashed a speculative attack on the peso, which lost half its value in a matter of days as a flight to U.S. dollars by foreign and domestic peso holders depleted Mexico's foreign exchange reserves. Immediately thereafter, authorities were forced to free the exchange rate, which fell further. The collapse of the peso cheapened Mexico's exports, leading North Americans to buy more Mexican products and fewer U.S. and Canadian ones. It also pushed Mexico's inflation rate close to triple digits in 1995; and as they always do under such circumstances, nominal wage rates lagged behind inflation, so that real wages fell (OECD 1999, annex tables 38 and 39; Larudee 1998, tables 1 and 2). During 1995, GDP contracted 8 percent and unemployment soared, adding to downward pressure on wages and giving foreign companies even more incentive to invest in Mexican production.

Emergency economic and financial measures locked these comparative advantages into place. Out of fear that the new Mexican government might repudiate NAFTA or do something equally drastic, the Clinton administration, with the IMF, swiftly put together a bailout package of close to $50 billion in short-term credits; the IMF's share, $18 billion, was the largest ever approved for a member country. Mexico agreed to keep its foreign exchange windows open, and to implement tight monetary and fiscal policies. The follow-up was inevitable. In 1992, with NAFTA on the drawing boards, President Salinas had secured commitments from business and union leaders to limit wage increases (Darling 1992). Now, in January 1995, President Zedillo announced a severe austerity plan calling for limits on wage and price increases, cutbacks in government spending, and privatizations in previously untouched areas (e.g., railroads, airports, seaports, telecommunications, electricity generation, and even the sacrosanct petrochemical industry). He conceded that devaluation and wage controls would mean "a drop in real earnings" for nearly all Mexicans over the next year (Fineman and Darling 1995, A1). Two months later, a peso stabilization plan brought more wage restraints, coupled with increases in the prices of water, natural gas, electricity, and other public-sector services (Crawford 1995). Higher interest rates damaged Mexico's middle class, many of whom had taken on mortgages and loans for small businesses. Average real wages in the industrial sector plunged, and in 2000 they were still 12 percent below their 1993 level (Mexico 2000).

Mexico's economy recovered in 1996 and 1997. Real GDP growth averaged 4.2 percent per year, spurred by a strong performance of the export sector and a rebound in oil prices, and unemployment fell. But even with the peso stabilized, the damage to real wages has proved hard to reverse. Separating the effects of the currency crisis and NAFTA would be difficult, but there is little need to do so. NAFTA draws Mexico more deeply into global economics and finance, and real wages took another hit with the depreciation of the peso in the fall of 1998 in the wake of the Russian debt crisis. Austerity, liberalization, and privatization have also reduced the size of government in the Mexican economy to little more than half the U.S. level (table 2.1), itself the lowest of all high-income countries.

For the United States, the NAFTA years have brought a distinct shift in the balance of merchandise trade with Mexico. The United States has consistently run a trade deficit (imports exceeding exports) with Mexico over the past two decades, with the exception of 1991–1994. The post–NAFTA surge in Mexican exports to the United States was given an initial boost by the devaluation of the peso, but it was soon reinforced by policies that curb wages and stifle labor unions, widening the gulf between wages and working conditions of Mexicans compared to U.S. and Canadian workers. NAFTA backers in the United States forecast an increase in American exports to Mexico if NAFTA were passed, and that did happen: U.S. exports to Mexico rose from $51 billion in 1994 to $87 billion in 1999, and Mexico has now replaced Japan as the second-largest market for U.S. exports, after Canada. But imports from Mexico rose faster, and so has the bilateral U.S. trade deficit. In 1998–1999, Mexico was responsible for 7 percent of the U.S. trade deficit, more than triple its 1980s level, and trailing only four countries. Canada accounted for 9 percent, but its lead over Mexico has been narrowing.[18]

NAFTA supporters, with two presidents in the lead, also promised that more jobs would be created in the United States. The claim was withdrawn after two academics, whose predictions of 175,000 new jobs by 1995 were cited by the Bush administration, reported that any net increase in jobs would evaporate after fifteen or twenty years, and that the NAFTA agreement would displace 324,000 jobs from the United States (figures that were left out of their previously published book on the topic) (Bradsher 1993).[19] Between 1993 and 1998, according to a later study, trade with Mexico and Canada destroyed 440,000 American jobs (1.1 million jobs gained from exports, more than 1.5 million lost from imports). Displaced workers have generally been able to find new jobs during the long expansion of the U.S. economy in the 1990s, but their earnings dropped by an average of 16 percent (Scott 1999).

FREE TRADE OR FREE ENTERPRISE? THE NAFTA TESTAMENT

Economic globalization as we know it is three decades old, and its distinguishing feature is the high mobility of capital across borders. Capital is not only more mobile than labor, but is itself immensely more mobile than ever before: It can be packaged with the newest technologies and supported by funds transmitted electronically to any place anytime.

Among economic models of NAFTA, the great majority rely on the standard theory of free trade, a descendant of David Ricardo's nineteenth-century concept of "comparative advantage." The main assumptions are that capital is immobile internationally and that countries gain when they specialize in producing goods in which their labor has a relative productivity advantage. Of nineteen NAFTA forecasts reviewed by the U.S. Congressional Budget Office (CBO) in 1993, only five looked at possible movements of capital. The CBO's reviewer acknowledged that investment outflows could wipe out potential job gains in the United States but reported that "no one has looked at it much" (Bernstein 1993, 34). The conclusion reached by economists about the effects of NAFTA was no more cogent even within the framework of their own model: The way trade generates gains is precisely by restructuring production inside trading nations, and while some opponents exaggerated the possible costs of NAFTA in terms of jobs lost and wages reduced, proponents downplayed the fact that trade expansion creates losers, destroys jobs, and often has negative income distribution consequences.

The massive, furiously pursued campaign to sell NAFTA to the U.S. Congress and the American public was framed in terms of "free trade" and benefits for participating nations. NAFTA was promoted as a way of creating high-paying, export-related jobs inside the United States. President Bush, who negotiated NAFTA, told Republican Party leaders that it would be "a vote-winner" for all of them. Another alleged benefit, less openly advertised, was reducing the large-scale illegal immigration of Mexican workers into the United States. The only way to slow it down, Clinton administration officials and congressional supporters of NAFTA let it be known, was to create better jobs in Mexico (MacArthur 2000, 117–119, 290–291). When asked by a member of a private-sector NAFTA advisory board whether he really believed that "NAFTA will create jobs in the U.S. net of the losses of jobs that will occur," one of the chief negotiators replied, "Hopefully, it will slow down illegal immigration" (Simmons 2000, 20).[20]

The real goals lay elsewhere. Rather than embodying the Ricardian theory of comparative advantage, NAFTA more closely resembled the Archimedean principle of "give me but a place to stand, and I can move the world." The pact was an effort by U.S. MNCs to gain quick and convenient leverage in a globalizing economy in which every market and every productive resource is challenged, and nothing is secure, even in one's own bailiwick. The practical goals, as the fight over NAFTA in Washington made clear, were to make Mexico safe for private investment, by making sure that its government's history of expropriating foreign-owned assets could not be repeated, and to guarantee open access for U.S. manufacturers to the country's supply of low-cost labor (see MacArthur 2000). As a California consulting firm specializing in "start-up management and ongoing operations in Mexico" advised potential customers, "production sharing assembly and manufacturing in Mexico [are] safe, easy, and profitable." A U.S. company could "remain competitive by reducing direct labor costs, avoid the cost and burden of mandated government programs (including worker's compensation), stay in close proximity to your low cost, foreign manufacturing facility, [and have] limited availability of quality labor."[21]

The great leap toward formal economic integration in North America, between 1988 and 1993, came after more than a decade of intensifying international competition that, like the mobility of capital fueling it, has few if any historical parallels. By the mid-1980s, America's "big three" automakers were controlling only 65 percent of all domestic sales, a market share that would have been lower in the absence of "voluntary restraints" on imports of Japanese cars negotiated with Tokyo in 1981. Other U.S. industries under siege by imports were lumber products, steel, machine tools, textiles and apparel, shoes, consumer electronics, and communications equipment, as foreign producers captured 30 percent to 70 percent of their markets by the mid-1980s. Seven of America's ten leading high-tech-oriented industries, including pharmaceuticals, electrical equipment, and professional and scientific instruments, also lost ground in world markets (Du Boff 1989, 156–160).

The corporate strategies that NAFTA embodied were largely extensions of those pursued for years inside the United States and abroad, and by MNCs of several industrial nations, not only the United States. America's automakers are one of the best examples of an industry looking to restructure operations and to make use of production-sharing arrangements like those offered by the *maquiladoras*. In some respects, the United States itself is a low-wage country with an attractive investment environment. In the view of the managing director of Germany's Dresdner Bank, more European FDI may be headed to the United States, with a labor market "far more flexible than the labor market in Europe. Not only is the mobility of job-seekers far greater than in Europe, but also the differentiation of wages and salaries meets with hardly any problems of acceptance" (Federal Reserve Bank of Atlanta 1997, 3). U.S. MNCs have been effectively moving capital and labor to Mexico for a quarter century—and using the threat of moving operations southward to wring wage and working condition concessions from their workers. Plant closing threats "appear to be extremely effective in undermining union organizing efforts," even when the majority of workers seem predisposed to support a union at the beginning of the organizing drive. Based on union certification elections from 1993 to 1995, half of all employers threaten to close plants when facing a union vote. In manufacturing, storage, and warehousing, and some transportation and service industries, 60 percent of union organizing efforts were met by management threats to close the plants, compared to 29 percent before NAFTA. When organizing drives nonetheless succeeded, employers closed the plants fully or partially 15 percent of the time within three years, triple the postelection plant closing rates in the 1980s (Bronfenbrenner 1996).

For the United States, NAFTA is a tactic to advance its own liberal economic policies, rather than to change any of its policies to fit a set of regional institutions. The need, for U.S. MNCs, was liberalization of Mexico's investment rules and access to its supplies of lower-cost labor, along with wider access to Canada's markets and economic assets. Canada sees NAFTA as guaranteeing surer access to the markets of its dominant trading partner in a time of increasing global competition (Clement et al. 1999, chapter 7). During NAFTA negotiations, another Canadian objective was to secure relief from U.S. antidumping and countervailing duty actions. Direct trade between Canada and Mexico was relatively minor—it is now growing—but Canada also sought Mexican support against U.S. use of contingent protection, the case-by-case application of "Section 301" duties when U.S. producers were found to be injured by subsidized or dumped imports (after section 301 of the 1974 Trade Act requiring the president's trade negotiator to retaliate against any nation judged to be engaging in "unfair trade practices").

For Mexico, a regional trade agreement appeared to be the best way to solidify domestic policy changes, as well as to broaden links to a giant neighbor's market, its capital, and its technologies. There was also pressure to join the rush toward global free markets before it was too late. In the words of the president of Mexico's Center of Research for Development, "Governments all over the world are moving in the same direction—deregulating, privatizing, cutting their deficits and vying for foreign investment" (Zachary 1997, A1). Through NAFTA, Mexico's own MNCs have a stronger base for extending operations in the hemisphere, through membership in the eleven-nation Latin American Integration Association (1980) and the Group of Three (1994, with Colombia and Venezuela), and links to the Mercado Común del Sur (1991; MERCOSUR), the most important trade bloc in Latin America, comprising Argentina, Brazil, Paraguay, and Uruguay (Millman 2000). But if these are the benefits for Mexico, the costs are clear: It will be harder if not impossible for Mexico to pursue any mode of economic growth based on spreading productivity increases to workers, increasing wage income, and expanding the social infrastructure of the economy. The country that nationalized foreign oil companies and redistributed land to peasants in the 1930s is now in thrall to the World Bank, the IMF, the World Trade Organization (WTO), and the economic and financial establishments of the G-7 nations (United States, Canada, Japan, France, Italy, Germany, and United

Kingdom). The neoliberal economic policies of the past two decades have had predictable effects, and in the era of NAFTA itself, the Zedillo austerity measures imposed great pain on the mass of Mexican workers. It is unlikely that the new administration will depart from this model of economic and financial management; during the election of 2000, Vicente Fox campaigned against almost everything the PRI stood for, but his promise of sweeping changes did not extend to economic policy.

None of the policy structures of NAFTA are inward-looking, but they are forms of globalization insurance rooted in regional arrangements. For all three countries, they create a larger tariff and investment unit for bargaining with other countries and regional trading groups, especially the European Union. A major provision of NAFTA is free trade and investment in the service industries. Many of these industries harbor intellectual property, the protection of which was so important for the United States in the negotiations leading to NAFTA. The worldview inherent in this tenaciously pursued goal is underscored by the fact that services trade with Canada and Mexico has developed more slowly than with Europe and Pacific Asia.

Expansion of this trade could target essential public services that have been provided by the government in Canada and to a lesser degree in Mexico; the idea would be to open them up for investment by U.S. corporations operating in for-profit industries. NAFTA specifies "law enforcement, correctional services, income security or insurance, social security or insurance, social welfare, public education, public training, health, and child care" as services that any "Party" shall be able to provide (NAFTA, article 1201). But this NAFTA provision, and most others, "are essentially replications and extended versions of the respective GATT provisions as formulated throughout the Uruguay Round of negotiations (1986–1994). Thus, as NAFTA goes further than GATT in establishing freedom for international capital, it also almost ensures that the next round of the GATT [now WTO] negotiations will dig deeper in this direction than did the Uruguay Round" (Hossein-zadeh 1997, 247). In fact, NAFTA contains not only a much-enhanced definition of investment and services, but also an "accession clause" enabling other countries to join the pact subject to approval of the member countries (NAFTA, article 2204).

REGIONALIZATION AND GLOBALIZATION: SUBSTITUTES OR COMPLEMENTS?

The history of the past fifty years is marked by the decline of U.S. economic hegemony. The United States emerged from World War II in a position of supremacy probably unparalleled in history. Within a quarter century, it began to encounter serious challenges, from both Japan and the newly constituted European Common Market, to its competitive position in world markets and its leadership in international economic and financial institutions. Through the 1970s, the United States still preferred the multilateral approach to free trade, which seeks to minimize trade barriers among all nations, and opposed the idea of preferential trade agreements (PTAs) among a limited number of countries usually within the same region of the world. But when a GATT ministerial meeting in 1982 was adjourned without agreement on a new round of trade negotiations because of European resistance to American proposals, the U.S. response was that henceforth it would seek to expand trade on a "two-track" approach. This U-turn from multilateralism led to the 1984 Caribbean Basin Initiative, which extended unilateral trade preferences to twenty-one beneficiary countries in the region. A bilateral agreement with Israel quickly followed (Frankel 1997, 4–11). Two years later Canada and the United States opened the talks that led to CUSFTA, and in 1991 negotiations began with Mexico when it indicated its desire to join a North American PTA.

The NAFTA countries were not alone in their pursuit of economic integration through bilateral or preferential lowering of trade and investment barriers. The Association of Southeast Asian Nations, formed in 1967, set up a PTA that joined Indonesia, Malaysia, the Philippines, Singapore, Thailand, Brunei, and Vietnam in 1995; it also plans a free trade area for 2003. The European Community decided in 1987 to adopt the Single Market Initiative to turn a free trade area into a comprehensive economic union; it took effect in 1992 with the Maastricht Treaty. The 1991 Andean Trade Preference Act (Bolivia, Colombia, Ecuador, and Peru) was granted preferential access to the U.S. market for certain goods, a "carrot" aimed at reducing Andean economic dependency on drugs smuggled into the United States. MERCOSUR is pursuing links with countries outside the bloc; in the summer of 1999, it invited fifteen European and thirty-three Caribbean and Latin American nations to Rio de Janeiro to explore possibilities of an economic alliance as a counterweight to U.S. economic influence and the Clinton administration's push for a wider free trade area of the Americas (Rohter 1999). In late 1999, the European Union made an accord with Mexico setting up a free trade area that went into effect on July 1, 2000. By 2003, when industrial products will be fully liberalized in NAFTA, all Mexican exports will enter the European Union duty-free, and tariffs on imports from the European Union will be virtually eliminated by 2007 (Smith 2000).[22]

All these nations, and their PTA groupings, are looking to protect their own turf, increase their economic weight and bargaining power, and find extranational ways of dealing with production, trade, and investment in a global marketplace. Regionalization and globalization are mutually reinforcing, not mutually exclusive; they allow nation-states to pursue the same goals with a greater variety of means. The prime mover is corporate capital, and its instrument is the "representative firm" of our day—the MNC, which is by its nature a globally competitive institution. It is unreasonable to expect it to pursue, or accommodate, policies that work against global reach. With primacy given to economics and finance above all else, NAFTA is one more tool that helps both industrial and financial MNCs carry out business as usual to the exclusion of politics, except when the state is needed to create new national and international institutions to further the globalization process.

Comparing NAFTA with the European Union is illuminating. The European Union is a holistic structure of political, economic, and monetary institutions, tied together in a legal and parliamentary framework. The essence of the move toward a common internal market (Maastricht) is the standardization of regulatory regimes for financial services, insurance, and telecommunications, as well as of laws covering business practices, product safety, and technical and licensing requirements. There is an uneasy coexistence between the economic-monetary side and the political side of the European Union. The former seems no less dominated by corporate and banking capital than it is in NAFTA, but the European Union's political and judicial institutions, underdeveloped as they may be, are in place and could become focal points for anticapitalist and reformist opposition.

NAFTA, by contrast, is purely an economic integration scheme. Any law or regulations embodied in it apply to engagement among private parties or the resolution of disputes among them. There are no elements of political supranationality: formal national sovereignty over economic affairs remains intact. Unlike the European Union, NAFTA does not allow for the free movement of labor across borders, and it provides no intraregional subsidies for agriculture or industrial development. Liberal economics rules, and political and other nonmarket institutions must adapt themselves to it—if they can. It is hardly surprising that the NAFTA side agreements covering labor rights and the environment have become a virtual dead letter, particularly in Mexico, which was the area of concern that prompted them. The reality is that NAFTA, like the WTO, the IMF, and even the European Union itself at this stage in its history, elevates the rights of private capital over the state. It draws new boundaries between the public and the private by strictly limiting the former and reclassifies the services it supplies as "tradable" and open to private-sector takeover. It wrests control from democratically elected bodies, transfers it to unelected bureaucrats, and could preempt further public-sector expansion.

The symbol of NAFTA's unpopularity in the United States is imports from Mexico and the job losses they represent, despite the fact that imports from Canada are more than 80 percent larger and the U.S. trade deficit with Canada 30 percent higher (table 2.2).[23] U.S. investment in Canada is greater than in Mexico (table 2.5), and the total stock of U.S. FDI in Canada is four times larger.[24] In Mexico's automotive industry, the level of integration with the United States has not reached that of the U.S. and Canadian industries. The reason for distrust of NAFTA is nonetheless understandable: Unlike for

Canada, the division of labor that investment and production-sharing arrangements with Mexico make possible is a threat to the jobs and incomes of lower-wage workers in the United States. That threat will grow. For U.S. firms, improving competitiveness against foreign rivals is more difficult than years ago. Since the 1950s and 1960s, U.S. share of world GDP, manufacturing production, and exports has dropped by more than half; its share of world FDI, 60 percent in 1950, is now 25 percent. Of the top one hundred corporations ranked by foreign-held assets in 1997, twenty-seven were American; together, Germany, France, Switzerland, and the United Kingdom, with a combined GDP seven-tenths that of the United States, had forty, and Japan had seventeen more (Dicken 1998, tables 2.2, 2.5, 2.8; UNCTAD 1999, tables III.1 and annex table B.4). Even in the new "information" sector, where U.S. companies have been the leaders, foreign capital has made inroads at home and abroad. French and German firms own 20 percent of Sprint, the third largest telecommunications operator, and non–U.S. firms own half of the six major Hollywood film studios, several leading record distributors, and a number of book and periodical publishers (Schiller 1999, 85).

NAFTA is part of, facilitates, and advances globalization—the restructuring of economic and financial capital through international flows of production, trade, investment, and assets. Its continental manifestations are not to be dismissed: they are significant, and they revolve mainly about Mexico. Non–NAFTA FDI in Mexico has spurted over the past decade, and Mexico's own integration into the global system has accelerated and is not likely to be reversed. Mexican exports have also increased sharply since NAFTA took effect; but it must be recalled that relatively more of them are going to the United States itself, continuing a trend that precedes NAFTA (table 2.4). The same holds true for Canada (table 2.3).

Special aspects of post-1994 North American economic integration that would differentiate it from the globalization process are not evident. Japan's domestic market and its labor force are affected by backyard competition from Asian countries. Since 1989, Poland, Hungary, and other eastern European countries are being drawn into the free market orbit, and German, French, and Italian firms have already moved operations to that region to take advantage of lower labor costs (see Andrews 1998). If Mexico—the poor relation of NAFTA—shows signs of closer links with the United States, and even sports an economic and political elite enjoying lifestyles and professional and managerial work modes like those in the United States and Canada, it is no different from a number of other developing countries and their links to one or more high-income industrialized countries. Globalization, if uneven, leaves few areas untouched, and the "convergence" it brings about can be seen on the North American continent, and everywhere else.

INTERNATIONAL TRADE AND INVESTMENT: WINNERS OR LOSERS?

International trade has always taken place in the context of free market capitalism. The same questions that can be raised about capitalist economic growth can be raised about capitalist trade—two sides of the same coin. Neither can be called a zero-sum game: Over time, both increase incomes and employment opportunities by creating new markets and stimulating investments that add to a country's productive and technological base. But trade, like industrial change, destroys old jobs and forces large numbers of workers into jobs that pay less. Economists insist that the gains from foreign trade and investment are large enough so that the winners could compensate the losers and still leave themselves better off. But the political reality is that winners do not compensate losers. Even the long-acknowledged "dislocations" caused by trade are getting no public hearing, seemingly less than they did twenty years ago. In the United States, the trade adjustment assistance promised during the NAFTA negotiations is invisible. In 2000, the Clinton administration pointed to "a funding stream for dislocated workers" through several programs, but cited no dollar amounts (U.S. President 2000, 224).

A century ago, the capitalist accumulation process transformed disconnected local and regional economies into national economies dominated by corporate capital in the form of continent-spanning oligopolies. Globalization represents a further step in this historical process, with the global economy superseding the national economy as the relevant economic space for finance and production for a steadily larger, and dominant, fraction of capital. Just as the previous wave of accumulation did, globalization will generate higher levels of production and income for large numbers of people. It will also generate enormous economic and social costs, with real wages lagging behind property incomes and the welfare of nations recurrently threatened by economic and financial instability.

This time around, the cost-benefit trade-offs of globalization could well be steeper. The crisis of the 1930s opened the floodgates for long-delayed and fiercely resisted reforms to achieve some measure of economic justice and security for the mass of the nonpropertied population. One must wonder whether it will be as easy—and it was not at all easy then—for working classes to make good their earlier losses the way they finally did during the golden age of postwar capitalism (1948–1973). Now, multinational capital, both physical and financial, has far more mobility than ever before; and technologies and productive capacity can be redeployed throughout the world with unprecedented freedom. Across national borders, the bargaining power of capital is on the rise relative to both labor and government. Constraints on domestic policy choices are tightening; it will be harder for lower-income countries to follow the government-promoted, export-led industrialization model pursued so successfully by East Asian countries from 1965 to 1990. Already the epochal world trade and investment expansion of the past three decades has been accompanied by sharply widening income and wealth gaps both between and within countries (UN Development Program 1999, 1–12). NAFTA is part and parcel of this process—nothing less, nothing more.

NOTES

Unless noted otherwise, all dollar amounts are in U.S. currency.

1. On these developments, see Randall (1996) and Lustig (1998).

2. Automotive Branch of Industry Canada data supplied by Garry Emond of Industry Canada, <http://www.strategis.ic.gc.ca> [last accessed: 15 February 2001].

3. On the NAFTA negotiations, see Mayer (1998, chapter 3), Hufbauer and Schott (1994, 219–222), Shoch (2000, 122–127).

4. The NAFTA text is at <http://www.sice.oas.org> [last accessed: 15 February 2001]. The "side agreements" are chapters 27 and 28 of the NAFTA text.

5. *Survey of Current Business*, October 1999, table B, 58.

6. *Survey of Current Business*, April 2000, table 2, 175–176.

7. *Survey of Current Business*, June 1985, table 3, 48.

8. The 85 percent figure excludes extractive-based industries (food, beverages, tobacco, paper, and wood products), which would push the 1998–1999 total to 90 percent.

9. *Survey of Current Business*, July 1999, table 2, 100; June 1993, table 2, 82.

10. The other eight were China, Hong Kong, Korea, Malaysia, Singapore, Taiwan, Thailand, and Brazil.

11. Calculated from UNCTAD (1998; 1999, annex tables B.1 and B.2).

12. This is a summary of several estimates, all affected by the inadequacy of data on worldwide IFT.

13. In 1992–1993, the figures for Canada and Mexico were 34.3 and 10.9 percent, respectively. See *Survey of Current Business*, July 1999, table 18, 29; June 1995, table 10, 43.

14. *Survey of Current Business*, July 1999, table 2, 100; June 1995, table 2, 98; June 1977, table 3, 44.

15. *Survey of Current Business*, July 1999, table 2, 100.

16. *Survey of Current Business*, October 1997, table 3, 56; July 1999, table 3, 22.

17. *Survey of Current Business*, September 1999, table 16, 82.

18. *Survey of Current Business*, April 2000, table 2, 176. Japan accounted for 24 percent of the U.S. trade deficit, China 21 percent, and Germany 9 percent.

19. One of the authors, Gary Hufbauer, later estimated that the surging trade deficit with Mexico cost the United States 225,000 jobs by 1996.

20. The advisory board member is chairman of Allegheny Technologies, Pittsburgh.

21. The consulting firm offering these services is North American Productions, <http://www.napsmexico.com> [last accessed: 15 February 2001].

22. The agreement can be found at <http://www.europa.eu.int/comm/trade/bilateral/mexico/fta.htm> [last accessed: 15 February 2001].

23. *Survey of Current Business*, April 2000, table 2, 176.

24. *Survey of Current Business*, July 1999, table 3.2, 57.

REFERENCES

Andrews, E. L. 1998. "Germany Cut Labor Costs with a Harsh Export: Jobs." *New York Times*, 21 March, A1.

Bernstein, Aaron. 1993. "An Anti-NAFTA Argument You Haven't Heard." *Business Week*, 8 November, 34.

Bradsher, Keith. 1993. "Trade Pact Job Gains Discounted." *New York Times*, 22 February, D1.

Bronfenbrenner, Kate. 1996. *Final Report: The Effects of Plant Closing or Threat of Plant Closing on the Right of Workers to Organize*. Ithaca: New York State School of Industrial and Labor Relations, Cornell University.

Canada. 2000. *Statistics Canada*. <http://www.statcan.ca> [last accessed: 19 February 2001].

Clement, Norris C., et al. 1999. *North American Economic Integration*. Northampton, Mass.: Edward Elgar.

Crawford, Leslie. 1995. "Anger on the Streets As Mexico Swallows the Economic Medicine." *Financial Times*, 11 March, 4.

Darling, Juanita. 1992. "Mexico's Inflation Fight Hurts." *Los Angeles Times*, 31 August, D1.

Dicken, Peter. 1998. *Global Shift*. 3rd ed. New York: Guilford.

Du Boff, R. B. 1989. *Accumulation and Power*. Armonk, N.Y.: Sharpe.

Federal Reserve Bank of Atlanta. 1997. *Economics Update* (January–March): 2–4.

Ferguson, Jonathan. 1993. "Did Chrétien Get a Good Deal?" *Toronto Star*, 3 December, A27.

Fineman, Mark, and J. Darling. 1995. "Zedillo Outlines Rescue Plan, Calls for Deep Sacrifices." *Los Angeles Times*, 4 January, A1.

Frankel, Jeffrey A. 1997. *Regional Trading Blocs in the World Economic System*. Washington, D.C.: Institute for International Economics.

Freeman, Richard B. 1995. "Are Your Wages Set in Beijing?" *Journal of Economic Perspectives* 9 (Summer): 15–32.

Hossein-zadeh, Esmail. 1997. "NAFTA and Sovereignty." *Science and Society* 61 (Summer). 243–254.

Hufbauer, Gary C., and J. J. Schott. 1992. *North American Free Trade*. Washington, D.C.: Institute for International Economics.

———. 1994. *Western Hemisphere Economic Integration*. Washington, D.C.: Institute for International Economics.

Industry Canada. 1999/2000. *Trade and Investment Monitor*. Ottawa: Industry Canada. <http://www.strategis.ic.gc.ca> [last accessed: 19 February 2001].

Inter-American Development Bank. 2000. *Statistics and Quantitative Analysis Unit*. <http://www.iadb.org> [last accessed: 19 February 2001].

Kamel, Rachael, and A. Hoffman, eds. 1999. *The Maquiladora Reader*. Philadelphia: American Friends Service Committee.

Larudee, M. 1998. "Integration and Income Distribution under NAFTA." In *Globalization and Progressive Economic Policy*, ed. Dean Baker, G. Epstein, and R. Pollin. New York: Cambridge University Press.

Lustig, Nora. 1998. *Mexico: The Remaking of an Economy*. 2nd ed. Washington, D.C.: Brookings Institution Press.

MacArthur, John R. 2000. *The Selling of "Free Trade."* New York: Hill and Wang.

Mayer, Frederick W. 1998. *Interpreting NAFTA*. New York: Columbia University Press.

Mexico. 2000. *Mexican National Statistics*. <http://www.inegi.gob.mx> [last accessed: 19 February 2001].

Millman, Joel. 1998. "Mexico Is Becoming Auto-Making Hot Spot." *Wall Street Journal*, 23 June, A17.

———. 2000. "The World's New Tiger on the Export Scene Isn't Asian; It's Mexico." *Wall Street Journal*, 9 May, A1.

North American Production Sharing Incorporated. 2001. <http://www.napsmexico.com> [last accessed: 15 February 2001].

Organization for Economic Cooperation and Development. 1998. *Economic Outlook*, no. 63 (June).

———. 1999. *Economic Outlook*, no. 66 (December).

———. 2000. *OECD Statistics*. <http://www.oecd.org/std> [last accessed: 19 February 2001].

Randall, Laura, ed. 1996. *Changing Structure of Mexico*. Armonk, N.Y.: Sharpe.

Rohter, Larry. 1999. "Latin America and Europe to Talk Trade." *New York Times*, 26 June, C2.

Sachs, Jeffrey D., and H. L. Shatz. 1994. "Trade and Jobs in U.S. Manufacturing." *Brookings Papers on Economic Activity*, no. 1: 1–84.

Schiller, Dan. 1999. *Digital Capitalism*. Cambridge: Massachusetts Institute of Technology Press.

Scott, Robert E. 1999. *NAFTA's Pain Deepens*. Washington, D.C.: Economic Policy Institute.

Shaiken, Harley. 1993. "Will Manufacturing Head South?" *Technology Review* 96 (April): 28–29.

Shoch, James. 2000. "Contesting Globalization: Organized Labor, NAFTA, and the 1997 and 1998 Fast-Track Fights." *Politics and Society* 28 (March): 119–150.

Simmons, Richard P. 2000. "The Truth about Free Trade." *Business Week*, 5 June, 20.

Smith, Geri. 2000. "Mexico Pulls Off Another Trade Coup." *Business Week*, 7 February, 56.

Swardson, Anne. 1993. "Canada Set to Enact NAFTA." *Washington Post*, 3 December, A31.

Uchitelle, Louis. 1993a. "Northern Mexico Becomes a Big Draw for High-Tech Plants—and U.S. Jobs." *New York Times*, 21 March, F3.

———. 1993b. "Those High-Tech Jobs Can Cross the Border Too." *New York Times*, 28 March, F5.

United Nations. 1998. *Economic Survey of Latin America and the Caribbean 1997–98*. Santiago, Chile: United Nations.

UN Conference on Trade and Development. 1997. *World Development Report 1997*. New York: United Nations.

———. 1998. *World Investment Report 1998*. New York: United Nations.

———. 1999. *World Investment Report 1999*. New York: United Nations.

UN Development Program. 1999. *Human Development Report 1999*. New York: Oxford University Press.

UN Statistical Office. 1999. *1997 International Trade Statistics Yearbook*. New York: United Nations.

U.S. Department of Commerce. Office of Automotive Affairs. 1999. *Fifth Annual Report to Congress Regarding the Impact of the North American Free Trade Agree-*

ment upon *U.S. Automotive Trade with Mexico.* Washington, D.C.: U.S. Government Printing Office.

U.S. International Trade Commission. 1999. *Production Sharing: Use of U.S. Components and Materials in Foreign Assembly Operations, 1995–1998.* Washington, D.C.: U.S. International Trade Commission.

U.S. President. 2000. *Economic Report of the President, February 2000.* Washington, D.C.: U.S. Government Printing Office.

U.S. Tariff Commission. 1970. *Economic Factors Affecting the Use of Items 807.00 and 806.30 of the Tariff Schedules of the United States.* Washington, D.C.: U.S. Tariff Commission.

Zachary, G. P. 1997. "Global Growth Attains a New, Higher Level That Could Be Lasting." *Wall Street Journal*, 13 March, A1.

3

Globalization and Latin Media Powers: The Case of Mexico's Televisa

Andrew Paxman and Alex M. Saragoza

In the summer of 2000 in Fez, Morocco, two traveling U.S.–born college students of Mexican origin struck up a conversation in Spanish with a group of native youngsters. The conversation turned to television, and the students confessed to watching soap operas produced in Mexico and broadcast in the United States through a Spanish-language network. At the mention of a particular soap opera, the Moroccans shouted their surprise and gleefully invited the students to watch the program with them. The encounter led to a number of dinner invitations to the youngsters' homes for the American students, where the Moroccans found an unexpected measure of commonality in discussing the villains and heroines of a Mexican *telenovela* (Negrin 2000). The chance conversation and its aftermath disclosed commonalities engendered by the lingering consequences of Spanish colonialism, but it also offered a telling and complicated example of the globalization of mass communications.

The Mexican media conglomerate known as Televisa Group produced the soap opera that made its way into the United States through the Univisión Network, in which the Mexican firm holds a minority interest (though at one point in the past its stake was much larger). Through satellite transmission and/or rebroadcast, the *telenovela* was seen in Spanish-language markets elsewhere in the world, including former colonial possessions of Spain, such as parts of Morocco. The imperialism of a bygone era was complicit with the global expansion of a contemporary media company. In this sense, the previously mentioned encounter disguised a complicated process over time and space reflective of the distinctive relationship that developed over six decades between an authoritarian regime founded in 1929 and the corporation that became Televisa.[1] This special relationship facilitated importantly the emergence of a radio-based company in the 1930s that quickly dominated Mexico and soon spread into large parts of Latin America, using radio as the initial spearhead to penetrate markets akin to those in its homeland; later, its influence deepened through the use of television and ancillary commercial activities, beginning in the early 1950s and solidified by the late 1960s. Throughout this process, the connection between the Mexican company and Mexico's one-party state remained critical to its domestic dominance of the electronic commercial media, and it was this dominance that nourished the firm's ability to sustain an important media presence outside of Mexico.

But much of the evolving power of the Mexican company took place largely in the shadows of the United States and American economic interests, not an insignificant factor in the development of Televisa, as the Mexican company benefited from its geopolitical location and the relatively benign posture of American media interests for decades. However, it was an order subject to instability, and the expansion of multinational and transnational corporations in the post–World War II era inexorably lessened the ability of nation-states to shape easily the movements of corporate capitalist development. And the rapid and quickening pace of technological change underscored the inability of states or corporations to maintain with any assurance their established perches. As numerous scholars have noted, the volatility of the international political economy accelerated, particularly by the 1980s, as borders became ever more porous to the flows of corporate capital and technology (Dicken 1992). The collapse of the Soviet bloc was perhaps the most dramatic of these signs, but the fluctuating fortunes of large corporations, from Sony to News Corporation, were not any less dramatic for the observers of international capital.

In this context, the Mexican company inevitably faced a growing competition from within its regional stronghold as well as from without. Equally important, the tides of internal politics in Mexico shifted, at first slowly, and then with increasing force, undermining the moorings of Televisa's privileged place in a political order increasingly suspect. Thus, in recent years, Televisa has been hard-pressed to sustain its position as market forces and new technologies challenged its dominance at home and its influence abroad. However, foreign media interests and domestic rivals today confront a company with substantial assets, notably the huge advantages accumulated from its long association with an authoritarian regime and leadership capable of renegotiating Televisa's position when necessary without much loss of power. Televisa continues to be a formidable player in international Spanish-language broadcasting and a significant if not powerful presence in the globalization of the media. For the near future, the prospects for Televisa are generally bright, though the company must be vigilant to the mercurial global flows of the new media and the less predictable political economy of Mexico.

The contemporary challenges facing Televisa are not without precedent. In this sense, the story of Televisa must take into account the extraordinary leadership of the company over time, from its founder, Emilio Azcárraga Vidaurreta (1895–1972) and his son, the more flamboyant Emilio Azcárraga Milmo (1930–1997), to the current head of the corporation, Emilio Azcárraga Jean (1968–). To date, at each decisive turn in its fortunes, the house of Azcárraga has possessed the leadership capable of maintaining the formidable interests of the company. In this sense, the present position of the company in Mexico reflects in no small measure the capability of its captains to negotiate the fluctuations of markets, technology, and politics. In this regard, the year 1997 marked a critical moment for the Mexican media giant, as the conjunction of four events threatened the foundation of the house of Azcárraga.

In that year, the ruling party (Partido Revolucionario Institucional [PRI; Institutional Revolutionary Party]) lost its hold on the country's congress; no longer would the dominant party's president enjoy the predictable control of the legislative process, such as the routine control of federal communications policies and their implementation. In another sign of historic political change, a left-center opposition candidate won the mayorship of Mexico City, a major setback for the one-party state. And, as if to confirm the passing of the old political order, the death of Mexico's most important labor leader, and loyal soldier to the ruling party for decades, Fidel Velázquez, signaled a further weakening of the hand of the regime; predictable support from the country's largest labor federation for the ruling party was in question. In the midst of these ominous events for the ruling party, Emilio Azcárraga Milmo, the fiery head of Televisa, succumbed to cancer. The dominant political order had lost a crucial ally, whose control of the nation's dominant media company had constituted a virtual ministry of propaganda for the party for twenty-five years.

The death of Azcárraga Milmo in April 1997 spelled yet another complication for the embattled PRI, but for Televisa, the passing of its powerful leader was the cause of grave concern.[2] At the time, Televisa was struggling to recover from its worst year. Audience and advertising share had reached their lowest levels since 1972, as the inventiveness of its recently privatized rival, Televisión Azteca (TV Azteca), combined with the lethargy and complacency of Televisa to produce a real crisis for the media giant. The credibility of the company witnessed a consequent fall, nowhere more apparent than in the faltering viability of its news programming. The growing contempt for the PRI paralleled the widespread loathing for the party's cheerleader at Televisa, news anchor Jacobo Zabludovsky, whose reports belied the three-year economic downturn spawned by the policies of the discredited former president, Carlos Salinas de Gortari (1988–1994). A neoliberal hero for the party for most of his administration, Salinas had left office with his reputation tarnished by an economy in disarray (the Salinas family fell into utter disgrace shortly thereafter due to charges of various forms of corruption). Despite salvaging the presidency at his departure, the party had suffered irreversible political damage by Salinas, but Zabludovsky remained ever the loyalist to the regime.

Nonetheless, Azcárraga Milmo had kept his tottering empire from collapse. Bankers rolled over loans, relatives remained patient with their debts, and investors continued to hold on to stock. Televisa's past record of success combined with Azcárraga Milmo's sheer force of personality to stave off disaster for the struggling company. Then, with stunning swiftness, El Tigre—a sobriquet meaning "the Tiger"—was gone within a few weeks of the public disclosure of his illness. Stakeholders in the company, Wall Street analysts, and *priísta* leaders feared for the allegedly insipid, inexperienced, and insecure heir, Emilio Azcárraga Jean, and for the future of Televisa. With stock prices at a low ebb and in the face of a mountain of debt, the ownership of the company seemed on the brink of a takeover.

On Wall Street, Televisa's share price squirmed at around $25, far below its precrisis high three years earlier of $74. Broadcast performance languished, profit margins shrank, and investors worried over a $400 million gamble on international direct-to-home (DTH) television. Indeed, Televisa's cable and DTH enterprises, Cablevisión and Sky Latin America, respectively, were both running a distant second to rivals Multivisión and Galaxy Latin America. The internal workings of Televisa represented still another concern for stakeholders in the company. Azcárraga Milmo's newly appointed chief financial officer and prince regent had proven unpopular among ranking executives, while the owner's twenty-nine-year-old son and heir learned the ropes of managing the firm. The awkward situation at the top of the company spurred feuding among Azcárraga Milmo's offspring, nephews, and wife, and even his mistress became involved in the internecine machinations that surrounded the boardroom of Televisa. The problems of the media conglomerate were compounded by the huge debts of Azcárraga Milmo (estimated at $1.8 billion)[3] that were backed largely by his shares.

Four years or so later, the state of Televisa has changed completely.[4] Azcárraga Jean has proven to be an effective leader of the corporation, forming an efficient circle of senior executives that has put the company on solid footing. His managers have revived ratings, boosted advertising sales, and streamlined operating costs, including reductions of a bloated workforce. Confidence in the company has soared in comparison to 1997, allowing Azcárraga Jean to attract new investment by native businesspeople and to shun foreign suitors. Buoyed by healthy profit margins and the general optimism of investors, company stock tripled in price in 1999 alone. Cash flow margins grew from 18.6 percent in 1997 to 29.0 percent in 2000.[5] And in a more recent confirmation of the company's recovery since 1997, Televisa's holding company raised more than $1 billion in a public offering in January 2000, easing dramatically the debt burden inherited by Azcárraga Jean. Currently, there are few doubts as to the ownership of the house of Azcárraga.[6]

Today, Televisa's media hegemony over Mexico persists with surprising tenacity, taking into account its precarious position in 1997. The threat of greater competition—by the entry of U.S.–based pay channels, the emergence of TV Azteca, and the activation of the North American Free Trade Agreement (NAFTA)—has to date failed to pose a serious, sustained challenge to Televisa's dominance of Mexico's media market. Televisa's share of viewers and advertising sales currently surpasses 70 percent. Cablevisión since 1997 has enjoyed renewed growth and Sky has overtaken Galaxy as the leading DTH company both in Mexico and in Latin America as a whole.

For 2000, Televisa posted revenue of $2.165 billion, up from $1.929 billion in 1999, with broadcast operations contributing around 60 percent of the total in both years. In contrast, Televisa's competitor, TV Azteca, reported 2000 revenues of $558 million, almost all from broadcasting. In short, Televisa overwhelms its Mexican counterpart. Among Latin American media companies, Televisa ranks third. Based on 1999 figures, Brazil's Globo Group media conglomerate reported revenues of $2.6 billion, while Argentina's Clarín Group generated $2.2 billion ("The Global 50" 2000, 100). Nonetheless, the Mexican company continues to be the world's primary Spanish-language broadcaster. Its exported productions rake in roughly $100 million a year, and Televisa produces more than half the global market for Latin soap operas, or *telenovelas*, easily outdistancing its Latin American rivals in the programming trade ("Telenovelas" 1998). Moreover, Televisa programming provides the staple offerings of Univisión, the U.S.–based Spanish-language network whose revenues have climbed dramatically, from $321 million in 1995 to $737 million in 1999. Thus, Televisa has solidified its lofty perch in Spanish-language broadcasting both within and outside of Mexico.

But the future of Televisa is not without its questions. In new media, Televisa has been slow off the mark, as it avoided, perhaps mistakenly, joining an existing alliance between U.S. software giant Microsoft Corporation and the powerful Mexican telecommunications firm Teléfonos de México (Telmex). In addition, other international rivals, notably Spain's Telefónica de España and the U.S. venture America On-line (AOL), have entered the fray. As a consequence, the prospects for the Televisa venture (esmas.com) remain in doubt, though the company's programming library, reservoir of talent, and production capability sustains its Pan-American potential.

Mexico's political environment presents perhaps the most intriguing and difficult question facing Televisa. The centrality of the one-party state to the historic dominance of Televisa over the Mexican media has ended. Since the disastrous end of the Salinas administration, Televisa has distanced itself from the once dominant PRI, culminating in January 1998 by the removal of Zabludovsky as the voice of the company's news programming. Indeed, since the 1995 economic crisis and until his death, Azcárraga Milmo, the once self-proclaimed soldier of the PRI and stalwart supporter of Salinas, had noticeably shifted his political stance toward a more pragmatic position as the PRI reeled from the effects of the Salinas debacle. Taking his cue from his father, Azcárraga Jean has moved even further toward a centrist position. In the 2000 presidential elections, Televisa astutely afforded each of the three major parties qualitatively equal coverage during its major national newscasts (Academia Mexicana de Derechos Humanos 2000), though its coverage of President Ernesto Zedillo Ponce de León basically sustained the conventional, respectful norms toward the office. Televisa's disassociation from the PRI contrasts markedly from the virulent charges of political bias against the company in the past by human rights activists, news critics, and opposition party leaders.

The platforms of the three major parties in the 2000 presidential elections raised the issue of media regulation, where the victorious Partido Acción Nacional (PAN; National Action Party) and its left-of-center opponent the Partido de la Revolución Democrática (PRD; Party for Democratic Revolution) suggested a watchdog type of agency. According to one knowledgeable observer, there is interest within the two parties to establish an autonomous, civil body to monitor the media.[7] Yet events in February 2001 suggested a different tack, as the new administration of President Vicente Fox announced plans to resurrect a National Television and Radio Council, defunct since the early 1970s (Luhnow 2001b). Designed to consist of four government officials and two representatives each from the television industry and its unions, the body theoretically has broad censorship powers. Currently, Televisa and TV Azteca were trying to convince PAN officials of the merits of self-regulation, but the broadcasters' poor track record in this regard put them at a disadvantage. In addition, early 2001 witnessed tension between the state and Televisa on other fronts. Televisa contested a ruling by the monopolies commission that forbade it to acquire additional radio assets.[8] Rumors even arose of interest within the PAN in dissolving two of Televisa's four national broadcast networks. However, it remains unclear whether the dramatic turn in Mexican politics signified by the defeat of the PRI and ascendancy of the PAN will truly weaken Televisa's competitive position within and outside Mexico. After all, the state has moved to curtail the house of Azcárraga several times in the past—even threatening to nationalize its networks—only to back down in the knowledge that a strong and compliant Televisa can be of great service to the ruling party.

TELEVISA AND THE STATE

In 1972, Telesistema Mexicano, the broadcasting company controlled by the Azcárraga family, merged with Televisión Independiente Mexicano, the upstart broadcaster in the hands of the elite business interests of Monterrey, Nuevo León, that had begun operations in 1968. The new corporation took the name of Televisa. The deal renewed the monopolistic pattern in television broadcasting, reminiscent of an earlier merger in 1955 that had brought together three competing networks under the roof of the house of Azcárraga. (This second merger explains the anomalous situation whereby Televisa is not a network in the U.S. sense of the word, but a conglomeration of four national networks under one roof.) The pact of 1955 reflected the wealth and power accrued by the Azcárragas from their powerful position over radio broadcasting that dated from the early 1930s. Throughout the history of the Azcárragas and their dominance over the media, the state has been a complicit actor. First, the state permitted the establishment and growth of private radio, and later television, although the federal government also maintained a broadcasting apparatus since the 1930s. And despite the fact that the laws of Mexico prohibited monopolies, the political order contributed to the obvious dominance of the Azcárragas over commercial radio and television through subsidies, licensing agreements, and broadcasting concessions (Mejía Barquera 1989). Second, for over fifty years, the official economic nationalism promoted by the state inhibited the easy entry of foreign media interests into the ownership of commercial radio and television. As a result, the Azcárragas were in a position to mediate the capacity of foreign companies to penetrate Mexican media markets (Bartra 1987; Montalvo 1985). Third, given their dominant place in the media, the house of Azcárraga amassed enormous cultural capital that afforded the company an extraordinary influence over the shaping of radio listening and television viewing formulas, that is, the production of taste (Monsiváis 1982). The state, in spite of its broadcasting ability and authority over the media, failed to offer a viable alternative to the cultural production of the house of Azcárraga. Under these conditions, the Azcárraga interests earned huge dividends. From its state-sanctioned position in Mexico, the house of Azcárraga reached into Latin America, the United States, and eventually to the rest of the world. In exchange for these advantages, the Azcárragas generally supported an authoritarian regime controlled by one party since 1929 and whose grip over political power in Mexico lasted until the end of the century.

In building its powerful domain, condoned if not aided by the state, the company now known as Televisa has succeeded in no small measure because of its effective entrepreneurial leadership. Azcárraga Vidaurreta, the founder of the company's first radio station, XEW, used his uncommon talent, ruthless drive, and political savvy to build a radio empire that eventually encompassed most of Mexico and much of Latin America. From the profits of his radio-based empire, he pioneered the introduction of television to Mexico in the early 1950s and engineered the merger that created Telesistema Mexicano. His son, Emilio Azcárraga Milmo, extended decisively the television interests of the company and spearheaded the application of satellite technology to television broadcasting in Mexico and subsequently from Mexico to the United States and Latin America; and of course Azcárraga

Milmo presided over the company's famed and lucrative soap opera productions. Most recently, Emilio Azcárraga Jean has proven adept at leading the company through a difficult transition with impressive results.

In brief, the benefits of the relationship between the house of Azcárraga and the state was accentuated crucially by the business acumen of the leaders of the company with enduring consequences for the development of the media in Mexico. In this historical process, four decisive turning points were critical in the building of the empire of Televisa: the early 1930s; the years spanning World War II; the founding years of television in Mexico, from 1952–1955; and the recent crisis period of the late 1990s (Saragoza forthcoming).

The founding of XEW in 1930 by Azcárraga Vidaurreta reflected a pattern that accrued to the favor of the radio entrepreneur. The American company Radio Corporation of America (RCA) coveted a radio network in Mexico to develop a market for RCA radio parts, radios, phonographs, and records under their RCA Victor label. But Mexican laws prohibiting foreign ownership of radio stations forced the U.S. corporation to use Azcárraga Vidaurreta to front their interests, allowing the Mexican businessman to control the "mother" station, XEW, and to have an interest in the formation of affiliate stations in key cities of Mexico. More importantly, the federal government refused to exercise its legal authority to restrict the development of commercial radio stations, though the government maintained its own radio broadcasting operations. Rather, the state permitted the emergence of a dual system of both private and public radio operations. In this context, Azcárraga Vidaurreta's entrepreneurial abilities, combined with the technical assets provided by RCA, soon put XEW in the lead of the crowded field of commercial radio operations in Mexico. The success of the flagship station depended in large measure on a popular programming format, featuring musical variety shows, that facilitated the signing of affiliates in the country's major cities and towns. The soaring popularity of the XEW network also lured the best talent in the radio and recording industry, which only added to the clout of the "W" in Mexico. Indebted to RCA, Azcárraga Vidaurreta often carried programs from the National Broadcasting Company (NBC), a subsidiary of the American corporation, but it was the Mexican mogul who decided the programs and the terms. The rapid accumulation of cultural capital by the XEW network gave Azcárraga Vidaurreta the leverage to negotiate with foreign media interests, as evidenced by the establishment of a second network in 1938, anchored by XEQ station, but linked to the Columbia Broadcasting System (CBS). Thus, the wily Mexican radio mogul incorporated the two most powerful radio networks in the United States into his web, but again, on his terms. By the end of the decade, over half of Mexico's radio stations were under the aegis of either XEW or XEQ. On the one hand, the state failed to block the clear dominance of the house of Azcárraga over commercial radio, while government broadcasting languished in quality and in the number of listeners. On the other hand, the state promoted a vibrant,

pervasive policy of cultural nationalism that contributed to the popularity of
Azcárraga Vidaurreta's programming, given its reliance on various forms of
Mexican popular music. From his Mexican stronghold, Azcárraga Vidaurreta
branched out into Latin America, making deals from Argentina to Cuba and
spearheading the organization of Latin American radio owners. By 1940,
there was no doubt that Azcárraga Vidaurreta was the leading figure in Latin
American radio.

The World War II years represented a key period for Azcárraga Vidaurreta, as
the Mexican government was quick to join the Allied effort against the Axis
powers. U.S. concerns for security, exaggerated by the attack on Pearl Harbor
and Nazi influence in Argentina, fueled an American-sponsored propaganda
campaign in the region. With his links to NBC and CBS, Azcárraga Vidaurreta
was the favored conduit for the radio-based campaign, and the Mexican entrepreneur took full advantage of the opportunity, earning huge profits
from the programming paid by U.S. dollars carried on his stations and on his
American-financed Pan-American network. No effort was made by the Mexican
state to distribute the monetary benefits of the Allied propaganda campaign to
other Mexican broadcasters; the state essentially was passive to the enormous
gains made by Azcárraga Vidaurreta in these years, as he extended his grip over
entertainment promotion, recordings, advertising, movie production, and ancillary activities. By 1945, the wartime profits of Azcárraga Vidaurreta's domain
served to solidify his hegemonic position in the Mexican media and encouraged him to move to a new medium, television, as he reduced his radio holdings to finance his ambitious plans for television. In this endeavor to bring television to Mexico, however, Azcárraga Vidaurreta was not alone.

The agreement signed in 1955 climaxed the contentious arrival of television
to Mexico. The Mexican state faced two choices: a government-run broadcasting system similar to that of the British Broadcasting Corporation in
Britain, or a private, commercial system like that of the United States. As with
radio, the state chose to do both. But the evidence suggests that the decision
to allow a commercial system involved the self-interest of then president of
Mexico, Miguel Alemán Valdés (1946–1952), when a close associate received
the first license to operate a television station. Although Azcárraga Vidaurreta
was in a more capable position for television transmission, he was forced to
wait several months for government approval of his request for a television
concession. Meanwhile, the government had authorized a third channel. After a nasty and costly fight for advertisers, talent, and programming ascendancy among the three contestants, the merger led to the formation of Telesistema Mexicano (TSM), with the Azcárraga Vidaurreta interests in
command. A transparent monopoly, TSM was greeted with governmental as-
sent. Subsequent competitors found it difficult to challenge the house of
Azcárraga and usually succumbed to the vast assets of TSM. Similar to the experience with radio, government-sponsored television productions suffered
from a lack of investment, talent, and, not surprisingly, an audience. In short,

the state basically made no effort to offer a viable alternative to the dominance of TSM over television broadcasting. Government regulators limited the entry of foreign material, forcing American producers, for example, to negotiate with the house of Azcárraga to air their shows. Furthermore, much of Azcárraga Vidaurreta's accumulated cultural capital was transferred to television, including scheduling formats and programming content. Thus, television in Mexico sustained a decidedly "Mexican" inflection, to which a new genre, the soap opera (*telenovela*), was added from 1958 with highly lucrative results (Fernández and Paxman 2000, 74ff.). In 1968, the industrial elite of Monterrey mounted a challenge to TSM, but four years later, the rival initiative was forced to throw in the towel, leading to the formation of Televisa. And, again, the state maintained its benign stance toward the strengthening of the grip over television by the house of Azcárraga interests, now led by the son of the founder, Azcárraga Milmo. In the years that followed, the tentacles of Televisa spread further to embrace publications, video distribution and production, and professional sports, among other activities that deepened the presence of Televisa in Mexican society and culture. Equally important, Televisa exported programming to Latin America and to the United States, where it maintained a substantial stake in the Spanish International Network (SIN), which later became known as Univisión. In this respect, the Mexican company sustained much of its "Mexican" flavor and refused to simply translate U.S. programming, for instance, into Spanish. Throughout the 1970s and 1980s, the state generally supported the growth of Televisa by subsidizing, for example, the introduction of satellite capability for television broadcasting and routinely renewing the licenses for the network's affiliate stations. Anchored by its dominant base in Mexico, Televisa was to expand its presence in South America and retain its foothold in the United States. Thus, though occasional tensions arose between government officials and Televisa, the symbiotic nature of the 1955 merger persisted for another forty years.

Finally, as noted earlier, the year of the death of Azcárraga Milmo witnessed a critical turning point for Televisa, ushering in a distinct new era for the powerful Mexican media conglomerate. In light of the 2000 elections in Mexico, the relationship of Televisa to the state has changed fundamentally. Nevertheless, the Mexican media giant retains much of its cultural capital, which foreign interests have found difficult to reproduce with sufficient success to challenge the cumulative strength of the house of Azcárraga. This durable asset is perhaps best expressed in the contemporary success of the *telenovela*, which has keyed Televisa's growth since the 1960s.

TELEVISA IN THE INTERNATIONAL ARENA

Telesistema's short-form soap operas, or *telenovelas*, paved the way to the programming success of the Mexican company as it assumed a new level of international prominence.[9] Technical improvements made by Telesistema, such as the introduction of tape-to-tape recording in 1965, fueled the exports of its popular soap operas, and its pioneering use of color in 1968 extended TSM's lead over its Latin American rivals, such as Brazil's Globo and Venezuela's RCTV, which started productions in color four years later. Thus, the Mexican company gained or expanded a competitive foothold throughout South America and deepened its thrust into the Spanish-language television market north of the border through its U.S.–based SIN network. Equally important, the popularity of the *telenovela* combined with the production capability of TSM to induce the genre's best talent to move to the well-equipped studios (called Televicentro) of the Mexican company. With its relatively strong production values, TSM's soap operas were the core of its programming exports. By 1970, the Televicentro studio facility shipped an average of seven hundred half-hour shows per month to thirteen countries in Central and South America, and it provided the bulk of the programming for Spanish-language broadcasting stations in the United States. Emboldened by the genre's success, Azcárraga Milmo relocated his production facilities to the south of Mexico City, making his San Angel studio complex the centerpiece of the growing output of *telenovelas* and other genres at Televisa, as the company was now called.

Still, Televisa was not immune to setbacks. The anchor of its success was embedded in its Mexican market, and the country's dramatic economic swings inevitably held repercussions for the house of Azcárraga. The heady optimism of the oil boom of the mid-1970s in Mexico gave way to the gloom of falling petroleum prices by the end of the decade that precipitated a severe economic crash by 1982. Hurt by the recession that followed, the Mexican company's ambitious European plans fell apart, as its Spanish subsidiary was forced to close. But the slow recovery of Mexico's economy, prompted by its neoliberal schemes and huge infusions of foreign financial aid and investment (Cypher 1990; Maxfield 1990), soon induced the Mexican media conglomerate toward another round of expansive activity outside of Mexico. The early success of the Salinas administration exaggerated expectations of a Mexican economic miracle, and the house of Azcárraga embarked on an aggressive foreign strategy.[10]

The key to the strategy was to create a greater dependency on Televisa programming among foreign broadcasters. The initial effort centered on gaining an interest in networks outside of Mexico, and then using that influence to sell to those networks more programming produced by Televisa. The Mexican company acquired a stake in broadcasting systems in Chile, Peru, and Bolivia in 1991 and 1992 and solidified its ties with the U.S.–based Univisión network (the new name for the SIN operation). The scheme was blocked in Argentina, Spain, and Russia by local political resistance, but the intent of Televisa was clear, as demonstrated most forcefully in the case of Univisión. In South America, however, this approach failed to produce the expected results and ultimately cost the Mexican company an estimated $90 million. Thus, Azcárraga Milmo started to shed his South American holdings and began a different policy, based on affiliate deals along the lines established with Univisión. In exchange for first option on an unlimited supply of Televisa-produced programming, the Mexican company would take a 10 percent to 15 percent share of the broadcaster's total advertising revenue. For stations and networks with limited production capabilities, Televisa programming boosted ratings, while the house of Azcárraga reaped the benefits of increasing advertising sales. Through this strategy, the Mexican firm eventually signed five-year contracts with over a dozen Central and South American broadcasters, improving annual sales to the region from $10 million in 1994 to $35 million in 1997. Cognizant of the popularity of his *telenovelas*, Azcárraga Milmo pressed the international sales of the genre, seeking new markets in Europe, the Middle East, and Asia. Spurred by the tremendous draw of the *telenovela, Los Ricos También Lloran (The Rich Also Cry)*, in Russia, Televisa pushed into eastern Europe and Southeast Asia, where the *telenovela* phenomenon proved incredibly profitable for the Mexican company. In 1996, Televisa's total programming exports passed the $100 million mark, where 85 percent of the amount derived from the sales of its soap operas that appeared on television screens from Guatemala City and Los Angeles to Istanbul and Manila. According to one estimate, in 1997 Televisa programming export revenues totaled slightly more than half of the entire $200 million market for Latin American productions around the globe ("Telenovelas" 1998). The only slight pale on the gloss is the fact that there are few new territories for Azcárraga Jean's productions to conquer: Asia and eastern Europe were basically penetrated by the mid-1990s, and the global market for soap operas has been saturated by cheaply made fare from producers in Colombia, Venezuela, and Peru. Significant growth will likely come from Televisa's affiliate deals within the Americas, where advertising revenue is being shared.

Televisa's programming success facilitated Azcárraga Milmo's intent to enter into a series of strategic partnerships with media corporations of much greater international clout, among them News Corporation and Tele-Communications Incorporated (TCI). In this move, the Mexican corporate head expected to expand beyond his core business in broadcast television and to ally his company with potential competitors. Through these maneuvers, Azcárraga Milmo evidently hoped to shape the interface between Mexico and the globalization of media to his advantage. In the early 1990s, there was initial speculation that U.S.–based pay channels (starting with Entertainment and Sports Programming Network [ESPN], Cable News Network [CNN], and Home Box Office [HBO], which debuted in the region between 1989 and 1991) would encroach upon the markets of established broadcasters in Latin America. But these foreign-based offerings depended on distribution deals with local cable-television operators. As a consequence, Televisa's Cablevisión, one of Mexico's two largest systems, benefited from the enriched programming supply. In fact, the initial fears surrounding pay television failed to materialize, as the growth in Mexican cable homes lagged and advertising sales for cable were slow to climb (Paxman 1998). In this regard, the entrenched structure of income inequality in Mexico has constrained the potential for pay television, and more so in the uncertain economic climate that characterized the mid-1990s. The country's 2.8 million pay television homes constitute just 16 percent of households, compared with close to 70 percent in the United States (*Private Advisor* 2000, 48).

More significantly, in 1995 Azcárraga Milmo struck a deal with News Corp., TCI, and Globo for the $1 billion DTH project named Sky Latin America. He was a reluctant partner. Azcárraga Milmo's preemptive effort came too late to thwart that of two other major competitors for the DTH market, including Hughes Communications International (the Galaxy Latin American project) on the one hand, and News Corp. and Globo on the other. The profitability of a three-way competition, certainly in the short-term, was much too risky for Televisa as it recovered from the battering of the post-Salinas recession in Mexico. The joint venture with News Corp. and Globo gave Televisa a 30 percent stake and conceded the Mexican platform to the house of Azcárraga with majority participation. By 1998, Sky had overtaken its rival in numbers of subscribers in Mexico and Latin America as a whole, and, to date, it has maintained its lead.[11]

Televisa retains control of both of its principal pay television operations, 60 percent of Sky Mexico and 51 percent of Cablevisión, and the two platforms make Televisa the leading pay television service provider, with 800,000 of Mexico's 2.8 million subscribers at the end of 1999; the rest of the market is highly fragmented. But outside Mexico, Televisa's pay television ambitions have fallen short. Sky's multinational platform by mid-2000 was confined to only two countries, Colombia and Chile. Meanwhile, competitor Galaxy Latin America, backed by Hughes Communications, rolled out throughout the region in just two years, 1996–1998. Agreements with Univisión and Globo have barred Televisa from the DTH arena in the United States and Brazil, respectively. Televisa also participates in the Spanish DTH service, Via Digital, through an agreement with Spain's Telefónica corporation, but this platform trails its rival, a fact that has pushed the Mexican company to reduce its share in its Spanish venture from 17.5 percent to 8.8 percent as of 2000. Furthermore, the powerful influence of the Clarín interests in Argentina and the Cisneros Group in Venezuela has favored Sky's competitor, allowing Galaxy Latin America to monopolize the DTH market in those two countries. Televisa's potential benefit from overseas DTH growth, therefore, appears limited, as Televisa lacks a substantial presence in most of the major Spanish- and Portuguese-speaking markets.

Televisa's most important foreign market, by far, is the United States, to which Televisa exports broadcast programming, magazines, and music recordings. Key to this relationship is the thirty-million-strong U.S. population that is of Latin American descent, which represents—relative to the Mexican market—a high-income consumer group for Televisa's exports. Here, the business is grounded in a programming supply deal with Univisión, in which it retains a 5.8 percent holding and a seat on the board. The deal guarantees Televisa 9 percent of the U.S. network's advertising revenue until 2017; effectively, it also ensures cross-promotion of the stars that appear in Televisa's magazines and on its record labels. The importance of the Latino market in the United States for Televisa accents the Mexican company's recording and publishing interests. Televisa publications, such as *TV y Novelas, Vanidades* (a woman's magazine), and the teen-oriented *Eres*, are all big sellers in Mexico and the United States. Through licensing arrangements, for instance with the Hearst Corporation and the European publisher Hachette Filipacchi, Televisa publishes Spanish-language versions of *Cosmopolitan, Good Housekeeping, Elle*, and *Quo*, to mention just a few examples. Indeed, Televisa is the world's largest publisher of magazines in Spanish, with more than 30 titles, circulation of about 133 million copies, and revenues of $181 million in 1999 plus $79 million in publishing distribution fees. In music recording, Televisa derives more of its revenues from the United States than from Mexican sales. In 1999, when sales reached $139 million, Televisa's music division sold fourteen million units in the United States, compared to seven million in Mexico and other countries combined. Indeed, its Los Angeles–based subsidiary, Fonovisa, represents the most important independent label in the U.S. Spanish-language market.

But the Mexican company's ability to expand north of its border is problematic. The deal with Univisión precludes Televisa from offering DTH services in the United States, since the U.S. broadcaster has first option on all Televisa programming, and could also hamper efforts to forge an Internet presence there. Furthermore, its music division has found it difficult to keep its talent, as homegrown Televisa artists have defected to major labels that can offer huge contracts and enormous promotional clout—a pattern that has plagued Televisa past and present. For example, the popular Spanish singer Enrique Iglesias, originally discovered by Televisa, signed with Universal Records for a reported $40 million in 1999 (Sandler 1999). The Mexican company's efforts to strengthen its musical distribution have thus far been less than satisfactory. Cognizant of the consolidation taking place in the recording business (Polygram Records for instance has merged with Universal Records), Televisa continues its six-year search for a powerful partner.

Uncertainty also marks the Mexican company's Internet venture, esmas.com.[12] Beyond the misfortune of a shaky launch, including a public falling-out with the portal's U.S. designers,[13] three issues in particular weigh on Televisa's entry into the dot.com arena: the viability of the market in Latin America, the advisability of a partnership, and the popularity of its content. Latin America is one of the world's fastest-growing areas of growth of Internet service, where the number of users is projected to increase from 7.1 million in 1999 to 19.1 million in 2003, with Mexico's rate of expansion leading the way (Hussey et al. 2000). On-line advertising is expected to grow from $121 million in 1999 to $1.6 billion in 2003, and e-commerce from $459 million to $8 billion in the same period. These projections rest on skimpy figures, as only 2 percent of the region's population is currently on the Web, consistent with the income inequality that underlines the digital divide in Latin America. The market is similarly thin at present for Televisa to be an Internet service provider (ISP). In 1999, personal computer penetration per capita in Mexico was 4.9 percent (compared to 52 percent in the United States). The future of Internet access may lie, therefore, on the Mexican company's penetration of homes through pay television. Through cable and DTH, Televisa already reaches eight hundred thousand of Mexico's affluent households, and the company pledged in July 2000 to improve Cablevisión and to offer Internet service over it after a $200 million overhaul of the system (Millman 2000). But Televisa enters a market laced with horizontal portals and powerful competitors, suggesting the need for a strategic partnership. In fact, many media analysts expected the pact between Telmex (Mexico's hugely profitable telephone company) and Microsoft to induce Televisa to join the group to form an unbeatable trio. But Azcárraga Jean refused to be limited to a 33 percent stake (Tricks 2000), following a long-standing company tradition of avoiding minority partnerships. An attractive partnership still remains an option. In fact, Televisa has moved to do so in specific sectors of e-commerce, as indicated in the September 2000 launch of a health and beauty products portal with a Mexican department store chain.[14] Still, Televisa has more than Telmex and Microsoft to contend with in an Internet market crowded with rivals backed by the deep pockets of foreign, mainly U.S., investors.[15]

If there is an element of optimism for Televisa in this field, it derives from the company's programming strength. Televisa is by far Latin America's major audiovisual provider: it possesses a massive library of programs, its production facilities churn out forty-four thousand hours of annual television output, its soccer teams anchor its extensive sports coverage, and its music recording, radio, and publishing assets reinforce the company's exclusive hold on a number of leading actors, singers, and writers. In this sense, Televisa has an advantage unavailable to U.S. Internet competitors: it has exclusive ownership over most of the content that its portal features.

In the monthly ranking of the top twenty television shows in Mexico, it is a rarity for a foreign-made production to make the list—a list inevitably loaded with shows produced by Televisa. Though the house of Azcárraga operates four broadcast networks, just 37 percent of the programming it aired in 1999 was foreign-produced (largely in the United States). Dubbed Hollywood films occasionally crack the top twenty list, but the conclusion remains obvious: it is highly unlikely that foreign imports will increase substantially in the television slate of Televisa. Indeed, on average since the 1970s, approximately two-thirds of Televisa programming comes from the company's San

Angel and Chapultepec studios.[16] In this respect, the *telenovela*-laden Channel 2 signifies the consistent hold of Televisa over Mexican viewers and constitutes its most important asset. The popularity of the *telenovela* to some extent rests, according to critics, on the instability of daily life in Mexico for much of its population, buffeted by currency changes, economic swings, political shifts, and jarring social inequities (Cueva 1998, 71f.). This argument helps explain the lagging ratings of Televisa's Channel 5, with its reliance on U.S.–made weekly programs, which tend to be marked by their thematic and stylistic emphasis on novelty. Instead, *telenovelas* in Mexico offer melodramas with predictable characters and reliable story lines five times a week, for months at a time, and in which justice, love, and family prevail.

In summary, Televisa's international position is anchored in its domestic strength, which in turn raises three crucial considerations for its future. First, though a regional power, Televisa is dwarfed by such global titans as AOL/Time-Warner. In 1998 and 1999, Televisa ranked thirty-fourth and thirty-third, respectively, among the world's entertainment companies ("The Global 50" 2000, 88). Second, the economic fragility of Mexico, punctuated by the volatility of the peso, constrains the growth potential of Televisa, as its revenue base continues to be predominantly within the domestic market. The company's effort to increase dollar earnings, with its DTH strategy leading the way, has failed to meet expectations. Dollar-denominated revenues remained at about 20 percent in 1999, the same as in 1995. Third, competition has challenged Televisa's place in the front rank of Latin American media conglomerates. Brazil's Globo and Argentina's Clarín have overtaken Televisa in terms of annual revenue. Even smaller concerns, such as Telefónica's Latin American holdings and Univisión, are seeing revenues increase at a faster rate than they are for Televisa. Given the Spanish-language opportunities offered by the Internet, where its rivals launched products first, Televisa will likely have to ally with U.S. and/or European partners to maintain its position as a major regional player, as suggested by the deal to form Sky Latin America.

In the contemporary context of the globalized media, it appears that Televisa must forge strategic alliances to sustain its place in the Spanish-language market.[17] Currently, Televisa is singularly attractive.[18] Its domestic base is rock solid. The Mexican company's audience share reached 75 percent in 2000, while Televisa's management has been stellar. Corporate debt is low, thereby allowing the company large borrowing capacity to initiate new ventures. The Azcárragas have historically shunned partnerships, but the new era in Mexico and in the media compels a reconsideration of past practices.

CONCLUSION

Students of the media in Mexico, particularly in recent years, have questioned the longevity of Televisa. The passage of NAFTA and the privatization of TV

Azteca combined in 1993 to produce a spate of commentary that suggested the imminent decline of the media powerhouse. Critics noted the initial burst of enthusiasm for the rival network as an ominous sign for the house of Azcárraga, while the proliferation of U.S.–based Blockbuster Video stores in the same year pointed to the possible displacement of Televisa's video retail interests by its North American counterparts. On the contrary, Televisa enters the new millennium with its Mexican media supremacy largely intact. The threat of domestic rivals has been contained, and encroaching international competitors have been often transformed into allies. The imagined demise of Televisa at the hands of foreign interests has scarcely materialized. And the rampant speculation of the endangered fate of the Mexican firm in 1997 has been stilled by the deft leadership of the third generation of Azcárragas to head Televisa. Given low Internet penetration and heavy competition, new media remains a gray area, but Televisa's strength as a content provider brightens the long-term prospects. Furthermore, Televisa sustains a tenacious presence among Spanish-speaking audiences in the Americas, even though its expansive possibilities are less assured. Nonetheless, the foundations of Televisa appear solid, allowing the company to look toward the future with a measure of confidence.

The specter of political change does cast a pall over the rather positive scenario at Televisa. Politicians of several parties have begun to press for greater television regulation and will likely continue to do so. However, President Fox, a former executive for Coca-Cola in Mexico, has consistently been probusiness; despite several recent decisions by an emboldened monopolies commission, it is difficult to imagine Fox as a hard-nosed reformer of Mexican capital, when several corporations dominate each of various sectors of the Mexican economy. More importantly, Televisa has clearly bowed to the new order, as evidenced by its recent nonpartisan political coverage and its deliberate impartiality during the last presidential campaign. Indeed, Fox's party has historically opposed government intervention in the private sector and seems an unlikely source for any omnibus legislative scheme to restructure dramatically the media in Mexico. Thus, if Televisa continues its balanced representation of Mexican politics, Fox will have little justification to dismember Televisa's holdings, to cancel its broadcasting licenses, or to exercise heavy-handed censorship of its programming. It is plausible, however, that Fox will use the legal authority of the state over the media to restrict any renewal of Televisa's overt political influence. For all of his neoliberal credentials, Fox maintains a cautious attitude toward foreign interests; he will not facilitate, in our view, the opening of Mexico to international media competition. In this light, the prospects for Televisa appear far from bleak. Forged in an era of governmental favors, the accumulated strengths of the house of Azcárraga will figure importantly in its ability to negotiate the challenges of globalization.

NOTES

Unless noted otherwise, all dollar amounts are in U.S. currency.

1. The historical analysis in this chapter builds upon an extensive body of work on the evolution of Mexican radio and television. The principal titles are: the collections *Televisa: El quinto poder* and *Las redes de Televisa*, edited by Raúl Trejo Delabre; Fernando Mejía Barquera's *La industria de la radio y la televisión y la política del estado mexicano (1929–1960)*; Fátima Fernández Christlieb's *Los medios de difusión masiva en México*; Claudia Fernández and Andrew Paxman's *El Tigre: Emilio Azcárraga y su imperio Televisa*; Kenton T. Wilkinson, Omar Hernández, and Aída Cerda's paper "Have Monopolies Become a Part of Mexico's Past? Lessons from the Television Industry", and Alex M. Saragoza's *The State and the Media in Mexico: The Origins of Televisa*.

2. For a detailed discussion of the consequences for Televisa of Azcárraga Milmo's death and the subsequent attempts to restore the company to health, see Fernàndez and Paxman (2000, 481–500).

3. The $1.8 billion arose from Azcárraga Milmo's leveraged buyout of his sister Laura in 1993, effected to consolidate personal control of Televisa, and interest accrued thereafter. It consisted of: $1.3 billion in bank loans (the "Alameda Debt") held by Televisa holding company Televicentro Group, of which Azcárraga held a majority; and Azcárraga Milmo's personal debts to Laura and to several banks, of $320 million and $200 million, respectively (Fernández and Paxman 2000, 468).

4. For an overview of Televisa's recently renewed health, see Preston (2000) and Tricks (2000).

5. Financial and audience statistics for Televisa, TV Azteca, and Univisión are taken from these companies' annual reports to the stock market (see the references for these specific entries). Figures for 1999 are converted at the year-end exchange rate of $1 = 9.315 pesos and for 2000 at the year end rate of $1 = 9.61 pesos.

6. As of June 2000, when Azcárraga Jean's cousin Alejandro Burillo sold his voting shares, Televisa had the following controlling shareholders: Azcárraga Jean (53.94 percent); Sinca Inbursa, a financial group controlled by Mexican billionaire and Telmex chairman Carlos Slim (25.44 percent); and the Aramburuzabala and Fernández families, owners of the Mexican brewery Modelo Group (20.62 percent) (Ortiz 2000). While Azcárraga Jean appears to have full control, there remains the slight possibility of a future challenge. First, his majority appears to be contingent upon continued support from his three sisters, who granted him their voting rights. Second, following a 1999 restructuring that saw Slim become a Televicentro shareholder, it was rumored that Azcárraga family debt still owed to Slim was convertible, so that, in the event of nonpayment by the Azcárragas, Slim could assume enough of their shares to give him control of Televisa. How much of this debt remains outstanding is unclear.

7. Our thanks to Beatríz Solís, a professor of communications at Mexico City's Universidad Autónoma Metropolitana, who also provided us with the relevant portions of the major parties' 2000 manifestos.

8. Even before the PAN took office, Mexico's Federal Competition Commission (CFC) moved to restrict Televisa at least twice during 2000. In the spring, it instructed cash-rich telephone giant Telmex to reduce its participation in Televisa's subsidiary Cablevisión from 49 percent to 25 percent, in response to the cable-television operator's planned expansion into the provinces (*Private Advisor* 2000,

40). Then, in August, CFC pressure contributed to the collapse of an intended $400 million acquisition by Televisa of Mexico's top radio group, Radio Centro (*Wall Street Journal* 2000). Three days after Fox's December 1 inauguration, the CFC ruled against a second attempt by Televisa to expand its radio division, this time through a $101 million part-purchase of Radio Acir; Televisa appealed the ruling in early 2001 (Gomez Sparrowe 2000; Luhnow 2001a).

9. For a detailed discussion of the origins and rise of the Mexican *telenovela*, production, and export developments in the 1970s and 1980s, and Televisa's international strategy of the early 1990s, see Fernández and Paxman (2000, chapters 3 and 5, 8 and 10, and 13 and 15, respectively).

10. A complementary part of Azcárraga Milmo's new foreign strategy was news channel ECO, a Spanish-language answer to CNN, begun in 1988. Costing hundreds of millions of dollars, ECO was a moderately useful political tool—allowing Televisa to ingratiate itself with foreign governments in Spain and South America—but as a commercial product it was a failure. According to its former president Félix Cortés, ECO was still losing money eleven years after its launch, despite cost-cutting that brought its annual budget down to less than $20 million (Fernández and Paxman 2000, 329f., 488f.; Cortés 1999).

11. Comparisons are obstructed by differences in reporting methods. By December 31, 1999, according to totals derived from the reports of Sky partners Televisa and News Corp. and Galaxy owner Hughes Communication, Sky had 950,000 subscribers and Galaxy had 800,000 (Grupo Televisa 2000, 31f.; News Corporation 2000; Hughes Communications International 2000). However, Galaxy has always claimed, and third-party program suppliers affirm, that while it counts subscribers only once they begin to make monthly payments, Sky counts them as soon as they sign up; Sky's actual lead over Galaxy was therefore probably closer to 100,000. Program suppliers also report that by January 2000, Sky had 380,000 paying subscribers in Mexico to Galaxy's 149,000. Given the enormous costs involved, competition between Sky and Galaxy may well end in merger. Speculation over this possibility, frequently made since start-up, was renewed in February 2001 when Rupert Murdoch, the chief executive officer of News Corp., confirmed his engagement in talks to buy Hughes's satellite division. As consequent majority owner of Galaxy, Murdoch would undoubtedly seek a Pan–Latin American merger with Sky, thereby producing a likely tussle with Televisa and Globo over control of the Mexican and Brazilian platforms of the combined operation.

12. A consensus of views within the Latin American Internet community was derived through conversations in May 2000 between Andrew Paxman and Emilio Romano, chief executive officer of SportsYA!; Rudi Vila, New Business vice president of Yupi; and Manuel Blanco, general manager of ElSitio México.

13. Launched in May 2000 at a cost of $80 million, esmas.com suffered technical problems, a change of chief executive officers, staff layoffs, and a falling out with Chicago-based MarchFirst, the company contracted to design the portal ("Televisa Site Head Out" 2000; "Mexico's Televisa 'Disappointed' with Portal Design" 2000).

14. The new portal, estarbien.com, is a $16 million fifty-fifty joint venture between Televisa and Casa Saba, better known by its previous name of Casa Autrey ("Televisa, Saba Launch Web Portal" 2000).

15. The biggest regional competitors are ISP/portal AOL Latin America, owned by AOL and Venezuela's Cisneros Group; ISP/portal Terra Networks, majority-owned by

Spain's Telefónica; portal Yahoo! En Español, owned by Yahoo! Incorporated; ISP/portal UOL, from Brazilian groups Folha and Abril; portal Yupi, whose backers include Sony and News Corp.; portal ElSitio, whose backers include Argentina's Liberman Group, Venezuela's Cisneros, and U.S. investor group Hicks, Muse, Tate & Furst; and market pioneer StarMedia Network Incorporated, an ISP/portal backed by Chase Capital Partners. Within Mexico there are several more rivals of note, including Todito, 50 percent owned by TV Azteca, and the Telmex/Microsoft-owned MSN T1. Except for AOL's Mexican portal, all of these rivals launched before esmas.com.

16. Soon after Azcárraga Milmo took control of San Angel in 1972, Televisa was producing 70 percent of the content of its four broadcast channels (Fernández and Paxman 2000, 211). Today's ratings dominance by Mexican fare is shown in statistics from ratings agency Ibope. For example, in August 1999 there were just three U.S. programs in the top twenty, each of them films and ranked in the bottom quarter; in March 2000 there were four, again films and again in the bottom quarter (*Private Advisor* 1999, 2000).

17. Given Televisa's strong cash flow and low debt, acquisitions are another potential route to expansion. Indeed, in September 2000, rumors emerged of Televisa's interest in acquiring ISP/portal StarMedia. Despite a strong user base, StarMedia was believed to be in play due to concerns over its profitability ("Mexico's Televisa Said in Talks with StarMedia" 2000).

18. For example, investment bank Salomon Smith Barney initiated coverage of Televisa stock in September 2000 with a "buy" rating, calling Televisa's goal of doubling television advertising revenues by 2004 "highly achievable" and also predicting strong pay television and Internet revenue gains (Gutschi 2000).

REFERENCES

Academia Mexicana de Derechos Humanós. 2000. *Las elecciones federales de 2000 en seis noticiarios de televisión de la ciudad de México, del 8 de mayo al 30 de junio de 2000.* Mexico City: Academia Mexicana de Derechos Humanos.

Bartra, Roger. 1987. *Jaula de la melancolía: Identidad y metamorfosis del mexicano.* Mexico City: Grijalbo.

Cortés, Félix. 1999. Interview by Andrew Paxman. Mexico City, July.

Cueva, Alvaro. 1998. *Lágrimas de cocodrilo: Historia mínima de las telenovelas en México.* Mexico City: Tres Lunas.

Cypher, James M. 1990. *State and Capital in Mexico: Development Policy since 1940.* Boulder, Colo.: Westview.

Dicken, Peter. 1992. *Global Shift: The Internationalization of Economic Activity.* 2nd ed. New York: Guilford.

Fernández, Claudia, and Andrew Paxman. 2000. *El Tigre: Emilio Azcárraga y su imperio Televisa.* Mexico City: Grijalbo/Raya en el Agua.

Fernández Christlieb, Fátima. 1990. *Los medios de difusión masiva en México.* Mexico City: Juan Pablos.

"The Global 50" (a chart and a series of articles). 2000. *Variety* , 28 August, 87–108.

Gomez Sparrowe, Veronica. 2000. "Mexico Antitrust Body Blocks Televisa's Acir Buy." *Reuters*, 4 December.

Grupo Televisa. 2000. *Annual Report 1999*. Mexico City. (Reports for previous years also consulted.)

———. 2001. *Annual Report 2000*. Mexico City. (Reports for previous years also consulted.)

Gutschi, Monica. 2000. "Salomon Initiates Mexico's Televisa with 'Buy.'" *Dow Jones Newswires*, 11 September.

Hughes Communications International. 2000. *Hughes 1999 Annual Report*. (No date): 6. <http://www.hughes.com/ir/> [last accessed: September 2000].

Hussey, Chris, et al. 2000. "Latin American Internet Primer." Goldman Sachs (New York), 21 January, 39–49.

Luhnow, David. 2001a. "Tale of Televisa: A Mexican Tug of War." *Wall Street Journal*, 8 February, A16.

———. 2001b. "Broadcasters Decry Mexican Morals Move." *Wall Street Journal*, 15 February, A12.

Maxfield, Sylvia. 1990. *Governing Capital: International Finance and Mexican Politics*. Ithaca, N.Y.: Cornell University Press.

Mejía Barquera, Fernando. 1989. *La industria de la radio y la televisión y la política del estado mexicano (1929–1960)*. Mexico City: Fundación Manuel Buendía.

"Mexico's Televisa 'Disappointed' with Portal Design." 2000. *Reuters*, 29 September.

"Mexico's Televisa Said in Talks with StarMedia." 2000. *Dow Jones Newswires*, 6 September.

Millman, Joel. 2000. "Televisa's New Cablevision System Is First in Mexico to Link Net, Cable." *Wall Street Journal*, 10 July.

Monsiváis, Carlos. 1982. "La nación de unos cuantos y las esperanzas románticas: Notas sobre la historia del término 'cultura nacional.'" In *En torna a la cultura nacional*. Mexico City: SEP/Fondo de Cultura Económica.

Montalvo, Enrique. 1985. *El nacionalismo contra la nación*. Mexico City: Grijalbo.

Negrin, Diana. 2000. Interview by Alex Saragoza. Berkeley, California, September.

News Corporation. 2000. "Earnings Release for the Quarter Ended December 31, 1999." 9 February, 8. <http://www.newscorp.com> [last accessed: September 2000].

Ortiz, Fiona. 2000. "New Televisa Shareholder Seen As Neutral." *Reuters*, 19 June.

Paxman, Andrew. 1998. "Cablers Face Coin Crisis." *Variety*, 22 June, 30.

Preston, Julia. 2000. "A Firm Grip on Mexico's Dial." *New York Times*, 25 April, C1.

Private Advisor, the Latin American Media Newsletter (Buenos Aires). 1999. 20 September.

———. 2000. 20 April.

Sandler, Adam. 1999. "Iglesias, U in Tune: Latin Singer to Ink $40 Mil, Multi-Disc Pact." *Daily Variety*, 10 June.

Saragoza, Alex M. Forthcoming. *The State and the Media in Mexico: The Origins of Televisa*.

Solís, Beatríz. 1999/2000. Interviews by Andrew Paxman. Mexico City, December and June, respectively.

"Telenovelas" (a series of articles). 1998. *Variety*, 28 September, M38–M42.

"Televisa, Saba Launch Web Portal." 2000. *Dow Jones Newswires*, 26 September.

"Televisa Site Head Out." 2000. *Variety*, 25 August. <http://www.variety.com> [last accessed: September 2000].

Televisión Azteca. 2000. *Annual Report 1999.* Mexico City.

Trejo Delabre, Raúl, ed. 1985. *Televisa: El quinto poder.* Mexico City: Claves Latinoamericanas.

———. 1988. *Las redes de Televisa.* Mexico City: Claves Latinoamericanas.

Tricks, Henry. 2000. "Monarch of the Mexican Airwaves." *Financial Times,* 15 May, 14.

Univisión Communications Incorporated. 2000. *1999 Annual Report.* Mexico City. (Reports for previous years also consulted.)

Wall Street Journal. 2000. "Televisa, Radio Centro Fail to Form an Alliance." 10 August. <http://www.wsj.com> [last accessed: September 2000].

Wilkinson, Kenton T., Omar Hernández, and Aída Cerda. 2000. "Have Monopolies Become a Part of Mexico's Past? Lessons from the Television Industry." Paper presented at the fiftieth annual conference of the International Communications Association, Acapulco, Mexico, June 1–5.

4

Globalization, Cultural Industries, and Free Trade: The Mexican Audiovisual Sector in the NAFTA Age

Enrique E. Sánchez-Ruiz

This chapter presents a historical-structural analysis of the Mexican audiovisual sector's asymmetric articulation to the new global order, especially during the "neoliberal era," which has as a special high point the signature and implementation of the North American Free Trade Agreement (NAFTA) among Canada, the United States, and Mexico. The starting point of view is the differential insertion of nation-states into the so-called globalization process, which to some appears to be an overpowering, inexorable process that apparently leaves no alternatives or options, but only one way to assume it. Being the current phase of capitalism, globalization is a form of unequal and asymmetric articulation, but it seems that there is more than one way for nations to link to it. This means that globalization has not (yet?) completely substituted or deleted *national* realities, and *national states*. As a country and as a complex national reality, Mexico has not (yet?) disappeared from the map: neither from geopolitics, neither from geoeconomics, nor from "geoculture." So, Mexico (with its institutional arrangements, government, and so on), just as many other nations of the world, continues to exist and to act upon the international arena. This remains the case, in spite of the wishes and projections of postmodern vanguards, as well as from the transnational entities that are hegemons of global economics, politics, and culture (Beck 1998; Castells 1999a; Saxe-Fernández 1999). Therefore, it is still quite useful to analyze how the cultural industries behave as a *national* economic sector, but which has significant political and cultural implications, for example, in terms of competition and competitiveness, within the nation-state as well as in the international terrain. Likewise, it is valid and important to explore whether or not, and how, the state intervenes to contribute to the national and international performance of domestic firms and sectors (as well as the nationally based transnational corporations).[1]

Cultural industries produce and circulate commodities that do not simply "realize," when consumed, but which have wider cultural and political consequences. For example, they may contribute to the democratic processes, to the development of certain forms of political culture, including the "symbolic design" or social representation of the nation itself as an "imagined community" (Anderson 1992). Therefore, it is important to assure that within as well as between countries the cultural industries operate in an environment of competition and plurality. One might guarantee the other.

GLOBALIZATION, REGIONALIZATION, AND FREE TRADE

It is necessary to single out the new traits of the contemporary world that imply globalization as a real historical novelty, setting aside myths, fashions, and the "fetishization" of the phenomenon (Bolaño 1995). And we should differentiate what is actually new from what comes from previous long historical processes (Sánchez-Ruiz 1996a; Ferguson 1992; Ianni 1996; Ortiz 1994). It is referred to as a "fetishized" notion especially as a main component of the dominant "neoliberal ideology," which pretends "that the developing countries must insert swiftly, precisely the neoliberal way (with unflinchingly commercial opening, liberalization of foreign investment and the withdrawal of the state from its economic functions as investor, regulator, planner and promoter of economic growth and social welfare), under penalty of staying at the margins of progress and of the passage to the First World" (Calva 1995a, 13). Here, I am interested in emphasizing that, although globalization certainly can be considered descriptively a real and to a great extent inexorable process, it does not take place linearly, in only one way. History is multidimensional and open, not linear and predetermined. There are multiple possible ways for history to unfold (Castells 1999b). Hence, it is still a function of nation-states to decide (within limits) the ways that they shall articulate to the complex historical processes, in economic and political terms, as well as regarding some of their cultural exchanges.

Despite its naturalization in everyday discourse, globalization seems to be a novelty for many people, although some others think that it is the contemporary stage of a process that has been occurring along with the expansion of Western civilization and the world capitalist system. U.S. scholar Marjorie Ferguson seems to think likewise:

My first point is that questions about power and influence and trading in cultural products call for an historical as well as a critical perspective. For instance, if the globalization process began with the fifteenth and sixteenth-century explorers and discoverers, they foreshadowed their twentieth-century counterparts by exporting the technology, goods and cultural industry of their day. True, then it was Christianity rather than Madonna, but . . . it is important

to recall that exporting influence via economic and cultural goods has characterized international power relations over the centuries. (1993, 3)

Thus, from a long-term, or *long durée*, perspective, in the sense of Fernand
Braudel (1980), the insertion of Latin America to the world system did not begin with television, the "new communication technologies," or the Internet
(Ferrer 1999). The end of the "long fourteenth century," in the words of Immanuel Wallerstein (1976), departing from the expansion of commercial capitalism, foreshadowed (and configured) historically what is known today as
the "modern world system." From this long-term point of view, then, the
globalizing process is actually the result of the contemporary acceleration of
historical movements, whose principal engine has been the internationalization of capital (Pallois 1977a), although it does not exhaust itself in economic
factors (Ortiz 1994). In cultural terms, the constitution of the modern world
system has meant the Westernization of cultures and civilizations; sometimes
through armed conquest, sometimes by influence and imitation, but most of
the time by the mediation of economic domination (Fossaert 1994; Braudel
1991; Wallerstein 1990; Ianni 1974, 1993). But continental, regional, national,
and local cultures have always resisted, or at least have always been creative,
so that throughout the world, in different historical moments, there have
arisen new hybrid versions of the diverse dominant forms that Western civilization has adopted. Located in different moments in diverse historical centers of dissemination (hegemonic centers), Western civilization has been
influenced, modified, and enriched by other cultures and civilizations. Thus,
we are not referring to an unchanged, essentially pure "monolith," imposing
itself historically, totally obliterating what existed before, notwithstanding
its domination in the last instance (García Canclini 1989; Mattelart 1993;
Ochoa 1995).

The latter part of the twentieth century witnessed the acceleration of historical time, in terms of the internationalization-transnationalization-
globalization of economies, politics, and cultures.[2] This has happened
through the emergence and development of the large transnational corporations that do not know of frontiers, other than profitability on a global scale,
through the advent of the third technological-industrial revolution, and of
the information society (Sunkel and Fuenzalida 1979; Lacroix and Tremblay
1997; Castells 1999a). This long historical process has brought about changes
and reaccommodations in the international division of labor. They have consisted of the gradual articulation and (unequal) interdependence of nation-
states to the modern capitalist world system. Unequal interconnectedness is
the sign of cybercapitalism.

Thus, from an economic point of view, we understand by globalization the
contemporary process of ever greater—and accelerated—articulation and unequal interdependence between countries and world regions because of the
intensification of the functional articulations, in diverse territories of the earth,
among the phases of the circuit of capital: financing, purchase of inputs—raw

materials, labor force, production, distribution, and consumption—realization of the value thus generated, and conversion to new financial capital.[3]

For the sake of clarity, let me explain that in this use of "globalization" I refer to the result of such articulations among whole economies. "Globalization" is the configuration of the world economy. Seen from below, it is a whole national economy, not just one company, that "globalizes." In the case of so-called global corporations, maybe we should continue to call them "transnational corporations" (or "multinational corporations" as they are called in the English-speaking world). So, one can say that a company internationalizes when it begins to connect to the external markets, by exporting/importing, or through foreign investments.[4] It becomes a transnational enterprise when operating preferentially not in its own country of origin, but across several countries simultaneously (i.e., preferentially in the international markets), which consolidates by strategic alliances and associations, fusions and acquisitions, and so on, between companies and corporations from several different nations. Finally, the expansion of this form of international/transnational operation, intensified by the mobility of financial capital and of strategic information fostered by technological advancement, constitutes the process of globalization proper, as the configuration of the contemporary world economy.[5] The observations of the intensification of all kinds of economic connections (international trade, flows of direct and indirect foreign investment, and so on) are but partial indicators of globalization.

This global process, economic in principle, is accompanied by new political configurations of the world map. These redefine the roles of national actors (states, governments, corporations, social classes, and social movements) as well as non- or extranational actors (old and new international organizations, transnational corporations, nongovernment organizations, and so on) in the world scenario. The larger and faster (although still asymmetric) contacts among the multiple cultures that populate the planet constitute another fundamental feature of the new map of the world (Scarlatto et al. 1994).[6] Anthropologist Néstor García Canclini illustrates with some examples of "global articulation":

> we purchase a Ford car assembled in Spain, with windshields made in Canada, Italian carburetor, Austrian radiator, English cylinders and battery, and French transmission axis. I turn on my TV, manufactured in Japan, and what I see is a world-film, produced in Hollywood, directed by a Polish filmmaker with French assistants, actors and actresses of ten nationalities, and scenes shot in the four countries that financed it. The big enterprises that supply food and clothing, make us travel and jam in identical freeways throughout the whole planet; they fragment the production process, manufacturing every part of the goods where the cost is smallest. Objects lose the fidelity relationship to their original territories. Culture is a process of multinational assembly, a flexible articulation of parts; an assembly of features that any citizen of any country, religion or ideology can read and use. (1995, 15–16)

García Canclini seems to present in the quoted paragraph a process of equalization whereby everyone, everywhere, has access to the "democratic" consumption of such wonders of the world economic cultural integration. However, he has commented elsewhere that: "In spite of the diversity and intensity of the globalization processes, they do not imply either the undifferentiated unification or the simultaneous establishment of relationships of all societies amongst themselves. Countries access in an unequal and conflictive way to economic and symbolic international markets" (1996, 17). Globalization, then, does not imply the horizontal and egalitarian articulation of all (one possible image of the "global village"). As I said before, the expansive process of the world capitalist system and of Western civilization has never been able to avoid hegemonies and inequalities.

Contrary to what has been claimed, the world has not reached the "end of history" or the reign of Utopia after the fall of the Berlin Wall. Actually, it seems that polarization between rich and poor countries is growing. The UN 1999 *Human Development Report* indicates that two-thirds of humanity have not benefited from the new economic model and they are excluded from participation in the information society. In the 1997 *World Economic Outlook*, the International Monetary Fund concluded that:

> To put it simply, during the last thirty years, most developing countries—84 of 108 (with figures available)—have remained in the lowest fifth in terms of income or have fallen into this bracket from a relatively higher position. Moreover, there are less middle income developing countries now and their upward mobility seems to have declined over time. During the period 1965–1975 there was a certain tendency for countries to move towards higher levels and make progress with respect to the advanced economies, but since the beginning of the 1980's, the forces of polarization seem to have become stronger. (78)

On the one hand, a 1997 report of the Sistema Económico Latinoamericano (SELA; Latin American Economic System)[7] indicates that in the Western Hemisphere the situation is just a little less dramatic. We have two countries with very advanced economies, the United States and Canada, that in 1995 had a gross national product (GNP) per capita of $26,890 and $19,380, respectively. And on the other hand, there are Latin American countries with an average per capita GNP of $3,320. If the extremes are considered, the United States has a per capita GNP 108 times larger than that of Haiti ($250).

Within countries also inequalities have ensued and increased. For example, the Comisión Económica para América Latina y el Caribe (CEPAL; UN Economic Commission for Latin America and the Caribbean) estimates that in 1997, 36 percent of Latin American homes were under the poverty line (54 percent in rural areas). The range goes from Uruguay, with only 6 percent, Costa Rica and Chile with 20 percent, to Honduras with 74 percent, El Salvador with 48 percent, Bolivia with 47 percent, and Mexico with 43 percent (1998).

Today, we are witnessing the constitution of large political-economic blocks that are in their turn articulated to the world system (Varis 1993; González Casanova and Saxe-Fernández 1996). Paradoxically, "globalization" is taking the form of a process of regionalization of the world political economy (Oman 1994; Calva 1995b). Part of this relatively recent process is the signing and enforcement since 1994 of NAFTA among Canada, the United States, and Mexico. By virtue of this trilateral agreement, a combined market of nearly four hundred million consumers is being constituted, with an economic product that is similar or larger than that of the European Union (Calva Mercado 1998; Randall and Konrad 1995). However, some sectors of the three countries' populations have been concerned from the beginning with NAFTA's consequences and implications for justice and equity, both within the nations and especially regarding their multiple links (MacEwan 1996; Cardero 1996). The following description of NAFTA clearly states that it constitutes a form of asymmetric articulation:

> Because of the size of the United States' market, this grouping is a trading block of global scope.
>
> For this very same reason differences are observed between the free trade members themselves. The GDP of the USA (in 1996 it was US$7,342 billion) is twelve times larger than Canada's GDP (US$579 billion) and twenty-two times greater than Mexico's (US$335 billion). Their levels of development are also significant. While GNP per capita in 1996 was US$28,020 for the United States and US$19,020 for Canada, in Mexico it was only US$3,670. And yet another trait of this group is that prior to joining this trade agreement, its members already had a high level of trade with each other. (Sistema Económico Latinoamericano 1999)

In the case of Mexico, NAFTA constituted a sort of corollary of a process that had begun in the previous decade, with the implementation of so-called neoliberal economic policies. This process consisted of the reduction of the government apparatus and the privatization of state and parastate companies, liberalization and deregulation of diverse economic sectors, swift commercial opening to external markets, and so on (Calva 1995a; Meyer 1995). The previous inward-oriented development model, based mainly on protectionist import substitution policies, had entered into crisis in the 1970s, so it began to be substituted by an "outward-oriented" free market development model, by the Miguel de la Madrid administration (1982–1988). Mexico's neoliberal way to globalization was called "authoritarian liberalism" (Meyer 1995). Although immediate effects were expected from NAFTA's implementation, regarding diverse economic sectors in the three countries, in Mexico many processes that have unfolded recently have simply been the consequence of such previous trends, a result of the prevailing neoliberal policies (Sánchez-Ruiz 1996a).

Canada had the previous experience of a bilateral agreement with the United States, signed in 1989, of which there is still not consensus on whether or not it was beneficial for that country (Thompson and Randall 1994; Randall and Konrad 1995). In particular, Canada has shown resistance to include the cultural industries sector in this kind of negotiation, under the same conditions as any other economic area, because the Canadian government thinks that the cultural industries have important consequences for their national identity and sovereignty: "For almost a century, Canadian governments have attempted to assert this cultural sovereignty, and to control the allegedly deleterious effects of U.S. newspapers, popular fiction, magazines, comic books, motion pictures (and now videotapes), radio, and eventually television and the associated recording industry" (Thompson 1995, 394).

In Mexico, there are still concerns about whether the greater and faster economic integration that is happening will translate into a larger economic, political, and cultural subordination, with regard to the neighboring country to the north (Calva 1995b; Cardero 1996; Dietrich 1997; Sánchez-Ruiz 2000). The NAFTA signature is but one of many bilateral and multilateral agreements that Mexico has signed since 1986, when it joined the General Agreement on Tariffs and Trade and more recently a free trade agreement with the European Union. By June 2000, Mexico had twenty-seven free trade agreements signed with all types and sizes of nations ("México en el Mundo" 2000). It appears that the Mexican government has sought to diversify the country's international economic links. However, CEPAL, for example, observes that: "Actually, the growing connection of Mexico with the international market is equal to a greater integration of its economy to the North American bloc, especially to the United States. . . . Between 1990 and 1998 the importance of North America in Mexico's total trade increased from 69% to 82%, and over two thirds of foreign direct investment in Mexico had its origin in United States and Canada" (2000, 104).

Those "over two thirds" break down to 60 percent from the United States and 2.7 percent from Canada. What repercussions are all these recent facts and processes having on Mexico's cultural industries, in particular on the audiovisual sector? In the case of the cinema industry, for example, it seems that "market forces" are reducing a country that came to be an important film producer and exporter, to a mere consumer of imports from abroad. In any event, NAFTA accelerated tendencies that were already taking place, in terms of "asymmetric interdependence" (Straubhaar 1993) between the Mexican and U.S. markets.

NAFTA AND THE MEXICAN AUDIOVISUAL SECTOR

As I mentioned before, Canada refused to include the cultural industries in the negotiations of the agreement, as it had already done before with its previous bilateral agreement with the United States. Even though the Mexican government did not oppose to negotiate the cultural industries, they were not included in NAFTA, although there were some aspects of them, such as copyright issues or telecommunications, that related to the audiovisual sector.[8] So, because of this exemption much of what has happened in this area has been due, more than directly to NAFTA proper, to the acceleration and reinforcement of previous tendencies, and because of economic policies that already were being implemented, of which NAFTA itself was one of many consequences, and the motor, after its implementation (Sánchez-Ruiz 1996a). For example, regarding the audiovisual cultural industries, we should add some other changes to privatization, liberalization, and opening of markets that already had begun to happen: the modernization, adoption, and generalization of new technologies for signal distribution that did not begin, but simply accelerated with the NAFTA environment. So for instance, pay television (pay–TV; e.g., cable, satellite, and multichannel multipoint distribution service [MMDS]) expanded rapidly worldwide during the 1990s, and therefore it has developed in Mexico just as everywhere else, although hastened by the wider effects of Mexico's economic globalization. Thus, we see a process of technological modernization beginning to occur before NAFTA, accelerating and producing further changes. In the case of cinema, the new multiplex halls have produced a significant recovery for the exhibition business (just as throughout the world). It is also pertinent to add that movies have become the paramount program form in pay–TV, and that they rank second in the supply on broadcast television. So we find a considerable increase in film imports, caused by growing demand not necessarily directly related to NAFTA.

In any event, some actions were not taken in preparation for NAFTA's signature, but rather asystematically. For example, the federal 1992 Law of Cinematography broke with the long protectionist tradition of the 1941 law, which reserved 50 percent of screen time to the national cinema.[9] The new act reduced the Mexican movie quota in cinema halls to 30 percent in 1993, decreasing 5 percent every year until 10 percent on December 31, 1997. The corresponding federal Law of Radio and Television was not modified, but the cable television regulation was modified so as to allow 49 percent foreign ownership. Another important action, which took place during the NAFTA negotiations, was the privatization of Televisión Azteca (TV Azteca), the former parastate company. The deal included a national network (Channel 13) and a seminational network (Channel 7), along with a "media package" that included COTSA, then the largest chain of cinema outlets (Sánchez-Ruiz 1999a). As I suggested before, the NAFTA negotiation, as well as this series of measures, can be thought of as a result of the sequence of neoliberal changes that began to occur in Mexico since the early 1980s, in tune with dominant world trends.

Based on the analysis of such previous tendencies, I maintained a rather "gloomy" hypothesis regarding the Mexican audiovisual space and its exchanges with the NAFTA partners—especially the United States—before the enactment of the agreement (Sánchez-Ruiz 1992; De María y Campos 1992). Even being aware, as I was, that the most important Mexican media group, Televisa Group, was (and still is) the main producer and exporter of television programs in the Spanish-speaking world, my doubts and critique were based on the highly oligopolistic structure that has characterized the Mexican television system as well as the film industry. Since the 1970s, Televisa went through processes of horizontal and vertical integration that translated into too few other alternatives for television content production, which the big Mexican corporation did for distribution by its own networks, and for export. However, Televisa did not have practically any experience in actual, full competition, in a competitive market, either in Mexico, or in the United States, where it had expanded during the 1970s until the mid-1980s. During that time, the Spanish International Network, later on renamed Univisión Network, constituted the monopoly of Spanish-language television in the United States. My concern referred also to the already existing unequal flows and exchanges in the audiovisual market of the North American area, regarding the competition for *all* of the linguistic-cultural markets of the area (including the Anglo-Saxon market, which is a majority in the United States and Canada) (Sánchez-Ruiz 1986).[10] Finally, such skepticism was based on the knowledge of the production and export strength in the audiovisual sector of NAFTA's major partner: the United States. Pay–TV modalities (cable, MMDS, and satellite), which had begun to expand in the beginning of the 1990s, brought about new needs for programming, both for generalist television as well as for specialty television, that just one single Mexican corporation, huge as it could be, would not be able to solve. There were too few audiovisual production companies, either for cinema or television, and barriers to entry of the size of Televisa itself. The result would be that new possible actors in the Mexican audiovisual space, for example, new independent pay–TV stations, would have to resort mainly to imports for programming, which in turn would increase the deficit in the audiovisual trade balance with the United States (Sánchez-Ruiz 1992, 1993).

On the other hand, the Mexican film industry was in a sort of "eternal crisis" since the 1960s after having been a strong and creative cultural business in the 1940s and 1950s. With one-third of the current population, during the 1940s Mexico produced an average of almost eighty films per year. In the 1970s and 1980s, Mexican cinema had a production average of nearly one hundred long films a year, and a high proportion were exported to Latin America and to the Hispanic market of the United States. According to available data, from 1976 to 1979, Mexico had an average surplus of $6.5 million per year in its "cinematographic trade balance." By the late 1980s, it became a chronic deficit: for example, during the years 1984–1988, there was an average deficit of $2.5 million (Ugalde 1998). Therefore, there was pessimism about the destiny of the Mexican cinema as an industry (Ugalde and Reygadas 1994). The video rental and sale sector showed a structure in its supply (with a corresponding almost identical demand) in which U.S. movies prevailed (80 percent) over those from Mexico (10 percent) and "foreign cinema" (10 percent) (García Canclini 1994).

Finally, my concern departed from the hypothesis that cultural products are not simple commodities that can be left adrift at the mercy of blind market forces. Cultural products, especially those of the audiovisual sector—and this is a hypothesis that I could not substantiate in one single research—have cumulative and long-term consequences in the cultural realm and in terms of their contribution to the construction of sociocultural identities (Sánchez-Ruiz 1995a). Since then, I have been exploring empirically the concrete forms of the internationalization of the audiovisual cultural industries. In general terms, the hypotheses regarding the unequal flows and exchanges will be sustained later in this chapter (Sánchez-Ruiz 1996b, 1998a).

THE MEXICAN AUDIOVISUAL SECTOR: A BRIEF EXAMINATION OF UNEQUAL FLOWS

Television

Mexican television at the end of the twentieth century was highly concentrated and centralized. Even though there are optimistic viewpoints that see the coming end of monopolies in Mexico (Wilkinson, Hernández, and Cerda 2000), the cultural industries sector still shows a very concentrated market structure. Besides, in consonance with the prevailing economic and political centralism, most of the industry is controlled in Mexico City. For example, Televisa controls almost half the broadcast television stations in the country (see table 4.1).

However, according to its own account, Televisa had a 78 percent share of the television audience during 1999: "Additionally the company's networks broadcast 187 of the 200 most popular programs during 1999" (Televisa 2000, 1). It is estimated that around 80 percent of television ad expenditure goes to Televisa (while 70 percent of media ad expenditure goes to broadcast television) (Sánchez-Ruiz 1999a).

Table 4.1 Distribution of Broadcast Television Stations in Mexico, 1999

Company/Institution	Number of Stations	Percentage
Televisa	326	46.2
Televisión Azteca	251	35.6
Government	91	12.9
Other	37	5.3
Total	705	100.0

Source: Televisa website at: <www.televisa.com.mx/gts/CENTROpart.HTM> [last accessed: 10 August 1999].

Broadcast television has a 98 percent penetration in the Mexican population, while pay–TV reaches only 15 percent (see table 4.2). Even though in cable television there seems to a be greater competition than in broadcast television, according to data from the Chamber of Cable Television eight companies control 70 percent of the market. The largest share of wired homes is for Cablevisión, the cable division of Televisa (around six hundred thousand subscribers) in which Teléfonos de México (Telmex), the giant monopoly of local telephony, holds 49 percent interest. Likewise, in MMDS the largest share is for Multivisión (MVS), which owns five of the nineteen operating systems, and is still expanding throughout the country. One of the two direct-to-home (DTH) outlets, Sky Latin America, belongs to Televisa in partnership with Rupert Murdoch's News Corporation and the Brazilian Globo company; the other, DirecTV, belongs to MVS in partnership with Hughes Communications International, the Brazilian Abril, and the Venezuelan Cisneros Group. Sky leads the DTH race with "more than 410 thousand active subscribers" (Televisa 2000), while DirecTV had only 150,000 by the end of 1999 (Cacho López 2000). Thus, we see that Televisa still controls a large part of the Mexican television system overall.

Table 4.3 describes the evolution of the distribution in terms of origin of the programs broadcast by Mexican broadcast television during the 1980s and 1990s. There is a clear trend towards "Mexicanization" of programming during the 1980s, which reverses in 1995 and then makes a slight recovery in 1997. Partially, the increase of imports in the early 1990s was due to the competition that was energizing the newly privatized TV Azteca against Televisa. However, in 1995 TV Azteca also imported a good portion of Latin American *telenovelas* (soap operas), besides the U.S. fare. Before TV Azteca began producing some successful soap operas, its main competitive weapons were imports, such as *The Nanny* or *The Simpsons*. It should be noted that for all of the years included in the sample, in prime time the proportion of programming imported from the United States increases, while the Mexican part decreases correspondingly, although remaining the largest portion.[11]

Although it is true that in general terms the programs preferred by the Mexican audiences are of national origin, especially soccer broadcasts, soap operas, news, and feature films, I should differentiate between what they like from what they actually see. For example, in a survey that I conducted

Table 4.2   Distribution of Pay–TV Stations in Mexico, 1999

	Systems in Operation	*Subscribers*
Cable Television	310	1,900,000
MMDS	19	700,000
DTH	2	529,000
Total	331	3,129,000

Source: National Chamber of Cable Television, several reports and interviews with Chamber staff, 2000.

Table 4.3   Origin of Samples of Mexican TV Programming, Selected Years (percentages)

Year	Mexico	United States	Latin America	Europe	Canada	Other	Total
			Total Time				
1983[a]	65.58	29.42	N/A	N/A	N/A	5.00	100.00
1984[a]	68.63	24.02	N/A	N/A	N/A	7.35	100.00
1990[a]	69.49	22.96	1.88	N/A	N/A	5.67	100.00
1995[b]	52.79	36.65	5.24	3.64	0.16	1.52	100.00
1997[a]	60.41	35.18	2.09	0.97	0.15	1.20	100.00
			Prime Time				
1983[a]	54.00	44.35	N/A	N/A	N/A	1.65	100.00
1984[a]	54.32	39.67	N/A	N/A	N/A	6.01	100.00
1990[a]	54.22	33.92	1.58	N/A	N/A	10.28	100.00
1995[b]	47.72	41.88	6.22	2.90	0.21	1.07	100.00
1997[a]	57.78	38.76	1.79	0.33	0.33	1.01	100.00

[a]Mexico City and Guadalajara.
[b]Mexico City, Guadalajara, León, and Uruapan.
Note: The category "Other" is different for the years 1983 and 1984 than for the following years.
Sources: Sánchez-Ruiz (1986, 1996b).

in 1993, most people said that they preferred to watch the movies in the cinema halls; however, of these, only 39 percent actually did so, and the rest used videocassette recorders (VCRs) (28 percent) or regular television (34 percent) (Sánchez-Ruiz 1994).[12] Something similar but more relevant arises from a survey performed by Jorge González in several Mexican cities.[13] Although, for example, only 31.4 percent of his respondents indicated that the foreign miniseries were their favorite programs, 59.4 percent stated that they used to watch them regularly.[14] Foreign movies were reportedly the favorite of 51.4 percent of the total, but 77 percent viewed them frequently.[15] Thus, for the case of television, I have found that although national programming prevails in the supply as well as in the demand, it is clear that in both cases there is a significant component of imported programs, mainly U.S. movies (which I have realized are a central television genre).

Let me illustrate the rank and role of foreign feature films for Mexican television audiences. In 1996, the competition for the Mexican broadcast television market reached an unusual high, so that other media called it the "TV broadcasters war." As part of such "war," Televisa published in local and national newspapers a series of ad inserts, one of which showed the "100 most viewed programs in Mexican TV during 1996."[16] Of the first ten in the list, seven were national soccer games and two Mexican soap operas; there was only one "program" from the United States: the *Karate Kid II* movie. But from the total of one hundred programs, forty-six were U.S. movies, broadcast by Televisa's national network of Channel 5, which specializes in imported programming. In the list corresponding to the one hundred weekend programs with highest ratings,[17] I find exactly the same number of forty-six U.S. films, all broadcast by Channel 5. According to Televisa's own published data,[18] then, almost half of the most popular "TV programs" in 1996 were Hollywood films. This tells me that to observe only the list of ten or twenty most popular programs is not enough to have an adequate image of the actual tastes and consumption patterns of television viewers. It is necessary to consider, for example, the diverse television genres and their relationships to sociographic and cultural variables.

As a matter of fact, Televisa's programming is also present in the United States, especially through its participation with Univisión, which is the one with greater coverage and highest audience ratings in the Spanish-speaking community (around 11 percent of the total U.S. population) (Sinclair 1999). However, in the "big market," which is the Anglo-Saxon majority, neither Televisa, nor practically any other company from anywhere else in the world, can penetrate. According to multiple measurements spanning the 1970s to the 1990s, on average foreign programs constituted around 2 percent of the total television programming in the United States (Straubhaar, Campbell, and Cahoon 1998). From these data and from my own measurements of Mexican programming throughout the years, I have maintained that the television trade balance has systematically favored the United States. This unequal exchange becomes still more uneven if I take into account pay–TV (cable, MMDS, and DTH satellite), video, and long films in cinema halls.

Cinema

The Mexican cinema industry, as I have suggested before, has been sinking in its worst crisis yet, even though there has been a handful of critical and box office successes during the past few years. My conclusion from the analysis of the sector is that, although differentially in its three subsectors, it is going through a process of contraction, concentration, and transnationalization (Sánchez-Ruiz 1999b). The recent evolution of feature film production in Mexico can be observed in figure 4.1.

Although during the 1980s there was an average of about 84 films per year, and the following decade began with a high 104, production fell to 36, tumbling and decreasing to around 10 in 1998, with a slight recovery in 1999. Correspondingly, many producers have closed down, especially the small independents. For example, in 1985 there were 152 production companies in Mexico registered by the National Chamber of the Cinema Industry; by 1994, there were 128. In the Mexican Institute for Cinematography, the federal government's cinema authority, there were eighty-nine registered production companies in 1997; by 2000 I found only fifty-four (Sánchez-Ruiz 1999b). The grand winner was the most important production company: Televicine, the cinema division of Televisa, which also has its own distribution company, Videocine. For example, in 1995 Videocine was the distributor that premiered

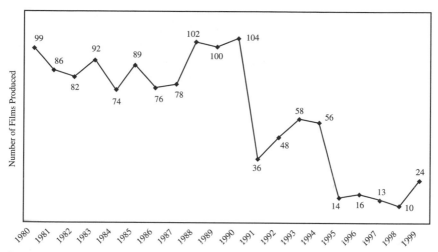

Figure 4.1 Feature Film Production in Mexico, 1980–1999. *Source:* **National Chamber of the Cinema Industry, several reports and interviews with Chamber staff, 2000.**

the most films (forty-five, or 20 percent of the total). Videocine and two other distributors (Columbia Pictures and United International Pictures) accounted for 53 percent of premiers that same year. These same three companies accounted for 91.7 percent of the revenues produced by the "one hundred blockbusters" in 1995 (Sánchez-Ruiz 1998a). Distribution has turned out to be such a good business for Televisa that its production activities have recently slowed down and it has devoted more efforts to the distribution activity. In its 1997 *Annual Report*, regarding its cinematographic activities, one can read:

> Grupo Televisa is the exclusive distributor in Mexico of the films produced by Warner Brothers, and of some of the New Line Cinema and Polygram productions. In 1997, the company distributed a total of 46 feature films, most of them from the United States of North America. The most successful films in box office distributed by the company include *Space Jam, Batman and Robin, The Plot, Selena, Contact, Mortal Kombat 2* and the *Devil's Advocate.* (Televisa 1998)[19]

Data about the distribution, attendance, and revenues of the one hundred most popular films in Mexico in 1998 are shown in table 4.4. Ninety-five percent of the revenues earned by the one hundred most successful films in Mexico corresponded to Televisa plus the three U.S. majors. There were only three Mexican movies, while eighty-seven were from the United States and the rest from Europe.

The contraction of the sector has been followed by concentration in a few companies and a rapid transnationalization process, even in the exhibition subsector, which had traditionally been owned by Mexican capital. Table 4.5 eloquently shows the decrease in exhibition and premiers of Mexican films and the corresponding growth of Hollywood movies.

I have already indicated that in the case of video stores, their stock is predominantly from the United States (80 percent). I have also indicated that cinema is by its own right an important television genre. In the measurements that I have done, cinema has occupied one of the top places in the television supply, with an average of 20 percent of total time, as well as in prime time. For example, in my 1995 sample, of the total time dedicated to movies, 61 percent corresponded to U.S. films, while 37.2 percent were Mexican. However, in prime time the U.S. share increased to 75.8 percent. Table 4.6 shows the Chamber of the Cinema Industry's estimate for Mexico City's free and pay–TV.

Cablevisión is the cable division of Televisa, and Multivisión the most important MMDS operator. Pay–TV is expanding in its several modalities throughout the Mexican social space, beginning nowadays with the upper and upper-middle classes, but at a pace that will probably surpass the speed of the diffusion of VCRs since 1985. With their expansion, these alternatives to broadcast television are demanding ever more audiovisual programs for specialty television, as well as for more generalist options. Such potential de-

Table 4.4   Results of the Top One Hundred Blockbusters in Mexico, 1998

Distributor	Number of Films	Spectators		Revenues[a]	
Columbia	31	14,301,849	33.51%	314,614,507	33.56%
Videocine	30	8,923,305	20.91%	202,292,409	21.59%
UIP	17	8,894,217	20.84%	195,076,198	20.81%
Fox	14	8,768,141	20.55%	186,242,857	19.87%
Gussi	6	1,380,645	3.24%	29,826,618	3.18%
Quimera F.	2	406,185	0.95%	9,308,865	0.99%
Total	100	42,674,342	100.00%	937,361,454	100.00%

[a]Mexican pesos.
Source: Telemundo (1999).

Table 4.5   Mexican and U.S. Feature Films Shown in Mexico, 1980–1993 (percentages)

Years	United States	Mexico	Other
1980	34.04	54.01	12
1981	35.28	53.45	11
1982	35.36	52.02	13
1983	38.29	48.64	13
1984	40.46	46.82	13
1985	40.17	48.11	12
1986	40.97	48.34	11
1987	40.2	47.40	12
1988	46.78	46.87	6
1989	48.53	46.55	5
1990	49.90	45.62	4
1991	53.02	42.73	4
1992	61.27	34.62	4
1993	62.86	32.09	5

Source: Estadísticas de Cultura (1995).

mand comprises all types of formats and genres, including feature films. Given the information about the Mexican audiovisual sector, I believe that such a production capacity has not yet been developed, other than by Televisa and incipiently by TV Azteca and MVS.[20]

In table 4.7, I confirm that the audiovisual trade balance between Latin America and the United States is negative for the former and highly positive for the latter.

Table 4.6 Feature Films Transmitted through TV in Mexico City, 1996

Company	Mexican Films		Foreign Films	
Televisa	1,136	43.63%	1,468	56.37%
Televisión Azteca	351	33.69%	691	66.31%
Cablevisión	4,618	16.94%	22,649	83.06%
Multivisión	2,192	11.65%	16,623	88.35%
Channel 22	17	7.36%	214	92.64%
Channel 11	0	0.00%	1,065	100.00%

Source. National Chamber of the Cinema Industry, several reports and interviews with Chamber staff, 2000.

Table 4.7 Mexican Audiovisual Sector, Foreign Trade Balance, 1997 (in U.S. millions of dollars)

	United States	Latin America	Europe	Other	Total
Exports, Television					
Signals	2.0	4.0	0.0	0.0	6.0
Programs	43.9	43.0	8.1	17.5	112.5
Total	45.9	47.0	8.1	17.5	118.5
Imports, Television					
Signals	84.0	2.8	2.4	2.0	91.2
Programs	45.0	3.0	1.0	1.0	50.0
Total	129.0	5.8	3.4	3.0	141.2
Exports, Long Films					
	0.1	0.2	0.0	0.0	0.3
Imports, Long Films					
	37.2	0.3	2.4	0.6	40.5
Total Audiovisual Exports					
	46.0	47.2	8.1	17.5	118.8
Total Audiovisual Imports					
	166.2	6.1	5.8	3.6	181.7
Difference, Exports – Imports					
Television	−83.1	41.2	4.7	14.5	−22.7
Cinema	−37.1	−0.1	−2.4	−0.6	−40.2
Total	−120.2	41.1	2.3	13.9	−62.9

Source: Cámara de Diputados, "Iniciativa de Reforma y Adiciones a la Ley Federal de Cinematografía," April 1998, in Toussaint (1999).

Again, it is evident that Mexico's deficit is larger in cinema than from the exchange of television programs. But regarding television, the deficit is much larger when I consider only the exchanges with the United States than for example with Latin America (where the balance is positive for Mexico). It is important to emphasize that in spite of the fact of Televisa's exports, Mexico is still a *net importer* in this field.

Table 4.7 shows that the greatest part of Mexico's deficit in its audiovisual exchanges is explained by those corresponding with the United States, especially with regards to television programs. According to a Spanish analysis of the Ibero-American market (i.e., Latin America, plus Spain and Portugal), Mexico appeared as the largest audiovisual exporter of the region. According to the data, in 1997 Mexico controlled 50 percent of the overall audiovisual exports of the area. However, it imported much more than it exported, so according to that analysis it had a deficit of $117 million (Media Research and Consultancy–Spain 1998). Ibero-America and the "rest of the world" produced a surplus of $40.6 million and $13.4 million, respectively, but the exchanges with the United States generated a deficit of $170.8 million (and $700,000 with Europe). In 1996, Mexico's audiovisual deficit appeared still larger: $158 million (Media Research and Consultancy–Spain 1997). Because of the exports and worldwide presence of Televisa's programs, many people, including scholars and politicians, have thought that Mexico is a net exporter, but there are more grounds to cast doubt on such a "certainty."

The outcomes of the so-called neoliberal policies that have been implemented in Mexico do not seem to favor the development of competitiveness *in the sector as a whole.* By virtue of the instrumentation of an "imperfect neoliberalism," which hinders competition and favors concentration, the Mexican government has advanced in several sectors, the formation and operation of highly oligopolistic and monopolistic market structures.

Televisa is a "global" giant of the industry and is Mexico's transnational corporation in the cultural industry, which maintains an important presence in many countries of the world as an exporter and foreign investor. Actually, Televisa exports even beyond the Spanish-speaking cultural-linguistic markets (Sinclair 1999). However, *one* successful, quasi-monopolistic enterprise does not necessarily make an economic sector. Neither monopoly nor duopoly—which characterizes Mexican broadcast television—are market structures that allow the development of competitive diversity in the production and distribution of cultural goods.[21] The main competition of Televisa in Mexico, TV Azteca, has incipiently developed some production and export capacity, and has manifested very ambitious plans of international expansion, including the project for establishing its own film division. However, in order for a country to build up a strong audiovisual sector, a competitive environment is required. Barriers to entry should be set aside, allowing the establishment of a good number of independent enterprises to compete with each other and with the major players, for the different segments of the market (production, distribution, and exhibition/retail). This in turn guarantees a greater diversity of expression and of choices for the audience. For example, in the United States the seven major producers of audiovisual cultural products, associated in the Motion Picture Association of America (MPAA), compete for national and international markets with the more than 130 "independent" companies grouped in the American Film Marketing Association (AFMA). Although there is a certain greater inclination of the majors for the production of feature films, both produce a good proportion of the series and movies that are shown in television in practically all the world (Bedore 1997). A recent report performed by a consulting firm for AFMA shows that over 60 percent of the feature films produced in the United States are made by so-called independent companies, which generate almost $1.6 billion for the North American economy (Arthur Anderson Economic Consulting 1998).

However, I believe that Televisa's exports are sometimes exaggerated a bit. Of its net sales in 1997, 18 percent originated abroad (which, however, almost duplicated the corresponding proportion in 1990), and 82 percent from Mexico. In terms of the operating profit, the foreign portion was slightly smaller: 15 percent (85 percent from Mexico). Of the revenues in foreign currency that Televisa reports to have obtained in 1997, $1.33 billion, only $364.5 million (less than one-third) are said to have originated from exports (Televisa 1998). Now, even though Televisa has boasted of the diversification of its sales abroad, at least in terms of monetary value, there is one predominant market: According to Televisa's 1997 *Annual Report,* 75.3 percent of the value of the firm's exports, and 97 percent of its imports in 1997 took place with the United States. The predominance of the high value of Televisa's exports to the United States is explained by the way that prices are set in the international markets. For lack of more recent data, table 4.8 shows the distribution of Televisa's sales abroad during 1990.

There is in table 4.8 a reflection of the differential ways of setting prices in the international markets of television programs (richer countries pay more for the same program, and vice versa) that affects Televisa's form of operation. For example, Central and South America appear as the main buy-

Table 4.8   Televisa, Program Exports by Region, 1990

Country/Region	In Millions of U.S. Dollars		Programming Hours Sold	
United States	35.4	52.3%	2,645	9%
Central and South America	25.0	37.0%	21,040	71%
Europe	2.1	3.1%	1,775	6%
Asia and Australia	1.6	2.4%	1,340	4%
Other	3.6	5.2%	3,042	10%
Total	67.7	100%	29,842	100%

Source: Morgan (1992).

ers of programs, with 71 percent of the hours sold. However, the actual best market for Televisa's exports, with a little more than half the value in U.S. dollars, is the United States, which buys only 9 percent of the programming hours. Thus, the great presence of Televisa's programs in the southern part of the continent may translate into some form of cultural influence, but it does not necessarily translate into spectacular revenues. It was shown before—and here I corroborate it—that the most important market for the Mexican audiovisual industry is the United States: 11 percent of its population is of Hispanic origin.

The main source of income for Televisa is still the sale of television advertising in the Mexican domestic market. For example, according to Televisa's 1997 *Annual Report:* "Net sales of television derive mainly from the sale of advertising time in the Company's channels. The principal source of income from television advertising comes from national sales. . . . The percentage of the net sales of television derived from advertising sales was 87%, 85% and 88% in 1995, 1996 and 1997, respectively; the remaining is generated mainly by the sale of programming rights" (Televisa 1998, 45).

This allows Televisa's own cultural products to have recovered most of the initial investment in the domestic market by the time they are offered to the world market. Again, Televisa's capacity to produce and export audiovisual cultural goods is not in question, but rather the possibility of the emergence and consolidation of a diversified, plural, and competitive Mexican audiovisual sector, in principle larger than one or two companies.

The advent of digitization and the convergence of telecommunications, information technologies, and the traditional media, especially the audiovisual, are already producing a vast new demand for all sorts of programs. A solid and diversified "content industry" has not developed yet because of the highly concentrated structure of the market, particularly in the production subsector. In the case of cinema, it seems that the "new international division of labor" is reducing a country that used to be an important producer and exporter to a mere consumer of imported feature films. Is that what Mexico's current "comparative advantage" allows for the national audiovisual sector? I believe that a more active government policy in Mexico may help the audiovisual sector to become more plural, competitive, and diversified. More options have to emerge so that the audiovisual media can contribute to a more democratic order, to Mexico's more active insertion to the new stage of cybercapitalism, and to build its own cultural identity based on its rich and plural cultural diversity.

IS THERE A "NEOPROTECTIONIST" ALTERNATIVE TO NEOLIBERAL POLICY?

The inward-oriented, protectionist, and import substitution development model—with a great deal of state intervention—which practically all of Latin

American nations implemented during the 1960s and 1970s, entered into crisis in Mexico since around 1968.[22] The crisis actually lasted—with short periods of recovery—for the following three decades (Levy and Székely 1983; Oppenheimer 1996). It was not until the 1980s that a new "technocratic" elite took power in Mexico, during the De la Madrid administration, and a policy shift began to take place. In what political scientist Lorenzo Meyer (1995) called "authoritarian liberalism," the new administration began transferring most economic and social issues from the control of the previously interventionist state to market forces, thereby reorienting the development strategy from reliance on the internal market to the opening to external markets. The evolution of the world system of capitalism, which brought about the new global order, made the old kind of inward-oriented development style obsolete, even for countries that could have seemed almost self-sufficient, such as China (Fossaert 1994). But it was clear: The old development model was actually a variant of capitalism, although not corresponding to the "ideal" image of capitalism offered by neoclassical economics (Blaug 1982).

The seeming real alternative to capitalism, socialism, collapsed with the Berlin Wall by the end of the 1980s. The world was freed from the excesses of socialist totalitarian statism and left to the "benefits" of the market forces (Fossaert 1994). But the market does not seem to be delivering the goods that neoliberalism has promised. I have corroborated before that even an institution like the International Monetary Fund, which can hardly be suspect of anticapitalism, recognizes that the new global order is producing and enlarging inequalities. One can read in its most recent *World Economic Outlook*:

> A core issue in this regard—and perhaps the most striking exception to the otherwise remarkable economic achievements of the twentieth century—has been the persistent failure to break the cycle of stagnation and poverty in the poorest countries. The global income distribution across countries is somewhat less skewed today than 25 years ago when weighted by population, largely on account of rapid growth in China, as well as in India. But this is no consolation for the large number of very poor (living on a dollar or less per day) that has remained stubbornly high in the range of 1.2 to 1.3 billion—about one-fifth of the world's population. Moreover, per capita incomes have been regressing in absolute terms in a large number of countries during the past 25–30 years. As a result, the world is entering the twenty-first century with the largest divergence ever recorded between rich and poor. The widening income gaps within many countries and the gulf between the most affluent and most impoverished nations are, in the words of the then Managing Director of the IMF, morally outrageous, economically wasteful, and potentially socially explosive. (2000, 36)

The market utopia of full employment and relative income equalization seems to be far from becoming a reality. Very often, the state has to take actions to solve serious social problems (e.g., environmental or human) generated by blind and insensitive market forces. It is interesting to remember that the communist utopia predicted, just like neoliberalism, the necessary "withering away of the state" (Lenin 1976).[23] The Leninist theory of the state bumped into basically the same historical stubbornness of concrete reality as the neoliberal utopia: the need for government intervention to regulate social processes and issues that just cannot be left adrift to the tide of supply and demand. Social access to health and education, wealth redistribution, protection of biodiversity, protection of cultural diversity, and so on, are issues for which the market does not guarantee any *social* efficiency.[24] It is necessary, then, to stop thinking in simplistic binary terms: It is not a dilemma of "state v. market," but rather some kind of "third way" (Giddens 2000; Castañeda and Mangabeira Unger 1998). In any case, it has to be the coexistence of the market with the *democratic* (therefore, representative, plural, and legitimate) state.

The nation-state that has been the bulwark of the neoliberal model, the United States, based its international competitive strategy, from the 1960s until practically the present, on selective "neoprotectionism" and intensive state intervention (e.g., recall Ronald Reagan's administration's enormous deficits). Writing about two of the most conservative governments in recent history (Reagan's and Margaret Thatcher's), Brazilian scholar Theotonio dos Santos comments that:

> However, they still present themselves as movers of a colossal neoliberal wave. It is therefore the neoliberalism of state monopoly capitalism, which consists of the increase of state intervention to guarantee the survival of capital, above all of the great monopolies and financial capital. When it is about these interests, the market economy is sent to fry potatoes, for it does not combine with the world of monopolies, oligopolies and transnational corporations that dominates the economic life of our day. (1992, 12)

Thus, even if sometimes disguised by ecological concerns, or by apparent social considerations, the advanced industrial nations do exert oftentimes neoprotectionist measures that hinder free trade, in order to gain extra benefits or maintain positions of market power (García Menéndez 1996). The Economic Commission for Latin America and the Caribbean (ECLAC) makes a yearly assessment, the *Barriers to Latin American and Caribbean Exports in the U.S. Market* (1999), perhaps in response to the Office of the U.S. Trade Representative's annual *National Trade Estimate Report on Foreign Trade Barriers* (2000). Of course, overt and covert neoprotectionist measures and other barriers to trade are found every year by the ECLAC report. In the case of the cultural industries, I know of a couple of reports that analyze measures that affect trade with the United States. One, by the Strategic Research and Analysis unit of the Department of Canadian Heritage, concludes with regards to the United States:

> The image of a free and open market environment projected by the United States is clearly not the case in the cultural sector. The US maintains a system of

measures which have real or potentially adverse effects on cultural trade with Canada. The majority of these measures can be categorized as foreign investment restrictions, although the US affects cultural trade by restricting the movement of persons, border measures and licensing practices among other measures. (Cowl and De Santis 1996, 2)[25]

Another study conducted for the European Union is a bit more comprehensive, in the sense that it includes barriers that originate from market factors, as well as those that derive from government policy. The United States is found to present these barriers to trade and investment in the audiovisual industry:

Sector	Barrier
General	Unilateralism as a feature of U.S. trade policy, and the use of Special 301 can lead to bilateral trade agreements that can have negative effects on EU trade with target countries.
Copyright	U.S. copyright law does not recognize the "moral rights" of the author.
Cinema	Vertical integration of the production and distribution chain by the major studios leads to control of resources and market access.
Cinema	Net profit accounting practices by the major studios obscure profits, limiting profit shares for non–U.S. major organizations from U.S. distributors.
Cinema	Cultural barriers in the form of censorship limit market access of European productions.
Cinema	Language barriers require the use of dubbing technologies that are prohibitively expensive.
Cinema	Video piracy is increasing, with New York as the center of illegal operations in the United States.
TV and radio	Differences in technical standards cause additional expenses for European exports.
TV and radio	Foreign ownership of television and radio broadcasting is limited under the Communications Act to 25 percent.
Sound recordings	Restaurants and retail establishments are exempted from obtaining licenses to play background music at their premises.
Sound recordings	Piracy of sound recordings is growing, particularly over the Internet.

(Solon Consultants 1998, 6)

Actually, it is very well documented that the U.S. audiovisual media developed and expanded throughout the world, from the beginning of the twentieth century, but especially during the world war periods, aided by direct government intervention, support, and protection: "contrary to official rhetoric, the history of international trade of American cultural goods in the twentieth century is not founded on the values of freedom and formal equality nor on the principles of trade liberalization, reciprocity or transparency.

These values and principles were promoted in the cultural sector only once the American domination of world markets had become firmly established" (Gingras 2000, 3).

So I realized that even the United States, which seems to be the world "watchdog" of free trade, has been historically found to erect barriers for its realization (Schiller 1976, 1992). However, nowadays the U.S. government is very persistent in its yearly assessment of foreign trade barriers (U.S. Trade Representative 2000). In this report, Mexico appears in general terms as a "very well behaved" country, particularly in relation to the cultural industries. For example, in the 1999 edition Mexico appeared as presenting "a troublesome restriction against film dubbing" (U.S. Trade Representative 1999, 309). Even if the new 1999 Law of Cinematography was not modified so as to eliminate such a restriction, it seems to have been negotiated informally at the highest level.[26] In the following year's edition, such complaints had disappeared (2000). But the United States' best client for audiovisual commodities and services, the European Union, appears with lots of problems, barriers, and protectionist measures. So does Canada.

What is relevant here is to recall the fact that there exist alternative policy options, other than the alleged sheer reliance on the market forces, without denying some role and function to supply and demand (Sánchez-Ruiz 1998b). For example, the Canadian government exerts actions that to an extent not only protect, but also—and mainly—*promote* the development of the cultural industries (Thompson 1995). Even though there are recent negative assessments of the results of Canada's neoprotectionist policies (Acheson and Maule 1999), and cultural nationalism is said to be in crisis (Straw 1996), the Canadian government still judges it important to support the production and distribution potential of its domestic cultural industries (Canadian Heritage 1999, 2000; Canadian Radio-Television and Telecommunications Commission 1999; Sectoral Advisory Group on International Trade [SAGIT] 1999). One report for the Department of Foreign Affairs and International Trade begins by synthesizing this belief:

> Culture is the heart of a nation. As countries become more economically integrated, nations need strong domestic cultures and cultural expression to maintain their sovereignty and sense of identity. Indeed some have argued that the worldwide impact of globalization is manifesting itself in the reaffirmation of local cultures.
>
> Canadian books, magazines, songs, films, new media, radio and television programs reflect who we are as a people. Cultural industries shape our society, develop our understanding of one another and give us a sense of pride in who we are as a nation. Canada's cultural industries fulfill an essential and vital role in Canadian society. . . .
>
> The Canadian government uses a combination of financial incentives, Canadian content requirements, tax measures, rules on foreign investments and intel-

lectual property tools to promote Canadian culture. Working together, government and the cultural sector have been able to develop a policy and regulatory environment that ensures that Canadians have access to the best the world has to offer while preserving a space for Canadian culture. (SAGIT 1999, 1)

The European Union has also enforced policies to foster a European presence in television and on cinema screens. The point of departure is that: "The audiovisual industry is therefore not an industry like any other and does not simply produce goods to be sold on the market like other goods. It is in fact a cultural industry *par excellence*. It has a major influence on what citizens know, believe and feel and plays a crucial role in the transmission, development and even construction of cultural identities" (Commission of the European Communities 1999a, 8).

Thus, during the last decade, the European Union has developed a series of tools to enable it "to guarantee the creation and operation of a European area for audiovisual services, to contribute to the strengthening of the European programme industry and to promote cultural diversity and take societal aspects into account" (European Union 1998b, 5). The support policies have a legal basis in the "Television without Frontiers Directive," which was "modernized" in 1997. Among other measures, article 4 of the directive stipulates that "Member states shall ensure, where practicable and by appropriate means, that broadcasters reserve for European works . . . a majority proportion of their transmission time" (European Union 1998a, 11). Article 5 complements this with the requirement to reserve "at least 10% of their programming budget, for European works created by producers who are independent of broadcasters" (11). Furthermore, the MEDIA Program provides the means to encourage "and supports the development of projects and undertakings, the transnational distribution of productions and the training of highly-qualified professionals, thus boosting the structures of the industry" (European Union 1998b, 5). In 2001, a second revision of the five-year program will enter into effect with the title "MEDIA Plus" (Commission of the European Communities 1999b).

None of these types of policies and programs is perfect, just as neither are the workings of the market by itself. However, there are some positive results already. For example, it seems that at least at the local level European fiction productions are regaining television screens, especially in prime time (Vilches, Berciano, and Lacalle 1999; European Audiovisual Observatory 2000a, 2000b). European cinemas are also reversing gradually the dominance of U.S. films in their multiplexes (European Audiovisual Observatory 2000c). Even though Canada has not been able to make a spectacular advance in the Canadian presence in its own television and movies, its audiovisual exports have been gradually increasing during the last decade (Attallah 1996; Canadian Film and Television Production Association 1999). There are some other cases of relative success of active policies toward cultural industries. For example, the Argentinean and Brazilian cinematographic industries are showing signs of fast recovery as a consequence of the implementation of new legislative and fiscal support mechanisms (Bonet 2000). Even the Chilean government, which has implemented market-oriented economic policies, is analyzing possible ways to aid its television system and increase its production and export capacity (Secretaría de Comunicación y Cultura 1999).

The times of "statism" and authoritarian interventionism are fortunately long gone. But again, that does not mean that nation-states and governments have disappeared or lost meaning in the global order of cybercapitalism. There is still much room for legitimate, democratically elected governments to exert active promotion of their own nations' cultural industries. They are too socially important to be left adrift in the "invisible" (but blind and insensitive) hands of market forces. This does not mean the return to the authoritarian state interventionism of the past, but rather that the state, as the legitimate representative of the diverse (and multiple) classes and sectors, be able to regulate and guide the blind forces of the market in the direction of the fulfillment of social needs and aspirations. It is not then a matter of "betting" for the state *or* for the market. To be sure, supply and demand *do* exert structural constraints on the production, distribution, and consumption cycles of any kind of commodities. But neither supply nor demand possess intelligence or consciousness, or human sensibility, or ethnic identity, and so on. As I have pointed out before, cultural goods are, besides commodities, sense proposals about the surrounding world; they constitute proposals of social definitions of who we are (and who we are not). The symbolic contents of the cultural products propose—and sometimes impose—socially aesthetic patterns (i.e., what and who is beautiful, and what and who is not); and they propose ethical and moral standards (i.e., what is correct/incorrect, normal/abnormal, proper/improper, and so on). The media propose social representations of possible "imaginary communities," from the closest (local) to the farthest (global). They may be symbolic carriers of new sociohistoric utopias. But also and principally, they are devices that can potentially show us the enormous diversity, plurality, and richness of the cultural manifestations that exist in one's own nation as well as in the several regions of the world. That deserves more than "neoliberal" jungle laws.

NOTES

In 2000, Mexico elected a new president from the rightist opposition party Partido Acción Nacional, after seventy-one years of hegemony of the Partido Revolucionario Institucional. The new president, Vicente Fox, was a former Coca-Cola executive and governor of the state of Guanajuato, and is described as a "right wing populist." But it is too early to speculate whether the issues and policies dealt with in this chapter might suffer any changes. Also note that unless stated otherwise, all dollar amounts are in U.S. currency.

1. For example, the U.S. Department of Commerce advocates against barriers to trade in favor of all U.S.–based film companies, which includes some foreign-owned transnational corporations, such as Sony (U.S. Trade Representative 2000; U.S. International Trade Commission 1999).

2. However, a fundamental point to keep in mind in order to read this work appropriately is that the economic-financial and technological movements and mutations are much quicker than cultural changes. That is to say that the domain of production and circulation-consumption, or of supply and demand, or of transnational cultural products, does not have an immediate and direct correlate with the cultural affectations of the reception processes, especially regarding mid- and long-range cultural transformations in space and time.

3. Among others, during the 1970s Christian Pallois (1977a, 1977b) theorized this process from the viewpoint of Marxist economics, calling it "the internationalization of capital."

4. This mode of operation, most probably, contributes in principle to the "globalization" of the wider economy. But not because one firm imports or exports one kind of commodity—for example, some *telenovelas*—has it "gone global."

5. Néstor García Canclini (1999) recently proposed the "internationalization-transnationalization-globalization" flow in terms of historical stages of capitalism. Both uses are in principle compatible.

6. I should make clear that, although I consider that the economic processes constitute a fundamental motor of the globalization process, the historical flows do not necessarily follow the causal order that could be inferred from the order of presentation of the three main dimensions (economic, political, and cultural).

7. SELA is a regional intergovernmental organization that groups twenty-eight Latin American and Caribbean countries. Its headquarters are in Caracas, Venezuela.

8. To be precise, actually the cultural industries were included, but in the annexes in the chapter on exceptions, as requested by Canada.

9. That unfortunately was almost never quite fulfilled, especially since Mexican film production began to decline.

10. Actually, the exchanges between Mexico and Canada were practically nonexistent. An interesting view of the NAFTA television market, that sees it in terms of five "television cultures," with their respective programming markets, can be found in Straubhaar, Campbell, and Cahoon (1998). The problem is that this view gives the impression of a very clear-cut, ordered, symmetric, and respectful "linguistic-cultural division of labor," which I think has to be problematized. However, the existence of the several linguistic television markets in the area is a fact.

11. Similar findings for Mexico City, Monterrey, and Guadalajara can be found in Crovi and Vilar (1995), Lozano and García (1995), and Sánchez-Ruiz (1995b), respectively.

12. Incidentally, in this research I corroborated that currently the main medium that people use to watch movies is regular, broadcast television.

13. In this case, I had access to the database thanks to the kindness of Jorge González and María Guadalupe Chávez. Some other findings can be found in González and Chávez (1996).

14. The differentials by social class are: 68 percent of the higher stratum regularly watched foreign series, while 61 percent of the middle class did so, and 57 percent of the lower echelon.

15. That is, 86 percent of the higher class, 79 percent of the middle, and 73 percent of the lower.

16. *Siglo 21*, 20 October, 1996.

17. *Siglo 21*, 30 October, 1996.

18. The reported source of the data is Ibope, the most important Latin American firm in ratings research.

19. This is my free translation of the titles in Spanish. Some of them may not correspond exactly to the original title in English, because they are often changed for marketing reasons.

20. MVS is the operator of Multivisión and partner of Hughes in the DirecTV DTH service.

21. At least, those are the teachings of neoclassical economics, which is the economic theory behind so-called neoliberalism, and for which the market is more imperfect as it gets closer to the monopolistic structure. For example, see Samuelson (1973).

22. Actually, in order to be congruent with my open conception of history, I should use the plural: "What are the *alternatives* to neoliberalism?" But here I want to discuss a "neoprotectionist" option, which consists of government intervention to breed plurality and competition for its domestic strategic sectors, *in order to succeed later on in the market itself.*

23. For example, see Lenin (1976, chapter 5).

24. The problem in so-called real socialism was exactly that it went from the Leninist call to the "withering away of the state" to its excessive—and even oppressive—presence in society.

25. There is another report on some Latin American countries (De Santis 1998). The Chilean government made an extensive comparative market analysis of the NAFTA countries' cultural industries (Secretaría de Comunicación y Cultura 1995).

26. One newspaper note reads: "Ernesto Zedillo to receive Hollywood ambassador. State visit of Jack Valenti, President of the MPAA" (*El Financiero*, 20 July 1999, 28).

REFERENCES

Acheson, Keith, and Christopher Maule. 1999. *Much Ado about Culture: North American Trade Disputes.* Ann Arbor: University of Michigan Press.

Anderson, Benedict. 1992. *Imagined Communities: Reflections on the Origins and Spread of Nationalism.* London: Verso.

Arthur Anderson Economic Consulting. 1998. *The Economic Consequence of Independent Film Making.* Los Angeles: Arthur Anderson Economic Consulting, Research Report.

Attallah, Paul. 1996. "Canadian Television Exports: Into the Mainstream." In *New Patterns in Global Television: Peripheral Vision,* ed. J. Sinclair, E. Jacka, and S. Cunningham. Oxford: Oxford University Press.

Beck, Ulrich. 1998. *¿Qué es la Globalización? Falacias del globalismo, respuestas a la globalización.* Barcelona: Paidós.

Bedore, James M. 1997. "U.S. Film Industry: How Mergers and Acquisitions Are Reshaping Distribution Patterns Worldwide." In *Industry, Trade, and Technology Review* (January): 17–33.

Blaug, Mark. 1982. *The Methodology of Economics—or How Economists Explain.* Cambridge, Mass.: Cambridge University Press.

Bolaño, César Ricardo. 1995. "Economía política, globalización y comunicación." *Nueva Sociedad* (Caracas, Venezuela), no. 140 (November–December): 138–153.

Bonet, Lluís. 2000. "La Producción y el Mercado Audiovisual Iberoamericano Frente a los Retos de la Mundialización." *Diálogos de la Comunicación* (Lima, Peru), no. 57 (March): 61–75.

Braudel, Fernand. 1980. *On History.* Chicago: University of Chicago Press.

———. 1984. *La historia y las ciencias sociales.* Mexico City: Alianza Editorial.

———. 1991. *Las civilizaciones actuales. Estudio de historia económica y social.* Mexico City: REI.

Cacho López, Yalín. 2000. "DirecTV en Busca de más Canales para sus 150 mil suscriptores." *El Financiero,* 28 February, 45.

Calva, José Luis. 1995a. "Prólogo." In *Globalización y bloques económicos. Realidades y Mitos,* ed. J. L. Calva. Mexico City: Juan Pablos/University of Guadalajara/Universidad Autonoma de Puebla.

———, ed. 1995b. *Globalización y Bloques Económicos. Realidades y mitos.* Mexico City: Juan Pablos/University of Guadalajara/Universidad Autonoma de Puebla.

Calva Mercado, Alberto. 1998 "Particularidades de la Unión Europea y el TLC" (part 1). *El Financiero,* 11 July, 10.

Canadian Film and Television Production Association. 1999. *The Film and Television Production Industry: A 1999 Profile.* Ottawa: Canadian Film and Television Production Association, Association des Producteurs de Films et de Télévision du Québec.

Canadian Heritage. 1999. *The Road to Success: Report of the Feature Film Advisory Committee.* Quebec: Department of Canadian Heritage, Cultural Industries Branch.

———. 2000. *Culture and Heritage: Connecting Canadians through Canada's Stories.* Quebec: Department of Canadian Heritage, Cultural Industries Branch. <http://www.pch.gc.ca/mindep/misc/culture/htm/1.htm> [last accessed: 1 February 2000].

Canadian Radio-Television and Telecommunications Commission. 1999. "The New Policy on Canadian Television: More Flexibility, Diversity, and Programming Choice." Ottawa: Canadian Radio-Television and Telecommunications Commission, news release. <http://www/crtc.gc.ca/ENG/NEWS/RELEASES/1999/R990611e.htm> [last accessed: 6 June 1999].

Cardero, Ma. Elena, comp. 1996. *Qué ganamos y qué perdimos con el TLC.* Mexico City: Siglo XXI/UNAM.

Castañeda, Jorge G., and Roberto Mangabeira Unger. 1998. "Después del Neoliberalismo: Un nuevo Camino." *Nexos,* no. 243 (March). (Also published in the *Economist,* 17 January. <http://www.nexos.com.mx/nexos/mar243/temcen/tc4.html> [last accessed: 11 May 1998].)

Castells, Manuel. 1999a. *La era de la información. Economía, sociedad y cultura.* 3 vols. Mexico City: Siglo XXI.

———. 1999b. *La era de la información. Economía, sociedad y cultura.* Vol. 1, *La sociedad red.* Mexico City: Siglo XXI.

Comisión Económica para América Latina y el Caribe. 1998. *Panorama Social de América Latina.* Santiago de Chile: Naciones Unidas, Comisión Económica para América Latina y el Caribe.

———. 2000. *La inversión Extranjera en América Latina y el Caribe. Informe 1999.* Santiago de Chile: Naciones Unidas, Comisión Económica para América Latina y el Caribe.

Commission of the European Communities. 1999a. "Principles and Guidelines for the Community's Audiovisual Policy in the Digital Age." Brussels: Communication from the Commission to the Council, the European Parliament, the Economic and Social Committee, and the Committee of the Regions (COM [1999] 657 final).

———. 1999b. "Proposal for a Programme in Support of the Audiovisual Industry (MEDIA Plus—2001–2005). Brussels: Communication from the Commission to the Council, the European Parliament, the Economic and Social Committee, and the Committee of the Regions (COM [1999]).

Cowl, Terrence, and Heather De Santis. 1996. *An International Comparative Review of Measures Which Affect Trade in the Cultural Sector: The United States, Mexico, and Chile.* Quebec: Strategic Research and Analysis/International Comparative Research Group, Department of Canadian Heritage.

Crovi, Delia, and J. Vilar. 1995. "Canales abiertos de la ciudad de México: Programación y preferencias del público." In *Desarrollo de las industrias audiovisuales en México y Canadá*, ed. D. Crovi. Mexico City: UNAM.

De María y Campos, Mauricio. 1992. "Las Industrias Culturales y de Entretenimiento en el Marco de las Negociaciones del Tratado de Libre Comercio." In *La Educación y la Cultura ante el Tratado de Libre Comercio*, ed. G. Guevara and N. García Canclini. Mexico City: Nexos/Nueva Imagen.

De Santis, Heather. 1998. *Measures Affecting Trade in the Cultural Sector: Focus on Cultural Policy in Latin America.* Quebec: Strategic Research and Analysis/International Comparative Research Group, Department of Canadian Heritage.

Dietrich, Hans, ed. 1997. *Globalización, exclusión y democracia en América Latina.* Mexico City: Joaquín Mortiz.

Dos Santos, Theotonio. 1992. "Trucos del Neoliberalismo. Auge de la Economía mundial, 1983–1989." In *Política*, a supplement to *El Nacional* (Mexico City), 4 June, 12–14.

Economic Commission for Latin America and the Caribbean. 1999. *Barriers to Latin American and Caribbean Exports in the U.S. Market, 1998–1999.* Washington, D.C.: United Nations, Economic Commission for Latin America and the Caribbean (Washington Desk), November.

Estadísticas de Cultura. 1995. *Cuaderno Núm. 1.* Mexico City: INEGI.

European Audiovisual Observatory. 2000a. "Domestic TV Fiction Back in Prime Time." <http://www.obs.coe.int/oea/docs/00002305.htm [last accessed: 14 February 2001].

———. 2000b. *European Films on European Televisions.* Strasbourg: European Audiovisual Observatory.

———. 2000c. "The Trend of Admissions' Growth Survives the Titanic. The Film Market in the European Union." Strasbourg: European Audiovisual Observatory Press Release, in Cannes Film Festival 2000.

European Union. 1998a. *Television without Frontiers: The Text of the New Directive.* Brussels: European Parliament–Council, European Union.

———. 1998b. *Audiovisual Policy of the European Union.* Brussels: European Commission, Directorate General X.

Ferguson, Marjorie. 1992. "The Mythology about Globalization." *European Journal of Communication* 7 (1) (March): 69–93.

———. 1993. "Globalisation of Cultural Industries: Myths and Realities." In *Cultural Industries: National Policies and Global Markets*, ed. Marcus Breen. Melbourne: CIRCIT.

Ferrer, Aldo. 1999. *De Cristóbal Colón a Internet: América Latina y la globalización.* Mexico City: Fondo de Cultura Económica.

Fossaert, Robert. 1994. *El mundo en el Siglo XXI. Una teoría de los sistemas mundiales.* Mexico City: Siglo XXI.

García Canclini, Néstor. 1989. *Culturas Híbridas. Estrategias para entrar y salir de la Modernidad.* Mexico City: Grijalbo.

———, ed. 1994. *Los nuevos espectadores. Cine, televisión y video en México.* Mexico City: Instituto Mexicano de Cinematografía–Consejo Nacional para la Cultura y las Artes.

———. 1995. *Consumidores y ciudadanos. Conflictos multiculturales de la globalización.* Mexico City: Grijalbo.

———. 1996. "Políticas culturales e integración norteamericana: Una perspectiva desde México." In *Culturas en globalización. América Latina–Europa–Estados Unidos: Libre comercio e integración,* ed. N. García Canclini. Caracas: Nueva Sociedad.

———. 1999. *La globalización imaginada.* Mexico City: Paidós.

García Menéndez, José Ramón. 1996. "Neoproteccionismo, Dumping Social y Eco-Dumping." *Nueva Sociedad,* no. 143 (May–June): 124–141.

Giddens, Anthony. 2000. *La tercera Vía. La renovación de la Socialdemocracia.* Mexico City: Taurus.

Gingras, Anne-Marie. 2000. "International Conflict Resolution in Culture and Communication: Values and Principles." Paper presented at the International Political Science Association Congress, Quebec, August 1–6.

González, Jorge, and María Guadalupe Chávez. 1996. *La cultura en México I. Cifras Clave.* Mexico City: Conaculta/Universidad de Colima.

González Casanova, Pablo, and John Saxe-Fernández, eds. 1996. *El mundo actual: Situación y perspectivas.* Mexico City: Siglo XXI/CIICH–UNAM.

Ianni, Octavio. 1974. *Sociología del imperialismo.* Mexico City: SepSetentas, Secretaría de Educación Pública.

———. 1993. *A Sociedade Global.* Rio de Janeiro: Editora Civilização Brasileira.

———. 1996. *Teorías de la Globalización.* Mexico City: Siglo XXI–UNAM.

International Monetary Fund. 1997. *World Economic Outlook.* Washington, D.C.: International Monetary Fund, May.

———. 2000. *World Economic Outlook: Asset Prices and the Business Cycle.* Washington, D.C.: International Monetary Fund, May.

Lacroix, Jean-Guy, and Gaëtan Tremblay. 1997. "The 'Information Society' and Cultural Industries Theory." Special Issue of *Current Sociology* 45 (4) (October).

Lenin, V. I. 1976. *The State and Revolution.* Peking: Foreign Language Press.

Levy, Daniel, and Gabriel Székely. 1983. *Mexico: Paradoxes of Stability and Change.* Boulder, Colo.: Westview.

"Ley Federal de Cinematografía." 1992. *Diario Oficial de la Federación,* 29 December.

Lozano, J. C., and J. García. 1995. "Oferta de programación audiovisual extranjera en la televisión aérea de Monterrey, Nuevo León." In *Desarrollo de las industrias audiovisuales en México y Canadá,* ed. D. Crovi. Mexico City: UNAM.

MacEwan, Arthur. 1996. "Globalización y estancamiento." In *El mundo actual: Situación y perspectivas,* ed. Pablo González Casanova and John Saxe-Fernández. Mexico City: Siglo XXI/CIICH–UNAM.

Mattelart, Armand. 1993. *La comunicación-mundo. Historia de las ideas y de las estrategias*. Madrid: Fundesco.

Media Research and Consultancy–Spain. 1997. *La Industria Audiovisual Iberoamericana: Datos de sus Principales mercados. 1997.* Madrid: Media Research and Consultancy–Spain.

———. 1998. *La Industria Audiovisual Iberoamericana: Datos de sus Principales mercados. 1998.* Madrid: Media Research and Consultancy–Spain.

"México en el Mundo. ¿Nos Sirve ser uno de los Campeones Mundiales en la Negociación de Acuerdos de Libre Comercio?" 2000. *Expansión* 31 (792) (June 7): 1.

Meyer, Lorenzo. 1995. *Liberalismo Autoritario. Las Contradicciones del Sistema Político Mexicano*. Mexico City: Océano.

Morgan, A. Sassan. 1992. *Grupo Televisa—Company Report*. 28 May.

National Chamber of Cable Television. 2000. From several reports and interviews.

National Chamber of the Cinema Industry. 2000. From several reports and interviews.

Ochoa, L., ed. 1995. *Conquista, transculturación y mestizaje. Raíz y origen de México*. Mexico City: UNAM.

Oman, Charles. 1994. *Globalisation and Regionalisation: The Challenge for Developing Countries*. Paris: Organization for Economic Cooperation and Development.

Oppenheimer, Andrés. 1996. *México: En la Frontera del Caos*. Mexico City: Javier Vergara Editor.

Ortiz, Renato. 1994. *Mundialização e cultura*. São Paulo: Editora Brasiliense.

Pallois, Christian. 1977a. "The Self-Expansion of Capital on a World Scale." *The Review of Radical Political Economics* 9 (2): 1–28.

———. 1977b. *Las firmas multinacionales y el proceso de internacionalización*. Mexico City: Siglo XXI.

Randall, S. J., and H. W. Konrad. 1995. *NAFTA in Transition*. Calgary: University of Calgary Press.

Samuelson, P. A. 1973. *Economics*. New York: McGraw-Hill.

Sánchez-Ruiz, Enrique E. 1986. "La agenda televisiva en México y Guadalajara (O las apariencias engañan)."*Cuadernos* (Guadalajara), Nueva Epoca, no. 2 (September–December): 33–42.

———. 1992. "El espacio audiovisual mexicano ante el Acuerdo de Libre Comercio Canadá–Estados Unidos–México." *Comunicación y Sociedad* (Guadalajara), no. 14–15 (January–August): 177–197.

———. 1993. "Internacionalización de la televisión mexicana: Perspectivas para la descentralización cultural." *Revista Universidad de Guadalajara* (Guadalajara) (Winter–Spring): 22–28.

———. 1994. "Guadalajara: Cine, televisión y video." In *Los nuevos espectadores. Cine, televisión y video en México*, ed. N. García Canclini. Mexico City: Instituto Mexicano de Cinematografía–Consejo Nacional para la Cultura y las Artes.

———. 1995a. "Remarques sur la globalisation, l'ALENA et l'espace audiovisuel mexicain." In *Le Projet Monarque. Étude comparée des industries québécoises et mexicaines de l'audiovisuel*, ed. Gaëtan Tremblay and Jean-Guy Lacroix. Montreal: GRICIS/Université du Québec à Montréal.

———. 1995b. "La agenda televisiva en Guadalajara." In *Desarrollo de las industrias audiovisuales en México y Canadá*, ed. D. Crovi. Mexico City: UNAM.

———. 1996a. "El nuevo carácter de la dependencia: La globalización y el espacio audiovisual." In *Miradas latinoamericanas a la televisión*, ed. G. Orozco. Mexico City: Universidad Iberoamericana.

———. 1996b. "Flujos globales, nacionales y regionales de programación televisiva. El caso de México." *Comunicación y Sociedad* (Guadalajara), no. 27 (May–August): 43–88.

———. 1998a. "El cine mexicano y la globalización: Contracción, concentración e intercambio desigual." In *Horizontes del Segundo Siglo. Investigación y Pedagogía del Cine Mexicano, Latinoamericano y Chicano*, comp. J. Burton-Carvajal, P. Torres, and A. Miquel. Mexico City: University of Guadalajara/Instituto Mexicano de Cinematografía.

———. 1998b. "Industrias culturales y libre comercio. México, Canadá y la Unión Europea: Hacia un análisis comparativo de políticas de comunicación." Paper presented at the Latin American Studies Association Conference, Chicago, September 24–26.

———. 1999a. "La Televisión Mexicana: ¿Globalización exitosa?" *Voces y Culturas* (Barcelona), no. 14 (second semester): 83–106.

———. 1999b "O cinema no Mexico: Globalização, concentração e contração de uma indústria cultural." *Estudos de Sociologia* (Araraquara, S.P., Brasil), 3 (6) (first semester): 79–122.

———. 2000. "La Industria Audiovisual Mexicana ante el TLC. Radiografía de Flujos Desiguales." *Revista Mexicana de Comunicación* 12 (61) (January–February): 6–14.

Saxe-Fernández, John. 1999. "Globalización e imperialismo." In *Globalización: Crítica a un paradigma*, ed. J. Saxe-Fernández. Mexico City: Plaza y Janés/UNAM.

Scarlato, F. C., et al, eds. 1994. *O novo mapa do mundo. Globalização e espaço Latino-Americano*. São Paulo: ucitec/ANPUR.

Schiller, Herbert I. 1976. *Communication and Cultural Domination*. White Plains, N.Y.: Sharpe.

———. 1992. *Mass Communications and American Empire*. 2nd ed. Boulder, Colo.: Westview.

Secretaría de Comunicación y Cultura. 1995. *NAFTA e Industria Cultural*. Santiago de Chile: Secretaría de Comunicación y Cultura, Departamento de Estudios.

———. 1999. *Exportación en la Televisión Chilena*. Santiago de Chile: Secretaría de Comunicación y Cultura, Departamento de Estudios. Resena 36, August.

Sectoral Advisory Group on International Trade. 1999. *Canadian Culture in a Global World*. Report to the Department of Foreign Affairs and International Trade. Ottawa: The Cultural Industries Sectoral Advisory Group on International Trade.

Sinclair, John. 1999. *Latin American Television: A Global View*. Oxford: Oxford University Press.

Sistema Económico Latinoamericano. 1997. *El Tratamiento de las Asimetrías en los Procesos de Integración Regionales y Subregionales*. Caracas: Sistema Económico Latinoamericano (SP/DD/Di6).

———. 1999. *Guía de la Integración de América Latina y el Caribe 1999*. Caracas: Sistema Económico Latinoamericano/UN Educational, Scientific, and Cultural Organization, <http://www.lanic.utexas.edu/sela/libro/index.htm> [last accessed: 26 May 2000].

Solon Consultants. 1998. *Audiovisual Industry, Trade, and Investment Barriers in Third Country Markets: Final Report*. DG1 Market Access Unit. London: Solon Consultants.

Straubhaar, Joseph D. 1993. "Más Allá del Imperialismo de los Medios. Interdependencia Asimétrica y Proximidad Cultural." *Comunicación y Sociedad* (Guadalajara), no. 18–19 (May–December): 67–107.

Straubhaar, Joseph, Consuelo Campbell, and Kristina Cahoon. 1998. "From National to Regional Cultures: The Five Cultures and Television Markets of NAFTA." *Comunicação nas Américas: O Diálogo Sul-Norte*, special issue of *Leopoldianum* (Santos, Brazil) 1 (1) (September): 113–133.

Straw, Will. 1996. "La Crisis del Nacionalismo Cultural." In *¿Sentenciados al Aburrimiento? Tópicos de Cultura Canadiense*, ed. Graciela Martínez-Zalce. Mexico City: UNAM–CISAN.

Sunkel, Oswaldo, and Edmundo Fuenzalida. 1979. "Transnationalization and Its National Consequences." In *Transnational Capitalism and National Development*, ed. José J. Villamil. Sussex: Harvester.

Telemundo. 1999. No. 46 (March–April).

Televisa. 1998. *Informe Anual 1997*. Mexico City: Grupo Televisa, <http://www.televisa.com.mx/info97/e_on22.html> [last accessed: 20 August 1998].

———. 1999. "¿Qué es GTS?" <http//:www.televisa.com.mx/gts/CENTROpart.HTM> [last accessed: 8 October 1999].

———. 2000. "Grupo Televisa Reportó Margen Récord de 26.4% y Mejores resultados de Operación en 1999." Mexico City: Bolsa Mexicana de Valores (Mexican Stock Market), February 23.

Thompson, John H. 1995. "Canada's Quest for Cultural Sovereignty: Protection, Promotion, and Popular Culture." In *NAFTA in Transition*, ed. S. J. Randall and H. W. Konrad. Calgary: University of Calgary Press.

Thompson, John H., and Stephen J. Randall. 1994. *Canada and the United States: Ambivalent Allies*. Athens: University of Georgia Press.

Toussaint, Florence. 1999. "NAFTA's Impact on Mexican Audiovisual Industry." Paper presented at the II Coloquium NAFTA–MERCOSUR of Communitacion and Cultural Industries, University of Texas at Austin, June 1–2.

Ugalde, Víctor. 1998. "Panorama del cine en México: cifras y propuestas." *Estudios cinematográficos* 4 (14) (October–December): 45–59.

Ugalde, Víctor, and Pedro Reygadas. 1994. "La construcción del futuro cine mexicano ¿Yankees welcome?" In *Bye Bye Lumière . . . Investigación sobre cine en México*, comp. E. de la Vega Alfaro and E. Sánchez-Ruiz. Guadalajara: Universidad de Guadalajara.

UN Development Program. 1999. *Human Development Report*. New York: United Nations.

U.S. International Trade Commission. 1999. *Recent Trends in U.S. Services Trade: 1999 Annual Report*. Washington, D.C.: U.S. International Trade Commission, Publication 3198.

———. 2000. *Recent Trends in U.S. Services Trade: 2000 Annual Report*. Washington, D.C.: U.S. International Trade Commission, Publication 3306.

U.S. Trade Representative. 1999. *1999 National Trade Estimate Report on Foreign Trade Barriers (NTR)*. Washington, D.C.: U.S. Trade Representative.

———. 2000. *2000 National Trade Estimate Report on Foreign Trade Barriers (NTR)*. Washington, D.C.: U.S. Trade Representative.

Varis, Tapio. 1993. "Cultural Industries and the Post Cold War World." In *Cultural Industries: National Policies and Global Markets*, ed. Marcus Breen. Melbourne: CIRCIT.

Vilches, Lorenzo, Rosa A. Berciano, and Charo Lacalle. 1999. "La Ficción Nacional, Por Fin a Escena." *Anàlisi* (Barcelona), no. 23: 25–57.

Wallerstein, Immanuel. 1976. *The Modern World-System*. New York: Academic.
————. 1990. "Culture As the Ideological Battleground of the Modern World-System." In *Global Culture: Nationalism, Globalization, and Modernity*, ed. Mike Featherstone. London: Sage.
Wilkinson, Kenton, Omar Hernández, and Aída de los Angeles Cerda Cristerna. 2000. "Have Monopolies Become a Part of Mexico's Past? Lessons from the Television Industry." Paper presented at the fiftieth annual International Communication Association Conference, Acapulco, Mexico, June 1–5.

5

The Reorganization of Spanish-Language Media Marketing in the United States

Mari Castañeda Paredes

This chapter examines the transformation of Hispanic marketing and investigates the role of new media industries in the reorganization of Spanish-language media and the transborder commodification of the burgeoning Hispanic audience. The creation of these new marketing practices is important because it both pushes forward the transnationalization of economic activity as well as extends the commodification process of audiences in the new era of "digital capitalism" (Schiller 1999, xiv). In order to understand the logic of the processes under way, Vincent Mosco (1996) suggests that we should foreground how practices such as marketing and e-commerce create and extend the value of commodities, in this case the Hispanic audience. The rise of Spanish-language and bilingual new media industries is not, as some firms have advertised, a response by business to connect "communities that have long-suffered from a lack of [on-line] access" (Kong 1999, B1). Rather, it is an explicit political-economic attempt to control the emerging Hispanic market across the media landscape, including in cyberspace, in order to "intensify the exchange process and create marketable information about the users" (Mosco 1996, 148).

However, the transborder commodification of audiences is a dynamic process involving many dimensions such as advertising, content programming, language use, market research, trade pacts, public policy, and various forms of labor (Brooke 1999, 98). In this chapter, I focus specifically on a range of marketing and advertising practices—such as crossovers (the sale of a commodity within multiple markets), bilingual advertising campaigns, and multimedia promotions—as examples of how the conglomerate media-marketing complex is both recognizing Hispanics as a newly attractive demographic and transforming Spanish-language media into a newly competitive and well-integrated marketing and distribution network. By focusing on these practices, I wish to illustrate how the reorganization of Spanish-language media marketing is in fact a complicated, competitive, and at times inconsistent process that nonetheless embodies an intense drive to transnationalize the market economy as well as to produce a saleable transcultural audience.

Although cultural differences within the Hispanic population have caused many marketing and advertising campaigns to fail in the past, the sheer mass of this ethnic group and its economic impact in the Western Hemisphere are facts that marketers, including those working for political candidates, can no longer afford to ignore (Campo-Flores 2000, 24). The growing size of the Hispanic population on the North American continent, and throughout the world, represents a market demographic that is constituted from millions of people bounded together by the common tie of the Spanish-language and "la historia de la cultura Hispana," the history, or emergence, of a Hispanic culture. The proliferation of Spanish-language and bilingual media outlets in the past two years is a testament to the growing importance of this Hispanic audience, and the future of how Madison Avenue is increasingly intertwined with emerging attempts to target Hispanics (see Zbar 1999a, 46).

Since 1999, the number of Hispanic-oriented on-line media services has grown sharply with the dominant players on the U.S. front forming alliances with telecommunications behemoths in Mexico, Latin America, and Spain, thus creating new Internet services such as American On-line (AOL) Latin America, Yahoo! En Español, and Microsoft Corporation's MSN T1. It is important to note that the heightened interest in the Hispanic audience is not limited to the population south of the border. The inclusion of U.S. Hispanics in the new landscape of transborder ethnic marketing is central to the strategy that is increasingly being adopted across all media. Far from being an altruistic recognition of culture, the boom in Hispanic marketing and advertising is a response to intense global competition and the commercial necessity to directly target large and potentially profitable niches within the general market.

THE CHANGE IN DEMOGRAPHICS AND HISPANIC PURCHASING POWER

In a study on the history of the Hispanic audience, America Rodriguez notes that the consumer group was initially conceived as culturally and linguistically "foreign" and therefore commercially unattractive (1997, 287–288). The rise of Spanish-language radio, television, and print outlets in the 1960s and 1970s did little to convince marketers that the Hispanic audience was becoming a legitimate and lucrative consumer market in the United States. By the early 1980s, however, marketers were increasingly inclined to engage the ongoing changes in America's demographics. The U.S. Hispanic population, the cultural group most resistant to assimilation, was quickly becoming "the largest ethnic minority." The census estimated that by 2010, Hispanics would comprise 13 percent of the total U.S. population. The populations in Mexico and Latin America were also expected to grow, whereas non-Hispanic white communities in the United States and Canada would continue to decrease as a proportion of total population well into the twenty-first century (Strategy Research Corporation 1998, 58; Zbar 1995, 35).

Resistance to assimilation, legal and illegal immigration, and rising birth rates are some of the factors that explain the Hispanic population boom in late-twentieth-century America. As table 5.1 illustrates, this population surge reflects a long-term shift in the U.S. demography (Turow 1997, 17; "Sound of Success" 1999, 20).

As the U.S. Hispanic population shoots upward, its neighbors south of the border also anticipate a population explosion over the next twenty-five years. Mexico is expected to outrun all other Latin American states, with an estimated population reaching 136 million people by 2025. Following Mexico, Colombia and Argentina are expected to swell to forty-nine million and forty-six million people, respectively (Strategy Research Corporation 1998, 40). All told, by 2050 there are projected to be 950 million people living in Mexico and Latin America, generating an increasingly significant mass of Hispanic consumers (40).

In the United States, in 2000 there were over 32 million Hispanic individuals out of a total population of 269 million (Smith 2000, C1). According to the census, the United States has become the fifth largest Spanish-speaking country in the world; and the agency forecasts that by 2020 the U.S. Hispanic population will qualify as the world's second largest (Strategy Research Corporation 1998, 52). Additionally, U.S. Hispanics are young with an average age of twenty-four years old compared to forty-six years old in the non-Hispanic white population. Hispanic households are also the largest (approximately 4.0 persons), the youngest (34 percent of Hispanics are under the age of eighteen), and the poorest among families in the United States. Despite economic hardships and racially prejudiced public policies, the long-term

Table 5.1 Minority Populations of the United States as a Percentage of the Total Population, 1998–2050

	Hispanic	Non-Hispanic Black	Non-Hispanic Asian	White
1998	11.4	12.1	3.7	72.8
2000	11.4	12.2	3.9	72.5
2005	12.6	12.4	4.4	70.6
2010	13.8	12.6	4.8	68.8
2020	16.3	12.9	5.7	65.1
2030	18.9	13.1	6.6	61.4
2040	21.7	13.3	7.5	57.5
2050	24.5	13.6	8.2	53.7

Source: U.S. Bureau of the Census (quoted in Strategy Research Corporation 1998, 49).

potential of the U.S. Hispanic demographic is great enough that Christy Haubegger, the founder of *Latina* magazine, can suggest that Hispanics no longer constitute merely an ethnic niche, but represent "the new mainstream."

As noted previously, marketers have historically paid very little attention to the U.S. Hispanic audience; that is until the turning point of the 1980 census (Rodriguez 1997, 287). Advertising agencies assumed that mainstream ad campaigns in English-language media would eventually reach this largely low-income, immigrant, and Spanish-speaking population, and therefore did not require extensive "target[ing] efforts" (Wilson and Gutierrez 1995, 67; Bachman 1999, 2). The scarcity of Spanish-language media outlets in the United States, their historically underfunded endeavors, and the cultural/racial diversity within the Hispanic population further exacerbated the difficulty of marketing to Spanish-speaking consumers. Lastly, a ratings system for Spanish-language media did not exist, thus complicating the marketer's goal to "locate and label," segment, and target consumers by tracking their media consumption habits within the larger context of the mass market (Turow 1997, 19).

The regulatory, technical, and economic changes in the U.S. telecommunications industry throughout the late 1970s and 1980s expanded the industrial production and reach of the U.S. Spanish-language media sector, and spurred the formation of a specific profile known as the (pan-ethnic) Hispanic audience (Rodriguez 1997, 290). The "profiling" of Hispanic consumers required detailed viewer statistics and the discovery, perhaps even the creation, of distinctive characteristics that defined this diverse demographic in general terms, for instance income, language, and brand loyalty. The attempt here was to constitute a critical mass that was worth tracking and targeting. Such market research was perceived as critical for fully developing a triad relationship between advertisers, media outlets, and consumers (Schenker 1999, 35). The 1987 study on U.S. Hispanic media audiences, titled *Hispanic USA*, sponsored by Telemundo Group Incorporated and carried out by the Strategy Research Corporation (SRC), was developed to dispel the negative perceptions about Hispanic consumers, especially that they "refused to blend into the mythical melting pot" (Turow 1997, 45). More importantly, the study was also an attempt to quantify the media consumption habits of Hispanics across the United States and classify the growing consumer group as a distinctive niche worth pursuing through marketing and advertising campaigns.

Telemundo hired consultants from SRC Market Research in order to "conduct a comprehensive market study of Hispanics in the USA. Objectives were many but one of the sets was to gain insights about the Hispanic market: Telemundo viewers, Spanish television viewers in general, and non-viewers alike" (*Telemundo–Los Angeles* 1988). The study examined the top ten U.S. cities and states with the highest Hispanic market potential, and found that in the number-one market (Los Angeles) 84 percent of Hispanic adults were "Spanish language dependent," and they primarily watched Spanish-language television as a form of news gathering and entertainment (40).[1] Most salient to advertisers was the fact that in Los Angeles, 99 percent of the Hispanic audience owned television sets, 66 percent owned videocassette recorders, and 53 percent owned home stereo or portable stereo systems. Additionally, 49 percent of the population had a checking account, 45 percent owned a credit card, and 30 percent predicted that their income would rise in the following decade (22–23). As a result, marketers were determined to influence how Hispanics spent their available yet limited disposable income. They also saw a heightened need for a more generalized Hispanic consumer group that could be packaged and marketed to corporate advertisers.

Building on the preliminary Hispanic audience study from four years earlier, Telemundo and the Univisión Network joined forces in 1992, and contributed $35 million each in order to help launch the National Hispanic Index (NHI), a Spanish-language audience measurement system. Developed by AC Nielsen Incorporated, NHI was specifically created to research the television-viewing behavior of Hispanics. Joseph Turow emphasizes that NHI was an attempt by Telemundo and Univisión to "gain credibility with national advertisers" in the wake of the 1990 census, which confirmed the skyrocketing growth of the U.S. Hispanic population (1997, 85). Leon E. Wynter (1991) agrees that by the mid-1990s, as Hispanics' combined purchasing power climbed and their value as an audience commodity accordingly increased, marketers were beginning to target Hispanics, particularly in Spanish-language media (B1). Although most of the Hispanic population resided in big city markets, the U.S. census predicted that virtually every state would be affected, including those municipalities that were historically dominated by non-Hispanic white families. Indeed, the demographic statistics were indicating a new social reality: the Hispanicity and Latinization of North American society (see Rodriguez 2000). The expansion of liberal trade policies between Mexico and the United States in the 1990s, in this context, offered a framework within which to restructure not only production flows, but also the flow of marketing and advertising across the United States and its southern border.

A year before the North American Free Trade Agreement (NAFTA) was passed, Emilio Pradilla Cobos reports that advertising agencies were already looking "covetously" to Mexico's booming trade with the United States and the potential "Hispanic floodgates" that a successful free trade agreement would open (1996, 97). Marketers and advertising agencies anticipated that the trade policies would produce "positive market effects" on both sides of the border (Fisher 1992, 25). According to Jeffrey D. Zbar, the erosion of transnational barriers would in time produce a shift in the advertising industry as agencies expanded their "workload from solely a U.S. Hispanic orientation to the new wave of pan-regional work throughout the Americas. Thus, the budget . . . [in] the U.S. has [been magnified] to target another 479 million [Hispanics] in Latin America" (1998, S16).

NAFTA's passage legitimated the transnational race to expand the pool of available consumers, and companies ranging from consumer products, banking, life insurance, health insurance, and telecommunications (such as

Proctor and Gamble, Washington Mutual, Allstate Insurance Company, Blue Shield, and American Telephone and Telegraph (AT&T), respectively were all joining the race to target the "newest mainstream" of North America and, increasingly, the global Hispanic market. The Hispanic populations in Mexico and Latin America presented an opportunity for marketers to target a specific and growing pool of Spanish-speaking consumers while "not losing sight" of the Hispanic audience in the United States (Lynch 2000, 1B). Furthermore, Mexico, like other developing countries around the globe (e.g., India), was newly welcoming of foreign marketing, and often regarded the increase in "advertising as a barometer of economic development, industrial growth, consumer culture, and investment capital" (Pendakur 1991, 251).

However, the various policies that promote liberalization, privatization, deregulation, and industrialization do not of themselves guarantee the success of capitalist expansion within developing countries, including those in Latin America. Marketing and advertising projects are therefore becoming increasingly critical practices within this broader transnational economic initiative. Manjunath Pendakur notes that these commercial-based attempts to create and manage demand are "imperative in the [creation] of a consumer culture" (1991, 252). Currently, the big marketing dilemma is how to develop advertising messages that "move" Spanish-speaking consumers to buy more diapers, eyeliner, toilet paper, cereal, and increasingly advanced telecommunications and new media services—on both sides of the border. Marketers are responding to the challenge in various ways, most evidently in the development of transborder corporate partnerships and the application of crossover ethnic marketing in both traditional Spanish-language and multimedia outlets. These practices are reorganizing capital and pushing forward the transnationalization of communications and cultural sectors. What are the political, economic, and cultural implications of such reorganization?

According to Eduardo Porter (2000), these changes translate into consumer choice and increased empowerment for Hispanics. In the following pages, I will suggest that, to the contrary, the emerging transnational regime is merely reproducing the entrenched tendency to commodify "most-needed" audiences on behalf of marketers, and the rise of commercial Spanish-language media therefore has little to do with providing new channels for the voices of marginalized, indigenous, or poor Hispanics (Traber 1986, 154–155). What types of advertising projects, media content, and new information channels, we may ask, has the reorganization of Spanish-language marketing produced?

MARKETING IN THE NEW ERA OF THE HISPANIC CONSUMER

For the first time ever in 1999, General Motors (GM) launched a Spanish-language broadcast, print, and Internet advertising campaign in an effort build brand loyalty and recognition for its Buick Century automobiles among Hispanic consumers. Its television advertisements boasted that

Buick's Spanish-language website, company magazine, operator manuals, and sales catalogs comprised examples of GM's commitment to Hispanics. According to Buick's public relations manager, however, the purpose of the advertising blitz centered on GM's desire to expand the company's market share of Hispanic automobile purchases and establish a firm footing within the larger trend of Spanish-language media reorganization (Green 1999, 76). African Americans have historically held the favored position in ethnic advertising (which is to say that they have been treated as the leading group of second-class citizens), but the Hispanic population is swiftly overtaking the dominant position, thus fueling the creation of Hispanic-oriented commercial spaces and the expansion of already established venues ("Assimilation No Threat to Hispanic Media" 1997, A2).

One such venue is the Superbowl. During the televised half-time performance of the thirty-fourth Superbowl football game in January 2000, dancers from multicultural backgrounds filled the field while the two fastest-selling crossover music performers, Christina Aguilera and Enrique Iglesias, emerged on center stage singing a bilingual (English-Spanish) duet. Aguilera, a singer who was originally marketed as a mainstream artist, had just released the Spanish-language version of her pop album, while Iglesias, a famous Spanish-language performer, had just crossed over into the general market with the release of a bilingual, primarily English-language album. The duet by these new multiple-market artists was followed by another performance by the reigning queen of crossover (bilingual) music, Gloria Estefan, and a brief narration by crossover actor Edward James Olmos.

Not only was Superbowl Sunday 2000 the biggest television advertising event of the season, but this "American tradition" also attracted more Hispanics than ever before. By showcasing a "multicultural" half-time show with a Latin flavor, the show's executives were able to capitalize on the general market's growing acceptance of selected Hispanic cultural products, while also appealing specifically to the growing number of Latino Superbowl fans. For Anheuser-Busch—the leading sponsor of televised football and soccer games in the United States—Superbowl Sunday 2000 was an important event since not only do Hispanics consume more beer than any other ethnic group, but also Anheuser-Busch's Budweiser brand dominates the U.S. Hispanic alcoholic beverage market.

The Superbowl advertising blitz is just one example of the critical changes taking place. Marketers are using mainstream media and creative extensions of Spanish-language media, such as Internet Web portals and websites, in an effort to target bilingual and monolingual Hispanic consumers while concurrently attracting Middle American audiences. The utilization of crossover content and advertisements with popular bilingual Hispanic celebrities like Oscar de la Hoya is one of the ways in which advertisers can dig their hands into the most attractive markets. The technique, in effect, opens the possibility of attracting a variety of desirable consumer groups in the United States and Latin America while capitalizing on the popularity of "Latin-themed" cultural products. It is the transnational and transcultural character of Hispanics that makes transborder and crossover efforts so appealing to marketers (Turow 1997, 56). For instance, Chevron Corporation announced that its 2000 television advertising strategy would include airing a Spanish-language television ad with English subtitles in the top general market stations as an effort to target bilingual Hispanic consumers who also watch mainstream television. The crossover marketing technique will essentially "kill two birds with one stone." It tries to reach the various segments of the Hispanic market while "keeping ties" with general market consumers (Johnson 1999, C1).

The crossover effort is evident across all Spanish-language and mainstream media outlets. The president and chief executive officer of the National Academy of Recording Arts and Sciences, which sponsored the 2000 Latin Grammy Awards, notes that "with the phenomenal growth of Latin music around the world, crossover does not only mean Latin artists recording in English, but [also] non-Spanish-speaking consumers buying music from Latin artists." The executive manager of the number-two rated radio station in Los Angeles, KIIS FM, admitted that the station's decision to grant radio play to the newest crossover musical star, New York–born salsa singer Marc Anthony, was an attempt to "appeal to the Hispanic audience and the Anglo audience simultaneously" (Valdes-Rodriguez 1999, F1). The same was true for the mainstream commercial success of other pop bilingual performers like Iglesias, Aguilera, Jennifer Lopez, and Ricky Martin.

In the cable television sector, Nickelodeon, an advertiser-supported English-language children's cable television network, unveiled a weekly show, the *Brothers Garcia*, and two cartoon programs, *Dora* and *Rocket Power*, that feature Hispanics as main characters. These cable television programs are consistently bilingual. The same is true for Showtime's weekly drama *Resurrection Boulevard*, which is about an East Los Angeles Hispanic family with a boxing legacy. The Disney Channel also capitalized on the Hispanic-theme programming in the summer of 2000, by televising a television original movie titled *Ready to Run*, which is about a young Latina who cleaned horse stables but dreamed of becoming a jockey. The emergence of the new bilingual cable channel Si TV and the pay-cable channel Playboy TV en Espanol are also signs of the times.

Released in June 1999, Playboy TV en Español aims at Spanish-speaking men between the ages of twenty-one and forty-nine in the United States. According to Anthony J. Lynn, the president of Playboy Enterprises, "Latinos are the fastest growing and increasingly economically empowered segment of the audience. The move is both strategic positioning and ethnic marketing. The Spanish-language channel will help the company beat the rush of other broadcasters vying for channel space as digital television is expected to roll out in the coming months. We felt it was important to stake our position in this marketplace sooner rather than later" (Collins 1999, C1). Similarly, AudioLibros del Mundo, a new Spanish-language audio books company, is betting on the exponential growth of Spanish-speaking markets, especially immigrants. The company is paving the way for another extension of a small but growing niche. The founder of AudioLibros, a former marketing executive, claims the Hispanic market is "both invisible and elusive to audio book publishers" although the Spanish-language and bilingual mass market is on the cusp of demanding the availability of inexpensive creative fare (Romney 2000, C1).

The contemporary $13 billion Christian music industry has also recently jumped on the Hispanic transborder bandwagon. Jaci Velasquez, a nineteen-year-old Christian pop singer born in New Mexico but now based in Nashville, released a Spanish version of her top-selling album *Heavenly Place*. The Spanish-language album *Llegar a Ti* was nominated for a Latin Grammy Award, and as evidence of its crossover success, the religious-theme album became a listener favorite among Latin pop stations in the United States, Mexico, and throughout Latin America. Sony Discos, one of the largest distributors of Hispanic music along with EMI Latin Records, predicted that by Christmas 2000 *Llegar a Ti* would reach gold status and indeed it did (Valdes-Rodriguez 2000, 9; Cobo 2000, 26). Described as "the next Amy Grant and Ricky Martin all rolled into one" (Valdes-Rodriguez 2000, 9), the crossover appeal of Velasquez was evident at a sold-out concert in Los Angeles where Spanish-speaking and English-speaking fans filled the Universal Amphitheater as did bilingual advertisements for *Latina* magazine and Sony Music. The chief executive officer of EMI Latin Records explains that the crossover technique transcends language and culture; it "means being able to identify with many fans" (Lechner 1999, 61). In market terms, it means broadening the consumer base of what had been a niche commodity, in this case, Spanish-speaking Hispanics.

The appeal of ethnic marketing thus goes beyond the fact that the buying power of Hispanics is expected to surpass $440 billion in the next decade, although Spanish-language media are indeed also becoming a more significant means for realizing "the full sales potential" of Hispanics (Kane 2000, C6). Spanish-language media comprise a key nexus in the production of a comparatively affluent Hispanic consumer market and therefore are coming to constitute "a core media buy for advertisers" (Porter 2000, B1). The dominant Spanish-language television networks in the United States, Telemundo and Univisión, indeed are showing "phenomenal growth," and along with other media outlets (including radio broadcasting, the print industry, and the Internet) reaped over $1 billion in advertising from some of the biggest corporate marketers: GM's Chevrolet Motor Division, Shell Oil Company, McDonald's Corporation, and AT&T (Porter 2000, B1; Vrana 2000, C1).

There are many other examples of how business (either through crossovers, multimedia outlets, or corporate alliances) is exploiting Spanish-language media channels in order to influence the development of what has become a hot commodity in the United States—"a consumer audience with Latin flair" (Kane 2000, C6). GM, for instance, advertised its autos through Telemundo and Univisión and "partnered" with *VISTA* magazine, a weekly Spanish-language newspaper supplement. Like GM, the consumer conglomerate Proctor and Gamble also joined forces with the two-year-old Spanish-language Internet Web portal yupi.com, in order to launch a free bimonthly, bilingual magazine titled *Avanzando* (*Progressing*). The magazine is overflowing with Proctor and Gamble product coupons and "helpful" articles on how to best access the Spanish-language world of the Internet, and it uses yupi.com as the prime source of information. In the spirit of alliances, *Avanzando* also sponsors yupi.com's advanced Internet search engine. The editors of the new Latino-oriented food magazine *Gusto*—from the publishers of *Cooking Light*—also announced similar alliances with food marketers on and off the Internet. The publishers explained that a non–U.S. edition of the magazine for the Australian and European markets was abandoned once the market statistics pointed to "*Gusto*'s niche as wide open and underserved" (Green 1999, 76, Fine 2000, 8).

McDonald's also developed a synergy based marketing campaign that targeted Hispanics in a variety of venues including its franchised restaurants and the Internet. Through its "Points of Pride" campaign, the burger chain sponsored a promotional "Latin music contest" that was linked to major Latino music festivals and a website that provided news "about the fast-food chain and stories about contributions to world events made by Hispanics. The site also link[ed] back to McDonald's main [web]site" (Kramer 1999, 6). Toyota Motor Sales USA launched a similar campaign to target bilingual, but especially Spanish-language Hispanic consumers via television commercials, print ads, and radio spots. According to Saatchi and Saatchi, the advertising shop responsible for the campaign, "marketers [cannot] afford to ignore the population growth of the Hispanic population. [Although] the niche is [near] 13% of the U.S. population, ad budgets usually never come close to the general-market ad budget," but the tide is turning as evidenced by the growth of Hispanic-directed magazines and Internet services (Halliday 2000, 16).

Editorial Televisa, a U.S. subsidiary of the Mexican media conglomerate Grupo Televisa, publishes the largest selection of Spanish-language magazines in the world and reaches 4.2 million consumers in the U.S. Hispanic market. The magazines are a combination of Televisa and U.S. company–originated titles such as *Vandidades, Cosmopolitan en Español, Christina la Revista, TV y Novelas, Furia Musical, Eres, Tu, National Geographic en Español, Men's Health en Español, Deporte Internacional, Mecania Popular, Geomundo, Buenhogar, Ideas ParaTu Hogar, Marie Claire, Bazaar en Español, Elle, People en Español, Newsweek en Español,* and *Discover en Español.* Editorial Televisa also offers regional editions according to market sales in Spain, Mexico, Latin America, and the U.S. Hispanic market.

The push toward "narrowcasting," that is, further segmenting Hispanic audiences, is apparent not only in magazine, television, and radio marketing and advertising campaigns, but increasingly on Spanish-language Internet websites as well. As an emerging, multifaceted commercial sector, the Internet lends itself to the practice of creating and extending niche segments within established markets in the United States and beyond. Yupi.com's "gratis" main Web page, for instance, provides hyperlinks to its other websites according to country (e.g., Mexico, Argentina, and Spain) or region in the United States (e.g., Los Angeles, New York, and San Antonio). Thus, cyberspace is becoming an audiovisual medium with great potential for assembling, segmenting, and targeting a relatively affluent transnational audience—a cross-cultural pool of Spanish-speaking and bilingual consumers.

According to International Data Corporation (IDC), over the next few years Internet users in Mexico and Latin America will increase by 32 percent annually, and in the United States, Hispanic Internet use will grow by 75 percent (Cororan 2000). In 1999, there were fifteen million Spanish-speaking Internet users worldwide with five million of them residing in the United States (Petersen 1999, B6; Hafner 2000, 6). According to the market research by espanol.com, the average Hispanic on-line user is thirty-two years old, has an income above $51,000, and purchases products 76 percent of the time when on-line. These affluent Hispanics are the consumers Internet advertisers and marketers are interested in targeting, while the IDC estimates that, in general, the Internet markets in the United States, Mexico, and Latin American will become "the fastest growing e-commerce" sectors in the world as more consumers sign up for on-line services (Corcoran 2000). The way is being readied for the future growth of on-line sales to this favored group.

Proliferating partnerships between U.S.–based and major Latin American as well as Iberian media conglomerates, which in turn are endorsed by sponsors and advertising agencies, signify that Spanish-language marketing on the North American continent is rapidly moving onto the Web. The prospect of "e-comercio" is indeed driving a whole range of untested (and sometimes vulnerable) transnational alliances. For instance, StarMedia Network Incorporated, a high-profile Latin American new media company, and Mexico's phone company Teléfonos de México (Telmex) were among the big players aiming to capture the global Hispanic "e-business." StarMedia's chief executive office, a former AT&T advertising executive, planned to build the company as global brand, "as the Coke of the Internet," and focused on using the Web portal to reach English, Spanish, and Portuguese speakers throughout the Americas and in Europe ("Sound of Success" 1999, 62). StarMedia therefore explicitly viewed the Internet as a "powerful targeting tool" with the means to draw a transnational audience. More generally, Mercedes Cardona notes that marketers are betting on the prospect that "Internet commerce will bind Latin American countries" with each other and the United States, and eventually produce a "borderless" system of e-trade (2000, 34).

Other pairings of domestic and transnational media companies are shooting at the same target. AOL, the dominant Internet service provider in the United States, formed a partnership with Venezuela's Cisneros Group, the second largest Spanish-language media content producer, in order to create AOL Latin America as a contender in the important Latin American Internet world (Wingfield and Ewing, 2000). Mexico's Infosel, the dominant Internet service provider owned by Telmex, is already growing more than 100 percent each year with its purchase of Prodigy On-line, the first Internet service provider in the United States to offer Spanish-language services. Telmex executives announced that the combination of Infosel and Prodigy provides "natural conduits for on-line sales on both sides of the border of well-known brands and product lines available through partner holding companies" (Petersen 1999, B6). In the last year, the transborder Internet space was corralled into even fewer hands when Spain's Telefónica de España and Mexico's Telmex, the two largest Spanish-language telecommunications service providers, formed an alliance with Terra Networks, a major European Internet provider. According to Infosel, the alliance was created to "balance economies of scale with local content needs" (B6). This same approach was utilized when Telmex and Microsoft joined forces to develop MSN T1, a Spanish-language version of the established MSN brand. James F. Smith reports that "as a result of the MSN T1 alliance, the majority of the new PC's sold in Latin America with Microsoft software will have T1 set up as the default homepage for Internet Explorer, Microsoft's Internet software" (2000, C1; see also Smith 1999, C1). Bill Gates aims to build "T1 [as] the leading Spanish-language portal everywhere in the world. Although 80% of the Internet users are currently U.S. residents, it is not going to stay that way. It is estimated that by the end of 2000 there will be 13.3 million users in Latin America and that number will jump to 29.6 million by the end of 2003" (Lynch 2000, B1).

Even the established media industries are expanding their ventures into the transborder market of Spanish-language and bilingual media. The *Miami Herald*'s insert "El Nuevo Herald" will now be published as its own newspaper. With the rise of Hispanic media consumers, the *Miami Herald* hopes that the Spanish-language version becomes the "leading news source in the Western Hemisphere" ("Sound of Success" 1999, 54). California-based Entravision Communications Corporation is also hoping to "capitalize on investors' appetite for the growing and lucrative Hispanic media market" (58). As the owner of the leading daily, *El Diario/La Prensa*, thirty-one television stations, seventeen Univisión affiliates, sixty radio stations, and ten thousand billboards, Entravision markets itself to advertisers as the link to U.S. Hispanics. Not coincidentally, Univisión, the largest Spanish-language broadcasting network in the United States, is one of Entravision's major investors.

The move to restructure capital as a result of the changes in media capabilities, and changes in population demographics, has also impacted the advertising industry. Beginning in the late 1990s, *Advertising Age* found it crucial to publish a section in its trade magazine titled "Multicultural Media and Marketing" and in 1999 the magazine held its first annual Hispanic Creative Advertising Awards (Zbar 1999b, S1). Since then, the ad industry has experienced several major changes, the most important consisting of the "buy outs" of multicultural (Hispanic, African American, and Asian American) ad agencies and their placement on the rosters of some of the largest marketing agencies (Fitch 1999, S1). The three biggest multicultural ad agencies were fully or in part acquired by mainstream agencies, boosting the potential ad billings for the dominant media groups and extending their targeting potential into ethnic markets. For mainstream players like True North Communications, and Young and Rubicam, the acquisition (or the creation) of multicultural marketing departments is quickly becoming the "cornerstone" of the industry it is calling the "New America," the lucrative ethnic sector estimated to reach $1 trillion in consumer sales in the next decade (Chura 1999, 1). Without a doubt, the transnationalization of Spanish-language media will continue to deepen the ongoing process of audience commodification and the commercialization of Latino cultural outlets across the Americas.

CONCLUSION

The expansion of Spanish-language marketing across old and new media is being rapidly assimilated by the largest U.S. and foreign commercial media companies as a means of creating and exploiting a valuable commodity: the Hispanic audience.

Leading Latino advertising executives assert that the rise in purchasing power and continued population growth will give Hispanics greater power to negotiate Spanish-language and bilingual promotional campaigns and Latino-oriented products. This belief that growing recognition of the Hispanic market will bring forth real choice for the large majority of Hispanic consumers is, however, very problematic. The development of commercial crossovers and of Spanish-language campaigns throughout old and new media alike does not signify that democracy finally is reaching the Latino masses. Rather, it points merely to the emergence of a long-term strategy for exploiting the Pan-American commercial potential of the Hispanic audience. In this context, it seems more likely that, as William A. Orme puts it, "the danger is that this new pan-American trading system may perpetuate old patterns of dominance and resentment" in both the United States and across Latin America (1996, 256).

NOTES

Unless noted otherwise, all dollar amounts are in U.S. currency.

1. The study looked at television viewing hours per week, language of strong emotion, reading ability, Spanish television use among Hispanics who understand

English (47 percent), attitudes toward advertising in Spanish, and the best media for information (*Telemundo–Los Angeles* 1988, 20–21).

REFERENCES

"Assimilation No Threat to Hispanic Media." 1997. *Advertising Age* 68 (13) (March).

Bachman, Katy. 1999. "Hispanic Broadcasting." *Mediaweek*, 13 December.

Brooke, John. 1999. "Cyber Profits: Doing Business on the Web." *Hispanic Magazine* (July).

Campo-Flores, Arian. 2000. "The Bogeyman Will Get You." *Newsweek*, 24 July.

Cardona, Mercedes. 2000. "HBA Sales Increase Sans Niche Support." *Adverting Age*, 27 March.

Chura, Hillary. 1999. "Suitors Pursue Minority Agencies." *Advertising Age*, 7 June.

Cobo, Leila. 2000. "The Year in Latin Music." *Billboard*, 30 December.

Cobos, Emilio Pradilla. 1996. "NAFTA and Territorial Integration in Mexico." In *Economic Integration in the Americas*, ed. George E. Eaton, Ricardo Grinspun, and Christos C. Paraskevopoulos. Brookfield, Vt.: Edward Elgar.

Collins, Scott. 1999. "Bunny's about to Make Big Hop into Spanish-Language TV." *Los Angeles Times*, 16 June.

Corcoran, Cate. 2000. "New Study Seeks to Profile Hispanic Web Users in the US." *Wall Street Journal*, 5 January.

Fine, Kate. 2000. "Cooking Light Concocts Title on Hispanic Cuisine." *Advertising Age*, 21 August.

Fisher, Christy. 1992. "Trade Talks Could Open Hispanic Floodgates." *Advertising Age*, 3 February.

Fitch, Stephane. 1999. "Surviving a Heat Wave." *Forbes*, 25 January.

Fitzgerald, Kate. 1999. "Latino Lifestyle Missing from English-Language Fare." *Advertising Age*, 30 August.

Green, Jeff. 1999. "Buick Embraces Hispanics Via New TV, Print Ads, and Carnival Fest." *Brandweek* 40 (42) (November).

Hafner, Kaite. 2000. "Hispanics Are Narrowing the Digital Divide." *New York Times*, 6 April.

Halliday, Jean. 2000. "Toyota Leads in Hispanic Niche." *Advertising Age*, 3 July.

Johnson, Greg. 1999. "A Chevron Car Speaks Spanish on English TV." *Los Angeles Times*, 21 May.

Kane, Courtney. 2000. "ACCENT Marketing." *New York Times*, 30 August.

Kong, Deborah. 1999. "Niche Sites Court Ethnic Groups." *San Jose Mercury News*, 20 September.

Kramer, Louise. 1999. "McDonald's Consolidates Hispanic Marketing Efforts." *Advertising Age*, 13 December.

Lechner, Ernesto. 1999. "Crossover Mania." *Hispanic Business* 21 (7) (July–August).

Lynch, David J. 2000. "Net Company Terra Aims for Hispanic Connection." *USA Today*, 20 January.

Mosco, Vincent. 1996. *The Political Economy of Communication*. London: Sage.

Orme, William A. 1996. *Understanding NAFTA: Mexico, Free Trade, and the New North America*. Austin: University of Texas Press.

Pendakur, Manjunath. 1991. "Indian Telecommunications." In *Transnational Communications: Wiring the Third World*, ed. John A. Lent and Gerald Sussman. Newbury Park, Calif.: Sage.

Petersen, Scott. 1999. "Prodigy Plans Interest and Service for Spanish-Language Speaking in the US." *Wall Street Journal*, 6 April.

Porter, Eduardo. 2000. "TV Takes Off in the US: Spanish-Speaking Americans Will Get Third Network and Investors Take Notice." *Wall Street Journal*, 7 September.

Rodriguez, America. 1997. "Commercial Ethnicity: Language, Class, and Race in the Marketing of the Hispanic Audience." *The Communication Review* 2 (3).

Rodriguez, Gregory. 2000. "Taking the Oath: Why We Need a Revisionist History of Latinos in America." *Los Angeles Times*, 20 August.

Romney, Lee. 2000. "Latinos Old Guard Passing the Torch." *Los Angeles Times*, 15 September.

Schenker, Jennifer L. 1999. "Reading the Mind of the Market." *Time International* 154 (4) (August).

Schiller, Dan. 1999. *Digital Capitalism*. Cambridge: Massachusetts Institute of Technology Press.

Schlesinger, Jacob. 2000. "Despite Boom, Americans Are More Likely to Fall Below the Poverty Line." *Wall Street Journal*, 29 June.

Smith, James F. 1999. "Latin America Is On-line for an Internet Sales Explosion." *Los Angeles Times*, 26 July.

———. 2000. "Spanish Language Web Portal Unveiled by Gates, Mexico's Slim." *Los Angeles Times*, 22 March.

"The Sound of Success." 1999. *Hispanic Business* (July–August).

Strategy Research Corporation. 1998. *US Hispanic Market. 1998*. Miami: Strategy Research Corporation.

Telemundo–Los Angeles: The Power of the Hispanic Market. 1988. Miami: Telemundo Television Group.

Traber, Michael, ed. 1986. *The Myth of the Information Revolution: Social and Ethical Implications of Communication Technology*. Beverly Hills, Calif.: Sage.

Turow, Joseph. 1997. *Breaking Up America*. Chicago: University of Chicago Press.

U.S. Department of Commerce. 1996. *U.S. Global Trade Outlook, 1995–2000: Toward the 21st Century*. Washington, D.C.: U.S. Government Printing Office.

Valdes-Rodriguez, Alisa. 1999. "In Ever-Expanding Musical Universe, Crossover Rules." *Los Angeles Times*, 26 June.

———. 2000. "A Higher Authority Is at Work." *Los Angeles Times*, 6 February.

Vrana, Debora. 2000. "Hispanic TV, Radio Firm Entravision Plans IPO." *Los Angeles Times*, 22 April.

Weston, Ann. 1994. *The NAFTA Papers: Implications for Canada, Mexico, and Developing Countries*. Ottawa, Canada: The North-South Institute.

Wilson, Clint C., II, and Felix Gutierrez. 1995. *Race, Multiculturalism, and the Media: From Mass to Class Communication*. Beverly Hills, Calif.: Sage.

Wingfield, Nick, and Terzah Ewing. 2000. "AOL Faces Challenge Picking Up Latin America." *Wall Street Journal*, 2 August.

Wynter, Leon E. 1991. "Choose Your Language for Reaching Hispanics." *Wall Street Journal*, 22 November.

Zbar, Jeffrey D. 1995. "Dynamic Hispanic Audience Expands." *Advertising Age*, 6 February.

———. 1998. "Power Up Internet en Español." *Advertising Age*, 29 November.

———. 1999a. "Marketer Leads AOL into Latin Markets." *Advertising Age International* (September).

———. 1999b. "Marketing to Hispanics." *Advertising Age*, 30 August.

6

Telecommunications after NAFTA: Mexico's Integration Strategy

Gerald Sussman

Since achieving independence in 1821, Mexico has gone through alternating periods of nationalization and denationalization in its critical investment sectors, including telecommunications. Under one ruling party, the Partido Revolucionario Institucional (PRI; Institutional Revolutionary Party) from 1929–2000, the country generally has followed regional and world political currents, pursuing a national bourgeois direction during the Lázaro Cárdenas administration in the 1930s and again in the 1970s—and without resorting to the militarization that swept much of Latin America in this period. In the 1970s, however, the Mexican state, lured by easy lending terms of the international banking community, became entrapped in the following decade by heavy debt dependency. Exacerbated by falling oil prices after 1981, the debt burden reached $154 billion by 1997.

Throughout the 1980s, Mexico was pressured by the International Monetary Fund (IMF), the Ronald Reagan administration, and the General Agreement on Tariffs and Trade (GATT) to sell off state-operated enterprises (SOEs) to the private sector and open them to foreign investment. Between 1988 and 1992, the market value of SOEs that were sold was $22 billion, as Mexico paralleled the neoliberal policies pursued in Argentina and Venezuela. The flagship target of the IMF and its Mexican allies and one of the most profitable of the SOEs was the national telephone monopoly, Teléfonos de México (Telmex), whose privatization was secured in 1990 with the active engagement of President Carlos Salinas de Gortari (1988–1994). The sale of Telmex represented 30 percent of all privatization revenues generated by the Salinas administration (Clifton 2000, 68).

Although this round of privatization and denationalization was under way before the North American Free Trade Agreement (NAFTA) went into effect (1994), the agreement nonetheless represents a major phase of expansion of transnational capital through individual and cooperative corporate ventures among the leading players in the three participating countries. NAFTA opens up markets in leased lines, terminal equipment attachment, interconnection, and switching, signaling, and processing functions. It also calls for "cost-based pricing," eliminating restrictions (including ownership limits and cross-border data transfers) on foreign companies engaged in value-added, enhanced, and packet-switched services, and ending duties for telecommunications and computer equipment by 2004.

U.S. corporations are the major suppliers of Mexico's expanded telecommunications infrastructure. They also are assured of access to public telecommunications networks in Mexico and the right to set up intracorporate communications on both sides of the border. For its part, Telmex originally agreed as part of the privatization scheme and as recommended by the International Telecommunication Union to establish twenty lines per hundred population by the year 2000 (Gonzalez, Gupta, and Deshpande 1998, 351). From a teledensity rate of 6.4 percent at the time of privatization, the company achieved only half its goal (10.7 percent) by the target year. Further expansion will likely be limited mainly to the more affluent sections of the populace still on the wait list, that is, the top 20 percent of households that control 58.2 percent of the country's income as of 1995 (up from 54.2 percent in 1992) (Warnock 1995, 183; World Bank 2000).

Telecommunications is key to NAFTA's success or failure. For Mexican elites, telecommunications investment is seen as a critical determinant of whether the country will be able to engage in the wider trade and investment agreements with any degree of parity. With the U.S. government's $52 billion bailout of the Mexican economy in 1995 and a veto power over key elements of its economic policy, Mexico's development is bound by its relations with its northern neighbor. The United States is the largest foreign investor in Mexico (about 60 percent of foreign direct investment [FDI]), receives 88 percent of Mexican exports, and is the source of 74 percent of Mexico's imports (in 1998).

Mexican officials have argued that NAFTA's insistence on deregulation, privatization, and liberalization of markets, including those in telecommunications, is necessary if Mexico is to become a player in the world economy and the "information revolution." This chapter looks at how NAFTA's demand for and the Mexican government's compliance with an open door investment strategy has changed the structure of telecommunications and how denationalization and transnational control of this sector is related to social distribution and poverty. Telecommunications as addressed here includes wired and cellular telephone, broadcast and cable television, and Internet services. The main focus, however, is on telephone. Space constraints permit only brief discussions of the fuller spectrum of communications—including television, satellite communications, and the Internet.

MEXICAN TELECOMMUNICATIONS IN RETROSPECTIVE

National identity, based on its cultural, religious, and ethnic traditions, the Spanish language, and a political iconography of, among others, José María Morellos, Emiliano Zapata, and various pre-Columbian rulers, has buffered U.S. hegemony for most of Mexico's modern history. Periodically, nationalist economic policy, as during the oil nationalization in the 1930s and the telephone nationalization in the 1970s, encouraged the recovery of domestic resources, although the economy as a whole has been and continues to be largely controlled by U.S. corporate interests. NAFTA threatens to be the coup de grace of latent nationalist economic tendencies, state ownership, and the retention of capital resources in Mexico and in the hands of Mexicans.

In actuality, the postcolonial Mexican state never had full control of its informational resources. Its early telecommunications development emerged within the footprint of its northern neighbor. International telegraphy was started in 1867 by an affiliate of Western Union and was expanded in 1897 through an international monopoly operating agreement between Western Union and Compañía Telegráfica Mexicana. A telephone network was set up in Mexico City in 1881 by an American businessman, M. L. Greenwood. With three foreign partners, Greenwood organized under a concession from the Porfirio Díaz government the Compañía Telefónica Mexicana (later the Compañía Telefónica y Telegráfica Mexicana), with technical and financial links to the Western Electric Telephone Company. A telephone concession was also given to L. M. Ericsson (Sweden) in 1905,[1] but by 1924 the Swedish subsidiary was forced to compete with International Telephone and Telegraph Corporation (ITT), which had taken over Compañía Telefónica y Telegráfica Mexicana. The two phone systems were not interconnected until the 1950s (*Enciclopedia de México* 1978).

What became the national telephone monopoly, Telmex took over the Swedish company in 1941, Ericsson remaining a major shareholder, and ITT in 1950.[2] Majority Mexican ownership did not occur until 1958, followed by the government's 51 percent stock acquisition in 1972, rising to 56 percent by 1990. At this point, Salinas arranged to have the company (re)privatized. Carlos Slim Helú, a rising real estate investor, retail entrepreneur, and investor in mining, manufacturing, and tobacco, and a close business associate of the president, acquired with Mexican partners the major stock holding in Telmex while the rest went to foreign investors.

The government's current foreign investment law formally restricts foreign equity ownership of basic telecommunications services to 49 percent, a share in fact more liberal than that permitted by either the United States or Canada. NAFTA rules may force a lifting of this limitation, as it already has in other industries. Ericsson, meanwhile, no longer has an ownership stake in Telmex but remains its principal equipment supplier. U.S. companies, however, account for about half of Mexico's overall telecommunications equipment purchases. With a near total monopoly over domestic telephone and a commanding position in cellular and long-distance services, Telmex is Mexico's second largest enterprise behind the national oil company, Petroleos Mexicanos. It is the largest telecommunications corporation in Latin America, the biggest of any industry in the region by market value, and is reported to be one of Wall Street's most coveted stocks (Preston 2000b, C4).

Nationalist currents have periodically influenced telecommunications policy. Under the 1917 constitution, following a revolutionary phase and the withdrawal of U.S. military forces that Woodrow Wilson had sent south to "teach" Mexicans "to elect good men," the state took over the management of the telegraph and other means of communications. In 1938, the regulation of the nation's telecommunications systems was given to the national Secretaria de Comunicaciones y Transportes (SCT). With telecommunications under state ownership, the government took the lead in 1985 in contracting Hughes Communications International for the building of the *Morelos* communications satellites, a system primarily used for the transmission by the private monopoly television network, Televisa Group, and for long-distance telephony [3] *Morelos I* failed to live up to the state's promised objective of delivering social services. A second satellite, *Morelos II*, was sent into orbit a year later. Meanwhile, technical upgrades in telephone service, including digital pulse code modulation, digital microwave, and fiber optic networks, were installed principally to serve the border areas (Ciudad Juárez, Nogales, Reynosa, Nuevo Laredo, and Matamoros) and originating at the industrial sites of foreign companies in the *maquiladoras*[4] (border assembly plants) (Griffith 1998, 168–175).

Mexico launched a second generation of satellites, *Solidaridad I* and *II* in 1993 and 1994, respectively (built by Hughes Aircraft and launched by the European Ariane rocket at a cost of $452 million for the two satellites), and *Satmex 5* (originally called *Morelos III*) in 1998. The latest three satellites, now under the Satmex logo, are operated in part by Loral Skynet, a U.S. company that earlier bought the Skynet satellite business from American Telephone and Telegraph (AT&T). The results of this investment have been disappointing. As of late 1997, Mexico's three functioning satellites were operating at a low 65 percent capacity (Sutter 1997b).

Encouraged by the 1995 Mexican Telecommunications Law (anticipating the U.S. Telecommunications Act of 1996) that privatized and denationalized Mexican satellite communications, Loral became a 49 percent joint owner of Satmex. Loral runs the company with a private Mexican telecommunications startup, Telefónica Autrey (chaired by Sergio Autrey), and a 25 percent government interest (to be sold as public stock offerings). Loral and its Mexican partners had beat out bids by two other U.S. companies, General Electric and Panamsat.

Public use of the satellite is marginal at best. Mobile telephone users and Internet service providers are expected to absorb part of the three newest satellites' unused transponder capacity, and Loral is also targeting as clients the increasing number of U.S. transnational corporations (TNCs) entering the country (Case 1998). The owners of the two *Solidaridad* satellites initially allocated 35 percent of capacity to private telephone services, 30 percent to private television stations, 10 percent to government, and the rest to nineteen radio stations and twenty financial institutions (Vandenack 1993).

LIBERALIZATION AND TRANSNATIONALIZATION

Following Mexico's 1985 earthquake, in which the national telephone network was severely damaged, and under pressure from the IMF and the World Bank, the Mexican government under Salinas organized the selling off of the country's telephone monopoly. Telmex was sold in 1990 to a group of foreign and Mexican investors at the undervalued price of $1.757 billion (Leppman 1996, 14). The Ivy League–educated Salinas (doctorate in economics and public administration from Harvard)[5] had declared during his 1988 presidential campaign that "telecommunications will become the cornerstone of the program to modernize Mexico's economy" (Griffith 1998, 166). For transnational interests on both sides of the border, his presidency could not have been more timely. Two business journalists observed that Salinas "flaunted his Harvard education and readily spoke English with foreigners—a first for Mexican Presidents. He hired McKinsey & Co. to reorganize state-run companies in preparation for privatization, and Wall Street investment banks were given plum roles. . . . With the personal attention of Salinas and Cabinet officers, U.S. corporate paperwork zipped through ministries. CEOs raved over Salinas and his team" (Smith and Baker 1995, 56).[6]

The biggest stockholder in Telmex is a consortium, Grupo Carso, led by Mexican billionaire Carlos Slim Helú,[7] with 28.2 percent (voting) shares. Southwestern Bell International Holdings Corporation, and France Cable et Radio, a France Télécom subsidiary, each hold 24.5 percent AA shares, and the remaining 22.8 percent is shared among fifty other Mexican investors (Sussman 1997, 247; Tandon 1992, 14–15).[8] The New York brokerage house of Goldman Sachs (at the time cochaired by Robert Rubin, who would become Bill Clinton's secretary of the treasury) took 4.5 percent in the selling off of Telmex in 1990–1991 and an additional 3 percent fee for the underwriting of another Telmex offering the following year (Herman 1997, 11) (see table 6.1).

Slim's Grupo Carso and Inbursa financial group also invested $1.5 billion in 1999 in other telephone businesses, including companies in Guatemala, Puerto Rico, and the U.S. mainland,[9] as well as in Apple Computer, CompUSA, the on-line music seller CDnow, and the dominant Mexican television network, with 85 percent of the national market, Televisa (G. Smith 1999, 55). Slim also advanced $350 million in loans and investments to the holding

Table 6.1   Telmex Share Ownership (percentages)

	Before Privatization	After May 1992
Government	55.9	4.8
Private Domestic	21.3	35.0
Private Foreign	22.8	55.8
Employees	0.0	4.4

Note: Both preferred and common shares.
Source: Tandon (1992, 16).

company of Televisa and received 23.9 percent of its stock value, which rose a remarkable 13 percent on the day the investment news went public. Slim, a son of Lebanese immigrants (born 1940) and married to the niece of Lebanon's former phalangist president, Amin Gemayel, is reported to be the richest man in Mexico, estimated to be worth $12.5 billion, and probably in all of Latin America. He was the biggest of the country's five billionaires invested in communications, according to a *Forbes* 1995 listing (Friedland 1999a, A17; Preston 2000a, C4; Smith and Forest 2000, 161).

Slim's rapid absorption of highly profitable telecommunications holdings on the strength of his presumed connections with Salinas drew charges of high-level political corruption. Salinas left office at the end of 1994 in the midst of a political scandal,[10] but his NAFTA telecommunications policies, including the statutory lifting of foreign ownership restrictions, were carried on by his Ivy League successor, Ernesto Zedillo Ponce de León (who holds a doctorate in economics from Yale).[11] In 1995, Zedillo pushed through the telecommunications law that required companies to lower long-distance and raise local telephone rates and to allow nondiscriminatory interconnection by all competing telecommunications corporations. The 1995 law also required Mexico to open all segments of the telecommunications market, including uses of the radio spectrum, Mexico's satellite orbital slots, and local and long-distance telephony, to competitive bidding, with foreign corporations entitled to own up to 49 percent, previously 40 percent, of voting stock and a larger share of nonvoting stock. Cellular telephone service is not bound by the 49 percent foreign equity limitation—additional participation may be approved by the state foreign investments authority (Wellenius and Staple 1996, 9).

NAFTA forced Mexico to open its international telephone business to at least a dozen telecommunications companies, including the biggest in the United States, which have established joint venture partnerships with local financiers and businesspeople (Ramamurti 1996). In rivalry with Telmex and its foreign partnership with Southwestern Bell and France Télécom, the U.S. company Microwave Communications Incorporated (MCI; now MCI World-Com) and Grupo Financiero Banamex-Accival, Mexico's biggest financial group, formed a joint venture, Avantel, in 1996 to build a long-distance telephone network linking Mexico with the United States and Canada. With 49 percent ownership, AT&T is linked in a similar project, Alestra, with Alfa Group, Mexico's second largest financial group. Already wielding a combined 25 percent share of the market, AT&T and MCI WorldCom have forged an alliance to try to force the Mexican government to further reduce Telmex's dominant 75 percent share and grab a bigger slice of the $4.4 billion in international long-distance revenues (Preston 2000b, C4).

The U.S. government has weighed in on this "free market" issue. Acting on behalf of U.S. carriers in Mexico, the Federal Communications Commission (FCC) accused the U.S.–based office of Telmex in San Diego of resisting the opening of private lines and circuits in Mexico and imposed a $100,000 fine on the company (Garcia 2000, C2; Preston 2000b, C4). At home, Telmex has been widely criticized for its low rate and poor quality of telephone access, especially outside the largest cities. And even within Latin America, Mexico is said to have one of the worst systems of telephone service delivery. (See table 6.2 for regional comparisons.) In fact, Mexico's telephone line to population ratio falls behind some of the poorest countries in the region, including Guatemala, El Salvador, and Nicaragua (Gori 2001, W1). At the time of privatization, Telmex's owners promised to modernize and revamp the quality of service and to wire a major portion of the 94 percent of households without telephones.

Telmex also has been criticized by the European carriers. In 1999, the Organization for Economic Cooperation and Development (OECD) released a report that praised Mexico's general deregulation initiatives but complained about its high long-distance telecommunications service prices.[12] It also noted that Mexico had the worst per capita telephone access rate among the twenty-nine OECD countries. (It did not mention that Mexico is also the poorest of the OECD countries.) As a solution, the report urged the government to force Telmex to remove barriers to entry for other telecommunications firms and to standardize agreements on carrier interconnection rates (Friedland 1999b, A15). The report had little to say about how to make telephone service more affordable for ordinary Mexicans.

The previously anticipated cross-subsidies from international to local service that might have made telephones more accessible and affordable to most Mexicans are in fact being reversed as competition forces down long-distance rates and offers the greatest utilities to TNC users (Leppmann 1996, 15). Mexico once had the world's cheapest local and regional telephone rates, but this socially oriented telephone policy was reversed starting in 1987. After the deregulation and privatization of Telmex in 1990, the cost of residential installation rose rapidly, from $98 in 1987 to $543.33 in 1992 (554 percent), equivalent to four to five months' average Mexican wages and more than ten times the cost in the United States. In a more recent report, the front-end cost was said to be $120, with the average worker income at $200 per month (Gori 2001, W1). Residential monthly service went from $1.65 to $12.30 (745 percent), continuing to rise thereafter. Waiting times for connec-

Table 6.2 Media and Information Access, 1997 (and 1980)

	Number of Radio Receivers (per 1,000 pop.)	Number of TV Receivers (per 1,000 pop.)	Daily Newspaper Circulation (per 1,000 pop.)[g]	Cinema Attendance per capita	Telephone Lines (per 1,000 pop.)[f]	Personal Computers (per 1,000 pop.)	Internet Hosts (per 10,000 pop.)[g]
Mexico	329 (133)	272 (57)	97 (123)	0.7 (3.9)[a]	96 (40)	37.3	8.75
Argentina	681 (427)	223 (183)	123 (142)	0.2 (2.1)[b]	191 (73)	39.2	15.92
Brazil	434 (312)	223 (123)	40 (45)	N/A (N/A)	107 (39)	26.3	9.88
Canada	1,067 (721)	710 (432)	158 (221)	2.8 (4.1)[b]	609 (530)	270.6	335.96
Chile	354 (292)	215 (110)	98 (108)	0.6 (1.3)	180 (32)	54.1	15.44
Colombia	524 (116)	115 (79)	46 (49)	N/A (N/A)	148 (49)	33.4	2.91
Cuba	352 (300)	239 (131)	118 (108)	2.2 (8.3)[c]	N/A (N/A)	N/A	0.08
Paraguay	182 (112)	101 (22)	43 (51)	N/A (N/A)	43 (15)	N/A	1.64
Peru	273 (159)	126 (52)	84 (81)	N/A (N/A)	68 (17)	12.3	1.52
Uruguay	603 (559)	239 (125)	293 (240)	N/A (N/A)	232 (76)	21.9	49.67
United States	2,116 (1,973)	806 (675)	212 (270)	4.6 (4.4)[d]	644 (415)	406.7	975.94
Venezuela	472 (391)	180 (113)	206 (195)	0.9 (3.0)[c]	116 (N/A)	36.6	2.94

[a]Data available for 1995.
[b]Data available for 1990.
[c]Data available for 1993.
[d]Data available for 1994.
[e]1996 (and 1980).
[f]1997 (and 1981).
[g]1998.

Sources: AT&T Long Lines (1982); UN Educational, Scientific, and Cultural Organization (2000); World Bank (2000).

tion averaged two to three years, and the quality of local service, especially in Mexico City, remained as bad as, or worse than, the period before Telmex's privatization (Ramamurti 1996).

Commercial service installation fees also increased dramatically, from $217 in 1987 to $941.52 in 1992 (434 percent). Long-distance and international service tariff rates, now comparable to those in the United States, rose over the same period but at a much slower rate than local service (Ramamurti 1996, 82–83). In preparation for privatization in 1990, Telmex initially reduced international long-distance tariffs by 40 percent and raised domestic long-distance tariffs by as much as 100 percent. The World Bank complained that Mexico still had among the world's highest direct and indirect telephone tax rates (Tandon 1992, 22).

After privatization, the rapid rise of Telmex's local rates both in nominal and real terms made Telmex a more attractive takeover candidate by increasing its profits that year (1990–1991) by 126.54 percent (Pérez Chavolla and Samarajiva 1997, 154; Tandon 1992, 18). A World Bank senior economist, Ahmed Galal, acknowledged that the privatization scheme has negatively affected most Mexicans but is at the same time consistent with World Bank policy: "You have the winners and the losers—among these actors are government, the consumers, the workers. We do have numerical values as to who won how much. It is true that in the case of Telmex consumers were worse off and that is okay from an economist's point of view" (quoted in Avery 1994, 98).

Not only is the rate of telephone access very low nationally, but 40 percent of the country's telephones are also concentrated in Mexico City (Federal District), which has only 11 percent of the national population. The three largest cities, Mexico City, Guadalajara, and Monterrey, together with less than 15 percent of the total population, have 70 percent of the country's national and international long-distance traffic (Sutter 1997a, 5A).[13] Although Telmex still holds three-quarters of the provision of long-distance service (awarded on the basis of an extremely low turnout city-by-city ballot), with two U.S.–Mexican joint ventures holding the rest, the real winners in the opening of Mexico's markets are U.S. equipment investors and suppliers (see tables 6.3 and 6.4), joint venture–enhanced service providers, the largest corporate users, and the urban elite. The apparent losers thus far have been Mexican and American workers, measured in terms of lost jobs and lower wages on both sides of the border and the increased marginalization of the Mexican rural population.

In 1996, Mexican and foreign telephone service companies were allowed to form joint ventures, thereby interconnecting with the Telmex national telephone infrastructure. For U.S. telecommunications carriers, the capture of the Mexican long-distance telephone market is crucial. Of U.S. calls to Latin America, Mexico is the principal destination, followed by Brazil and Colombia, and U.S.–Mexico traffic is the second biggest international telephone route in the world, behind only the U.S.–Canada corridor.[14] U.S. carriers, in particular Southwestern Bell, have aggressively competed in capturing the long-distance call markets of the Hispanic/Latino community within the United States, which amounts to $2 billion in international calls or 5 percent of the domestic residential long-distance market.

NAFTA telephone agreements clearly are at the service of transnational interests, currently led by Telmex and its foreign partners. An emerging TNC in its own right, Telmex in recent years has found more interesting investment opportunities in the United States and its territories than in its home country. In 1999, the Mexican company took over Comm South companies in Texas, which provide local telephone service to 177,000 households in fourteen U.S. states. Also in 1999, it took over Sprint's share of Telmex/Spring Communications, a

Table 6.3   Leading Foreign Electronics and Communications Investments in Mexico

Company	Total Sales (in millions of U.S. dollars)	Employees
IBM	3,053	2,100
Hewlett-Packard	1,600	1,200
Siemens (Germany)	801	12,648
Compaq	390	300
Philips (Netherlands)	360	2,000
Motorola	350	2,500
Xerox	340	3,767
LG (South Korea)	238	600
EDS	169	1,950
AT&T	119	2,500
Olivetti (Italy)	75	N/A
Microsoft	70	100
NCR	70	198

Source: Castellanos (1999).

Table 6.4   Leading Destinations of U.S. Information Technology Exports, 1995 (in billions of U.S. dollars)

European Union	$23.6
Canada	$12.6
Japan	$9.1
Mexico	$6.0
Singapore	$5.6
Malaysia	$4.8
South Korea	$3.9
Hong Kong	$3.6
Taiwan	$2.8
Philippines	$2.0
Thailand	$1.9
China	$1.1

Note: Covering 1996 tariff agreement; excluding semiconductor manufacturing equipment.
Source: U.S. Trade Representative (1996).

subsidiary that provides long-distance service to the United States, bought up Topp Telecom and Cellular Communications of Puerto Rico, both in the cellular telephone business,[15] and with its partner, Carso Global Telecom, got a controlling interest in Prodigy's Internet services.

As the U.S. telecommunications carriers pressure the Mexican government in the name of free markets to open its economic terrain to foreign participation, they also rely on the leverage of the state apparatus at home to aid them in the process. The U.S. carriers and the Bill Clinton administration showed impatience with the strategy and pace of Mexico's liberalization. Despite the privileged positions they quickly gained after being allowed to enter the Mexican market, AT&T[16] and MCI WorldCom pushed the FCC, rather reactively, to block the entry of a joint venture in the United States between Telmex and Sprint (Beachy 1998, D3). AT&T and MCI WorldCom also got Charlene Barshefsky, then U.S. trade representative, to threaten Mexico with a trade grievance under the World Trade Organization (WTO) for "anticompetitive" practices and for limiting foreign penetration of its long-distance markets (Preston 2000d, C4).

Another continuing friction between the U.S. and Mexican telephone companies is the revenue sharing arrangements for calls between their countries. One of the ways that U.S. long-distance carriers, such as AT&T, increase their revenue share is by providing "callback" services that enable foreign-based callers to "originate" a long-distance dial tone in the United States at rates that undersell those offered at their actual calling locations. Callback takes away a large portion of Third World international carriers' call revenues, 15 percent in Hong Kong, for example ("Telecommunications" 1996, 67). AT&T and other callback providers are able to arbitrage the highest profit returns by arranging the cheapest traffic routes.

A similar system, "refile," offers bulk rates to large-scale users, mainly TNCs, that use third-country calling sites as call transfer points, playing them off against one another based on which provide the lowest international settlement rates (Silverman 1996, 70–71). Callback and refile undermine traditional international accounting procedures and the option of Third World carriers to charge premium rates to TNCs. Up to 1997, international settlements provided $10 billion to Third World carriers (Schiller 1999, 50). As the largest bloc of overseas businesses in the world, U.S.–based TNCs stand to reap the biggest gains from efforts to bring all international rates in line with the lowest offered and have allied themselves with AT&T and other U.S. service providers.

Many poorer countries rely on international settlement rates for a high proportion of their telecommunications service income, which is used in part to subsidize local call rates. China, India, and Pakistan received between $500 million to $650 million net settlement amounts in 1997; Vietnam received $260 million; and the Philippines received $230 million. Mexico's share declined from $876 million in 1996 to about $600 million in 1997 (De Sarkar 1998; International Telecommunication Union 1999).

NAFTV

Although Mexico's television system is often seen as relatively indepen-dent, there are nonetheless several points of external influence, if not con-trol. Under NAFTA rules, television and radio stations remain under Mexi-can ownership, while cable stations may be up to 49 percent foreign owned. And although much of Mexican television programming is domes-tically produced, a significant portion is of direct foreign origin or other-wise formatted along U.S. and other cultural and commercial styles. Mexi-can mass media also rely heavily on U.S. telecommunications equipment imports and advertising, on press agency news, and on syndicated reports and news magazines. Some authors (e.g., Cunningham, Jacka, and Sinclair 1998; Moran 1998) have attempted to refute the "cultural imperialism" the-sis by pointing out that a number of countries, not just the United States, export television programs as well as content ideas and formats. What these writers seem to miss in such a counterthesis is that it is not the na-tional origins of programming that matters so much as the commercial im-print, which is mainly derivative of Western (especially U.S.) advertising values and practices. In the long run, to the extent that Mexico opts for a commercial over a publicly oriented approach to mass media, the market-based approach will almost certainly favor U.S. corporate suppliers re-gardless of whether Mexican (or other domestic) capital demonstrates re-silience and relative autonomy in the short term.

Even where, and perhaps especially where, the language medium is the vernacular, as in Mexico's dominant commercial television network, Tele-visa, program formats remain largely creolized versions of U.S. urban, middle-class, and consumerist values, a design in which Indians and peas-ants are invisible (Sklair 1991, chapter 5). Through the airwaves, Mexican viewers are exposed to a high concentration of U.S. television program-ming and advertising, particularly those living along the border areas where there is direct reception from twenty-four American transmitting sta-tions along a 2,234-mile border contiguous with southern California, New Mexico, Arizona, and Texas. Even in central Mexico, around Mexico City, there are stations that transmit almost 100 percent American programming during prime time.[17]

Attracted by advertised commodities (78 percent of the consumption is on clothes, electronics, and perfumes) not available or too expensive in the home markets, the *maquiladora* industries' labor force of almost four hun-dred thousand people spends up to 40 percent of its income on the U.S. side of the border (Barrera 1996, 199). Entrepreneurs, including Slim and Emilio Azcárraga Milmo, anticipated the "free flow" of *norteamericano* media that would follow in the wake of NAFTA and expanded their holdings of not only broadcast television, but also cable (jointly owning Cablevisión S.A. de C.V.), video rental, and satellite program distribution and dish receiver businesses.[18]

One of Televisa's major investments (30 percent) is Sky Latin America, a joint venture satellite television delivery system with Rupert Murdoch's News Corporation (30 percent), the Brazilian media monopoly Globo Group (30 percent), and the U.S. cable giant Tele-Communications Incorporated (TCI) (10 percent). Media access indicators (see table 6.2) suggest that most Mexicans have not fared well in this category since Mexico entered into NAFTA, even when compared to other Latin American countries.

It is not only the political economic and media power of Mexico's northern neighbor that compromises its national sovereignty, but also the ambition and partnership of its own "nationals" collaborating in the process of transnationalization.[19] Televisa, which emerged in 1973 as a merger of several existing television stations, is, like Telmex, a conglomerate in its own right. Controlled by the powerful and politically well-connected Azcárraga family,[20] the multimedia giant owns four television stations (with an 85 percent television market share) and sixteen radio stations, a cable system in Mexico City, national film and dubbing studios, a publishing house, and direct-to-home television, and dominates Mexico's magazine, video distribution, musical recording, paging, billboard, and advertising industries and special events promotions. Televisa owns television stations in Chile and Peru, and its Tijuana station is a Fox Television Stations Incorporated affiliate. It is also the largest producer and publisher, respectively, of Spanish-language television and magazines in the world, and, together with Venevisión, has the major share of foreign investment in the U.S.–based Spanish-language network, Univisión Network, together with ownership of two professional soccer teams, Aztec sports stadium, and a major share of the regional satellite consortium, Panamsat (Griffith 1998, 181; Herman and McChesney 1997, 101; Mody and Borrego 1991, 154).

Azcárraga Milmo was well known as a ruthless media monopolist who tolerated no independence from hired talent, a reputation carried on after his death in 1997 by his son and successor. One study on Mexican television and film found that "Entertainers and artists work exclusively for enterprises—transgressors are blackballed throughout Latin America, their careers ruined." The system also requires advertisers to pay stations a year up front, and Azcárraga's companies absorb 80 percent of advertising money spent in Mexico. But the ultimate casualties are poor Mexican *campesinos* who are "dependent on the Azcárraga broadcasting empire for their political information" (Rodríguez 1995, 144).

In the NAFTA era, no domestic power base such as Azcárraga's will be left unattended by capital from the north. Deregulation and privatization has created openings for foreign investment. One immediate result was Televisión Azteca (TV Azteca), a joint venture of a domestic group (with financial ties to the brother of then-president Carlos Salinas de Gortari) and General Electric's National Broadcasting Company (NBC), with a 20 percent holding, formed in 1994 to create an "alternative" television network to the Televisa monopoly—

with at least 40 percent of its programming coming from the United States. NBC was to be involved in all aspects of the network: management, programming, and marketing. TV Azteca management later broke the agreement, arguing that NBC failed to live up to its commitments. The same year, Fox formed a joint venture with Televisa to produce *telenovelas* (soap operas), while Blockbuster Video expanded its Mexico holdings to become the country's second largest video chain (McAnany and Wilkinson 1996, 10). Mexico has also had a fairly rapid growth of cable television, with 1.2 million subscribers by the early 1990s, although 50 percent of these viewers are concentrated in Mexico City and Monterrey (Wellenius and Staple 1996, 11).

MEXICO ON-LINE

In Internet services, Slim and Telmex once again appear on the scene with an 80 percent holding in Prodigy On-line, a once failed Internet service provider previously owned by Sears, Columbia Broadcasting System (CBS), and International Business Machines (IBM) and now, as Prodigy de Telmex, the largest Internet service provider (ISP) in Mexico. In late 1999 and early 2000, Slim paid an estimated $884 million to take sole ownership in Comp-USA, the biggest computer retailer in the United States. And in late 1999, he started up a $100 million joint venture with Microsoft Corporation for a Spanish-language Internet portal for Latin America that would help the "Mexican Bill Gates" expand his telecommunications operations beyond telephony into data transmission and Internet services. The Slim–Microsoft joint venture plans to take on America On-line and Yahoo! Incorporated along with a Brazilian ISP, Universo On-line, for control of the Latin American Internet market and a major share of NAFTA markets in the United States and Canada (G. Smith 1999, 55; Preston 2000c, C3).

Although Internet usage is growing in Mexico, it is concentrated among a very small stratum. Almost 95 percent of Mexico's ninety-six million people could not use a computer as of 1999; there were 8.75 computer hosts per thousand people (1997), and only 10 percent of households had telephone service. An *Inter Press Service* story reported a Mexican government technology development plan that found that "almost all investment in the [Internet] field is carried out by large industrial, commercial and financial groups." For ordinary Mexicans, cost is the major exclusion factor. A household computer setup costs close to half of Mexico's annual per capita income, and monthly Internet service adds an additional 15 percent per capita earnings expense (International Telecommunication Union, 1999). The government study also found that although small- to medium-sized businesses employ 80 percent of the working people and produce 65 percent of the country's output, they have almost no access to information networks (Cevallos 1999; World Bank 2000).

ROLE OF THE UNIONS

Mexico's labor laws support the closed shop, that is, the recognition of only one union in each company. Although there is rivalry among the different labor organizations, chiefly among the Confederación de Trabajadores Mexicanos (CTM; Confederation of Mexican Workers), Confederación Revolutionaria de Obreros y Campesinos (CROC; Revolutionary Confederation of Workers and Peasants), and the independent Unión Nacional de Trabajadores (UNT; National Union of Workers, founded in 1997), most unions are PRI–controlled as part of a corporatist relationship with business and government. Salinas assured labor compliance with his policies by arresting recalcitrant union leaders, including the head of the oil workers union, Joaquín Hernández Galacia (known as "La Quina"), and in the latter case sending in the army to take over oil operations. But as workers have lost real wages of at least 40 percent between 1988 and 1997, the corporatist relationship has come under increasing criticism from rank-and-file movements within the various unions and federations.

Mexican unions in general supported NAFTA at its inception (the Authentic Labor Front is the only one that did not), believing it would bring benefits to Mexico and to the unions. In general, Mexican unions have acquiesced in government wage control and other policies and with the IMF's structural adjustment programs, a collaboration that goes back to the Venustiano Carranza era (Sepúlveda 2000).[21] Having seen that many of the guaranteed protections under NAFTA have not been enforced, the unions have since been less compliant.

The Sindicato de Telefonistas de la República Mexicana (STRM; often called Telephone Workers' Union by the U.S. media) was founded after the creation of Telmex in the early 1950s. It is now the largest nongovernment-aligned union, with some fifty thousand members, including most Telmex workers as well as nonvoting retirees, and over the years has been one of the most militant. Under Article 123 of the 1917 Mexican constitution, workers are assured the right to organize unions and to strike, but, in fact, the government has used a loophole, the *requisa* (which is backed by the army, the police, and private police), to force strikers back to work. Of the eleven applications of the *requisa*, seven have been directed against the STRM.

When privatization of Telmex was introduced, with direct pressure on the union by Salinas, the STRM leadership—then under the pro–PRI CTM–dominated Congreso de Trabajadores (CT; Workers' Congress), an umbrella of corporatist unions—supported it.[22] However, following a government attempt to privatize the country's social security system, the STRM broke ranks. The breakaway was led by former CT organizer Francisco Hernández Juárez, reportedly a former Salinas ally, who brought STRM into the UNT federation (with the social security and national university workers), which then made Hernández Juárez its secretary general. UNT has chartered a more independent path, recently opposing a CTM–backed plan to privatize the country's electrical utility industry (Diaz 1998; Donnelly 1998).

For Mexican workers, NAFTA provisions on labor fail to specify protections of basic universal rights. The absence of language guaranteeing free association or the right to organize collectively, protest, or go on strike, and the lack of simple enforcement mechanisms for correcting contract violations loads the trade accord with a potentially heavy bias against Mexican workers. The liquidation of special trade arrangements, such as the General System of Preferences, which have built-in clauses on labor rights as a condition for duty-free status, represents another threat to the universal rights of workers. Although NAFTA is a three-way agreement among Mexico, the United States, and Canada, the agreement overwhelmingly benefits U.S. corporations concentrated in Mexico's *maquiladoras*, that is, the border area export processing zones, in which 68 percent of the investing companies are American, and 25 percent are Mexican with contracts with U.S. companies (4 percent are Japanese, and 3 percent are European, Canadian, and South Korean) (Sampler 1997, 637–638). Low-wage work in the *maquiladoras* rose rapidly after NAFTA, from 560,000 in 1993 to nearly a million in 1998 (Marin 1999).

SOCIAL CONDITIONS AND DEPENDENCY IN MEXICO

In common with most Third World countries, Mexico has sharp class and social divisions, with a narrow stratum of extremely wealthy landowners and capitalists and a broad majority of people living in or close to poverty—a fifth paid the daily minimum wage of $3.50 (Rosen 1998, 25). In 1989, the top quintile of income earners held 57 percent of the national income; the poorest quintile received only 4 percent and the middle 60 percent earned the remaining 39 percent. The situation has since further deteriorated. According to the Economic Commission for Latin America and the Caribbean, only six countries outside of Africa have a more polarized income distribution than Mexico. In 1987, Mexico had one billionaire, but by 1994 there were twenty-four, together worth $44.1 billion, having more income than the poorest 40 percent of Mexican households (Camp 1998; Rozo 2000).[23]

The Mexican poor have little or no access to health care and their housing typically lacks basic amenities such as electricity, running water, and sewerage. Although the quality of housing has improved since 1970, by the mid-1990s approximately 12 percent of Mexican households remained without electricity, 11 percent were without running water, and 26 percent had no sewer facilities. A large percentage of children suffer from malnutrition and leave school at a young age to help support their families with meager income supplements. Mexico's fast-growing population has severely strained important government services, including education and health care, and the economy and job market lag behind its growth. Thousands of

skilled and unskilled workers, injured by NAFTA "free market" and privatization policies, have migrated to the United States in search of employment
(Camp 1998).

Other social indicators are equally stark. The average infant mortality rate,
for example, is thirty per thousand (1997) and is much higher in its rural
states: fifty-two per thousand in Oaxaca, fifty-five per thousand in Guerrero,
and fifty-six per thousand in both Chiapas and Puebla. In the urban region
of Mezquitic, Jalisco, the rate reaches 152 per 1,000. A 1996 study by Mexico's National Autonomous University found that 51 percent of Mexican families, unable to pay for a "basic basket of foodstuffs" at $5.39 a day, were liv-
ing in "extreme poverty"—a condition that dramatically worsened
immediately after NAFTA (32 percent in 1993 and 16 percent in 1989). Subsidies for basic items ended in 1999, including tortillas, a staple of the Mexican diet, whose price rose to $3.50 per kilo from $1.90 the previous year. The
World Bank reported in 1996 that a quarter of Mexicans were earning less
than $2 a day, with 17 percent earning less than $1 a day ("Mexico" 1999;
Camp 1998; World Bank 2000). A private-sector think tank in Mexico determined that real income fell 30 percent from 1995 to 1997 (Rozo 2000, 74).
Measures of physical quality of life indicators in table 6.5 reveal, moreover,
that Mexico is not only well behind the United States and Canada, as would
be expected, but also behind most other Latin American countries.

The Mexican government does not keep accurate statistics on unemployment (its poverty rate estimate reproduced in table 6.5 is grossly underesti-
mated), and official reports passed on to the United Nations and the World
Bank are often extremely misleading. Underemployment, which in not
counted in official data, is very high. Combined unemployment and underemployment may be more than 50 percent, as reported by the liberal Mexican newspaper *La Jornada* in 1995. The Monterrey Technological Institute,
a conservative research center, found real unemployment in 1994 to be
about 25 percent. The International Labor Organization indicated that 31
percent of the total Mexican labor force was in the informal sector, with an
average monthly income of $171. The informal sector in Mexico City alone
includes over two hundred thousand street vendors (Camp 1998; Cross 1998,
18; Warnock 1995, 169–170, 178–179).

CONCLUSION

From the World Bank's perspective, Mexico has to show the world that it is
"open for business." A bank report argued that this is best achieved by attracting foreign investment and establishing a free trade agreement with the
United States (with no mention of Canada). "How can the Mexican government credibly convey its attitude to the rest of the world? We believe that by
selling off a high profile company such as Telmex, and selling it at a relatively

Table 6.5 Physical Quality of Life Indicators, 1997 (and 1980)

	Population (in millions)	Wages in Dollars per Year[g]	Population % below $2 per Day	National Poverty Rate (%)	Life Expectancy at Birth	Infant Mortality (per 1,000)	Child Malnutrition % under Five Years Old	Higher Education % of Relevant Age Group[h]
Mexico	94.3 (67.6)	768 (1,343)	40.0	10.1[a]	72 (67)	38 (74)	14	16 (14)
Argentina	35.7 (28.1)	2,400 (N/A)	N/A	25.5[b]	73 (70)	22 (35)	2	42 (22)
Brazil	163.7 (121.7)	1,308 (1,690)	43.5	17.4[c]	67 (63)	34 (70)	6	12 (11)
Canada	30.3 (24.6)	7,897 (4,974)	N/A	N/A	79 (75)	6 (10)	N/A	90 (57)
Chile	14.6 (11.1)	1,781 (663)	38.5	21.6[d]	75 (69)	11 (32)	1	30 (12)
Colombia	40.0 (28.4)	1,128 (N/A)	21.7	16.9[b]	70 (66)	24 (41)	8	19 (9)
Cuba	11.1 (9.7)	N/A (N/A)	N/A	N/A	76 (74)	7 (20)	8	12 (17)
Paraguay	5.1 (3.1)	N/A (N/A)	N/A	21.8[b]	70 (67)	23 (67)	N/A	11 (9)
Peru	24.4 (17.3)	N/A (N/A)	N/A	53.5[e]	69 (60)	69 (60)	8	31 (17)
Uruguay	3.3 (2.9)	1,027 (1,262)	N/A	N/A	74 (70)	16 (37)	1	29 (17)
United States	267.6 (227.2)	8,056 (6,006)	N/A	N/A	76 (74)	7 (13)	4	81 (56)
Venezuela	22.8 (15.1)	1,463 (1,869)	32.2	31.3[f]	73 (68)	21 (36)	5	25 (21)

[a]Data available for 1988.
[b]Data available for 1991.
[c]Data available for 1990.
[d]Data available for 1992.
[e]Data available for 1994.
[f]Data available for 1989.
[g]1995–1999 (and 1980–1984).
[h]1996 (and 1980).
Note: In U.S. dollars.
Sources: World Bank (1999/2000, 2000).

low price, the government is trying to show that it is willing—indeed that it is eager—to see foreign investors make money in Mexico" (Tandon 1992, 42).

The collaboration of Mexican *compradors* with northern capital at the expense of the ordinary Mexican is nothing new. General Porfirio Díaz, who ruled Mexico from 1876 until his forced exile in 1911, brought in a wave of foreign capital and the dispossession of the Indian communal lands and the Mexican *campesino*. NAFTA is a more recent stage of this collaboration. As Noam Chomsky has observed:

> The main goal of NAFTA, we can now concede, was not to achieve the highly touted wonders of "trade" and "jobs," always illusion, but to ensure that Mexico would be "locked in" to the reforms that had made it an "economic miracle" (for U.S. investors and Mexican elites), deflecting the danger detected by a Latin America Strategy Development Workshop at the Pentagon in September 1990: that "a 'democracy opening' in Mexico could test the special relationship by bringing into office a government more interested in challenging the U.S. on economic and nationalist grounds." (1998, 366)

At the moment, no political movement appears poised to become that kind of government. Despite severe dislocations to Mexican farmers and workers caused by the PRI's embrace of neoliberalism and NAFTA, the mobilization of a serious challenge to its policies has yet to materialize. Some on both sides of the border look at the entrepreneurial achievements and wealth of Mexican capitalists, such as Helú and Azcárraga Milmo (and his son and successor Emilio Azcárraga Jean), and see evidence of a competitive, distributive, and developmental transnationalism—and the fallacy of cultural imperialism and neocolonialism. Mexico is seen to have produced a transnational base of its own.

Slim's star in the small galaxy of Mexican capitalism is so bright that reports of his heart problems in 1997 sent the Mexican stock market into momentary fibrillation. Slim may very well be a successful second-generation Mexican measured in terms of his personal accumulation, but whether this kind of success translates into positive returns to the majority of the Mexican people or whether most Mexicans even embrace him as a leader is not apparent. One section of the country that clearly does not is Chiapas.

Before its privatization, Telmex was the country's most profitable corporation, the crown jewel of Mexican state capitalism. The Salinas government determined that the neoliberal program of the state and the attraction of foreign capital required the modernization and denationalization of the telecommunications sector and the weakening of the unions. A Salinas ally, Slim was the most conspicuous beneficiary of this policy. The losers have been the Mexican working class, who have seen their wages decline and their telephone rates, for those with access, rise. At the time of the December 1994 peso devaluation, STRM workers had three times the average Mexican wage, but since then real wages for all Mexican workers have been sliding, though at a slower rate for the telephone workers. In recent years, the STRM workforce has been frozen, as Telmex has been subcontracting much of the expansion work to nonunion workers or to weaker unions (Dubb 1999, 283, 352).

The anticipated benefits of NAFTA have not trickled down to the majority of Mexicans by almost any measure. Telephone-line access has grown from 6.4 percent to nearly 10 percent (in 2000) since privatization in 1990, not a very impressive statistic. Mexico is last among the twenty-nine OECD countries in this category and also in the percentage of gross domestic product spent by government. The logic of neoliberalism dictates that Mexican capital seek profits wherever they are the most promising, and the private telecommunications companies have seen this opportunity mainly in long-distance, cellular, paging services, Internet, broadcasting, and cable television rather than in basic wired telephony. Foreign investment in Mexico's telecommunications system may make it operate more efficiently in terms of employing domestic resources, but the profits are more likely to flow out of the country than be used for domestic development.

Mexican resistance is likely to take several forms. The PRI, especially after the 2000 elections, has lost much of its credibility and electoral power base in the past decade. It is being challenged by parties on both the left (Partido de la Revolución Democrática) and the right (Partido Acción Nacional). A key element of resistance resides in a type of internationalism very different from what TNC alliances have in mind. One writer sees the formation of the independent federation, UNT, as an opportunity for the remobilization of Mexican workers and the rejection of the corporatist strategy of labor-state-capital collaboration. With a more progressive leadership, the American Federation of Labor–Congress of Industrial Organizations, which long followed a type of corporatist, business union approach, has taken in recent years a more critical, activist, and internationalist stance. In Mexico, it has pushed for a new "social clause" in a renegotiated NAFTA. The Teamsters and the United Electrical Workers have worked with the independent Frente Auténtico del Trabajo (Authentic Workers Front) in organizing efforts in the *maquiladoras* (Rosen 1998). There are also grassroots activist organizations in the United States and progressive nongovernmental organizations in Mexico working for social redistribution, such as the Red Mexicana de Acción Frente al Libre Comercio (Mexican Action Network on Free Trade).

In the long run, a revived and politically oriented labor movement, together with other natural allies in opposition to NAFTA and the WTO, including environmentalists and small businesses in Canada, Mexico, and the United States, is the best hope of putting the process of social change back in the hands of citizens and democratic interests.

NOTES

I wish to thank Alicia Sepúlveda for sharing her insights on Mexico's current labor conditions and to acknowledge the research assistance of Abeer Etefa and Carlos Vilalta. Note that unless stated otherwise, all dollar amounts are in U.S. currency.

1. One year after the first Mexican telephone company was set up with Mexican capital in 1878, it was sold off to American interests in the Continental Telephone Company, where it remained until it was nationalized in 1915 under the name Mextelco. Ten years later, it was reprivatized under the International Telephone and Telegraph Corporation (ITT), its chief competitor, Mexeric, run by the Swedish firm, L. M. Ericsson. Mexeric was taken over by a majority of private Mexican interests and began operations as Telmex in 1948. Telmex bought out ITT's controlling share of Mextelco in 1950 (Petrazzini 1995, 106–108).

2. The two foreign companies, together with American Telephone and Telegraph (AT&T), continue to be major suppliers to Telmex. ITT was taken over by Alcatel in the early 1980s.

3. The satellites' eponym is the nineteenth-century Mexican revolutionary priest and hero José María Morelos, who led his Indian and other landless followers to oppose foreign (Spanish) domination and control and declared, "You must regard as enemies all the rich, the nobles, and high ranking officials" (quoted in Galeano 1973, 57). The twist is that the control and use of the *Morelos* satellites is held primarily by the new representatives of foreign and domestic wealth and power.

4. The principal market for *maquiladora* exports is the United States. Export earnings grew more than tenfold from 1980 to the mid-1990s. "By December 1997, the U.S. Labor Department's Transitional Adjustment Assistance (TAA) program—which systematically undercounts job losses—certified that 151,256 U.S. jobs had been lost to NAFTA–related imports and plant shutdowns" (Medaille and Wheat 1997, 23–25). El Paso, Texas, just across the Rio Grande from Ciudad Juárez, Mexico, a major *maquiladora* production center, was particularly hard hit with some sixty-five hundred job losses, mostly in the garments industry. It has been estimated by the Economic Policy Institute, a liberal think tank, that because of the government's very restrictive counting procedures for job losses along with exaggerated claims of NAFTA job creation, the actual impact was a net loss of nearly four hundred thousand U.S. jobs (23–25). The Clinton administration's effort to win Congress's "fast track" approval for extending NAFTA to other countries in Latin America was defeated in 1997.

5. A darling of the U.S. media and major financial interests, especially after getting control of runaway inflation during his time in office, Salinas was put on the board of directors of Dow Jones and Company, which publishes the *Wall Street Journal*.

6. *Business Week* referred to McKinsey as "by far the most influential consulting firm in the world" (*Business Week*, 20 September 1993).

7. The privatization of telecommunications in Mexico has been part of a larger national wealth redistribution through sell-offs of state–owned and operated enterprises. This was achieved through tight financial-political linkages and kickbacks between the then–ruling party (the PRI) and the top executive class, led by the Council of Businessmen. Slim's takeovers of Telmex and other telecommunications properties was nearly fully funded by this inner business circle. The telecommunications industry in Mexico generated 2.6 percent of the country's gross domestic product (GDP) and 5.7 percent of its manufacturing GDP in 1998, which included companies

such as Hewlett-Packard with $1.6 billion invested (Castellanos 1999; Herman 1997, 11–12; Mandel-Campbell 1999).

8. Grupo Carso had a controlling interest with 20.4 percent, of which Slim held 51 percent, while Southwestern Bell and France Cable et Radio each held 24.5 percent, plus additional nonvoting shares. Shortly after the company was put up for sale, foreigners had bought 55.7 percent of its total stock (Tandon 1992, 11, 15; Wellenius and Staple 1996, 3). In May 2000, the parent company of France Cable et Radio, France Télécom, announced plans to sell off its remaining stake to Southwestern Bell Communications Corporation (SBC), the Houston-based Baby Bell, already a major player in the U.S.–Canada telephone market (Mandel-Campbell 2000).

9. Beyond Mexico, Telmex operates the major telephone company in Guatemala and is positioned to do the same in Honduras. In the United States, Telmex has acquired or is partnered with Cellular Communications in Puerto Rico, Topp Telecomm, Comm South, the Williams Communications Group, and SBC (Lindquist 1999, C1).

10. Salinas went into voluntary exile in Ireland after his brother, Raul, was jailed on various government charges, including illegal secret partnerships in the telephone and television industries and of being the mastermind behind the political assassination of José Francisco Ruiz Massieu, a PRI leader.

11. John Warnock comments on the consecutive presidencies from Harvard and Yale (Salinas's predecessor, Miguel de la Madrid, was also a Harvard graduate) and the heavy influence of the Ivy League–trained cabinet members in the Salinas and Zedillo administrations that was "symbolic of Mexico's shift from being part of the Latin American community to economic integration with the United States" (1995, 53).

12. Mexico also has one of the world's lowest international telephone calling rates, despite the fact that telephone service has been in the country since 1878 and the fact that currently millions of Mexicans are separated from family across the U.S. border. Almost all of these intrafamily calls originate in the United States (Frederick 1997, 273; Petrazzini 1995, 106).

13. Alestra, a competitor to Telmex, plans to concentrate future telephone-line investment in the same three cities. According to the company, it will focus on "mostly medium-sized and larger businesses, using a combination of wire and wireless technology" (Gori 2001, W1).

14. This is measured in minutes of international telephone traffic (1997). The International Telecommunication Union puts this information on-line at <http://www.itu.int/ti/industryoverview/top50int.html> [last accessed: 1 June 2000]. International traffic is overwhelmingly dominated by the leading OECD countries. Of the top fifty routes, the United States was featured in nineteen (and five of the top six); Germany eight; United Kingdom, the Netherlands, and Switzerland three; Japan and Sweden two; and France, Italy, Belgium, Spain, Australia, New Zealand, and Canada one. (Only the Ukraine and Singapore were non–OECD entries.)

15. Telmex is also the country's largest cellular telephone operator, with 70 percent of the market, followed by Iusacell, a joint venture of the powerful Peralta family and Bell Atlantic, which has a 42 percent equity share. Sprint pulled out of this partnership in 1994 to join the Telmex group (Griffith 1998, 182). In 1997, Telmex took in revenues of about $6.5 billion and had a total of 63,115 employees.

16. Until 1989, AT&T was the exclusive provider of telephone traffic between the United States and Mexico. Sprint and MCI have since gained a foothold in that

market, but Telmex's aggressive expansion has reduced foreign control of the market from a third to about 25 percent (J. Smith 1999, C1). One of Telmex's strategies in fending off AT&T was to stir up nationalist sentiments, including the use of a television ad series depicting a gringo-accented pitchman, "Burton Helms" (a poke at the U.S. Helms-Burton Act, which threatens retaliation against countries, such as Mexico, that trade with Cuba). Burton Helms is sometimes depicted as "a plump exec golfing indoors," in other ads "he is dressed in a poncho and sombrero, trying to convince Mexicans he's one of them" (Sutter 1997a, 5A).

17. Almost half of all Mexican prime time television programming is imported, as is 30 percent of the total (75 percent of which is from the United States). While some studies show that most Mexicans still prefer Mexican-produced television programs to those from the United States in order to demonstrate that "cultural imperialism" is a false construct, they do not discuss the influence of American or, in general, commercial, broadcast advertising on cultural practices. Moreover, such studies (e.g., Lozano 1996) do not consider the American influence on the commercial formats, if not content, of popular Mexican game shows, sitcoms, news broadcasts, and *telenovelas* (soap operas).

18. The percentage of American programming on these latter three media delivery systems is higher than in television.

19. Cultural intervention is a serious problem for Mexico's film industry as well. Barbara Trent describes the plight of award-winning Mexican filmmakers who cannot get their films exhibited in Mexican theaters, which, she says, are making too much money showing dubbed American films (1998, 231).

20. The media empire was founded by Emilio Azcárraga Vidaurreta. His son, Emilio Azcárraga Milmo, having acquired a $3 billion fortune by 1993, was named by *Forbes* magazine that year as Latin America's wealthiest individual (Rodríguez 1995, 143–144), and when he died in 1997 *Forbes* put Slim in the lead. Televisa was passed on to a third generation, Emilio Azcárraga Jean, who, emulating his father's callous reputation, laid off six thousand of his twenty thousand employees (Preston 2000a, C1).

21. According to Alicia Sepúlveda, secretary of foreign relations for the Sindicato de Telefonistas de la República Mexicana (STRM), Mexican state-labor relations are entrenched in a type of corporatism similar to the peronista variety. The founder of the Confederación Regional Mexicana (CROM; Regional Confederation of Mexican Workers), Luis Napoleón Morones, served as president of the confederation, minister of labor, and ministry of industry during the Calles-dominated era in the 1920s and early 1930s. The government's strategy was to deliver on jobs and wages and make symbolic appearances at major labor mobilizations in exchange for the delivery of the union vote. CROM disciplined workers and blocked strikes (Warnock 1995, 114). Sepúlveda sees the closed shop as double-edged: it guarantees union protection against yellow-dog contracts but also allows union bosses to expel and blacklist dissidents and collaborate with management to deny them severance benefits (Sepúlveda 2000).

22. Rank-and-file members along with hundreds of shop stewards and counselors initially put up considerable resistance until they were persuaded by STRM leadership that the company might suffer massive job losses without privatization (Dubb 1999, 183–184). In the end, the union membership was sold a 4.4 percent stock share of the new privatized Telmex for $325 million through a loan from a government

bank, but not enough to qualify them for a seat on the board of directors. The share value quadrupled within the first two years (Tandon 1992, 10–11). Only a few hundred of the original fifty-two thousand recipients still own shares (Sepúlveda 2000).

23. Globally, the 358 richest people have as much income as the poorest 2.5 billion, or 45 percent of the world's population (Broad and Cavanagh 1995/1996, 27; Chomsky 1999, 125). Bill Gates alone had a net worth in 1996 of $39.8 billion, an amount greater than all of Central America's combined GNP and more than the combined wealth of 40 percent of Americans. By 1999, his assets rose to $100 billion (Collins 1999; Ivins 1997, D8).

REFERENCES

AT&T Long Lines. 1982. *The World's Telephones*. Morris Plains, N.J.: AT&T Long Lines.

Avery, Natalie. 1994. "Stealing from the State." In *50 Years Is Enough: The Case against the World Bank and the International Monetary Fund*, ed. Kevin Danaher. Boston: South End.

Barrera, Eduardo. 1996. "The U.S.–Mexico Border As Post–NAFTA Mexico." In *Mass Media and Free Trade: NAFTA and the Cultural Industries*, ed. E. G. McAnany and K. T. Wilkinson. Austin: University of Texas Press.

Beachy, Debra. 1998. "A Little Border War over Mexican–U.S. Phone Traffic." *New York Times*, 11 April, D3.

Broad, Robin, and John Cavanagh. 1995/1996. "Don't Neglect the Impoverished South." *Foreign Policy* (Winter): 18–35.

Camp, Roderic A. 1998. "Mexico." In *Encarta 98 Encyclopedia*. Seattle, Wash.: Microsoft. Compact disc version.

Case, Brendan M. 1998. "Message from Space." *Latin Trade* (May). On-line version.

Castellanos, Camila. 1999. "Foreign Interest." *Business Mexico*, 1 July. On-line version.

Cevallos, Diego. 1999. "Development-Mexico: Internet Use Is Growing, But Only for a Few." *Inter Press Service* release, 7 July.

Chomsky, Noam. 1998. "Free Trade and Free Market: Pretense and Practice." In *The Cultures of Globalization*, ed. Fredric Jameson and Masao Miyoshi. Durham, N.C.: Duke University Press.

———. 1999. *Profits over People: Neoliberalism and Global Order*. New York: Seven Stories.

Clifton, Judith. 2000. "On the Political Consequences of Privatization: The Case of Teléfonos de México." *Bulletin of Latin American Research* (January): 12–13.

Collins, Chuck. 1999. "The Wealth Gap Widens." *Dollars and Sense* (September–October): 12–13.

Cross, John C. 1998. *Informal Politics: Street Vendors and the State of Mexico City*. Stanford, Calif.: Stanford University Press.

Cunningham, Stuart, Elizabeth Jacka, and John Sinclair. 1998. "Global and Regional Dynamics of International Television Flows." In *Electronic Empires: Global Media and Local Resistance*, ed. Daya K. Thussu. London: Arnold.

De Sarkar, Dipankar. 1998. "Telecoms: Global Accounting Rate System under U.S. Attack." *Inter Press Service*, 11 March.

Diaz, Roberto. 1998. "Side-Tracked." *Business Mexico,* 1 November. On-line version.

Donnelly, Robert. 1998. "Alicia Sepúlveda, Working on Behalf of Labor." *The News* (Mexico City), 19 October. On-line version.

Dubb, Steve. 1999. *Logics of Resistance: Globalization and Telephone Unionism in Mexico and British Columbia.* New York: Garland.

Enciclopedia de México. 1978. "Telecomunicaciones," "Teléfonos," "Telégrafos," and "Televisión." 4th ed. Coyoacan, Mexico: Francisco Sosa.

Frederick, Howard H. 1997. "Mexican NGO Computer Networking and Cross-Border Coalition Building." In *Democratizing Communication? Comparative Perspectives on Information and Power,* ed. Mashoed Bailie and Dwayne Winseck. Cresskill, N.J.: Hampton.

Friedland, Jonathan. 1999a. "International: Mexican Entrepreneur Embarks on Spending Spree." *Wall Street Journal,* 26 July, A17, A19.

———. 1999b. "Telecommunications in Mexico Lag behind Deregulation Effort." *Wall Street Journal,* 5 August, A15.

Galeano, Eduardo. 1973. *Open Veins of Latin America: Five Centuries of the Pillage of a Continent,* trans. Cedric Belfrage. New York: Monthly Review.

Garcia, Eduardo. 2000. "Telmex Disputes Allegations It Failed to Give Rivals Service." *San Diego Union-Tribune,* 15 January, C2.

Gonzalez, Adrian E., Amar Gupta, and Sawan Deshpande. 1998. "Telecommunications in Mexico." *Telecommunications Policy* 22:341–357.

Gori, Graham. 2001. "Mexicans Seen Waiting Some More for a Phone." *New York Times,* 24 January, W1.

Griffith, Kathleen A. 1998. "Mexico." In *Telecommunications in Latin America,* ed. Eli M. Noam. New York: Oxford University Press.

Herman, Edward S. 1997. "The Global Attack on Democracy, Labor, and Public Values." *Dollars and Sense* (September–October): 10–15.

Herman, Edward S., and Robert W. McChesney. 1997. *The Global Media: The New Missionaries of Global Capitalism.* London: Cassell.

International Telecommunication Union. 1999. *Challenges to the Network: Internet for Development.* "Executive Summary" (October), <http://www.itu.int/ti/publications/inet_99/> [last accessed: 15 February 2001].

Ivins, Molly. 1997. "The Rich Get Richer." *The Oregonian,* 25 October, D8.

Leppmann, Kevin. 1996. "Putting the Public on Hold: Notes on the Privatization of Telecommunications." *Dollars and Sense* (May–June): 14–17.

Lindquist, Diane. 1999. "Telmex Lines Crossed?" *San Diego Union-Tribune,* 28 December, C1.

Lozano, José Carlos. 1996. "Media Reception on the Mexican Border with the United States." In *Mass Media and Free Trade: NAFTA and the Cultural Industries,* ed. E. G. McAnany and K. T. Wilkinson. Austin: University of Texas Press.

Mandel-Campbell, Andrea. 1999. "Digital Slim." *Latin Trade* (October). On-line version.

———. 2000. "Ownership Shakeup for Telmex." *Financial Times,* 3 May. On-line version.

Marin, Mehmet. 1999. "Dependency Theory, Environmental Regulations, and the Movement of Manufacturing to the Periphery: The Case of Mexico's *Maquiladoras.*" Unpublished paper. Portland State University.

McAnany, Emile G., and Kenton T. Wilkinson. 1996. Introduction to *Mass Media and Free Trade: NAFTA and the Cultural Industries*, ed. E. G. McAnany and K. T. Wilkinson. Austin: University of Texas Press.

Medaille, Bill, and Andrew Wheat. 1997. "Faded Denim NAFTA Blues." *Multinational Monitor* (December): 23–26.

"Mexico: Let Them Eat Hamburgers." 1999. *The Economist*, 9 January. On-line version.

Mody, Bella, and Jorge Borrego. 1991. "Mexico's Morelos Satellite: Reaching for Autonomy?" In *Transnational Communications: Wiring the Third World*, ed. Gerald Sussman and John A. Lent. Newbury Park, Calif.: Sage.

Moran, Albert. 1998. *Copycat Television: Globalisation, Program Formats, and Cultural Identity*. Luton, U.K.: Luton University Press.

Pérez Chavolla, Lilia, and Rohan Samarajiva. 1997. "Privatization, Market Liberalization, and Regulatory Reform in the Mexican Telecommunication System." In *Privatization and Competition in Telecommunications. International Developments*, ed. Daniel J. Ryan. Westport, Conn.: Praeger.

Petrazzini, Ben A. 1995. *The Political Economy of Telecommunications Reform in Developing Countries: Privatization and Liberalization in Comparative Perspective*. Westport, Conn.: Praeger.

Preston, Julia. 2000a. "A Firm Grip on Mexico's Dial." *New York Times*, 25 April, C1, C4.

———. 2000b. "Competitors of Telmex Say It Still Acts Like a Monopoly." *New York Times*, 4 April, C4.

———. 2000c. "Mexican Retail Conglomerate Buying Rest of CompUSA." *New York Times*, 25 January, C3.

——— 2000d. "U.S. Trade Representative May Take Action against Mexico." *New York Times*, 5 April, C4.

Ramamurti, Ravi. 1996. "Telephone Privatization in a Large Country—Mexico." In *Privatizing Monopolies*, ed. Ravi Ramamurti. Baltimore, Md.: Johns Hopkins University Press.

Rodríguez, América. 1995. "Control Mechanisms of National News Making: Britain, Canada, Mexico, and the United States." In *Questioning the Media: A Critical Introduction*, ed. John Downing, Ali Mohammadi, and Annabelle Sreberny-Mohammadi. 2nd ed. Thousand Oaks, Calif.: Sage.

Rosen, Fred. 1998. "Breaking Away: Mexican Workers Rebel against Government-Dominated Trade Unionism." *In These Times*, 22 February, 25.

Rozo, Carlos. 2000. "Mexico's Failed Growth Strategy." In *Real World Globalization*, ed. Ellen Frank, David Levy, and Allejandro Reuss. 6th ed. Somerville, Mass.: Dollars and Sense.

Sampler, Maria-Luz Daza. 1997. "An International Division of Labor: Gender and the Information Technology Industry." *International Journal of Politics, Culture, and Society* 10 (4): 635–658.

Schiller, Dan. 1999. *Digital Capitalism: Networking the Global Market System*. Cambridge: Massachusetts Institute of Technology Press.

Sepúlveda, Alicia. 2000. Personal correspondence. 15 March.

Silverman, G. 1996. "Rebalancing Act." *Far Eastern Economic Review*, 5 December, 70–71.

Sklair, Leslie. 1991. *Sociology of the Global System*. Baltimore, Md.: Johns Hopkins University Press.

Smith, Geri. 1999. "Mr. Slim, Meet Mr. Gates." *Business Week*, 8 November, 55.

Smith, Geri, and Stephen Baker. 1995. "The Fall of Carlos Salinas." *Business Week*, 27 March, 52–56.

Smith, Geri, and Stephanie A. Forest. 2000. "Slim's New World." *Business Week*, 6 March, 161.

Smith, James F. 1999. "Debate Rages over Carlos Slim, the Wealthiest Man in Latin America." *Los Angeles Times*, 5 September, C1, C13.

Sussman, Gerald. 1997. *Communication, Technology, and Politics in the Information Age*. Thousand Oaks, Calif.: Sage.

Sutter, Mary. 1997a. "Telmex Holding Its Own in Phone Customer Wars." *Journal of Commerce*, 20 March, 1A, 5A.

———. 1997b. "US–Mexico Venture Mapping Plans for When It Takes Over Satellite." *Journal of Commerce*, 31 October. On-line version.

Tandon, Pankaj, with Manuel A. Abdala and Inder Ruprah. 1992. "Mexico: Background, Telmex, AeroMexico, Mexicana." A World Bank conference report on *Welfare Consequences of Selling Public Enterprises: Case Studies from Chile, Malaysia, Mexico and the U.K.* Washington, D.C., June 11–12. Chapter 16. Draft version.

"Telecommunications." 1996. *Asia Yearbook, 1997* (December): 64–68.

Trent, Barbara. 1998. "Media in a Capitalist Culture." In *The Cultures of Globalization*, ed. Fredric Jameson and Masao Miyoshi. Durham, N.C.: Duke University Press.

United Nations. 1993. *World Urbanisation Prospects, 1992*. New York: United Nations.

UN Educational, Scientific, and Cultural Organization. 2000. *Statistics*. <http://www.unescostat.unesco.org/en/stats/stat0.htm> [last accessed: 1 June 2000].

U.S. Trade Representative. 1996. Reported in *San Jose Mercury News*, 21 December, 1C.

Vandenack, Tim. 1993. "Mexico Launches Communications Satellite in South America." *United Press International* dispatch, 19 November.

Warnock, John. 1995. *The Other Mexico: The North American Triangle Completed*. New York: Black Rose.

Wellenius, Björn, and Gregory Staple. 1996. "Beyond Privatization: The Second Wave of Telecommunications Reforms in Mexico." World Bank Discussion Paper No. 341. Washington, D.C.: World Bank.

World Bank. 1999-2000. *World Development Report*. Washington, D.C.: World Bank. <http://www.worldbank.org/wdr/> [last accessed: 15 February 2001].

———. 2000. *Development Data*. Washington, D.C.: World Bank. <http://www.worldbank.org/data/databytopic/databytopic.html> [last accessed: 15 February 2001].

7

Networking the North American Higher Education Industry

Lora E. Taub and Dan Schiller

> NAFTA cannot succeed without a coordinated response from the higher education institutions in North America. For our nations to be effective trading partners, higher education must provide well-trained professionals adept at working in this emerging trilateral context.
>
> —Consortium for North American Higher Education Collaboration (2000)

In 1994, the World Bank diagnosed a "worldwide crisis in higher education." The dysfunction, declared the bank, stemmed from the fact that

> in all countries, higher education is heavily dependent on government funding. In an era of widespread fiscal constraints, industrial as well as developing countries are grappling with the challenge of preserving or improving the quality of higher education as education budgets are compressed. The crisis is most acute in the developing world, both because fiscal adjustments have been harsher and because it has been more difficult for developing countries to contain pressures for enrollment expansion. (World Bank 1994, 2)

The solution, according to the bank, was not to make available sufficient revenues to expand the existing public education sector, but rather to build a new set of institutions to deliver postsecondary education.[1]

This campaign to place postsecondary education on a radically reorganized structural foundation has markedly intensified since the mid-1990s,[2] and the ongoing overhaul of institutional practice and policy indeed has gained global momentum. The concrete social content of this metamorphosis comprises a powerful drive to discredit and dismantle existing systems of public instruction, and to open higher education institutions directly to market forces. Adam Miller, the founder of one of a new breed of commercial educational suppliers, CyberU, provides a candid summary of the underlying process: "In many ways, we are forcing capitalism into higher education" (Carr 2000a, A57). Dramatic changes on both the supply and the demand sides of the postsecondary education complex testify to an overarching tendency to commoditize education "more or less everywhere," one recent report declares (Educational International and Public Service International 1999, 14).[3]

Unfolding is not a process of "market entry," whereby enterprising outsiders muscle into an existing for-profit sector. What is occurring is better understood as a process of market *creation*, whereby a for-profit activity is fashioned out of what had been a quasi-public social function. Thereby, "a sector traditionally regarded as a public service is turning into an increasingly attractive market for major national and foreign corporations. Although the international trade in education is not a new phenomenon, it is today assuming new forms and undergoing rapid expansion" (Education International and Public Service International 1999, 14). Educational offerings by corporations and for-profit consortia incorporate network technology, in particular, to help alter the social relations of production within the sector. Cyberspace in turn has become a preferred mechanism for securing capital's hold within this vast, long mostly nonprofit, domain.

Why is this transformative process under way? The restructuring of educational provision is animated by two converging trends: first, rapidly expanding efforts by corporations and other organizations to use networks to supply for-profit educational programs and services; second, large corporations' growing attempts to rely on those same networks to create an appropriately skilled and internationally mobile labor force, in support of accumulation on a supranational scale.

This chapter reviews recent network-enabled efforts to catalyze the commoditization of postsecondary education, with specific reference to the United States and Mexico. We set the stage for our analysis of the institutional embrace of "distance learning" by detailing the concurrent, and far from coincidental, attempt to undercut the existing system of public provision.

THE ATTACK ON PUBLIC EDUCATION

Long the most prestigious and largest institution of higher education in Mexico, the Universidad Nacional Autónoma de México (UNAM; National Autonomous University of Mexico), lately has endured a period of protracted punishment. The mainstream media attribute the crippling of UNAM to a 292-day student-led strike, the longest shutdown in the 89-year history of the university, during 1999–2000. They hold up UNAM's enfeeblement as a symbol of the breakdown and inefficiencies of public education. However, the strike is more accurately understood as a response to revamped institutional priorities, which in recent years have worked to undercut both UNAM and Mexican public higher education in general.

Publicly provided education long played a central part in Mexico's so-called postrevolutionary project, which emphasized the responsibility of the state to ensure education for all, and thus contributed to the formation of one of the strongest—though still characteristically underdeveloped—national educational systems in Latin America.[4] Funding from the Mexican government constituted the bulk of the country's public institutions' budgets. On average, funding from the Mexican government amounted in the early 1990s to 60 percent of the total education budget, with an additional 30 percent from state appropriations, and less than 4 percent derived from tuition.[5] However, federal spending on higher education had stagnated, reaching a cap of 0.7 percent of the gross domestic product (GDP) compared to 2.4 percent in the United States (Organization for Economic Cooperation and Development [OECD] 1996).[6]

Since the late 1970s, postsecondary education in Mexico, and in Latin America more broadly, has been divided into public and private institutional segments. Of the former, schools are either autonomous or dependent on the federal government. Among the latter are historically religious institutions, nonprofit institutions, and most recently for-profit colleges or universities (including a number of technological and vocational training schools). By the late 1990s, in addition to the roughly 40 public universities in Mexico, there were 250 private institutions, more than 100 public technological institutes, and numerous public two-year postsecondary schools closely coordinated with regional job markets and local business interests (Kent 1999, 12–13; Marmolejo and León-Garcia 1997).

These numbers attest to substantial recent growth in the sector. Total enrollments by Mexican higher education institutions doubled from 1990 to 1997. The bulk of this expansion, however, was captured by private institutions. Enrollments in public-sector institutions actually stood still, while private institutions—in a very short time—secured roughly 30 percent of students enrolled throughout the country (Kent 1999).[7] A signal that this competition was cutting deeply into the core of the public system has been the "elite flight" from public to private universities. UNAM was once the unrivaled educational milieu for Mexico's comfortable strata, but increasingly middle-class families, not to mention members of business and national elites, have sent their children to private institutions, both within Mexico and abroad. Enrollments at public universities dropped from 87 percent to 79 percent of total national enrollments in just three years, 1990–1992 (Kent 1998, 3–4). Significantly, however, the core of UNAM's student population—fully three-quarters—remained students from families who earn less than $600 a month (Navarro 2000, 22).

The tilt toward private institutions was also apparent at the level of academic labor. In the 1990s, the number of employed academics in Mexico nearly doubled, from 86,188 in 1990 to 153,044 in 1997. Hiring by the private-university sector outpaced that by the public universities, growing by

92 percent over this interval; the overwhelming majority of these hires were to part-time positions (Kent 1999, 12–13).

The rapid growth of the private-education sector offered a sustained challenge to the existing financial basis of publicly provided education. Equally grave, it "delegat[ed] to the private sector . . . increasing elements of education policy that were formally the reserve of the academic community itself" (North American Congress on Latin America [NACLA] 2000, 11). As this power was handed over to private interests, not only research agendas but also teaching agendas were altered.

The conditions that have favored the emergence of private educational provision can be traced back to the 1970s, when an unexpected surge in enrollments exceeded the public universities' capacity and resources. Demographic pressures on existing public universities combined in the 1980s with high inflation and severe budget cuts to place public postsecondary education in severe difficulties: top faculty left for better-funded positions at private universities locally and abroad, while a 40 percent decline in the real purchasing power of their salaries forced others to work additional jobs. During the 1990s, even as an educational expansion commenced, neoliberal policies designed to open the economy to the market and to scale back the public sector plunged the public university system into crisis.

Beginning in 1991, public universities were forced to compete for increasingly scarce federal funds with private institutions. As funding became tied to so-called standards of quality and performance, and public universities grappled with declining salaries, revenues, and prestige, private institutions, already geared to middle-class market demands, powered their way forward. In this way, the federal government, once the guardian and provider of the nation's prestigious educational system, actively promoted the private-education sector—promoting the familiar but fundamentally flawed neoliberal assumption that diversification of services promotes competition, which in turn raises quality.

The Programa de Desarrollo Educativo 1995–2000 set forth by the Ernesto Zedillo Ponce de León administration explicitly provided that no new universities would be built and that the potential for federally supported growth in the public sector would be confined to the technological institutes (Kent 1998, 5). Public universities were spared the closures or auctions that other public-sector services suffered in the wake of privatizations and government cutbacks, but what one analyst calls a "severe retrenchment" within academia "had drastic effects on the institutional fabric and academic morale" and thrust many institutions into "downward spirals of factionalist struggles over decreasing resources" (4).[8]

In part, to be sure, the plight of public higher education was due to a general economic crisis. After the fall of the peso in 1994–1995, public universities were forced at midsemester to cut their budgets by 20 percent. Hit hardest by the devaluation of the peso—which lost 37 percent of its value between December 1994 and February 1995—were science and technology programs dependent on costly equipment and supplies. The then vice president for academic affairs at the University of the Americas in Mexico City voiced the widespread disillusionment across campus in the era of the North American Free Trade Agreement (NAFTA). "For one fleeting moment, we were part of the first world, and then we found ourselves unexpectedly stuffed into the third world again" (Statland de Lopez 1995).

But encompassing and deliberate policy measures comprised the chief trigger of radical institutional change. At some universities, new statutes were written that legally committed schools to generate their own revenues through tuition and other means—in an effort to demonstrate to the federal government a willingness to accept market-based discipline. As the rector of the University of Sonoma explained, "We understand that regular operating subsidies from the government will not grow. So, we must become entrepreneurial, earning extra income and involving faculty and students in this effort" (Kent 1998, 17). Recent fee hikes at the University of Puebla increased tuition-based revenues from $1 million to $7 million in one year (23).

Government policymakers and university administrators sought to depict this as a "modernization" of Mexico's education sector. Modernization, however, mandated an end to long-established practices that worked to the benefit of less-favored social groups as well as of student and faculty rights: open access for students, nominal tuition, unconditional government subsidies as the sole funding source, and autonomy in governance (Kent 1998, 23). Modernization has introduced entrance examinations for prospective students,[9] and "professional competency examinations" for graduates, substantial fee structures, the end of public funds as the sole source of funding, and new systems of assessing "managerial efficiency" and "financial accountability." (Competing for limited funds, university administrators responded to an "unwritten rule" basically holding that those funds would be more favorably allocated to "institutions that developed significant alternative financial resources" [8].) Concurrently, incentives have been developed for faculty to develop and sell a variety of consulting services, and commercial contracts with local businesses have been actively pursued (8).

According to the older norm, to recap, Mexican higher education comprised a social asset, and academic programs were to be designed according to the idea that "what is good for the society will be good for the student." Within this model, students had been at least nominally considered active agents in "a social transformational process" (Marmolejo and León-Garcia 1997). As public universities were defunded, however, middle-class students defected in growing numbers to newly established private institutions. Members of the poor and the working class, historically ill-positioned to gain access to higher or even secondary education, saw their scant opportunities dwindle further.

Current struggles within Mexico's public universities must be understood in this context. Many Mexican university students, like their peers in Chile (Olavarría 2000, 28), and for that matter at some public institutions in the United States, [10] have sought to ward off efforts to impose this market-driven agenda, which redefines students as "consumers" of educational services or products, clients of university corporations. In 1992, a strong student movement at UNAM beat back the university rector's effort to implement a differential fee system. After the failure in 1992 to impose tuition, university administrators pursued a neoliberal agenda by other means, including selling services to local industry, while faculty from engineering and administration became particularly entrepreneurial in creating programs in managerial and technical training, as well as in consulting.

The 1999–2000 strike at UNAM, which halted all campus activities except basic research, ended on Sunday, February 6, when an estimated 2,700 federal police raided the UNAM campus, wielding batons and riot shields, forcibly reopening the university, and jailing nearly 750 students. While media reports described the shutdown as, simply, a self-interested protest by anarchistically inclined hotheads against the rector's plan to impose tuition, more was at stake in the strike than the proposed $150 (or 1,360 peso) tuition fees. The strike emerged as a means of opposing the radical reorganization of the nation's preeminent publicly funded institution of higher education. It directly engaged what one analyst terms "the neoliberal World Bank–inspired transformation of the national education system" (Navarro 2000, 22).

Rejecting the rector's proposal to hike tuition while offering loans and scholarships for "needy" students, and rejecting the end of open admissions, the students in the broadest sense were fighting to preserve the nation's commitment to free public education for all Mexicans, regardless of social class.[11] The strike was waged, that is, against the prevailing trend toward "well-heeled private schools for the rich and upper-middle classes, and dilapidated, underfunded public schools for the poor" (NACLA 2000, 11). Students also contested the process whereby a university with a history of serving students from working-class families as well as children of the nation's ruling and business elite, would begin to implement selective admissions policies and narrow its liberal arts curriculum to one fine-tuned to the local Mexican job market. "The tuition problem was just a detonator," according to one administrator. "Now we're going to have to really decide how a national university should serve the nation" (Statland de Lopez 2000, A67).

The campaign to dismantle Mexican public higher education, however, comprises only half of a two-sided initiative to set educational provision on a new structural basis. The other side is the emergence of a for-profit complex of educational vendors. To gain a clearer conception of this market-deepening initiative, we must turn to developments originating within the political economy of Mexico's powerful northern neighbor.

THE RISE OF A FOR-PROFIT EDUCATION
COMPLEX BUILT AROUND NETWORKS

The introduction of market relations into educational provision is no mere in-house academic achievement. Nor does it testify only to the ascendance of neoliberal ideology. Nor, finally, is it a product of endeavor by a few high-tech Goliaths nosing around the groves of academe in search of hardware and software contracts. The process of change that is under way encompasses all this, and more. Educational contractors, entertainment conglomerates, software and information technology vendors, textbook publishers, proprietary schools, government leaders, corporate trainers, and entrepreneurial academic administrators and professors have set about to construct a new, transnationally organized and oriented learning industry. Although their interests may sometimes clash, and although they do not operate in light of any comprehensive blueprint or joint action strategy, there can be no doubt that they have generated powerful momentum behind for-profit education. Within the past decade, "postsecondary proprietary education has been transformed from a sleepy sector of the economy, best known for mom-and-pop trade schools, to a $3.5 billion-a-year business that is increasingly dominated by companies building regional and even national franchises" (Strosnider 1998, A36–A38). Actually, as we will see, leading suppliers maintain an increasingly transnational orientation. For-profit vendors tend, moreover, to focus their institutional energies on closing gaps between labor market supply (students) and demand (corporate employers): they are vocationally driven.

Distance education—that is, courses delivered via networks—lies at the core of this institutional makeover. Networked education constitutes, in the words of John Chambers, the chief executive officer (CEO) of Cisco Systems, "the next big killer application for the Internet" (Friedman 1999). With explosive institutional innovation around the Internet, already by 1997–1998, U.S. postsecondary institutions overall were offering more than fifty-four thousand different distance-education courses—most of which were college-level, credit-granting courses provided by public two-year and (especially) four-year institutions (Lewis et al. 1999, iv). As we will see, however, conventional universities had no monopoly over this burgeoning field.

Increasingly, publicly traded corporations developed around the use of networks to cater to education markets on a supranational scale. The Apollo Group's University of Phoenix (UOP), now the largest private university in the United States and also assuredly the best known of this new class of vendors, by 2000 reached ninety-eight campuses across eighteen states, plus Puerto Rico and British Columbia, Canada, and served sixty-eight thousand students—about one-seventh of whom were on-line. The ninety-five hundred students enrolled on-line came from the United States and twenty-one other countries, and had the option of completing an entire degree program on the Internet. While UOP has its critics, it is championed by others as a model for expanding and improving higher education in developing countries "at little or no cost to the public sector" (Jackson 2000, 34). According to education analysts at the World Bank, network technology makes it possible for "the best universities of any country" to "open a branch anywhere in the world or to reach out across borders using the Internet, . . . effectively competing with any national university on its own territory." The UOP is its model example here, praised as "one of the most dynamic new distance universities in the US," which uses "an incentive system to reward professors on the basis of the labor market outcomes of graduates" (34). UOP's "business approach" to education, however, actually involves the abandonment of full-time faculty, and of academic tenure, in favor of inexpensive part-time labor (remuneration is $900 to $1,280 per course without benefits) (34).

With support from the *Washington Post* (owner of Kaplan Incorporated) and other backers, the company that runs the UOP has established a new unit—Apollo International—to expand further abroad. According to the venture's president, Apollo intends to "develop, acquire, or create partnerships with institutions" in other countries so that by 2010 "the overseas operation should be able to match, in size, the domestic operation." Seeking to profit by selling educational services to an expanding pool of students—in Mexico, the number of college students is projected to increase from 1.8 million in 2000 to 4 million by 2010—Apollo will establish physical campuses as well as using distance-education delivery. It claimed to be in a position to complete deals with institutions in Mexico and other Latin American countries by mid-2001 (Blumenstyk 2000, A44).

U.S.–based but transnationally oriented networked education businesses are typically supported at both the supply and demand ends by major corporations: they are overwhelmingly vocational in orientation. Cenquest, for instance, is an e-commerce–based education provider "rapidly bringing the world of higher education into line" with the "new paradigm" of internationalization that "the information technology revolution" has wrought. A fusion of business, technology, and university partners, Cenquest delivers industry-specific content on "hot topics" that are "validated and accredited"—the company is careful not to say that courses are *created* or *taught*—by "respected university partners." Cenquest has formed an alliance with Monterrey Technology Institute in Mexico, Adelaide University in Australia, and the University of Texas at Austin (UT–Austin) that will deliver to students in Mexico and Australia coveted courses in American business education. Local faculty will teach course materials coproduced by UT–Austin faculty and Cenquest, as course materials are wrenched farther apart from instruction.[12] The CEO of Cenquest sees the partnership as "proof that our e-commerce education model works" and demonstrates "the growing international interest in gaining access to American graduate business content" ("Cenquest

First to Serve International Demand for e-Learning" 2000). And what is driving this interest is demand from transnational corporations (TNCs) with activities in dozens of countries, which possess a need—as in Mexico—for suitably trained managers, technicians, and professionals.

To break themselves of reputedly "medieval" habits, in turn, institutions of higher education in the United States and elsewhere are being advised that they "cannot continue to draw boundaries around themselves and say, 'We are the only legitimate players in the higher education business'" (Blustain, Goldstein, and Lozier 1998).[13] Responding to repeated warnings from business-oriented groups concerning the ostensible "failure in the educational community to reform itself and adjust to the new demands of the economy" (Global Information Infrastructure Committee [GIIC] 1998), conventional universities throughout the United States have jumped on the for-profit bandwagon—not least, via strategic alliances to provide courses in different fields with companies like unext.com (see Confessore 1999, 26).[14] Columbia University, for example, saw in unext.com a strategy "to use the hundreds of years of intellectual capital that has grown up at the university." What kind of price tag does access to this "intellectual capital" command? For the course materials it develops to sell to TNCs through unext.com, Columbia is guaranteed a minimum of $20 million in royalties over five years. Columbia also retains the right to trade royalties for equity in the company when the latter makes its initial public offering (McGeehan 1999, C1). A Stanford University administrator suggests the tantalizing allure of these new arrangements: "The idea that all of this content—we used to call it teaching and learning—can be turned into content with an economic value is extraordinary" (Woody 1999).

This is not the only commercial Web venture in which Columbia is involved. Elsewhere on campus, the university began a for-profit Web initiative to market itself internationally with several other elite institutions—that is, recognized "brands" in higher education and culture, including the British Library, Cambridge University Press, the London School of Economics and Political Science, the New York Public Library, and the Smithsonian Institution's National Museum of Natural History. The intent is ostensibly to "transplant into cyberspace the intellectual milieu of academe," but financial allurements are driving the process (Carr and Kiernan 2000, A59). The site, called fathom.com, lays bare the ways network technologies are being used to reorganize institutions of higher education. According to the CEO of fathom.com—a Columbia faculty member—the university chose to launch the project as a commercial website so that it would be "a nimble, entrepreneurial organization" capable of surviving in the high-speed and cutthroat competition of cyberspace. "I was talking to a professor at Harvard," chimes in an on-line education company CEO, "and I was pushing the concept of online learning. She said, 'We're scholars. We're supposed to move slow.' I told her, 'We're the Internet. We have to move fast'" (Berinato 1999). This for-profit status all but requires the adoption of a peremptory stance toward traditional policies of university self-governance and academic freedom. Faculty, with their faculty unions and professional paradigms, consultants allege, "inhibit, to one degree or another, an institution's ability to be proactive" in the new commercial environment (Blustain, Goldstein, and Lozier 1998, 17). Networked education, declares the CEO of hungryminds.com, is "the ultimate in capitalism. We don't care about tenured professors or teachers' unions. Our focus is on the customer" (Berinato 1999).

Lining up to help universities quickly get on-line are education "portals"—websites that function as a kind of "Yellow Pages" of on-line education—some of them, once again, developed by university faculty. Portal companies comprise a significant marketing arm of the for-profit networked education complex. The CEO of embark.com emphasizes to administrators, "now the fact of the matter is that if you don't market it correctly," the strengths of your on-line program and the faculty do not matter (Carr 2000a, A57). Another portal, hungryminds.com, benefits from an exclusive education link on Yahoo! Incorporated's website, and in turn is the most prominent advertiser on Yahoo!'s education pages. The partnership encompasses a variety of university and college partners, who pay for listings on hungryminds.com's website: University of California at Berkeley Extension Office, University of Maryland University College, Jones International University, Rensselaer Polytechnic Institute, Rochester Institute of Technology, Western Governors University, and the UOP. University on-line programs are listed alongside how-to courses, for example, those offered by ehow.com, courses by publishers such as Rodale Press and Princeton Review, and the Public Broadcasting System. "The easy way to think about it," says the company's CEO about the venture's hoped-for economies of scale and scope, "if we get about the same amount of money from each of the 40 partners, then we have about 40 times the marketing money that any one brand does" (Berinato 1999).

TNC employees stand to gain ready on-line access to prestigious U.S. programs through unext.com and other on-line companies. Though Harvard Business School (HBS) opted out of the unext.com dealings for a different on-line venture, its dean recognizes the school has a profitable role to play in "an era where organizations are much more fluid, the pace of change is much faster and much more international," rendering employees in need of "just-in-time, just-right education" (Woody 1999). International Business Machines (IBM)—which provides the software platform for unext.com's course delivery—will pilot the first on-line program with thirty employees. Crucially, with IBM as a technology partner, unext.com benefits from the help of IBM Lotus Development Corporation's salesforce to pitch unext.com products to its corporate clients internationally. "When we go in on a sales call and talk to a customer," beams a Lotus manager, "we will be able to register a company for a UNext course" (McGeehan 1999, C1). Plans for the future include creating its own accredited MBA–granting virtual university, called

Cardean University, named for the Roman goddess who, a press release tells us, had the power to "open what is shut and shut what is open" (Guernsey 1999, D1). Could the metaphor be meant to suggest throwing the doors of the university wide open to corporatization and slamming the door on publicly provided education?

Competing with unext.com in the international corporate education market is Pensare, a Silicon Valley company that offers stock warrants to universities in exchange for courses. Pensare sells "knowledge communities" to corporations with content from "world-class" business schools at Harvard, Wharton, Duke, and the University of Southern California. Also contributing to the "knowledge communities" are consultants, seminar providers, technology partners, and financial partners, including General Electric (GE) Equity, Media Technology Ventures, Associated Venture Investors, and Battery Ventures. "Thought leaders" from these universities—the company avoids calling them faculty—contribute to content production alongside a cast of motivational speakers and celebrity consultants.

Pensare signed a multiyear agreement with Harvard Business School Publishing (HBSP) to jointly produce on-line business courses to sell to corporations. HBSP provides the content (based largely on the research of HBS professors) for "performance courses" and Pensare the platform, instructional, and software design ("Pensare and Harvard Business School Publishing" 1998). Initially, HBSP committed six courses, from which it will receive royalties on the courses sold by Pensare. Subjected to the school's famed case study methodology, the deal was assessed favorably by faculty and students. "People worried about the brand, the diversion of resources, whether this would take the school down-market." But "people recognized that this is a very powerful technology and a good opportunity" (Woody 1999).

With Pensare, Duke's Fuqua School of Business will sell not only courses, but also its entire MBA program. Pensare won exclusive distribution rights to the jointly produced Global Executive program that it will resell to international corporate customers. Pensare will also sell the MBA program to other business schools, creating something similar to Duke franchises. The partners expect "the Duke brand and business curriculum to resonate with major corporations on several levels." In the past, Fuqua's corporate education courses have resonated favorably with such global corporations as Deutsche Bank, Siemens AG, and Ford Motor Corporation ("Pensare Announces Partnership" 1999).

A formidable newcomer to the "fast-growing international market for higher education and advanced training" with whom unext.com and Pensare will have to contend is Universitas 21, a British company originally to be led by media magnate Rupert Murdoch. With Universitas 21, Murdoch planned to enter into the "provision of a pre-eminent brand for educational services," garnered from a network of eighteen prestigious universities in ten countries in Asia, Australia, Europe, Canada, and the United States, and created to "leverage the reputation, resources and experience of its members on behalf of corporate partners."[15] Murdoch stated that the company would offer custom-designed academic programs over the Internet to college graduates who were already employed. Universitas 21, he explained, "has taken a strategic decision to enter the distance-learning market using our global distribution platforms, our advanced technologies, and our marketing reach. A mutually profitable partnership between leading providers in higher education and one of the world's leading media companies is a very strong proposition" (Maslen 2000b, A47). Collectively, Universitas 21 members enroll roughly five hundred thousand students yearly and employ about forty-four thousand academics and researchers. Combined, they deliver "international curricula" and "credentials that are internationally portable" to enhance graduates' positions in a "global professional workforce."[16] "We don't think the individual campus brands or the old-fashioned forms of pedagogy and their adaptation to distance education from face-to-face teaching is the way e-education will go," declared Alan Gilbert, the chairman of Universitas 21. "Nor do we think the individual university brand is any longer the most potent in the global market. A U.S. university brand, for example, would look somewhat imperialistic if offered in China." Graduates of Universitas 21 would receive a diploma issued by the consortium and carrying the names and logos of the eighteen member universities: "Properly branded, advertised, and promoted, it will be hugely powerful, much more so than any individual university trying to franchise its brand around the world" (Maslen 2000b, A47). Ultimately, Murdoch abandoned the venture, which quickly sought to forge ties with a different media corporation (Maslen 2000a, A53).

Corporate education suppliers are working to redefine education as a "private good" benefiting the "student/consumer" rather than a "public service" benefiting society.[17] It is a crucial but widely unknown fact that this is exactly the definition of education that NAFTA itself instances. Within the conditions set by NAFTA, higher education is among the nearly nine thousand categories of goods and services produced and sold in North America targeted to be free of all tariffs by 2008. Under this agreement, professors, administrators, and trainers receive most-favored-nation treatment. In turn, the education sector is moving to the center of the larger campaign to liberalize free trade in services.

Across the U.S.–Mexico border, we may glimpse what a market-oriented education industry geared toward the labor demands of TNCs offers in place of public higher education.

CROSS-BORDER LABOR MARKETS AS AN EDUCATIONAL NEXUS

Visions of cross-border education are igniting a variety of initiatives and experiments to close the gap between the university and the workplace. Corporate models and labor-market needs are strikingly dominant in these attempts. World Bank priorities in education for the Latin American region, for example, are now to "strengthen the integral role of the private sector in finance and delivery" of education, specifically via network technology (World Bank 1999b, 50–51). The rationale for this approach is worth noting.

A leading weakness of Latin American and Caribbean countries, claims the World Bank, "is a lack of human capital that has severely limited their capacity to do research and to introduce technological innovations." Whether these less-developed countries will succeed in the arena of international market competition thus "will depend on how rapidly they are able to diversify their economies, upgrade the skills of the existing workforce, and prepare children to adjust to changing economic circumstances when they enter the world of work" (1999b, 14–15).

The World Bank's education sector manager for the Latin American and Caribbean region issued a challenge to universities to respond to "radical changes in training needs." Specifically cited in this context was "the growing attractiveness" to TNCs "of university degrees with an international application." In a global economy, the World Bank's analyst continues, "where firms produce for overseas markets and compete with foreign firms in their own domestic markets, there is a rising demand for internationally recognized qualifications, especially in management-related fields" (Salmi 2000, 8).[18] Conventional educational institutions, in contrast, are invariably said to be inadequate to the task at hand. Another organization, the so-called Global Information Infrastructure Committee (GIIC), established the Task Force on Education in the Information Age to address the alleged inefficiencies of higher education that "will end up producing a workforce that is not suited to the global economy" (GIIC 1998).

In keeping with this emphasis on TNCs' labor market needs is a shift toward adult, as opposed to youth, education:

> Training is becoming an integral part of one's working life, happening in different contexts: on the job, in specialized higher education institutions, or even at home. This means that, in the medium term, the primary clientele of universities will no more be young high school graduates. Universities will have to organize themselves to accommodate the learning and training needs of a very diverse clientele: working students, mature students, part-time students, day students, night students, weekend students, etc. (Salmi 2000, 8)

Overall, as we have already observed, the call is to suffuse a new vocationalism throughout educational provision.

The Consortium for North American Higher Education Collaboration (CONAHEC) recently published a working paper promoting "the greater integration of higher education in North America" to "assist us in shifting NAFTA from what has been largely an economic trade partnership to encompass all areas that are critical to our societies' development and prosperity, particularly

education" (León-Garcia, Matthews, and Smith 1999, 1). CONAHEC emphasizes that "[w]hat is now needed is international academic integration. Academic integration includes such initiatives as the joint development of courses
and programs, shared faculty appointments, multinational student cohort-
based programs, and international delivery via distance education technologies" (1).[19]

Students and teachers have been studying and teaching abroad for
decades (disproportionately in the developed market economies of the
United States and western Europe). Cross-border education, however, no
longer simply refers to such traditional international education programs.
Mexico's educational leaders, for example, are "preaching the need to integrate more closely with NAFTA countries—which means stretching beyond
study-abroad programs" (Rymer-Zavela 1999, 3).

What this stretch entails, according to CONAHEC's president, is redefining
the mission of higher education to "prepare global citizens." "In North America," CONAHEC asserts, "it should be imperative to take advantage of information technology to move educational resources between institutions and
countries and promote academic integration. Use of technology is probably
the only way to assure that the internationalization of higher education is not
limited to just the participants in international exchanges" (Léon-Garcia,
Matthews, and Smith 1999, 12). This high-toned civic language notwithstanding, the overall effort under way turns on development and cross-
border distribution of work-related courses and programs.

At a recent CONAHEC–sponsored conference on NAFTA and higher education, a participating American Telephone and Telegraph executive stated
unambiguously that "[t]he theoretical mission of academics is to provide human resources to society, in this case business, where, how and when it is
needed" (Jamar 1998, 12). The express subordination of postsecondary education to labor market needs, and the vocationalism that is its hallmark, are
apparent at universities across North America and elsewhere, in partnerships
that involve many powerful TNCs. A survey of 247 higher education institutions from both public and private sectors in Mexico demonstrates a sharp
increase in corporate-university linkages. In 1994, according to the study,
2,560 such partnerships were operating within these institutions; by 1996 the
number of linkages nearly doubled to 4,861 (Williams 1997, 10).

Vocational university-to-university linkages are also proliferating. The Program for North American Mobility in Higher Education "is a grant competition run cooperatively by the governments of the United States, Canada, and
Mexico."[20] Each year, the program awards numerous multiyear grants in the
$200,000 range. Technology for Industry through Mobility in Educational
Sectors, for example, links Austin Community College in the United States
with St. Clair College in Canada and the Universidad Tecnológica de
Coahuila in Mexico in a bid to establish cross-border exchanges "that will
prepare students for technical jobs in high demand within the NAFTA coun-

tries." The Alliance for North American Mobility in Engineering joins North Dakota State University with the University of Manitoba and the Universidad Autónoma de Zacatecas in "preparing technically trained professionals, particularly engineers, who have a sound appreciation of the specific norms and business cultures of the three countries." The North American Consortium on Legal Education partners the University of Houston, the University of Ottawa, and the Instituto de Investigaciones Jurísticas "to increas[e] the capabilities of each member institution to provide quality legal education to meet the current and future demands of the legal profession in North America." All told, through mid-2000 the program had funded a total of thirty consortia involving no less than two hundred higher education institutions and related nonprofit organizations throughout the three countries.[21]

For proponents of academic integration, distance education holds up especially alluring possibilities within fields serviceable to TNCs, including management, engineering, information technology training, and English-language instruction. It thereby accentuates forms of vocational education that are aimed at middle-class strata. Even as nonprofit educational institutions whose students are drawn from every social stratum continue to be placed on starvation budgets, the human resource needs of TNCs are generating strong demand for new means of producing an appropriately skilled, highly mobile labor force drawn overwhelmingly from the privileged classes.

The Ibero-American Science and Technology Education Consortium (ISTEC), with support from the Organization of American States and the Inter-American Development Bank, resulted from a meeting between government, education, and industry members sponsored by the University of New Mexico in 1990. ISTEC is "a vehicle for educational enhancement" created to "open up avenues for transnational research and development, provide a mechanism for technology transfer, and improve international relations" (Martinez 1998). Beginning with a group of fifteen educational and industry members from just seven countries, by 1998 ISTEC had upwards of seventy-five research, industrial, and academic institutional members from seventeen countries. According to its director, a University of New Mexico faculty member, the project is shaped by the view that "Information technologies effectively reduce global time and distances, thus facilitating the exchange of products and services. In addition, the elimination of international trade barriers greatly helps global trade and commerce" (Martinez 1998).

ISTEC initiatives aim to eliminate international barriers to the flow of education products and services, barriers such as different course credit requirements among participating institutions. Under the Advanced Continuing Education initiative, ISTEC offers a "Sandwich Ph.D.," a nontraditional program in which course work at the home university is followed by "an appropriate period" of residence at a "specialization site"—industry site—purportedly to gain a broader research scope. The Advanced Continuing Education initiative has been ISTEC's early priority, producing educational content for compact disc–read-only memory and video delivery, and through the Internet—products and services that under NAFTA will be treated as any other kind of commodity for trade. In the future, ISTEC plans to become its own virtual university with degree accreditation.

ISTEC not only connects universities with industry partners who help make up for budget shortfalls on campus, it also gives industry direct access to educational resources to build up their training programs. Participation in ISTEC connects national and transnational companies to resources that can "enhance their presence in Latin American markets and tap into the enormous potential of human resources" in the region.[22] Striving toward this goal compels considerable expenditures. Between 1997 and 1998, information training and technology services in Latin America grew by 14.8 percent to $8.45 billion. And, according to the International Data Corporation, the regional market for technology training is expected to double by 2002. Thus, ISTEC promises to corporations "access to a network of highly skilled leading international professionals, conduits for intellectual creativity, and avenues for market development." The neoliberal market logic NAFTA helped construct is this: "If industry leaders continue to provide the necessary resources to universities, students will be better educated, and industry will gain an invaluable source for knowledgeable employees, creative minds, and new business opportunities."[23]

The director of ISTEC characterizes the consortium-led collaborations as more horizontal—between Latin American institutions—than vertical—between Latin American and U.S. or Canadian institutions. However, some of the organization's largest initiatives involve powerful TNCs operating in the Latin America region. Through ISTEC, in 1999, Motorola Incorporated, the largest producer of embedded processors, granted member Latin American universities licenses for its microprocessor core, and the Semiconductor Reuse Standards the company has developed. In March 2000, Synopsys Incorporated joined the deal, contributing approximately $25 million worth of licenses for its Electronic Design Automation Software. While the collaboration purports to give students "access to technologies used in the development of the newest electronic products in the world," the motor behind the collaboration is that it gives both companies direct access to the skilled labor force to perpetuate its great presence and competitive advantage in the region.[24]

In March 2000, both Motorola and Synopsys expanded their participation in ISTEC with new grants worth millions, involving sixty-four Latin American, U.S., and European universities. "For Motorola," concluded the president of Motorola's operations in Mexico, "this licensing represents a major step forward in enrolling Latin America in the global society of knowledge." It also, clearly, constituted an enormous step in enlisting the participation of greater numbers of universities in the training and preparation of a labor force on which Motorola and Synopsys can depend. Combined, the deals weave a widening web of direct university participation in leveraging the corporations' growth in eighteen different countries ("Motorola Extends Digital DNA Technology to Benefit 64 Universities" 2000).

There exist many kinds of cross-border collaborations, of course, some of them no doubt animated by humane visions. However, the driving force behind most such collaborations is TNC capital, which exploits a manipulated fiscal crisis to pursue its objectives. With public funding cutbacks throughout North America, more and more universities on both sides of the U.S.–Mexico border have embraced deals that put university programs directly at the service of industry. Consider the Partners for the Advancement of CAD/CAM/CAE Education (PACE).[25] PACE began as a joint venture among General Motors (GM), Unigraphics Solutions Incorporated, Sun Microsystems, and Electronic Data Systems Corporation (EDS), to beef up engineering education at North American academic institutions with pooled hardware, software, and technical resources valued at $190 million. While engineering education has been at the forefront of vocational, market-based education for some time, what is important here is the extension of educational exchange across national borders as the automobile industry seized hold of Mexico as a low-wage manufacturing platform from which to export cars back into the vast U.S. market.

"Our objective is to help set the 'pace' in the computer-aided engineering curriculum of our primary academic partners to ensure future engineers have the education and experience with relevant industry-leading technology," claims a GM executive. The operative word here is "relevant"—meaning technology owned by and crucial to the participating corporate partners. This deal does more than set the "pace" in the curriculum—according to partnership criteria for universities, it *defines* the curriculum. Michigan State University (MSU), in GM's onetime home state, was the first university to receive a PACE grant—a $30 million gift-in-kind, the largest ever received by the university. MSU meets criteria set by the corporate sponsors, which include a willingness to commit to a "long-term relationship with General Motors as a primary educational partner; strong product development and manufacturing curricula; adequate infrastructure of facilities; [and] maintenance systems and personnel to support the donated hardware and software." Two criteria merit special attention: "a willingness to integrate Unigraphics software into the engineering curricula" and a "dedication to providing distance learning to students at GM facilities around the globe." In exchange for technology and software, the university handed over the design of curricula to GM and Unigraphics so that courses directly teach toward industry needs, reducing what is "relevant" to engineering curriculum to specific skills related to the companies' proprietary technology. The key here is that the curriculum is designed not only for MSU engineering undergraduates, but for the training and retraining of current GM employees.

In 2000–2001, the PACE consortium expected to bring into its fold forty institutions throughout the United States, Mexico, and Canada. In Mexico, PACE gained a foothold in two institutions with long track records in developing and using distance-learning technology: the Instituto Politécnico Nacional and the Escuela Superior de Ingeniería Mecánica y Eléctrica (IPN–ESIME) and the Instituto Tecnológico y de Estudios Superiores de Monterrey campus at Toluca (ITESM–Toluca). Each received $14 million (140 million pesos) in equipment, software, and technical support. With software from Unigraphics, hardware from EDS, and technical support from Sun, the work of coordinating the project and providing assistance and training is left to GM—not the universities ("GM y socios donan US $28 millones al IPN y al ITESM" 2000). With its new partners in Mexico, the extensive consortium is now a force for integrating—through the use of network technology and teleconferencing—some of the best universities in North America with some of the most powerful TNCs operating on the continent. Crucially, the purpose of this integration is both to produce in undergraduates "engineers who can hit the ground running" and to provide globalized distance learning courses to keep GM employees around the world running throughout their careers.[26]

ITESM is a twenty-six-campus university system founded in 1943 by Mexican businessmen to cater to industry's needs with a technical education based on the model of Massachusetts Institute of Technology. Its educational priorities express the concerns and interests of what James D. Cockroft calls "the intermediate classes: the administrative and technocratic agents of capital and the state"; that is, a group that experienced itself as "a technocracy opposed to labor and enamored of bourgeois and foreign values," and which "increasingly came to define the continued presence of TNC techniques of distribution, exchange, and education, as being in [its] own class interests" (1998, 225).

While transnational-oriented education took root in ITESM in the 1950s, it has been solidified in the present. The director of ITESM's career placement office, Gerardo Salazar, notes that "some two dozen U.S. companies—including the likes of Microsoft Corp. and Texas Instruments Inc.—send recruiters to the school's annual fall career fair and year-round on-campus recruiting sessions" (quoted in MacDonald 1999, 20). ITESM graduates also operate the "complex global communications networks" of such large manufacturers as Cooper Industries and Ford Motor Company. ITESM "has sent scores of graduates north of the border to take high-paying jobs in software firms and large corporations in Boston, Chicago, Dallas, San Francisco and several other U.S. cities in the last few years," according to Salazar (20).

Indeed, ITESM comprises a spearhead of the ongoing reorganization of higher education that we have examined.[27] Unlike traditional universities in Latin America, hampered by what the World Bank terms "institutional inflexibility" (here the World Bank's analyst gives special mention to UNAM), ITESM is among the many corporate-oriented universities that are able "to react swiftly to establishing new programs, reconfiguring existing ones, and eliminating outdated programs without being hampered by bureaucratic regulations and obstacles" (Salmi 2000, 8).[28] ITESM also enacts the World Bank's priorities to promote network technology and has been a leader in the region with its own virtual university since 1989.

ITESM's distance-learning library includes 91 programs for undergraduate and master's levels, 327 faculty development programs, 129 programs for public administrators, and 1,010 virtual business programs. Its corporate-oriented education is matched by a vast distance-learning apparatus. ITESM's distance-learning infrastructure includes 114 transmitting sites for satellite and video delivery via a satellite television network managed by two uplinks in Monterrey and Mexico City, six channels provided through the *Satmex 5* satellite, and an additional shared satellite on a digital broadcast system. Downlinks to 1,457 receiving sites deliver ITESM's content across Mexico and throughout Latin America (Wolff 1999). Might ITESM's facilities not offer an ideal infrastructure for PACE—that is, the previously discussed cross-border partnership to deliver virtual training to GM employees throughout the Americas? Might the new-model educational programs tested in the NAFTA region soon be extended, to encompass much of the Spanish-speaking world?

It is, assuredly, its service to labor market demands through network technology that has led World Bank analysts to single out ITESM as a model institution, "especially considering the advent of NAFTA and Mexico's desire to compete internationally, which means that firms need to change the profile of their employees" (Wolff 1999). In fact, ITESM was "discovered" by U.S. corporate executives in the mid-1990s (MacDonald 1999, 20). In 1999, ITESM began a joint venture with Thunderbird, a private U.S.–based graduate school of international management, to offer the Master's of International Management in Latin America (MIMLA). MIMLA is essentially Thunderbird's popular and pricey master's degree in international management repackaged with a Latin American focus to appeal to transnationals operating in the region. In Mexico, MIMLA students come from companies such as IBM, Kraft Foods, Hewlett-Packard, Cisco Systems, Texas Instruments, Coca-Cola, GM, GE, Proctor and Gamble Mexico, Citibank, and many others.[29]

The ascending model of educational provision is replacing liberal arts education for all social classes with vocational skills, training, and values developed to prepare select students for careers in the production and sales systems of TNCs. The very forces hammering away at UNAM and imposing market-oriented structures on public universities thus also help to establish what the World Bank praises as "entrepreneurial university leaders," such as ITESM (Salmi 2000, 8). The contrast between UNAM and ITESM indeed brings the crisis in North American education into full view. On one side, we see a generalized attack on the right of public access to higher education. On the other, is an already-massive, U.S.–based, for-profit networked educational complex, shaped mainly in response to demands from TNCs for a more vocational curriculum. As events at UNAM and elsewhere suggest, however, the reorganization of educational provision is likely to remain a conflicted process.

NOTES

Unless noted otherwise, all dollar amounts are in U.S. currency.

1. It should be noted that the World Bank was not alone in identifying a crisis in higher education in countries around the world. In the same year, the UN Educational, Scientific, and Cultural Organization (UNESCO) published its own policy paper on higher education concerned with the "crisis in all countries of the world" in which "enrollments continue to grow but public funding diminishes; and the gap between the developed and developing countries continues to widen in the higher education sector." While the UNESCO document urged higher education to "reformulate its mission" and "develop new perspectives" and "priorities for the future," the document did not question higher education's status as a public good and cautioned against the deleterious effects of unbridled commercialism (see Kent 1995; 1996, 3–5; the original document is UNESCO 1994).

2. The World Bank ultimately elevated "knowledge for development" into its guiding policy: underdevelopment, the bank held in 1999, could be mainly attributed to so-called knowledge gaps and information problems—which in turn could and should be alleviated by innovating new network technologies and acceding to additional privatization and deregulation measures, not least, within education itself (World Bank 1999a).

3. Commercialization throughout public higher education worldwide is rapidly accelerating. For a selection of recent developments, see "Report from the Conference on Globalization and the University" (1999), Johnstone (1998, 10–11), Schiller (1999), Overland (2000, A48–A49), Cohen (2000, A50), and Bain (2000, 11–12).

4. Inter-American Development Bank statistics show that the poorest 30 percent of Mexican students attend school for only three years. On average, according to the Mexican government, Mexicans attend classes for eight years. Moreover, the class schedule affords just four hours of daily instruction (Dillon 2000, A3).

5. SEP–ANUIES 1993. The Mexican federal education budget for 2000 was $23.7 billion (Dillon 2000, A3).

6. In Uruguay, in comparison, federal spending on higher education constitutes 0.59 percent of the GDP. The Universidad de la República (UR), a public university, was the only university in the country until 1985, when a new crop of private institutions began to emerge. Today, the UR competes with these institutions but still enrolls the bulk of the nation's students—sixty thousand. Funded entirely by the state, the UR has always operated without tuition and without admissions restrictions, an open access policy that extended to all areas of study and research, including its medical school. Today, "salary levels are extremely low, and competition from the private sector and from abroad transform into a Sisyphean labor the effort to build up teaching and research infrastructures and staff." The effort is made more burdensome by recent government demands that the UR must do more to sell "knowledge services" to generate income. "This is easier said than done," two faculty note, since the country invests 0.25 percent of its GDP on research and development, "and neither the state nor private enterprises have generated a strong demand for domestically created or applied knowledge" (Arocena and Sutz 2000, 14–15).

7. The commanding role of private institutions is visible elsewhere in Latin America. In Brazil, Chile, and Colombia, more than 50 percent of students are enrolled in private universities (Gentili 2000, 14–15). In Peru, neoliberal reforms driven by Alberto Keinya Fujimori's government abdicated the state's role entirely to the private

sector. Between 1991 and 1997, twelve new universities were created—all of them private (Degregori and Molero 2000, 30).

8. Kent outlines the experiences of three public universities wrestling with near collapse under these multiple pressures.

9. At the University of Puebla, for example, after hiring the College Entrance Examination Board to administer entrance exams to all students, the university canceled its open admissions policy. In 1994, eight thousand of nineteen thousand applicants were denied a place in the university (Kent 1999, 12–13).

10. It has been aptly observed that "the struggle to keep the City University of New York easily accessible to lower-income students and recent migrants in the face of the onslaught of the Republican municipal administration of Rudy Giuliani is not dissimilar to the battles being waged from Mexico to Chile to keep public higher education open to all who desire to study at the university level" (NACLA 2000, 11).

11. "Students began the strike to stop what they saw as a conversion of constitutionally guaranteed citizen's rights into a class privilege combined with public assistance and charity" (Navarro 2000, 20).

12. On the paring apart of "content" from instruction, see Noble (1998).

13. Reprinted from Katz and Associates (1998).

14. Some universities are using their for-profit subsidiaries to get into the international high school education market. At the University of Nebraska, a for-profit subsidiary called class.com was spun off by a faculty member and is now being used to market and sell distance-education courses to high schools internationally. In a deal with edunexo.com, an educational portal focusing on Latin America and Spain, edunexo.com will advertise class.com products free of charge in exchange for a commission on every student who enrolls in class.com courses after visiting the website. But class.com is not just looking to advertise. It aims to create a whole virtual high school abroad. "We will do it tomorrow if we can find a partner." Students in Mexico, Brazil, Argentina, and Spain who enroll in the courses will take them in English and pay regular tuition rates, like their counterparts in the United States. The deal is similar to Stanford's partnership with nexted.com, which sells courses to gifted high school students in Australia and Asia. The company is aggressively targeting the international student population, especially in Asia, where, according to the nexted.com president, "services may be as important" to students as "brand names" (Carr 2000b, A49).

15. <http://www.universitas.edu.au/> [last accessed: 19 February 2001].

16. <http://www.universitas.edu.au/>.

17. On this shift, see Altbach (1998).

18. In the interests of academic integration in the wake of NAFTA, Mexican university administrators are pushing to establish standards comparable to those in the United States and Canada to promote the mobility of graduates across labor markets.

19. Other initiatives underwritten by the U.S. Department of Education are aimed at these goals, specifically within the NAFTA context. See <http://www.ed.gov/offices/OPE/FIPSE/northam> [last accessed: 19 February 2001].

20. The North American Regional Academic Mobility Plan was created by the U.S. Department of Education's Fund for the Improvement of Postsecondary Education (whose director has previously stated the mission of universities should be to serve student consumers by providing an education that guarantees a job) to integrate the different priorities of each country (Desruissex 1994).

21. <http://www.ed.gov/offices/OPE/FIPSE/northam/2000projects.html>.

22. <http://www.istec.org> [last accessed: 19 February 2001].

23. <http://www.istec.org>. What resources are corporations providing to ISTEC university partners? Nortel Networks directs a Multicom-21 project creating on various campuses "synergetic virtual centers of telecommunications for research, education, and service"; Motorola Incorporated partnered with the Universidade de São Paulo, Brazil, to "create virtual design centers." See the ISTEC website for details on the scope and nature of these partnerships.

24. <http://www.istec.org>.

25. The acronyms stand for computer-assisted design; computer-assisted manufacturing; and computer-assisted engineering.

26. Details on PACE come from company press releases posted on the websites of Unigraphics: <http://www.ug.eds.com/news/> [last accessed: 19 February 2001]; and Sun: <http://www.sun.com/media/> [last accessed: 19 February 2001].

27. Other spearheads, however, also are apparent. Sylvan Learning Centers, a U.S.–based provider of education services, purchased a controlling interest in the fourteen-campus Universidad del Valle de México for $50 million in December 2000. Meanwhile, Apollo International (owner of the University of Phoenix) also expects to announce a venture in Mexico, aiming exclusively at the upper middle class: "we are going after 5 percent of the market," declares the venture's CEO (Leovy 2001, A4).

28. Another example of institutional flexibility and willingness to change highlighted in this World Bank article is the University of South Florida at Tampa, a public university, where the engineering department offers a five-year warranty "just like the traditional warranty against manufacturing defects, which comes with any consumer good." The warranty provides that "if at any time during the five years immediately following graduation an alumnus/a is required to apply skills in his/her work but had not received the requisite training during university studies, he or she can re-enroll at the university to acquire these skills free of charge." The World Bank suggests universities could extend this logic by selling "training for life" packages; "under such a scheme new students would sign up and pay for not only their initial professional education, but also for all the retraining periods which they would require throughout their professional career" (Salmi 2000, 8).

29. "Thunderbird has established new, innovative means for business students and professionals overseas to earn the world's most prestigious international business degree." ("129 Latin American Executives" 1999).

REFERENCES

Altbach, P. 1998. "Private Higher Education: Themes and Variations in Comparative Perspective." *International Higher Education* 10 (Winter). <http://www.bc.edu/bc_org/arp/soe/cihe/newsletter/News10/text1.html> [last accessed: 19 February 2001].

Arocena, R., and J. Sutz. 2000. "Challenges for Public Higher Education in Uruguay." *International Higher Education* 19 (Spring): 14–15. <http://www.bc.edu/bc_org/aup/soe/clhe/newsletter/News19/text9.html> [last accessed: 19 February 2001].

Bain, O. 2000. "Public Higher Education and Tuition: The Russian Case." *International Higher Education* 18 (Winter): 11–12.

Berinato, S. 1999. "Coming after You." *University Business*, 20 March, <http://www.universitybusiness.com/0003/hungry.html> [last accessed: 19 February 2001].

Blumenstyk, G. 2000. "Company that Owns the U. of Phoenix Plans for a Major Foreign Expansion." *Chronicle of Higher Education*, 11 August, A44.

Blustain, H., P. Goldstein, and G. Lozier. 1998. "Assessing the New Competitive Landscape." *CAUSE/EFFECT* 2, <http://www.educause.edu/ir/library/html/cem9834.html> [last accessed: 19 February 2001].

Carr, S. 2000a. "Online Learning's Yellow Pages are Bracing for a Shakeout." *Chronicle of Higher Education*, 14 April, A57.

———. 2000b. "Online High-School Programs Plan to Market Courses Internationally." *Chronicle of Higher Education*, 5 May, A49.

Carr, S., and V. Kiernan. 2000. "A For-profit Web Venture Seeks to Replicate the University Experience Online." *Chronicle of Higher Education*, 3 April, A59.

"Cenquest First to Serve International Demand for e-Learning." 2000. *BusinessWire*, 23 March, <http://www.businesswire.com> [last accessed: 19 February 2001].

Cockroft, J. D. 1998. *Mexico's Hope*. New York: Monthly Review.

Cohen, D. 2000. "Hong Kong's Boom in Distance Education May Be a Sign of What's to Come in Asia." *Chronicle of Higher Education*, 14 July, A50.

Confessore, N. 1999. "The Virtual University." *New Republic*, 4 October, p. 26.

Consortium for North American Higher Education Collaboration. 2000. Request for Proposals, North American Higher Education Conference, <http://conahec.org> [last accessed: 19 February 2001].

Degregori, C., and J. Avila Molero. 2000. "The Decline of the Social Sciences in Peru." *NACLA Report on the Americas* 32 (4) (January–February): 30.

Desruissex, P. 1994. "Promoting Collaboration in North America: Educators Step up Calls for Joint Ventures in Canada, Mexico, and the United States." *Chronicle of Higher Education*, 15 June, <http://www.chronicle.com/che-data/articles.dir/articles-40.dir/issue-41.dir/41a03601.htm> [last accessed: 19 February 2001].

Dillon, S. 2000. "Mexican Election Spotlights Ailing School System." *New York Times*, 20 April, A3.

Education International and Public Service International. 1999. "The WTO and the Millennium Round: What Is at Stake for Public Education?" <http:www.ei-ie.org/educ/english/eedqd2_may99.html> [last accessed: 19 February 2001].

Friedman, T. 1999. "Next It's E-ducation." *New York Times*, 17 November.

Gentili, P. 2000. "The Permanent Crisis of the Public University." *NACLA Report on the Americas* 32 (4) (January–February): 14–15.

Global Information Infrastructure Committee. 1998. "Discussion Report of the GIIC Education Committee Consultations with International Experts." Washington, D.C., June 25, <http://www.giic.org/pubs> [last accessed: 19 February 2001].

"GM y Socios Donan US $28 millones al IPN al ITESM." 2000. *El Economista Internet*, 6 March, <http://www.economista.com.mx> [last accessed: 19 February 2001].

Guernsey, L. 1999. "Click Here for the Ivory Tower: A Start-up Enlists School for Online Learning and Raises Eyebrows." *New York Times*, 2 September, D1.

Jackson, G. 2000. "University of Phoenix: A New Mode for Tertiary Education in Developing Countries?" *TechKnowLogia* (January–February): 34, <http://www.techknowlogia.org> [last accessed: 19 February 2001].

Jamar, C. 1998. "A Learning Curve." *US/Mexico Business* (January): 12.

Johnstone, D. 1998. *The Financing and Management of Higher Education: A Status Report on Worldwide Reforms*. Washington, D.C.: World Bank.

Katz, R., and Associates. 1998. *Dancing with the Devil: Information Technology and the New Competition in Higher Education.* San Francisco: Jossey-Bass.

Kent, R. 1995. "Two Positions in the International Debate about Higher Education: The World Bank and UNESCO." Paper presented for the Latin American Studies Association, Washington, D.C., September 28–30, <http://www.lanic.utexas.edu/project/lasa95/kent.html> [last accessed: 19 February 2001].

——. 1996. "The World Bank and UNESCO on Higher Education." *International Higher Education* 4 (Spring): 3–5.

——. 1998. "Institutional Reform in Mexican Higher Education: Conflict and Renewal in Three Public Universities." Inter-American Development Bank Paper No. EDU-102. Washington, D.C.

——. 1999. "Reform in Mexican Higher Education: An Overview of the 1990s." *International Higher Education* 15 (Spring): 12–13, <http://www.bc.edu/bc_org/avp/soe/cihe/newsletter/News15/text7.html> [last accessed: 19 February 2001].

León-Garcia, F., D. Matthews, and L. Smith. 1999. "Academic Mobility in North America: Towards New Models of Integration and Collaboration." Working Paper No. 9. Consortium for North American Higher Education Collaboration, <http://www.wiche.edu/pubs/alphalist.htm> [last accessed: 19 February 2001].

Leovy, Jill. 2001. "Latest U.S. Export: Education for the Masses." *Los Angeles Times*, 20 February, A4.

Lewis, L., K. Snow, E. Farris, and D. Levin. 1999. *Distance Education at Postsecondary Education Institutions: 1997–98.* NCES 2000–013. Bernie Green, project officer. Washington, D.C.: U.S. Department of Education, National Center for Education Statistics: iv.

MacDonald, C. 1999. "Networking over Borders." *MB* 10 (April): 20.

Marmolejo, F. Forthcoming. "A Region in Transition: The U.S.–Mexico Borderlands and the Role of Higher Education." *The Border Pact Report,* <http://www.borderpact.org/paper/marmolej.htm> [last accessed: 19 February 2001].

Marmolejo, F., and F. León-Garcia. 1997. "Higher Education in the U.S.–Mexico Borderlands: A Profile." <http://www.borderpact.org/paper/marmolejhtm> [last accessed: 19 February 2001].

Martinez, F. 1998. "Reaching out with Technology: ISTEC Opens Doors for Transnational Research." *Quantum* (Spring), <http://www.istec.org/pubs/istecquant.html> [last accessed: 19 February 2001].

Maslen, G. 2000a. "College Group Ends Talks with Murdoch's Company." *Chronicle of Higher Education,* 24 November, A53.

——. 2000b. "Rupert Murdoch's Company Joins with 18 Universities in Distance-education Venture." *Chronicle of Higher Education,* 2 June, A47.

McGeehan, P. 1999. "Business School Links up with Internet Education Firm." *Wall Street Journal,* 2 April, C1.

"Motorola Extends Digital DNA Technology to Benefit 64 Universities." 2000. *PR Newswire,* 15 March, <http://www.prnewswire.com> [last accessed: 19 February 2001].

Navarro, L. 2000. "The UNAM Stalemate: Mexico's Student Strike." *NACLA Report on the Americas* 33 (4) (January–February): 22.

Noble, D. 1998. "Digital Diploma Mills: The Automation of Higher Education." *Monthly Review* (February).

North American Congress on Latin America. 2000. "The Crisis of the Latin American University." *NACLA Report on the Americas* 33 (4) (January–February).

Olavarría, M. 2000. "Student Activism in Chile's Universities." *NACLA Report on the Americas* 33 (4) (January–February): 28.

"129 Latin America Executives Begin Distance Learning Course at Thunderbird." 1999. Thunderbird Press Release, 13 August, <http://www.thunderbird.edu> [last accessed: 19 February 2001].

Organization for Economic Cooperation and Development. 1996. *OECD in Figures: Supplement to the OECD Observer.* Paris: Organization for Economic Cooperation and Development, <http://www.oecd.org> [last accessed: 19 February 2001].

Overland, M. 2000. "India Uses Distance Education to Meet Huge Demand for Degrees." *Chronicle of Higher Education*, 14 July, A48–A49.

"Pensare and Harvard Business School Publishing to Develop Intranet-based 'Performance Courses.'" 1998. Pensare Press Release, 21 September, <http://www.pensare.com/> [last accessed: 19 February 2001].

"Pensare Announces Partnership with Duke University's Fuqua School of Business to Develop Internet-enabled 'Top-Ten' Accredited MBA Program: Education and Technology Alliance Reinvents Business Education to Meet the Needs of the New Economy." 1999. Pensare Press Release, 11 October, <http://www.pensare.com/> [last accessed: 19 February 2001].

"Report from the Conference on Globalization and the University." 1999. <http://www.salsem.ac.at/csacl/universityprojects/99plenary.htm> [last accessed: 19 February 2001].

Rymer-Zavela, J. 1999. "Critical Needs: Higher Education Faces Globalization." *El Financeiro Weekly International*, 19 April, 3.

Salmi, J. 2000. "Higher Education: Facing the Challenges of the 21st Century." *TechKnowLogia* (January–February): 8, <http://www.techknowlogia.org> [last accessed: 19 February 2001].

Schiller, D. 1999. *Digital Capitalism: Networking the Global Market System.* Cambridge: Massachusetts Institute of Technology Press.

SEP–ANUIES. 1993. *Agenda Estatistica de la Educación Superior.* Mexico City: SEP–ANUIES.

Statland de Lopez, R. 1995. "Free Fall in Mexico: Universities Scramble to Cope with the Effects of the Country's Currency Crisis." *Chronicle of Higher Education*, 3 February, <http://www.chronicle.com/che-data/articles-41.dir/issue-21.dir/2104501.htm> [last accessed: 19 February 2001].

———. 2000. "Mexico's National University Is Free of Strikers, but Hardly at Peace." *Chronicle of Higher Education*, 18 February, A67, <http://www.chronicle.com/weekly/v46/i24/24a06701.htm> [last accessed: 19 February 2001].

Strosnider, K. 1998. "For-profit Higher Education Sees Booming Enrollments and Revenues." *Chronicle of Higher Education*, 23 January, A36–A38.

UN Educational, Scientific, and Cultural Organization. 1994. "Policy Paper on Change and Development in Higher Education." Paris: UN Educational, Scientific, and Cultural Organization.

Williams, M. 1997. "Is There Market Potential for Innovation?" *El Financeiro Weekly International*, 2 November, 10.

Wolff, L. 1999. "Mexico: The Virtual University of the Technological Institute of Monterrey." *TechKnowLogia* (November–December), <http://www.techknowlogia.org> [last accessed: 19 February 2001].

Woody, T. 1999. "Ivy Online: Elite Universities and Professional Schools Are Scrambling to 'Leverage Their Brands' and Make Extra Money through Online Education." *The Industry Standard*, 22 October. <http://www.thestandard.com/article/display/0,1151,7122,00.html> [last accessed: 19 February 2001].

World Bank. 1994. *Higher Education: The Lessons of Experience*. Washington, D.C.: World Bank.

———. 1999a. *Knowledge for Development. World Development Report 1998/99*. New York: Oxford University Press.

———. 1999b. *Educational Change in Latin America and the Caribbean: A World Bank Strategy Paper*. Washington, D.C.: World Bank.

8

Commerce versus Culture: The Print Media in Canada and Mexico

Catherine McKercher

The print media of Canada, the United States, and Mexico have much in common. For the most part, they are privately owned and operated on a for-profit basis. And unlike other goods or services covered by international trading agreements, newspapers and magazines in all three countries have a claim to constitutional protection, rooted in the idea that freedom of the press is critical to nationhood.[1] As Canada has pursued fuller participation in international trading regimes in recent years, however, its efforts to protect and promote its domestic print media have come under attack, mainly from the United States. In the process, Canada has found itself swimming upstream not only against a tide of globalization, but also against the current in the North American trading bloc as well.

This chapter describes how the barriers that successive Canadian governments have tried to erect to shield its domestic print media have been steadily eroded—under the Canada–U.S. Free Trade Agreement (CUSFTA), the North American Free Trade Agreement (NAFTA), and at the World Trade Organization (WTO). Imperfect though those barriers may have been, they represented an attempt to ensure that a distinctive Canadian voice would be heard among the massed chorus of American magazines shouting from the country's newsstands. Following its defeat at the WTO in 1997, Canada has been left with one tool at its disposal to help the magazine industry, and it is a clumsy tool at best: direct subsidies to produce Canadian content. Ironically, while Canada contemplates how to manage a subsidy program to counter commercial U.S. interests, its NAFTA partner Mexico has been moving away from subsidies (and other government press controls) and toward a U.S.–style model for its print media. In Mexico, recent developments in the print media represent, in many ways, a modernization of a press system once characterized by corruption and heavy-handed political interference. But there is awareness in both Mexico and Canada that the U.S. model, where press freedom is synonymous with commerce, offers little protection to domestic cultural interests.

PURSUING COMMERCE, PROTECTING CULTURE

Canadian publishers have complained about a flood of U.S. magazines sweeping north across Lake Ontario for more than a century. As early as 1894, Goldwyn Smith, the British-born intellectual who edited the most influential Canadian periodical of the day, *The Week*, wrote: "what chance can our Canadian publishers have against an American magazine with a circulation of 150,000 and a splendour of illustration such as only a profuse expenditure can support?" (quoted in Desbarats 1995, 77). His complaint was not an idle whine: American publishers operated in a larger and richer market than Canadian publishers, and had been quicker to move from the so-called class market to the low-priced mass press. Because U.S. publishers recouped their costs in domestic sales, exports across the border represented extra profit. By the mid-1920s, fifty million copies of American magazines were selling in Canada each year, and American magazines outsold Canadian ones by a ratio of eight to one (Vipond 1989, 24). The flood of American magazines was particularly hard on English-language publishers; French Canada, with its own language and distinct set of cultural practices, was affected to a lesser degree.

Beginning in the 1920s, Canadian magazine publishers began calling on the government to provide tariff protection for domestic magazines. Their argument relied on three main points (Vipond 1989, 25–26). One was puritanical, based on the idea that many U.S. magazines contained immoral or prurient material that might contaminate Canadian society. The second was economic: Canadians would lose work if the low-cost "overflow" publications were allowed to flood the domestic market. The third was nationalist: "[I]f Canada lacked its own magazines, it lacked a vital agency of national communication" (26). At the beginning of the twenty-first century, the first strand of this argument seems, to say the least, quaint. The other two strands, however, have been at the core of the debate over communications and cultural life in Canada for more than seventy-five years.

Those calling for protection were aware that, as Peter Desbarats puts it, the case for protection contains "the seeds of its own rebuttal" (1995, 79). If an essential attribute of a free press is freedom from government interference, and if the free flow of ideas forms part of the creed of Canadian journalism, then suggesting that the government intervene on behalf of the magazine business raises the fear of government influence—or perhaps even government control—over a business that both claims and requires immunity from such control. The contradictions inherent in the argument concerning protection help explain what Desbarats characterizes as halfhearted efforts by successive Canadian governments on behalf of the magazine industry, beginning in 1925. These included, at various times, tariffs on selected U.S. magazines,[2] relief from customs duties on imported paper and printing material, and postal subsidies for Canadian publishers. Desbarats notes, "This policy of combining a refusal to offer significant help, particularly if it threatened to annoy the United States, with minor concessions designed to alleviate the industry's most pressing problems became familiar to Canadian magazine publishers in the following decades as they followed a well-worn path to and from Ottawa" (80).

During World War II, a new problem arose for Canadian magazine publishers. In an attempt to get around paper rationing, the popular U.S. magazines *Time* and *Reader's Digest* opened offices in Canada and began producing Canadian editions, which supplemented the American editions with some Canadian content. By the mid-1950s, the Canadian editions of these two magazines accounted for 37 percent of total advertising revenues of general-interest magazines in Canada. In total, American magazines claimed 80 percent of the Canadian market in 1954 (Vipond 1989, 61). In 1956, the Liberal government imposed a 20 percent tax on advertising placed in Canadian editions of U.S. publications. The new Progressive Conservative government removed the tax in 1958. Almost immediately, five more American magazines launched Canadian editions and several more began enticing Canadian advertisers with split-run magazines, that is, those in which Canadian advertising was substituted for American advertising without any significant change in editorial content (61).

By 1960, the federal government was convinced that Canadian magazines were in crisis, and policymakers in Ottawa were equally convinced that this crisis threatened national culture and identity, not just commercial interests. The government appointed a Royal Commission on Publications, whose mandate was explicitly rooted in the idea of cultural nationalism. The order-in-council setting up the Royal Commission described Canadian magazines as "essential to the culture and unity of Canada" (quoted in Vipond 1989, 61). The Royal Commission's report concluded that while the flow of magazines across the border was inevitable, something could be done about what it saw as the unfair competition of split runs and Canadian editions. The editorial content of these magazines had already been paid for by U.S. advertisers and subscribers, which meant publishers could sell ads to Canadians at a discount and dump the magazine on the market, earning additional revenue without spending more on content. And the revenue was substantial: *Time* and *Reader's Digest* alone were taking in forty cents of every Canadian dollar spent on magazine advertising (Sutherland 1989, 182).

The commission made two key recommendations. First, it said that Canadian firms advertising in foreign magazines or in Canadian editions of foreign magazines should not be allowed to deduct the costs of this advertising as a business expense for tax purposes. Second, it suggested that foreign periodicals selling ads explicitly aimed at Canadian readers should be barred from entry under the Customs Act. The hope was that Canadian advertisers would divert their money away from foreign periodicals and toward Canadian magazines. The Royal Commission recommendations sought to offer freedom from what it saw as unfair foreign competition, which in turn would give Canadian publishers the freedom to create a viable and distinctive Canadian magazine industry, supported by Canadian advertising dollars.

However, the recommendations also brought into focus a long-developing clash between the Canadian and U.S. governments over the cultural value of commercial media. If the Royal Commission saw its actions as protecting (and promoting) a business that was inextricably linked to national culture, the U.S. government did not. Lobbied fiercely and persuasively by the proprietors of *Time* and *Reader's Digest* and their allies, the United States viewed the recommendations as an attempt by a foreign state to interfere in a business that was meant to be immune from government interference. The U.S. government reacted to the report in a way that would also set a pattern: it threatened retaliation against other Canadian businesses. The State Department warned that if Canada went ahead with the recommendations, the quotas on Canadian oil exports might be reviewed, the future of U.S. defense contracts offered to Canadian firms could be in jeopardy, and congressional approval of the Canada–U.S. Auto Pact might be denied (Sutherland 1989, 187–188).

Before the Progressive Conservative government could do anything with the Royal Commission's recommendations, it was defeated by the Liberals. The legislation the Liberals finally enacted in 1965 adopted the main recommendations of the Royal Commission—the ban on advertising tax deductibility and the customs rule prohibiting the import of foreign split runs—but it exempted *Time* and *Reader's Digest* from the provisions (Vipond 1989, 63). The legislation also extended the tax-deductibility provisions to newspaper advertising, effectively preventing foreign ownership of Canadian newspapers.[3] A dozen years later, in 1976, the Liberal government of Pierre Trudeau passed Bill C-58, which eliminated the tax-deductibility provision for *Time* and *Reader's Digest.* Again, the United States responded with threats of retaliation. *Time* almost immediately shut down its Canadian office, though it continued to publish a Canadian edition out of New York in which Canadian ads were not eligible for tax deductions. *Reader's Digest* set up a Canadian foundation and continued publishing its Canadian edition. Because of its presence in Canada, *Reader's Digest Canada* remained eligible for tax deductibility.

Ted Magder sees the passage of Bill C-58 as "the high water mark for Canadian cultural nationalism," noting that no measure undertaken since then "has so aggressively challenged entrenched American interests in the cultural sector" (1998, 15). The legislation had a number of consequences for the Canadian publishing industry. One was the creation of new magazine titles, and the expansion of others. Maclean-Hunter, one of the main beneficiaries of the legislation, relaunched its *Maclean's* magazine as a weekly in 1978, stepping into the market niche left vacant by the departure of *Time Canada. TV Guide*, one of the most popular magazines sold in Canada, was taken over by the Montreal-based Télémedia company. Between 1975 and 1985, the number of city and entertainment magazines more than tripled, from seventeen to fifty-six. And although U.S. magazines continued to dominate newsstand sales, the share of the national magazine market occupied by Canadian publications increased from 30 percent to 40 percent (Sutherland 1989, 263).

But there were unintended consequences as well. The most significant of these was a substantial concentration of ownership, in both magazines and newspapers, in the last quarter of the twentieth century. With tax laws preventing foreign ownership, Canadian publishers looking to sell their newspapers or magazines had to find Canadian buyers. By the time the Royal Commission on Newspapers reported on the problem in 1981, the share of English-language circulation controlled by newspaper chains had risen to 74.3 percent from 69.4 percent ten years earlier, and the Thomson Corporation alone owned close to 40 percent of all Canadian daily newspapers (Canada 1981, 2). More shockingly, the share of French-language circulation controlled by chains had almost doubled, from 49.2 percent in 1970 to 90 percent by 1980 (3). By the 1990s, concentration of ownership had reached an even more extreme level. In large part, this had to do with Thomson's decision to sell many of its Canadian papers. Conrad Black's Hollinger International—it also owns newspapers in the United States, Britain, and Israel—bought many of them, and also took control of Thomson's erstwhile rival, Southam. At its high point in the late 1990s, Hollinger owned or controlled 60 percent of the daily newspapers published in Canada and was about to launch a national daily newspaper, the *National Post*. Through its controlling interest in Southam, it also published more than a hundred Canadian magazines and specialty publications.

In mid-2000, Hollinger's holdings contracted almost as dramatically as they had expanded. The company sold $3.5 billion (CD) in assets—including the Southam Magazine and Information Group, more than two dozen daily newspapers, scores of community papers, and a half-interest in the *National Post*—to CanWest Global Communications Corporation, the owner of the Global Television Network ("Hollinger Inc." 2000). The deal was larger than the 1998 transaction that moved the leading publisher of general-circulation magazines, Maclean-Hunter, into the Rogers Communications empire. Between them, Rogers and Télémedia account for almost half the ad revenue generated by Canadian magazines ("Background Briefing" 1999). While there is no doubt that Bill C-58 protected the Canadian publishing business from outsiders and resulted in growth in some areas, the question of whether it promoted Canada culture or diversity is considerably less clear.

Canadian concerns about the flood of American cultural products were not, of course, limited to the newspapers and magazines. John Herd Thompson (1995) notes that in a lengthy history of groping for policies to deal with U.S. mass culture, Canadian policymakers have followed two broad paths: attempts to protect Canadian cultural industries with regulatory or tariff barriers, and attempts to promote indigenous Canadian mass culture through subsidies to individual arts, artists or publications, or government-sponsored creation of cultural infrastructures. "Polices were not always clear-cut; protectionist and promotional solutions were sometimes applied alternately or even simultaneously" (398). The Canadian approach has also tended to be piecemeal. At various times and with varying degrees of success, Canadian policymakers have sought to protect the Canadian feature film business, including production and distribution (e.g., see Pendakur 1990); public and commercial radio and television, including ownership and content (see Vipond 1989, 1992); telecommunications (see Babe 1990; Winseck 1998); magazines; and even the ownership of bookstores (see Browne 1998).

Beginning in the 1980s, cultural policy became more complicated. The newly elected Progressive Conservative government of Brian Mulroney began pursuing a neoconservative agenda that emphasized cost cutting and deregulation in all areas of federal responsibility, including culture. Increasingly, it treated communication and information as commercial products rather than as part of the DNA of the nation. Its successor, the Liberal government of Jean Chrétien, has continued along this road—at least in terms of domestic policy. The Chrétien government has imposed a series of cuts in the area of cultural funding, especially to the Canadian Broadcasting Corporation (CBC) but in other areas as well.[4] The Canadian Magazine Publishers Association estimates that between 1991 and 1997, government grants to Canadian magazines were cut in half, from $1.4 million (CD) to $665,000 (CD). Vincent Mosco notes, however, that under the Chrétien government there has been a growing disjunction between domestic and international cultural policy. Internationally, especially in regards to the United States, Canada continues to claim special status for communications and culture. Domestically, however, it is another story. "[It] treats communications and information as marketable products not unlike any other commodities. This has moved Canadian policy further away from the position that communications and information are public resources that are vital to citizenship and nationhood, and therefore fundamentally different from marketable products" (1997, 161).

FROM CUSFTA TO WTO

Given the Canadian sensitivities to American cultural exports, it is no surprise that when Canada sat down to negotiate with the United States on a free trade agreement in the mid-1980s, it staked out a position that culture would not be on the table, and that nothing in the agreement could threaten cultural sovereignty. That position was eventually enshrined in article 2005 (1) of CUSFTA, which declares that "cultural industries are exempt from the provisions of this agreement." This pledge is far from watertight, however. As Magder notes the deal includes some specific references to cultural issues, "and in every instance forces the Canadian government to make adjustments that favor the U.S." (1998, 24). These include provisions that Canadian cable companies pay copyright fees for the retransmission of foreign broadcasts; a repeal of the print-in-Canada requirements for magazines and newspapers from the list of conditions to be met before Canadian firms could deduct advertising expenses; and a commitment to liberalized cross-border telecommunications and information flow. In addition, the agreement includes a clause, annex 1404 (C), stating that if one country takes an action on behalf of a cultural industry that harms an industry in the other country, that country can respond with measures of equivalent commercial effect. Magder believes this language "concedes much to the U.S. view that culture is a viable trade issue" (25). Indeed, the very act of agreeing to permit commercial retaliation against cultural subsidies suggests that culture can be counted as a commodity.

Canada continued to insist that culture be kept off the table in NAFTA negotiations in the early 1990s. It was, however, considerably less of an issue the second time around. There was no significant cultural industry trade between Canada and Mexico, and relatively little between Mexico and the United States (Thompson 1995, 407). Mexico, protected not only by language, but also by popular preferences in film, television, and printed material that have more in common with other Latin America countries than with either of its northern neighbors, did not feel threatened by American cultural exports. The chief NAFTA negotiator for Mexico saw "no cause for concern" in the cultural arena (Galperin 1999, 631) and if culture was a "sacred cow" for the Canadians, it was not for the other two. Washington's "sacred cows" included immigration, government procurement policies, and shipping. For Mexico, the most sensitive areas were the petroleum business, agriculture, and financial services (Grayson 1995, 82). In the end, NAFTA created a double standard on culture. Between Canada and the United States, the cultural exemption that was part of CUSFTA was retained. Canada also kept the right to review any investment relating to Canada's cultural heritage or national identity. In Mexico, cultural industries are regulated by NAFTA provisions, with a few minor exemptions (Galperin 1999, 632).

Magazines again became a contentious issue for Canada in the early 1990s when Time-Warner, one of the world's largest media conglomerates, announced plans to launch *Sports Illustrated Canada* with six special Canadian editions of the popular *Sports Illustrated* magazine. In doing so, it had come up with not one but two ways around Canada's long-standing ban on split-run publications. Time-Warner planned to take advantage of the converging technologies of telecommunications and print and send the magazine electronically into Canada, where it would be printed and distributed. With nothing physically crossing the border, the threat of a customs seizure was moot. In addition, the corporation sought—and was granted—the approval of a branch of the Canadian government for its *Sports Illustrated Canada* plan. Magder writes that *Time Canada* submitted an outline of its business plan to Investment Canada in 1990 to determine the legal status of the proposed special issues of the magazine. The company argued that *Time Canada*'s existing exemption from the tariff code banning the import of foreign split runs should be extended to *Sports Illustrated*, since both were owned by the same company. Investment Canada concurred (Magder 1998, 26). There was apparently no discussion on this matter between Investment Canada and the Department of Communication, which was responsible for cultural issues. "*Time Canada*'s application was treated as a business issue pure and simple by an agency within the federal government ill-suited to evaluate the cultural impact of its decisions" (26).

The Magazine Publishers Association, supported by a number of other groups with an interest in the issue, immediately began a campaign to stop the plan. They appealed to Revenue Canada, seeking a ruling that the proposed magazine violated the customs code on split runs. This turned out to be a dead end: If the magazine was transmitted electronically and printed in Canada it would "effectively bypass the jurisdiction of Canada Customs" (Magder 1998, 26). Within weeks of Time-Warner's announcement, the federal communications minister promised action to ensure the survival of the Canadian magazine industry, and a task force was created to come up with measures to do so.

Like the Royal Commission of 1960, the task force found that the electronic split-run format posed a major threat to the Canadian magazine business. Because American publishers could cover the fixed costs of production in the United States, they could afford to sell ads in the Canadian edition at very low rates—low enough, in all likelihood, to compensate Canadian advertisers for their inability to deduct the advertising expenditures from their income tax. Even watered down, that money would be gravy for the American publishers. The task force estimated that as many as fifty U.S. magazines might decide to launch split runs. This could cost Canadian magazines almost 40 percent of their ad revenue, and reduce average operating profits by as much as 85 percent (Magder 1998, 28–29).

The final report of the task force recommended that Canada impose an 80 percent tax on the gross advertising revenue of split-run magazines as a strong disincentive. It also recommended that the government offer *Sports Illustrated Canada* a six-times-a-year exemption from the measure, apparently in recognition of the fact it had already received a green light from Investment Canada. The report came out after the Conservative government, which had appointed the task force, was defeated by Chrétien's Liberal party. The new Liberal government proceeded with the excise tax recommended by the task force, with one significant change: there would be no exemption for *Sports Illustrated Canada*. The legislation, Bill C-103, was passed in 1996.

The U.S. government moved quickly in response. In contending that the Canadian action violated the General Agreement on Tariffs and Trade (GATT), it bypassed the dispute resolution mechanism of NAFTA—and the cultural exemption carried over from CUSFTA—and took the issue directly to the WTO. The U.S. complaint did not center solely on Bill C-103, however. It also included the long-standing customs regulation and the question of postal subsidies for Canadian magazines. As Magder comments, "culture was now most definitely on the table" (1998, 35).

At the WTO, Canada was defeated not once but twice. The WTO panel charged with handling the complaint found that both the customs regulation banning imports of split runs and the excise tax were inconsistent with GATT rules. So was the postal subsidy for Canadian magazines, it said, but the maintenance of the subsidy could be justified under article III:8(b) of GATT (World Trade Organization 1997a). A few months later, an appeal panel upheld the original decision, with some modifications. The worst of these from Canada's point of view was a finding that the postal subsidy was not justified under GATT rules (World Trade Organization 1997b). Ivan Bernier writes that the immediate consequence was that if Canada wanted to subsidize postal expenditures, "it will have to make payments directly to (publishers) instead of offering a reduction on postal rates" (1998, 117). The WTO gave Canada six months to comply with its rulings. Canada promised new legislation to protect the magazine industry.

Over the next two and a half years, Canadian policymakers wrestled with how to come up with a plan that met three seemingly contradictory goals: supporting the Canadian magazine industry, complying with GATT, and satisfying the U.S. government. They did so in an atmosphere of increasing threats of retaliation from the United States against Canadian exports. The result was Bill C-55, which would prohibit Canadian advertisers from placing ads in foreign magazines and fine foreign publishers violating the rule up to $250,000. As required to comply with the WTO rulings, the bill eliminated the customs regulation and the excise tax on split runs, equalized the commercial postal rate for foreign and domestic magazines, and restructured the postal subsidy program.

Predictably, the United States objected to the bill. Former U.S. trade negotiator Bill Merkin told the CBC on the day the legislation was introduced: "Those measures on prohibition of split-run magazines are being replaced by this system of fines. Obviously the U.S. government is going to view this as not a useful step and I would imagine will take action to attack it" (King 1998). While the bill made its way through Parliament, Canadian and U.S. negotiators tried to come up with a compromise.

By January 1999, the Americans were talking seriously about retaliation. The United States was reported to be preparing a list of Canadian industries it would target unless Canada withdrew the bill. Canadian officials were quoted as saying the U.S. countermeasures could cost the country billions of dollars ("U.S. Vows Fight in Magazine Battle" 1999). By May 1999, news reports indicated the United States was just weeks away from launching retaliation against a range of Canadian imports—including textile, lumber, plastics, and steel[5]—unless Canada would come up with a plan that would meet U.S. concerns, and soon (Morton and Jack 1999).

A week later, negotiators for the two countries reached an accord. The prohibition on foreign publishers selling ads aimed mainly at the Canadian market would be eased in two ways. First, the publishers of split runs would be able to sell a limited number of ads to Canadians without making any changes in content. The limit was set at 12 percent of advertising in the first year, rising to 18 percent by the third year. Second, although foreign publishing concerns would not be able to buy Canadian publishers, those who wanted to sell more ads to Canadians could open new businesses in Canada and produce publications with a majority of Canadian content ("Ottawa and Washington Agree" 1999). Canada also agreed to change the rules on tax deductibility. Previously, tax deductibility was allowed for ads placed in periodicals with a minimum of 75 percent Canadian ownership and 80 percent original (or Canadian) content. This would be changed to allow full deductibility, regardless of the nationality of ownership, in any magazine with at least 80 percent original or Canadian content. Advertisers buying ads in magazines with between 50 percent and 79 percent Canadian content would be able to deduct 50 percent of the cost of advertising (1999).

With more ad dollars flowing toward split runs or foreign magazines, Canadian magazines were likely to run short of money. To round out the package, the government promised to create a new Canadian Magazine Fund. The Canadian Heritage department sketched out the broad outlines of the fund at the end of 1999 ("New Canadian Magazine Fund" 1999). Beginning in 2000–2001, it would provide $150 million (CD) over three years, or roughly $50 million (CD) a year. The fund would be renewed in the fourth year, and the level of funding reviewed. To be eligible for funding, a publisher would have to be Canadian-owned and Canadian-controlled, and an individual magazine would have to contain 80 percent Canadian editorial content. According to the Canadian Heritage department, the goal of the fund would be to "support the production of high levels of Canadian content while strengthening the long-term competitiveness of the Canadian publishing industry" (1). The level of assistance would be based on a magazine's investment in the production of editorial content. Funding would also be provided for professional development, adapting to new technology, marketing, and distribution, and to "strengthen the infrastructure across the industry as a whole" (1).

It took the Canadian Heritage department until the fall of 2000 to set out the specific details of the fund. News reports indicated that $25 million (CD) a year would go toward supporting editorial content, while $15 million (CD) would be spent on research into the marketing and distribution of magazines and $5 million (CD) would go toward administration of the fund and enforcement of Bill C-55. The final $5 million (CD) would be earmarked for small magazines (Honey 2000). While it remains to be seen exactly who will get the money and how it will be spent, it is clear that this fund represents a new kind of support for Canadian magazines. Unlike previous plans that attempted to direct advertising dollars one way rather than another, the new magazine fund is aimed specifically and directly at content. In other words, the government will use taxpayers' money to subsidize the editorial activities of privately owned publications.

THE SUBSIDY QUANDARY

In announcing that an agreement had been reached with the United States on the magazine issue, the Canadian Heritage minister claimed victory, saying: "For the first time in its history, the American government has recognized the right of a country, Canada, to require a majority of Canadian content in one of its cultural instruments" ("Ottawa and Washington Agree" 1999). It was at best a muted victory, however. As John Geddes writes in *Maclean's* magazine, the tidy statements of principle on which Canada based its cultural policy and the U.S. based its claim that the magazine business was a business like any other "were messed up beyond recognition" in the eventual agreement (1999, 54). The United States had grudgingly accepted the idea that trade involving cultural products needed some special consideration. "As for Canada, the federal government will never again be able to credibly claim that its national policies are excluded from the sort of compromises that emerge when over-caffeinated trade negotiators engage in prolonged, high-stakes bargaining" (54).

In addition, by changing the advertising deductibility provisions to emphasize Canadian content rather than Canadian ownership, the rules for magazines have become significantly different from those covering the ownership of newspapers. This raises the possibility of a review of ownership restrictions on newspapers (Craig 2000). A few months after the announcement of changes in the regulations on magazine ownership, Thomson's *Globe and Mail*, which calls itself "Canada's national newspaper," published a commentary by Tony Ridder, the chairman and chief executive office of the Knight-Ridder company, criticizing the ownership restrictions on newspapers (2000). Under the headline "Get Rid of the Outdated Law," Ridder argues that the foreign ownership restrictions prevent a greater diversity of media. Knight-Ridder is the second largest newspaper publisher in the United

States. At the time, Thomson and Hollinger both had Canadian newspapers on the market.[6]

There is little doubt, however, that the result of the magazine fight left Canada in an unenviable position. If it wanted to protect a cultural industry, it would have to do so through a direct subsidy to that industry—not through the trade or regulatory instruments it once had at its fingertips. Subsidies are an unwieldy tool to use, especially in the case of magazines. In Canada's highly concentrated print media, the idea that subsidies might go to conglomerates headed by millionaires is politically unpalatable to many. Also, in an era in which the Canadian government has steadily been withdrawing support from domestic cultural industries, the prospects for secure long-term funding do not seem bright. Finally, the very idea of the government giving money directly to media enterprises makes journalists, among others, uncomfortable. While the subsidies might offer some relief from foreign competition, one must wonder whether—or how—they might affect the freedom to publish without government interference.

Indeed, as Mosco notes (1997, 174), changes to the funding policy of the Canada Council for the Arts have already forced some smaller Canadian magazines to refocus their mandates, from politics to the arts. The Periodical Writers Association of Canada (PWAC), the organization of magazine writers, has been waging its own fight against Canada Council funding changes. It strongly protested when the Canada Council announced in 1999 that it would restrict funding to organizations representing "literary" writers only. In an urgent memo circulated on the eve of submitting its 2000 application for operating funding, PWAC's national office wrote: "We are now faced with having to convince the Canada Council jury that the important work PWAC does on behalf of writers is of specific benefit to 'literary' writers . . . and that a significant number of our members produce such writing" ("PWAC Needs Your Help" 2000).

Perhaps the biggest irony in the fight to protect Canadian magazines, though, is that Canada, pushed by one of its NAFTA partners, wound up swimming against the current in the NAFTA trade bloc. While Canada looks at more direct support of its printing and publishing sector, Mexico is heading in exactly the opposite direction. In doing so, the Mexico media system is moving closer to the U.S. model.

The Mexican government has had available for many years a number of ways to control the press, ranging from a monopoly on newspaper distribution to controls on the distribution of newsprint to threats to withhold government advertising to bribes paid to individual journalists (see Salwen and Garrison 1991; Fromson 1996). Jon Vanden Heuvel and Everette E. Dennis write that the Mexican media "have traditionally been a key part of the vertical, authoritarian political structure" of the Mexican state: "Indeed, it is sometimes difficult to separate the media from the political structure in which they operate" (1995, 21). The print media, owned by wealthy families, have tended to reflect various factions within the dominant Partido Revolucionario Institucional (PRI; Institutional Revolutionary Party). Few are genuinely oppositional (22).

José Luis Benavides (2000) argues that the cornerstone of the political economy of the Mexican press for much of the twentieth century was the *gacetilla*—a paid publicity notice inserted in newspapers or magazines in the guise of a work of journalism.[7] The ready availability of government or PRI money for *gacetillas* meant that the Mexican newspapers did not feel the same urge as their more northerly counterparts to scrounge for higher circulation. He argues that the *gacetilla*, more than other factors like low literacy rates and intermedia competition, helps explain why Mexico has a wealth of newspapers—close to three hundred dailies, including twenty-five in Mexico City (Vanden Heuvel and Dennis 1995, 27)—but remarkably few readers and subscribers.[8] As recently as 1996, 60 percent of the country's dailies listed advertising rates for *gacetillas*, and the rates were usually two or three times higher than those for commercial advertising (Benavides 2000, 92–93). The funds raised from *gacetillas* "are the key ingredient in a system of governmental press subsidy, essential in explaining the way in which the Mexican press has served as a propaganda tool" for both the government and the PRI (85). They are also key to the proliferation of newspaper titles: Without the income from *gacetillas*, the bulk of Mexico City newspapers would probably not be able to stay in business (93). Benavides notes that although the *gacetilla* remains a cornerstone in the Mexican print media system, there is growing opposition to continued reliance on this kind of funding. In part, this is linked to a growing professionalization of journalism in the country (98).

In recent years, Mexico has moved away from a number of its traditional control mechanisms. As part of a policy of privatizing state-owned industries, the government has privatized the Productora e Importado de Papel, Sociedad Anónima (PIPSA), the government newsprint monopoly, by selling it in 1998 for $112.4 million to the country's largest paper-packaging company ("World Watch" 1998). Interestingly, it did so over the objections of some newspaper publishers. When the government announced plans to privatize PIPSA in 1989, the Mexican publishers association asked it to reconsider. By providing newsprint at a reasonable price, the publishers argued, the government was serving as a guardian of press freedom. In addition, they expressed concerns that small, independent publishers might be harmed by the privatization (Salwen and Garrison 1991, 24).

The monopoly on distribution was challenged in the mid-1990s by Alejandro Junco de la Vega, the president and general director of *Reforma* in Mexico City and *El Norte* in Monterrey. The monopoly is controlled by the Unión de Voceadores, whose leadership has close ties to the PRI (Fromson 1996, 133). It operates all kiosks in the capital, thereby dictating which newspapers are available for sale and which are not. Traditionally, kiosks close on Sundays and holidays. Junco de la Vega, however, wanted to distribute newspapers seven days a week. He wound up organizing his own distribution system and selling the paper on the streets on the days that the union refused to do so. "In effect, Junco de la Vega's daring action broke the back of a monopoly that had existed in Mexico City since 1921" (134). Vanden Heuvel and Dennis point to Junco de la Vega's *Reforma* as a leader in practicing "a sort of profit-oriented U.S.–style journalism" (1995, 25). The newspaper accepts no *gacetillas* and its reporters are forbidden from accepting *chayotes*, or gifts, from officials or businesses they cover regularly.

Threats to withdraw government advertising from the printed media have been an effective means of silencing critics. Six advertising boycotts were documented from 1925 to 1982, most of them successful (Benavides 2000, 88). However, the PRI's policy of privatization has meant that government advertising has shrunk. As a result, "tailoring editorial policy in order to ensure an uninterrupted flow of government ads has become less a factor within the media" (Vanden Heuvel and Dennis 1995, 25).

In 1998, the Committee to Protect Journalists looked at the state of the media in Mexico, noting that "marked strides toward independence and enterprise" were made during the presidency of Ernesto Zedillo Ponce de León ("Country Report" 1998, 1). A year later, it reported that journalists were covering local politics "with greater confidence and independence" ("Americas" 1999, 1). In a report to the UN Human Rights Committee, the London-based human rights group Article 19, the International Centre against Censorship, notes freedom of expression has made significant inroads in Mexico. "Bribery of journalists continues, but the government recently enacted legislation to combat it" ("Submission on Mexico's Fourth Periodic Report" 1999, 1). This independence, however, has come at a price for working journalists: an increase in violence against journalists. At least three journalists were murdered in 1998, and reporters investigating public corruption and the drug trade "are frequent targets of death threats and brutal beatings" (1).

Nonetheless, it is clear that the Mexican media are in a period of transition, moving away from their traditional role as a partner of the government and the PRI toward a market-driven system that is the dominant feature of the U.S. media and that characterizes the Canadian press as well, though to a slightly lesser extent. While this movement is likely to continue, there are, however, some reservations about the long-term consequences. Benavides notes that while some Mexican publishers, such as the Junco de la Vega family, believe the U.S. model will solve the problems associated with press control, others disagree.

Some journalists, in contrast, believe that the state has an obligation to subsidize newspapers and news media in general because a system of free enterprise will eliminate precisely those sectors of the press that have given voice to marginalized groups in society. These journalists support a direct subsidy, with clear rules that will allow journalism to remain free from obligation to either state or private advertisers (Benavides 2000, 99).

Interestingly, this position echoes to a degree the debates in Canada over how to protect the Canadian magazine business. If the mass media are linked to the creation, promotion, or preservation of national culture, and if culture is defined as more than the sum of a series of commercial transactions, then a case can be made for government action to ensure diversity in the commercial and public news media. The recent experiences of Canada in the North American trading bloc and at the WTO show the difficulties inherent in making this case: It runs counter to the exuberant push toward globalization, the romantic ideal of the free market, and the rapid spread of commercial American cultural products. In the end, Canada was left with no choice other than direct subsidy. Difficult though they may be, the subsidies offered through Canada's new magazine fund hold some promise. By promoting content, they may be used to encourage a more diverse and perhaps even democratic model of communication. To succeed, though, the magazine fund will require a commitment to valuing the printed media as essential to promoting the rights of citizenship, not just of commerce.

NOTES

Unless noted otherwise, all dollar amounts are in U.S. currency.

1. The oldest, broadest, and most succinct of these guarantees is the First Amendment to the U.S. Constitution, promising that Congress shall make no law abridging freedom of speech or of the press. Article 7 of the Mexican constitution pledges: "Freedom of writing and publishing writings on any subject is inviolable." It specifically precludes censorship, but then quickly sets some boundaries on press freedom, saying it may be limited "by respect due to the privacy, morals and public peace." In Canada, press freedom is included in a list of "fundamental freedoms" in the Charter of Rights and Freedoms that is part of the 1982 constitution. The charter sets some vaguely phrased limits on "fundamental freedoms"—"such reasonable limits prescribed by law as can be demonstrably justified in a free and democratic society."

2. Canada imposed a duty on a few U.S. pulp magazines in 1925 and broadened it in 1930, depending on the ratio of ads to editorial content. The tariff was lifted in 1935 (Desbarats 1995, 80).

3. This drew mixed reaction from the Canadian Daily Newspaper Publishers Association. While some publishers approved, others feared it might lower the eventual value of their newspaper businesses. Still others objected to any infringement by the state on their rights as free-enterprise publishers (Desbarats 1995, 82).

4. The CBC's parliamentary appropriations have fallen 20 percent since 1995 alone, prompting the CBC to develop a plan to shut down its supper-hour newscasts (Rabinovitch 2000).

5. The steel threat was particularly painful for the minister in charge of Canadian Heritage, Sheila Copps, whose Hamilton, Ontario, riding is in the heart of Canadian steel country.

6. Less than two months after the Hollinger–CanWest Global sale, Thomson made a deal with the telecommunications giant Bell Canada Enterprises (BCE) to create a $4

billion (CD) multimedia company. It brought together the country's leading private television network, Canadian Television Network (CTV), with the *Globe and Mail* newspaper and the Sympatico-Lycos and Globe Interactive on-line businesses. BCE, which moved to take over CTV early in 2000, ended up owning 70 percent of the new company ("BCE, Thomson and Woodbridge Create Content Triple Play" 2000).

7. *La Jornada*, in an attempt to indicate that *gacetillas* are different from regular news, italicizes the headlines. Otherwise, *gacetillas* are indistinguishable from other stories (Benavides 2000, 85).

8. Vanden Heuvel and Dennis note that while Mexico City is the largest city in the world, the combined circulation of its two dozen daily newspapers is less than the circulation of the *San Diego Tribune* (1995, 21).

REFERENCES

"Americas: Country Report—Mexico." 1999. New York: Committee to Protect Journalists. <http://www.cpj.org.> [last accessed: 15 February 2001].

Babe, Robert E. 1990. *Telecommunications in Canada: Technology, Industry, and Government.* Toronto: University of Toronto Press.

"Background Briefing Via Conference Call Re: The Canada–U.S. Magazine Issue." 1999. Federal News Service, 26 May. Comments are attributed to a "senior trade official."

Baxter, James. 2000. "Beer Hero Enlisted in Copps' Culture War: Minister Taps 'Joe' to Explain How and Why Canadians Are Different." *Ottawa Citizen*, 1 May.

"BCE, Thomson and Woodbridge Create Content Triple Play—Print, Broadcast and Internet." 2000. Thomson Corporation News Release, 15 September.

Benavides, José Luis. 2000. "*Gacetilla:* A Keyword for a Revisionist Approach to the Political Economy of Mexico's Print News Media." *Media, Culture, and Society* 22 (January): 85–104.

Bernier, Ivan. 1998. "Cultural Goods and Services in International Trade Law." In *The Culture/Trade Quandary: Canada's Policy Options*, ed. Dennis Browne. Ottawa: Centre for Trade Policy and Law.

Browne, Dennis. 1998. Introduction to *The Culture/Trade Quandary: Canada's Policy Options*, ed. Dennis Browne. Ottawa: Centre for Trade Policy and Law.

Canada. 1981. *Royal Commission on Newspapers Report.* Ottawa: Supply and Services Canada.

"Country Report: Mexico." 1998. New York: Committee to Protect Journalists. <http://www.cpj.org> [last accessed: 18 April 2000].

Craig, Susan. 2000. "Ottawa to Review Newspaper Ownership." *Globe and Mail*, 2 May, 1.

Desbarats, Peter. 1995. "The Special Role of Magazines in the History of Canadian Mass Media and National Development." In *Communications in Canadian Society.* 4th ed. Ed. Benjamin D. Singer. Toronto: Nelson Canada.

Fromson, Murray. 1996. "Mexico's Struggle for a Free Press." In *Communication in Latin America: Journalism, Mass Media, and Society*, ed. R. R. Cole. Wilmington, Del.: Scholarly Resources.

Galperin, Hernan. 1999. "Cultural Industries Policy in Regional Trade Agreements: The Cases of NAFTA, the European Union, and MERCOSUR." *Media, Culture, and Society* 21 (September): 627–648.

Geddes, John. 1999. "A Run for the Money." *Maclean's*, 7 June, 54.

Grayson, George W. 1995. *The North American Free Trade Agreement: Regional Community and the New World Order*. Lanham, Md.: University Press of America.

"Hollinger Inc., Hollinger International Inc., and Its Affiliates Announce the Sale of CDN $3.5 Billion of Canadian Assets to CanWest Global Communications Corp." 2000. Hollinger Incorporated News Release, 31 July.

Honey, Kim. 2000. "The $150-Million Prescription." *Globe and Mail*, 4 October, R3.

King, Suzanne. 1998. "Copps Tables Magazine Legislation." *Canada at Five* (CBC Radio News), 8 October. <http://www.infoculture.cbc.ca> [last accessed: 2 May 2000].

Magder, Ted. 1998. "Franchising the Candy Store: Split Run Magazines and a New International Regime for Trade in Culture." Canadian American Public Policy Paper No. 34. Orono: The Canadian-American Center.

Morton, Peter, and Ian Jack. 1999. "U.S. Poised to Declare Trade War." *Financial Post*, 20 May.

Mosco, Vincent. 1997. "Marketable Commodity or Public Good: The Conflict between Domestic and Foreign Communications Policy." In *How Ottawa Spends, 1997–98. Seeing Red: A Liberal Report Card*, ed. G. Swimmer. Ottawa: Carleton University Press.

"New Canadian Magazine Fund to Benefit Canadian Publishers." 1999. Canadian Heritage Department News Release, 16 December.

"Ottawa and Washington Agree on Access to the Canadian Advertising Services Market." 1999. Canadian Heritage Department News Release, 26 May.

Pendakur, Manjunath. 1990. *Canadian Dreams and American Control: The Political Economy of the Canadian Film Industry*. Detroit: Wayne State University Press.

"Profitability of Canadian Magazines 1991 to 1997." Canadian Magazine Publishers Association. <http://www.cmpa.ca> [last accessed: 15 February 2001].

"PWAC Needs Your Help." 2000. Posted on the Canadian Association of Journalists' electronic discussion group, September 12. Toronto: PWAC National Office.

Rabinovitch, Robert. 2000. "Opening Remarks by the President of the CDC to the Standing Committee on Canadian Heritage." 16 May. <http://cbc.radio-canada/ca> [last accessed: 15 February 2001].

"Restructuring Process Announced—Newspaper Assets to Be Made Available for Sale, Merger, or Affiliation." 2000. Hollinger International News Release, 25 April. <http://www.Hollinger.com> [last accessed: 31 July 2000].

Ridder, Tony. 2000. "Get Rid of the Outdated Law." *Globe and Mail*, 1 May, A11.

Salwen, Michael B., and Bruce Garrison. 1991. *Latin American Journalism*. Hillsdale, N.J.: Erlbaum.

"Submission on Mexico's Fourth Periodic Report to the Human Rights Committee: Focus on Freedom of Expression in Mexico." 1999. Article 19, the International Centre against Censorship (July). <http://www.article19.org> [last accessed: 18 April 2000].

Sutherland, Fraser. 1989. *The Monthly Epic: A History of Canadian Magazines, 1789–1989*. Markham, Ontario: Fitzhenry and Whiteside.

Thompson, John Herd. 1995. "Canada's Quest for Cultural Sovereignty: Protection, Promotion, and Popular Culture." In *NAFTA in Transition*, ed. S. J. Randall and H. W. Konrad. Calgary: University of Calgary Press.

"U.S. Vows Fight in Magazine Battle." 1999. CBC Radio Report, 12 January. <http://www.infoculture.cbc.ca> [last accessed: 2 May 2000].

Vanden Heuvel, Jon, and Everette E. Dennis. 1995. *Changing Patterns: Latin America's Vital Media.* New York: Freedom Forum Media Studies Center.

Vipond, Mary. 1989. *The Mass Media in Canada.* Toronto: Lorimer.

———. 1992. *Listening In: The First Decade of Canadian Broadcasting, 1922–1932.* Montreal: McGill-Queen's University Press.

Winseck, Dwayne. 1998. *Reconvergence: A Political Economy of Telecommunications in Canada.* Cresskill, N.J.: Hampton.

World Trade Organization. 1997a. "Canada—Certain Measures Concerning Periodicals." Report of the Panel, 14 March. WT/DS31/R.

———. 1997b. "Canada—Certain Measures Concerning Periodicals." Report of the Appellate Body, 30 June. WT/DS31/AB/R.

"World Watch—The Americas: Briefly." 1998. *Wall Street Journal,* 17 December, 16.

9

Whose Hollywood?
Changing Forms and Relations
inside the North American
Entertainment Economy

Ted Magder and Jonathan Burston

At about 5 A.M. on July 6, 1999, nearly three hundred people gathered in the parking lot of the Los Angeles Zoo to join a caravan of buses and cars bound for Sacramento. The round-trip rides, plus breakfast, were free. The caravan was headed for the California State Legislature to join another seven hundred people from elsewhere in the state, with almost two hundred teamster-steered vehicles—cranes and Musco searchlight trucks among them—in flanking support. Although the demonstration went on for over two hours, the chants were direct and to the point: "Film American!" "Bring Hollywood Home!" This was the second of three rallies over the spring and summer of 1999 spearheaded by the newly formed Film and Television Action Committee (FTAC). The third rally, on August 15, was the largest such event in Hollywood history.[1] Somewhere between fifteen thousand to eighteen thousand industry workers—writers, electricians, grips, camera operators, makeup artists, hair stylists, drivers, wranglers, carpenters, boom operators, and directors—jammed Hollywood Boulevard from Mann's Chinese Theater all the way to Vine. Among the speakers was Jack De Govia, president of the International Alliance of Theatrical Stage Employees' (IATSE) Art Directors Local 876 and chairman of the FTAC. This is part of what he said: "We do not have to be victims of the market. We are not going to go quietly while our fate is decided in the columns of a spreadsheet. We are not disposable. We are not a commodity. . . . We will not stand by and let a foreign government buy our jobs and our lives and the future of our families. We helped build this industry and this town and state and nation, and we will not give up our lives without a fight!" (De Govia 1999) De Govia's rhetorical pitch was matched that day by other speakers. While Hollywood still commands the attention of the world as the nucleus of the film and televisual entertainment industry, for the people who make their lives in and around the back regions of the sets and studios, something was amiss. Stories had multiplied, and a study jointly commissioned by the Directors Guild of America (DGA) and the Screen Actors Guild (SAG) appeared to confirm even the most alarming ones: more and more film and television production was moving out of Hollywood and settling abroad. Moreover, the DGA/SAG report revealed that one country in particular had garnered the lion's share of what had come to be referred to as "runaway" productions. "Canada," declared the FTAC later that summer, "is actively participating in an effort to steal the film industry from the U.S." (Film and Television Action Committee 1999). Dawn Keezer, the director of the Pittsburgh Film Office and chairperson of an association of 196 local and state film commissions with the pointed moniker Film U.S., put it this way: "The industry was created here. It's now walking out the back door" (quoted in Pollack 1999, 19).

The furor and vitriol of the mounting campaign probably took most Canadians—even those working in the industry—by surprise. Canada has been a home away from home for American films since the beginning of Hollywood's expansion into foreign markets in the 1920s. Hollywood distributors have always treated Canada as if it were part of their domestic market. In an average year, Hollywood films account for over 95 percent of Canadian box office and video receipts. On television, almost 90 percent of the dramatic programming watched by English-speaking Canadians comes from south of the border. For much of the past century, Canadians have struggled to find homegrown stories on-screen that help define themselves. Back in the 1920s, when thoughts first turned toward the idea of building a Canadian film industry, Lewis B. Selznick, one of Hollywood's first moguls, declared that "if Canadian stories are worth making into films, then companies will be sent to Canada to make them" (quoted in Magder 1993, 47). But for the most part, Hollywood has made its movies about Canada in the studios and countryside of southern California. Between 1910 and 1957, more than five hundred pictures with Canadian themes were made, many populated with Mounties, braving the obligatory snowstorm in pursuit of gruff, hirsute French Canadians (Berton 1975).

Now, however, Hollywood was going to Canada to make movies about America—often in partnership with Canadian firms. According to the DGA/SAG report, what began as a trickle has lately become something of a flood: in 1998, 37 percent of all U.S.–developed film and television productions were made in foreign locations, almost triple the number in 1990, and of these 81 percent were made at least partly in Canada (DGA/SAG 1999). Among the more recent examples: *Battlefield Earth*, *The Whole Nine Yards*, *Good Will Hunting*, *The X-Files*, *The Jesse Ventura Story*, and *The Audrey Hepburn Story*.

But despite this upsurge of production activity, the accusation of foreign thievery—the idea that Canada is stealing the film industry away from the United States—is rife with problems. Most fundamental, the dilemmas now faced by Hollywood's workers are dilemmas associated with globalization across many industries, and in many countries. The target of American entertainment labor invective—Canada, mostly—is therefore misplaced. And while the plight of American entertainment labor—and for that matter, entertainment labor worldwide—is of significant concern, the notion that the Los Angeles basin is somehow the natural home for film and television is (indeed, has always been) untenable. The term "runaway" production itself reflects this problematic assumption. We intend to show how and why this is so by examining production decisions in both the United States and Canada, and the fluctuating economic and technological contexts in which these decisions are made. Although such an examination requires that we briefly descend into the realm of exchange rates, variable labor costs, tax policies, and other government incentives, bigger issues are at stake. Each of these elements contributes to a deepening interrelationship between the American and Canadian film and television industries. While the end result of this process might be described as the latest, accelerated phase in the ongoing continentalization of the North American film and television industry, there is no evidence that the levers of power and influence have shifted substantially. Indeed, the history of Canada–U.S. relations suggests that the term "continentalization" has never meant equal standing among its partners. What emerges as particularly noteworthy in turn-of-the-century Hollywood is how, despite increasing levels of activity and expenditure among a larger number of players from both sides of the border, the "disparate dyad" that has long characterized the Canada–U.S. relationship remains intact.

THE BIG PICTURE

As Hollywood labor representatives began to fret over the possibility that California was losing its near-monopoly on production, the real movers and shakers in Hollywood had reason to smile. Gross domestic box office receipts climbed to roughly $7 billion in 1998 and went to $7.5 billion in 1999 (Motion Picture Association of America [MPAA] 2000, 1–2). And though the remarkable success of *Titanic* (1997) features strongly in these record-breaking years, box office receipts grew by close to 50 percent over the 1990s (1–2). During a decade when so many prognosticators expected that audiences would increasingly prefer to be entertained at home, the movies were making an impressive comeback. Total admissions increased by almost 25 percent over the decade, from 1.2 billion in 1990 to 1.47 billion in 1999 (4), and the total number of screens went from 23,689 in 1990 to 37,185 in 1999, an increase of 57 percent (26). Of course, the major film distributors have more than one revenue stream: On an annual basis, foreign box office receipts now generate roughly the same revenue as domestic box office. In total, the MPAA distributors derive close to 40 percent of their total revenue from theatrical rentals; home video sales worldwide account for another 40 percent, while sales to television make up most of the remainder (Standard and Poor's 2000, 17).[2]

But in business, admissions, receipts, and sales only have value relative to costs. And costs soared in the 1990s. The average negative cost for MPAA feature films went from $26.8 million in 1990 to $53.4 million in 1997, an increase of almost 100 percent.[3] During the same period, the average marketing costs of new feature films went from $12 million to $22 million (MPAA 2000, 16–20). Exorbitant salaries for actors, lavish development contracts between studios and independent producers, the special effects and gadgetry that define the blockbuster genre—each of these contributed significantly to the rising costs of production. And while there was still a lot of money to be made with the right picture at the right time, the risks remained massive.

Moviemaking, American-style, has always been an unpredictable business. Over the years, Hollywood has found a variety of ways to weather the flops and duds, the most important being the studio system itself that has, over the years, variously combined an oligopolistic structure, personal charisma, assembly-line production, and creative accounting to make things work.[4] But over the past fifteen years, there has been one fundamental change to the architecture of Hollywood: the major studios, all of them, were absorbed (or transformed) into larger media conglomerates, combining movie studios with television units, networks (both over-the-air and cable), music companies, Internet ventures, video game outfits, theme parks, Broadway, other live-entertainment properties, and so on. The trend began in earnest with the News Corporation's purchase of Twentieth Century Fox in 1985; along the way, Sony purchased Columbia Pictures, Disney Corporation took over American Broadcasting Company (ABC), and Paramount Communication became part of Viacom. Warner twinned with Time, and then with America On-line. Most recently, Vivendi (of France) offered to purchase Seagram (of Canada), which owns Universal Studios and Polygram.

Increasing conglomeration means that the major studios, as well as networks and cable channels, generally exist as divisions within ever larger corporate umbrellas. In such settings, movies and television production represent shrinking portions of overall corporate revenue streams. For example, in 1988 film and television accounted for close to 70 percent of Paramount's revenues; in 1998 they represented 39 percent of Viacom's total sales. Similarly, 1998 film and television production represented 30 percent of sales for Time-Warner, down from 37 percent a decade earlier (Weinraub and Fabrikant 1999). Film and television units, then, are not necessarily the most lucrative divisions inside a conglomerate. According to one media analyst, the return on capital in the film industry hovers in "the midsingle digits" (1999). As a consequence, "under strict orders from their corporate owners to pay more heed to the bottom line, studios are making fewer films, forcing the people who work in the industry to carve up a smaller pie" (1999). Major studios are slashing the number of development deals they make with independent producers. According to senior *Variety* commentator Peter Bart, Twentieth Century Fox, "which had a total of 56 producing deals in 1997, now has 25" (Bart 2000; see also Lyons 2000). Disney, ever the pioneer in the cultivation of new revenue streams such as theme parks, stage musicals, and cruise ships, released only twenty feature films in 1999, down from an average of forty annually in the early 1990s (Bates 1999). And the pressure to cut costs has now penetrated to the core of the business. For two consecutive years, average production costs have dropped, from their peak of $53.4 million in 1997 to $51.5 million in 1999 (MPAA 2000, 17). In addition, for the first time over the last twenty years, marketing costs are down, totaling an average of $24.5 million in 1999—a $780,000 decline from the previous year (20).

This is probably a good moment to point out that while one often speaks of Hollywood as if it were a single entity, or perhaps an exclusive club of giant producers, as a site of production it is better understood as a checkerboard of small- and medium-sized companies and casual labor working in the shadows of the vast studio lots. Eighty percent of the industry is comprised of companies with four employees or fewer (Kyser 1998, 22). Moreover, most film workers are employed on a project-to-project basis, and despite the presence of unions such as the DGA, SAG, and IATSE, many productions employ nonunion labor.[5] Hollywood's big players deftly maneuver across this checkerboard, using a variety of subcontracting arrangements, minority investments, and licensing agreements (on everything from script development to postproduction sound editing and even to trailers) to cut costs and spread financial risk. Susan Christopherson has usefully termed this new patchwork system as being a "virtual," rather than a "vertical," integration, suggesting its simultaneous capacities for both flexibility and integration (1996).

Flexibility and integration, that is, for the purposes of management. The industry's newly "virtual" patterns of integration pose for labor a series of challenges that unions have to date been unable to meet effectively. For even as this new industrial paradigm aids—somewhat paradoxically—in the success of independents in a climate of increasing conglomeration, it hinders unions' capacities to negotiate effectively with so many new, affiliated, yet legally separate entities. Entertainment unions, both above and below the line, are fighting a greater number of uphill battles on matters pertaining to fragmentation, casualization, and compensation (Gray and Seeber 1996, 184–185). The full onset of digitization in the realm of production likewise presents a host of "mission critical" issues for Hollywood labor.[6] As Lois Gray and Ronald Seeber correctly point out, "the movie business . . . is undergoing its greatest period of change since the talkies" (182), and the very viability of certain unions now may be at issue:

The bargaining strength of unions representing below-the-line workers has greatly deteriorated as the skill levels required to operate new equipment have decreased and as the functional lines between labor and management have blurred. In an industry in which materials and equipment have traditionally been the basis for work rules and union jurisdiction, the existence and identity of unions are at stake as equipment becomes obsolete or as certain jobs are eliminated outright. The decrease in required skill levels has also weakened the unions' power to strike because management has found it relatively easy to replace striking workers with no appreciable effect on production. (184–185)

The weighty issues of digitization, spiraling costs, and the paradoxical dynamics of virtual integration would be enough in combination to produce a portrait of a contemporary Hollywood experiencing extraordinary change and flux. But in providing an adequate portrait for our purposes, there is still more to consider.

We need to turn our attention briefly to the relationship between Hollywood and the world beyond the borders of the United States. This much is well known: Foreign markets have always been enormously important to Hollywood's bottom line. And in order to maintain industrial dominance, Hollywood has always been eager to welcome foreign talent, whether actors, directors, writers, or cinematographers. Mary Pickford, Charlie Chaplin, and Erich von Stroheim helped establish Hollywood's original mystique; Jim Carey, Paul Verhoeven, and John Woo are more recent examples of Hollywood's centripetal power. Recently, however, more than just foreign talent is finding its way to Hollywood. Foreign capital and foreign suppliers have also become part of the Hollywood nexus. Foreign capital arrives in many forms. Bookending either end of the last fifteen years, Sony's purchase of Columbia, and Vivendi's pending purchase of Universal provide examples of a more familiar, gargantuan form of foreign investment. Munich-based Intertainment's $500 million picture deal with Hollywood producers Arnold Kopelson and Anne Kopelson (Duke and Foreman 2000), and Paris-based Studio Canal's $900 million alliance with Michael Ovitz (James 2000),[7] each reveal a more mundane level of integration between Hollywood and its international markets.

Hollywood has also learned how to work with foreign suppliers of film and television products. And it is here that Canadian companies have played a critical role. From an early stage, Canada's private producers have been compelled to look beyond their own borders—not for sites of ancillary profit, but for the core financing necessary to do business. At less than one-tenth the size of the U.S. market, the Canadian sector is not as forgiving of the sizable financial risks associated with the industry. By necessity, Canada's private producers have become masters of the international deal, learning early on how to raise foreign capital through the presale of distribution rights, coventures, and coproductions with European, Australian, Asian, and American partners. They have also learned how to work for hire on what, in Canada, are commonly referred to as foreign service or location productions. In both instances, the U.S. market and U.S. capital are key ingredients. The impressive growth of total production activity in Canada over the course of the 1990s, from $1.5 billion (CD)in 1992–1993 to $3.67 billion (CD) in 1999 (Canadian Film and Television Production Association [CFTPA] 2000) owes much to the increase of foreign service productions and the increasing willingness of American companies to purchase Canadian-produced content. Is it conceivable that Hollywood's dominance over film and television production is on the wane as we witness the emergence of a Hollywood North? It is to these questions that we now turn.

THE RUNAWAY PRODUCTION ISSUE

The Monitor Report: Runaway Productions and Their Impact

In January 1999, the DGA and SAG commissioned an investigation into the phenomenon of runaway film and television productions. The Monitor Company, a leading global management consulting firm, conducted the now famous study. Monitor was asked to quantify the extent to which runaway productions had been occurring since 1990, to identify the major causes of this trend, and to assess its economic impact.

The report defines a "runaway production" as one "that was developed in the U.S. and was intended for initial release/exhibition or television broadcast in the U.S. but filmed partially or entirely outside of the U.S." (Monitor Company 1999, 6). According to the report, runaway productions can be filmed either by a U.S. company or by a foreign-based production company working under contract with a U.S. film distributor, broadcast network, cable network, or syndicator. While much rides on the interpretation of this definition, the report provides only one concrete example: *Titanic*, which was partly shot off the coast of Mexico. The report does distinguish between two *types* of runaways: creative and economic. "Creative runaways" are defined as productions that are "filmed partially or entirely outside of the U.S. due to script or setting requirements, or actor/director preference." An "economic runaway" is "a production that was filmed primarily abroad to reduce costs incurred during production" (6). The report also provides a long list of exclusions from its analysis: commercials, daytime soaps, documentaries, game shows, infomercials, music videos, sports, talk shows, and television specials. Put another way, the report focuses on the more glamorous side of film and television production, concentrating only on feature films produced for U.S. theatrical release, direct-to-video productions, movies for television (telefilms), and dramatic television series.

The report provides evidence that there has been rapid growth in runaways of all types. In 1998, of the 1,075 U.S.–developed productions that were made, 399 ran away from the United States; an increase of 82 percent from the 219 productions that ran away in 1990. In 1990, runaways of all types comprised 29 percent of total production as compared to 37 percent of all productions in 1998. The growth was largest in the area of television productions. In 1990, television runaways comprised 28 percent of total television production as compared to 42 percent in 1998, with domestically produced television programming increasing by only 10 percent during the same period (Monitor Company 1999, 7).

According to the report, this growth is primarily attributable to economic runaways, which go from 100 productions in 1990 to 285 productions in 1998, an increase of 185 percent. During the same period, creative runaways remain virtually stable, with 109 in 1990 and 114 in 1998 (1999, 7). Of those projects deemed economic runaways, movies for television have exhibited the most significant growth; from 30 in 1990 to 139 in 1998, a 363 percent increase. Of all U.S.–developed television movies, 45 percent were economic runaways in 1998 (139 out of 308). Feature films have also become an important component of the runaway phenomenon, going from forty-four in 1990 to one hundred in 1998, with twenty-four of the latter classified as high-budget films (Monitor Company 1999, 8).

Despite this flight in U.S.–developed productions to foreign locations, the Monitor report acknowledges that production activity in the United States has been steadily increasing over the past decade. According to the report, between 1990 and 1998 the United States experienced average annual growth rates of 8.2 percent for feature films and 2.6 percent for television (1999, 9). The report suggests, however, that these modest annual increases have "masked the true impact of the runaway production problem" (10), because the comparable growth rates in other countries have been much higher. In Canada, according to the report, U.S.–developed film and television productions have increased annually by 17.4 percent and 18.2 percent, respectively, over the same period (10). And there is no mistaking the overall importance of Canada as the site of runaway activity. While a small proportion of runaways go to Australia and the United Kingdom, and a few highly visible runaways such as *Titanic* go elsewhere (such as Mexico), the biggest number end up north of the border. In fact, Canada's share of runaways has gone from 63 percent in 1990 to 81 percent in 1998, including 91 percent of all telefilm runaways (10).

The report makes an ambitious attempt to calculate the cumulative impact of economic runaways on the U.S. economy for 1998. It first estimates that the 285 economic runaways had $4 billion in direct production expenditures, of which $1.2 billion remained in the United States, either as pre- or postproduction, or as salaries paid to U.S. actors, directors, and other principals working in foreign locations. The remaining $2.8 billion becomes the basis for the report's calculation of the total economic impact. Using multipliers supplied by the U.S. Bureau of Economic Analysis that are applied to wages, salaries, goods, services, and lost tax revenues, the report concludes that the total economic impact of lost production was $10.3 billion in 1998, five times the total economic impact in 1990 (1999, 11–12). This figure represents almost 14 percent of the total economic impact for all U.S.–developed feature films and television production included in the study (13).

While overall production activity in Los Angeles has *not* decreased according to the study, other cities and states have not fared as well in recent years. North Carolina experienced a 36 percent decline between 1995 and 1998, while Texas, another miniproduction center, experienced a decline of 31 percent over the same period (Monitor Company 1999, 15–16).[8] Finally, despite the difficulties inherent in attributing job loss to any single fact in an industry characterized by contract employment, the report concludes that economic runaways were responsible for 23,500 lost full-time equivalent positions in 1998. Of these, SAG members lost roughly eleven thousand positions and DGA members lost close to six hundred. The majority of lost positions affected members of other unions and nonrepresented labor (16–17).[9]

Economic runaways, as Monitor defines them, are first and foremost intended to reduce production costs and, as we have seen, Hollywood is now in the midst of a cost-conscious cycle. But how do runaways generate cost-savings and why is Canada the main destination for runaway productions? The answers here are not much in doubt. First, both the Canadian and Australian dollars have declined in value by more than 20 percent relative to the U.S. dollar over the last decade. At sixty-five to sixty-eight U.S. cents for every Canadian dollar, the savings on salaries, as well as on goods and services (everything from hotel bills to catering costs), are considerable. Second, according to the report, wage rates for many below-the-line positions are much lower in Canada, on average 25 percent lower for key below-the-line positions, and as much as 50 percent lower for a unit production manager (Monitor Company 1999, 19). Third, though the value of the dollar and the wage-rates savings alone might be enough to explain the increase in runaways, there is one other factor that must be taken into account: government incentives. As we will explain in greater detail later on, the Canadian federal government offers a rebate of 11 percent on spending for all labor involved in a production shot in Canada. Most provincial governments sweeten the incentive with rebates of their own. The Monitor report concludes that runaways can realize savings of up to 25 percent if located in Canada.

The report concludes by speculating that runaway productions are not a passing phenomenon. For one thing, it notes that Ontario and British Columbia have developed into solid and reliable production "clusters" with experienced crews and sound stage space that rival New York and North Carolina combined. Moreover, most of the major studios have made sizable investments in offshore production facilities. For example, in 1997, Viacom invested over $10 million to construct four sound stages and a production office in Vancouver and to open a production support office in Toronto. Fox recently opened a new production facility in Sydney, valued at $130.5 million (Monitor Company 1999, 24). In one telling phrase, the report suggests that "the increased globalization of entertainment companies is likely to stimulate further 'runaway' production" (24). For those who commissioned the study, its final words are dispiriting: "Without a meaningful response (or some unforeseen development abroad), production opportunities and associated benefits will continue to leave the U.S. at a significant rate" (26).

The View from the Other Side

Despite the apparent rigor of its analysis, the figures and definitions of the Monitor report should not go unchallenged. Canadian players from both industry and government took immediate issue with two features of the report that involve day-to-day film and television business in Canada. The Directors Guild of Canada (DGC) led the charge, challenging Monitor's claim that close to $2.2 billion ended up in Canada on so-called runaways (DGC 1999).[10] "What we need is a reality check," said Allan King, a former president of the DGC. "When you actually look at the audited numbers, it turns out that the U.S. study has exaggerated the amount of U.S. production dollars coming to Canada by a factor of three or four" (quoted in Madigan 1999a). According to the DGC, foreign location shooting in Canada in 1998 totaled $573 million.[11] The DGC also took exception to Monitor's exclusive focus on feature films and dramatic television productions. If the intention of the Monitor report was to assess the overall economic impact of runaway productions, why not take as a comparative measure the total volume of production in the United States? Estimates for this figure run upwards of $30 billion. At $2.8 billion, U.S. economic runaways would be less than 10 percent of the total; at $573 million they would account for less than 2 percent.[12]

However, even the DGC's more modest estimate of runaway productions constitutes a sizable chunk of the industry in Canada. There is, in fact, no denying the growing importance of foreign involvement to Canada's production industry. Between 1992–1993 and 1998–1999, the foreign share of Canada's total volume of film and television production has nearly quadrupled from $414 million Canadian to $1.55 billion Canadian; the foreign contribution to Canada's total production activity now stands at over 40 percent. Although we cannot be precise about the U.S. contribution to this total, our best estimate is that it is roughly 95 percent.[13] We are confident that these figures are more reliable than those provided by Monitor because they are derived from audited figures used to calculate Canadian tax rebates. It is unlikely that producers would underreport such information (CFTPA 2000, 30).

The Canadian data also provide a clearer picture of how this money is spent. Among other things, they make distinctions of their own between several types of production in Canada enjoying foreign participation, two of which require our attention here.[14] "Foreign location shooting" describes "film or video production shot in Canada by U.S. studios and U.S. independent producers" (CFTPA 2000, 29). A second type of film or television product benefits from the participation of foreign financing, but its copyright is still held in whole or in part by a Canadian company. Foreign location shooting experienced a growth rate of 34 percent in 1998–1999, amounting to a total of $1.1 billion Canadian. Foreign financing of projects owned or partly owned by Canadian producers amounted to another $454 million Canadian (30). Unfortunately, the Monitor report failed to distinguish between these two types of production, a distinction that is crucial as we turn our attention to some examples of the practical ties that now bind the American and Canadian industries together.

A Continental Film Industry?

On the day of its opening, *Battlefield Earth* (2000), starring John Travolta, claimed the distinction of being the most expensive feature film ever shot in Canada. Produced by Elie Samaha's Franchise Pictures, the film nicely illustrates the advantages of foreign location shooting and the shifting dynamics of the film industry in Hollywood and elsewhere. Franchise Pictures may not be a household name, but aside from *Battlefield Earth*, it is also the producer of *The Whole Nine Yards* (2000) with Bruce Willis, *Get Carter* (2000) with Sylvester Stallone, and *The Pledge* (2000) with Jack Nicholson and Sean Penn (Hirschberg 2000). All of these films were shot, in whole or in part, in Canada. Unlike the major studios, Samaha's pockets are not deep. As a consequence, he has been particularly adroit at cobbling together financial packages that reduce risks and cut costs. For *Battlefield Earth*, Samaha raised 70 percent of the budget by selling its overseas rights in advance, a significant departure from the studio tendency to horde worldwide distribution rights in the hopes of garnering blockbuster returns. Shooting in Canada, according to Samaha, trimmed the film's total budget from $90 million to $65 million. And although the domestic box office for *Battlefield Earth* pales in comparison to the other big-budget film released on the same day (*Gladiator*), Samaha claimed that he needed only $35 million in *domestic* returns to break even.

What Samaha does out of necessity, larger independent producers, cable channels, networks, and even studios are now doing by choice. Producer Leonard Goldberg, who shot the 1999 Tommy Lee Jones feature *Double Jeopardy* in British Columbia, succinctly reflects Hollywood's new cost consciousness and the impetus this provides Canadian production: "Between the Canadian dollar and the tax advantage they give you, it's very hard to beat it" (quoted in Pollack 1999, 19). In 1998, ten of the fourteen original movies shown on Showtime and fourteen of the twenty-three films made for the USA Network were made outside the United States. In that same year, Columbia-Tristar made five of its twenty television pilots in Canada (1999). Sonny Gross, who came to Canada in 1983 to shoot *Nightheat*, the first made-in-Canada television series to air in U.S. prime time, now owns a studio in Toronto: "Me, I go to Canada and imitate New York, because of the

Table 9.1 Foreign Location Shooting: Examples of American Productions Shot in Canada

Title	Location	Credits
2000		
X-Men	Toronto/Ontario region	Patrick Stewart/Twentieth Century Fox
Shanghai Noon	Alberta/Beijing	Jackie Chan/Touchstone Pictures
Get Carter	Vancouver/Seattle/Las Vegas	Sylvester Stallone/Franchise Pictures/Warner Bros.
Battlefield Earth	Montreal	John Travolta/Franchise Pictures/Warner Bros.
The Pledge	Vancouver	Jack Nicholson/Franchise Pictures
The Audrey Hepburn Story	Montreal	ABC/Endemol (TV movie)
Take Me Home: The John Denver Story	Vancouver	CBS (TV movie)
1999		
Mission to Mars	Vancouver	Tim Robbins/Touchstone Pictures
Dudley Do-Right	Vancouver	Universal
The Jesse Ventura Story	Toronto	Hearst Entertainment/Global
Aftershock: Earthquake in New York	Vancouver/Los Angeles/ New York	CBS (TV miniseries)
Ricky Nelson: Original Teen Idol	Vancouver/Toronto	VH1 (TV movie)
Double Jeopardy	British Columbia	Tommy Lee Jones/Paramount/ BC Production Tax Credit/ Munich Film Partners
1998		
The X-Files	British Columbia/Los Angeles/ London/New Jersey	Twentieth Century Fox
Blade	Vancouver/Los Angeles	Wesley Snipes/New Line
Barney's Great Adventure	Montreal	Polygram
Down in the Delta	Toronto	Esther Rolle/Miramax
Bad As I Wanna Be: The Dennis Rodman Story	Toronto/Los Angeles	TriStar/Mandalay (TV movie)
1997		
Good Will Hunting	Toronto/Boston	Matt Damon/Miramax
Batman and Robin	Montreal/Texas/Vienna	George Clooney/Warner Bros.
La Femme Nikita	Toronto	Warner Bros./Baton (TV series)
Joe Torre: Curveballs Along the Way	Toronto/New York	Showtime (TV movie)

Note: Year refers to date of release and unless otherwise noted productions are feature films.
Source: Industry publications and the Internet Movie Database <www.imdb.com> [last accessed: 15 February 2001].

money. Anything is possible in America—with a little help from Canada" (quoted in Hamill 2000, 17). As American producers grow increasingly confident in the skill and size of Canadian talent pools both above and below the line, they have begun to treat production in Canada as an entirely routine option. According to the *Los Angeles Times*, studios now regularly require an economic assessment of shooting costs in Canada (Bates 1999). "Everybody in town is there," one Columbia-Tristar television executive remarks. "It obviously works" (Pollack 1999).

We have so far provided examples of U.S. producers who have chosen to shoot—in whole or in part—in Canada, what the Canadian industry refers to as foreign location or service production. But not every original idea for a film or television production originates south of the Canadian border. In fact, *Canadians* make many film and television products, some of which are developed with the American market in mind. No area of the television marketplace better illustrates this than children's television, where a number of Canadian companies have carved a strong niche for themselves in international markets. Two of the most prominent are Nelvana and Cinar. Founded in 1985, Montreal-based Cinar has produced more than fifteen hundred half-hours of children's programming in the last fifteen years. When *Caillou* made its debut on Public Broadcasting System (PBS) in the fall of 1999, Cinar became the only producer ever to have four children's programs on PBS's "Ready to Learn" morning schedule at the same time. The other three shows have become staples of the PBS lineup: *Arthur* (coproduced with WGBH Boston) recently overtook *Sesame Street* as the most popular show among children aged two to eleven; *Wimzie's House* and *Zoboomafoo* (in association with Earth Creatures Company) round out the list. In each case, PBS or its affiliates provide Cinar with foreign financing (in the form of up-front production money) and Cinar, like most Canadian companies, also presells these shows in other foreign markets. Indeed, Cinar recently announced that China's Central Television will be added "to the list of over 120 countries where the *Arthur* television series has been sold" (Cinar 2000). Toronto-based Nelvana has an equally impressive record as a provider of children's entertainment. Nelvana's programs are sold in over 160 countries. Among its television and feature film properties are *Franklin, Babar, Little Bear,* and *Pippi Longstocking.* In 1999, Nelvana signed a $40 million deal with PBS to produce six new book-based series for its Saturday morning lineup, with PBS agreeing to pick up at least two of the series as weekday strips (forty episodes) (Nelvana 1999). That same year, Nelvana produced three series for Columbia Broadcasting System (CBS), *Anatole, Flying Rhino Junior High,* and *Mythic Warriors: Legends of the Deep,* and accepted an order from CBS for three more ("Playback Takes a Look Back at '99" 1999).[15] Nelvana's business plan also reveals the importance of foreign financing and coproductions. In an average year, the company will embark on only two productions without foreign partners (Tillson 2000).

Canadian companies have also enjoyed some success in dramatic programming. Perhaps the best known of these companies is Toronto-based Alliance Atlantis.[16] In 1994, Alliance's *Due South* became the first Canadian-produced television series to air during network prime time in the United States. The series ran for two years on CBS, helping establish Alliance's reputation abroad as a reliable program supplier. Among Alliance's more notable productions are *Joan of Arc* (1999 miniseries shown on CBS), *Nuremberg* (2000 miniseries shown on Turner Network Television), *Thirst* (1998 telefilm shown on National Broadcasting Company [NBC]), and *PSI Factor: Chronicles of the Paranormal* (a four-year-old series distributed by Eyemark–CBS). Alliance also recently completed a package of six films produced for Viacom's United Paramount Network as part of that network's "Way out There" movie franchise (Alliance Atlantis 2000). Like Cinar and Nelvana, Alliance considers foreign sales crucial to its business plan. In 1999, more than 80 percent of its broadcast license revenue came from foreign sources, with almost half coming from the United States (16). Alliance also owns—in whole or in part—seven specialty cable television networks in Canada.

Other Canadian companies are making a stab at joining the Hollywood nexus. One of these, Vancouver-based Lions Gate Entertainment, has studio-like aspirations. The company enjoys a well-established position as a niche-market film distributor (e.g., *Affliction* [1997] and *American Psycho* [2000]), controls the largest studio space in Vancouver (North Shore Studios), holds 45 percent minority ownership in the Los Angeles–based Mandalay Pictures, and acquired Trimark Holdings, a Los Angeles–based producer/distributor, in June 1999 (Eller and Bates 2000; Warren and Edwards 2000). The company's recent productions include the feature-film version of *American Psycho*, shot and edited for sound in Toronto, and directed by Mary Harron, a Canadian (Dillon 2000). During the summer of 2000, Mandalay was shooting *The Score* in Montreal, with a cast that included Robert DeNiro, Marlon Brando, and Ed Norton. The film's production designer was De Govia, who stepped down as chairman of the FTAC in January 2000 (Robb 2000c).

Runaway Productions: What Is in a Name?

Now that we have a somewhat better sense of the relationships between the American and Canadian production industries, we should revisit the term "runaway production." Recall that the Monitor report initially defines a "runaway production" as any project "that was developed in the U.S. and was intended for initial release/exhibition or television broadcast in the U.S. but filmed partially or entirely outside of the U.S." (1999, 6). However, in the glossary that accompanies the report and in the rather brief discussion of the methods employed to calculate the data, the criteria used to identify a television runaway are modified. The change is slight but significant: Indeed, *this* would appear to be the Monitor report's working definition: "any TV show, series or television film first intended for exhibition in the U.S. but filmed in another country by either a U.S. or foreign-based production company under license agreements with broadcast networks, basic/pay cable networks, syndicators, etc." (27). Notice that it no longer matters whether the project was "developed in the U.S." The phrase has been dropped from the definition. If this was the definition used during the collection of Monitor data, then every single previously mentioned Canadian-produced television program would qualify as a U.S. program that has run away from its natural home. It now seems as if the key criterion is the phrase "first intended for exhibition in the U.S." But this raises two issues. First, a considerable number of television shows produced in Canada *share* initial broadcast (exhibition) dates with American dates (the same is true for film releases). If a television show airs on the same date in two countries and one country is the United States, is it only the United States that counts? Second, is it inconceivable that a foreign producer could design a project with the intention of selling it first and foremost to the American market? Is it not possible that some of the productions that the Monitor report defines as runaways are better understood as imports? Ultimately, the Monitor report and its use by the DGA, SAG, and others is premised on two incorrect and parochial assumptions. First, every English-language film or television project with even a trace of U.S. participation is by definition an American production. Second, all of these projects could and should be made in the United States.

We are close to the heart of the problem with the term "runaway production." In many instances, it is increasingly difficult to accurately employ or assess the phrase "developed in the U.S." or, for that matter, "developed in Canada." The development of a film or television project is rarely a straightforward process. Take *Joan of Arc* as an example. The original idea for the miniseries was pitched to CBS by Alliance. CBS signed on, but the project was expensive—at $25 million, reportedly the most expensive television miniseries ever ordered by CBS. As a result, Alliance lined up other partners such as the Canadian Broadcasting Corporation (CBC) and European producers. The project was shot in the Czech Republic. Is this an American television program? Granted, it was released first in the United States; CBS aired the program in May 1999, while CBC aired it in July. But should we presume that CBS would have developed the project without Alliance? And can we be sure that Alliance would have passed on the project if there was no U.S. money involved? It is hard to be certain. Indeed, even in the case of *Battlefield Earth*, which was developed in the United States, we cannot be sure that the production would have gone forward without the savings derived from shooting in Montreal. Without the mix of foreign partners and advantages of a foreign location shoot, these projects might never have gotten off the ground. While working in Montreal on Mandalay's *The Score*, De Govia explained that the project was not an example of an economic runaway because part of the story is "set in French Montreal. . . . It's a location picture. We are shooting Montreal for Montreal. We [at FTAC] are not saying it's wrong for an American company to make movies in Canada. We're saying that it's unfair to use Canada as an imitation United States" (quoted in Robb 2000a). But if location verisimilitude is to be the new criterion for runaways, Los Angeles could probably win any numbers contest hands down. After all, Hollywood was built to stand in for the rest of the world.[17]

It bears repeating: Hollywood is the nexus of a global business, and it has been for nearly a century. And as a global business, it has always been willing to share some of its *largesse* with foreign partners—when necessary. Hollywood is looking to foreign partners with increasing frequency because it cannot guarantee the outputs it hopes to generate in an industry boasting an ever-increasing number of end markets. In this respect, the Hollywood segment of the global entertainment business is, after a fashion, coming more and more to resemble its Canadian counterpart. Of necessity, Canadian producers have learned the art of the international deal, crafting projects on a case-by-case basis, without the deep pockets and large domestic market that Hollywood so long enjoyed. Hollywood is learning to do the same, cutting costs and minimizing risks by building new alliances with foreign partners. In this context, the term "runaway" clarifies little and obfuscates much. It would be best put to rest.

BRINGING IN THE STATE: WHAT CAN POLICY DO?

If the loose alliance of American film and television workers, film commissioners, and politicians have their way, the United States may soon adopt another aspect of the Canadian playbook. Canadian film and television producers are major beneficiaries of government support, making use of a wide array of tax incentives and subsidies (Acheson and Maule 1999; Dorland 1998; Magder 1993). Canadian government programs date back to the late 1960s, when the federal government established the Canadian Film Development Corporation (now Telefilm Canada) with the lofty goal of creating, almost from scratch, a Canadian feature film industry based in the private sector. From the beginning, the complex array of policy instruments used to achieve this goal have embodied two, somewhat competing, objectives. On the one hand, government assistance was designed to help Canadians express themselves and their collective identities through the media of film and television. On the other hand, government assistance was designed to create an industrial infrastructure for the production of feature films and television programs in Canada. Given the size of Canada's domestic market, the challenge has always been to ensure that private producers remain committed to the production of high-quality Canadian content even as they grow more confident in their ability to create product for the international (mostly American) marketplace. And though there is an ongoing debate concerning the details of this policy field, in one sense it has surely been successful, given that a viable commercial film and television production industry now exists in Canada.

But despite the recent success of companies such as Alliance, Nelvana, and Cinar, most independent producers in Canada would be hard pressed to stay in business were it not for the support of government programs. This is not to disparage the entrepreneurial talents of Canadians. It merely reflects the economic dynamics of the Canadian marketplace for film and television. As we have suggested, these dynamics have everything to do with the small size of the Canadian domestic market, and the overwhelming presence of American product therein. In 1998–1999, direct public funding accounted for close to $400 million (CD), roughly 17 percent, of total production expenditures (CFTPA 2000, 3). The single most important source of funding is the Canadian Television Fund, which contributed roughly $200 million (CD) to the production of over two thousand new hours of prime time television programming in 1999 (Canadian Television Fund 1999). These funds and others like them, such as Telefilm Canada's Feature Film Fund—are available only to Canadian producers, and can be applied to projects deemed to be "Canadian" in accordance with a set of criteria that include creative talent (e.g., director, screenwriter, principal actors, and others) and the employment of Canadian crews.[18] Awards are made on the basis of a competitive application procedure.

Canadian producers can also take advantage of two federal tax incentives, both of which are administered by the Canadian Audio-Visual Certification Office (CAVCO). The first of these is the Canadian Film and Television Production Tax Credit Program, which provides a 25 percent refundable tax credit for eligible wages and salaries on projects that qualify as Canadian. The second tax credit program, the Film and Video Production Services Tax Credit (PSTC) Program, was established in 1997. The PSTC is equal to 11 percent of salaries and wages paid to Canadian residents or taxable Canadian corporations for services provided to productions in Canada. It is available to any producer, regardless of citizenship, who chooses to shoot in Canada. As CAVCO's activity report for 1998–1999 makes clear, the goal of the PSTC is "economic, that is, to attract foreign productions to Canada and to employ Canadian residents" (CAVCO 2000, 11). Every province in Canada has a similar set of incentives that vary in their detail and breadth.[19]

There has been some speculation in the United States that Canadian government financial support violates the norms of international trade law and constitutes unfair subsidies.[20] This is patently not the case. Although the PSTC is designed to encourage foreigners to locate productions in Canada and to employ Canadians, this does not in any way violate international trade law. Because the PSTC is available on a nondiscriminatory basis to both Canadian and foreign producers, it is perfectly in keeping with what are commonly referred to as "national treatment" provisions in international trade agreements. These speculations are moot in any event, because the production activities of the film and television sector have not been incorporated into any such accords. Furthermore, there are no grounds for supposing that the subsidies targeted to Canadian producers violate even the spirit of liberalized trade between Canada and the United States. These subsidies could only be deemed "unfair" if it could be shown that they provide Canadian producers with an unfair comparative advantage, making it possible for them to "dump" a product into the U.S. and/or other markets. This would be a hard case to make, most especially because "dumping" a product requires that it be sold for far less in the foreign market than in the domestic one. There is no compelling evidence that such practices are occurring. Finally, it is worth recalling that American carriers of content (e.g., film distributors, television networks, and cable stations) derive a considerable benefit from the supply of Canadian product. It is hard to imagine that they would want to jeopardize their relationships with Canadian producers by supporting an ill-conceived challenge under international law.

Assuming that there is no international mechanism that can be used to address the runaway issue, what prospects exist for a solution on the American domestic front? One solution would be for labor to make substantial concessions on wage rates and benefits. Another, per the "Film American!" banners at recent California demonstrations, would involve summoning the collective loyalty and patriotism of American producers. Neither of these are particularly tenable prospects. In fact, at the 1999 summer rallies, little mention was made of the hard-edged business decisions that had driven some producers to go north, though Jack Shea, a former president of the DGA, made one cautious reference to "companies that have little loyalty and only care about profits" (1999). Instead, the goal of the demonstrations has been to raise the issue at a legislative level and convince American politicians that the film industry needs a certain measure of government support.

Of course, the film industry already derives considerable benefit from the U.S. government. The American federal government has always underwritten Hollywood's global expansion. Since 1918, the major Hollywood distributors have been permitted to act as a legal cartel in overseas markets (Guback 1969). At the state and local levels, a wide range of small tax benefits, such as exemptions on restaurant and hotel taxes, as well as logistical support with locations and permits, have helped grease productions. There is no easy way to quantify the amount of government support, and no reliable estimates are available. These government expenditures are, for the most part, indirect and hidden from public view.

But the DGA, SAG, and others were raising the stakes by asking for something more: A public acknowledgment that U.S. film and television production needs *direct* financial assistance from the state. This is by no means an easy sell. For anyone outside the industry, it is hard not to be taken in by Hollywood's glamour; making the case for any kind of financial support to the business of moviemaking would require a particularly deft lobbying touch. Not surprisingly, such efforts first bore fruit in California, where the film and television business has played a starring role in fueling the remarkably robust recovery of the state's economy following the collapse of the aerospace industry (see Cassidy 1998; MPAA 1998). The activities of the FTAC in the spring and summer of 1999 were timed to heighten public awareness of two bills that were working their way through the California State Legislature, one of which called for a 10 percent tax rebate for below-the-line labor (Robb 1999). Both bills were passed by the state assembly in June 1999. But over the summer and fall of 1999, as the California Senate deliberated the bills, Governor Gray Davis indicated his reluctance to sign either bill into law (Gettleman 2000).

Meanwhile, Hollywood's Washington allies began the push for nationwide incentives. In mid-July, three members of Congress brought the outlines of a U.S. Film Protection Amendment before the House Ways and Means Committee. It called for a 20 percent wage credit, tax-exempt film production bonds, and low-interest loans (Boliek 1999; see also Madigan 1999b). While support for the measures seem to have grown on Capitol Hill, the tax incentives and other financial measures never made it out of committee. Washington, it seems, is not yet ready to send public money to Hollywood bank accounts.[21] However, the issue is still alive in Washington. In September 1999, Vice President Al Gore, after bipartisan meetings with members of Congress, instructed the federal research division of the Library of Congress to conduct its own investigation into runaway productions (Boliek 2000).

California has inched ahead. With the signing of the state budget for 2000–2001, Governor Davis approved the Film California First Fund. Noting that "California has a proud history as the cornerstone of the film industry," Governor Davis committed $15 million annually over the next three years "to offer production companies one more reason to film here, while also boosting the economic prosperity of our state and local communities" (CA Trade and Commerce Agency 2000). To be administered by the California Film Commission, the fund is designed to help producers recoup the costs of location shooting throughout California, primarily by reimbursing them for the use of state employees such as the California Highway Patrol, State Park employees, and fire marshals. Needless to say, the fund represents a far more modest financial commitment than the two bills that were working their way through the state legislature.

But it is extremely unlikely that the fund will have any significant impact on the use of foreign location shooting by American companies. Quite possibly, its major impact will be to encourage American producers to choose California over states such as New York and North Carolina, after the decision to shoot in the United States has been made. Would a national tax incentive that mirrored the Canadian federal government's PSTC fare any better? We do not think so. As we have seen, the relative value of the Canadian dollar and Canadian labor costs already present American producers with considerable advantages, playing a greater role than tax incentives in the cost savings that American producers obtain. Moreover, such a program would likely be considered enormously expensive for a government that has no history of providing direct financial assistance to the private production of popular culture.

WHOSE HOLLYWOOD?

The DGA/SAG–commissioned Monitor report represents a dishearteningly simplistic and one-dimensional intervention in a much-needed debate on the globalization and digitization of film and televisual production. By placing all of its emphasis on *where* production takes place, and avoiding entirely a consideration of *how* production takes place, the report fails to shed light on a number of crucial factors contributing to the profound instabilities that entertainment labor—in southern California and elsewhere—are now experiencing. It does so, furthermore, at a time when cultural workers and policymakers in many countries would have welcomed a productive investigation of worldwide economic, regulatory, and technological changes by two leading American entertainment unions. "Blame Canada" may be an amusing refrain, but it has little analytical purchase.

We have already identified some of the profound challenges that ongoing digital innovations (from pre- to postproduction) pose to below-the-line labor in Hollywood. We expect such trends to deepen the instability that traditional entertainment labor now faces. But the new, digitally prescribed conditions of production are no longer specific to below-the-line work. Most of us by now are aware of the "synthespians" among us: deceased performers who come back to life to sing with their daughters (Nat King Cole) or dance with vacuum cleaners (Fred Astaire), and digitally created "actors" now appearing as extras on cinema, television, and computer screens everywhere (e.g., *Ace Ventura, Gladiator,* and *The Patriot*). Digital media companies have been crowing for some time about the benefits that rapidly improving "vactor" (virtual actor) technologies can provide Hollywood management, at the expense of labor. If you are thinking digital scabs at this point, you are thinking along the right lines. For example, Gray and Seeber warn that digital video synthesizers will shrink the need for photographers, actors, and directors, especially at the middle levels (1996). And although SAG executive Allen Weingartner rightly observed in a 1999 interview that the cost of the innovations necessary for the normalization of such events is still prohibitively high, such costs continue, inexorably, to fall. SAG already finds itself deliberating how best to secure adequate recompense to a stunt worker whose single performance is digitally reinserted, often many times, in the same film. And the prospect of carbon-based stars "working with" digitally created waiters, bartenders, and doormen seems less far off than it once did (Weingartner 1999). Indeed, it is "all just a matter of time," Industrial Light and Magic's Steve Williams recently remarked, before "blood actors" will face actors "who only exist in a digital medium."[22] As our synthespian event horizon approaches, then, we might consider whether *blaming Silicon Valley* might lead to more productive debate than blaming Canada. Not Silicon Valley, the place, but Silicon Valley the product. For at the end of the day, placing preponderant blame on any locality makes little sense in an international cultural economy so spurred (and convulsed) by the search for corporate profits from the maximum distribution of new technologies whose properties of speed and weightlessness are practically their defining features.

Of course, such commonly shared understandings of cybercapitalism's new, antigeographical fundamentals are useful only to a point, and Hollywood's features as a regional network of entertainment-related industries continue to repay attention. Its access to cutting-edge technologies and to end markets, its broad, deep pool of skilled labor, and its highly desirable, American pop-cultural product—all of these factors assure it a future as "global" in reach and substance as its thoroughly imperial past. However, a paradox has nonetheless emerged. Hollywood is becoming less important as an actual location for production, even as it remains the center of a global economic formation and a worldwide entertainment imaginary. Its executives continue to play decisive roles in determining the mix and feel of the media products that the world consumes, even as some production moves abroad. The result: Hollywood's upper echelons continue to thrive while labor bears the brunt of change.

But there is even more bad news for film and television labor in southern California. For the emergence of synthespians and vactors may well signal the beginning of an extended decline for conventionally defined cinema and television. We need to look no further than Las Vegas to get a sense of what may be in store. In Las Vegas and elsewhere, technologies of the live spectacular now include computer-generated animation and motion simulation, Disney-inspired animatronics, holography, and three-dimensional Imax technology. It is not just for theme parks any more. As Las Vegas events combine more traditional theatricals with interactive performance encounters, with immersive, computer-simulated action experiences, with drinking and "fine dining," and crucially with retail opportunities, twentieth-century distinctions between cinema, stage, interactive video game, and amusement-park ride are literally going up in smoke in the Nevada desert. Doug Trumball, the designer of the brain-exploding, spine-demolishing "Back to the Future" rides at Universal Studios theme parks has observed that "in Las Vegas you will see things happening that are far in advance of anything in Orlando or Hollywood" (Provost 1994, 253). Indeed, there is no longer much doubt about the impact of the "New Vegas" on the wider entertainment industry. The spectacular disintegration of conventional boundaries between popular entertainment genres under way in Las Vegas is a harbinger of things to come very nearly everywhere, as theme parks, themed restaurants, multiplexes and malls, and virtual reality–heavy "location-based entertainment" centers come to play an ever-greater part in the worldwide generation of transnational entertainment revenue.

Here, too, the innovators carry passports from north of the border. Williams leads a long line of Canadians who work at the cutting edge of digital animation in Hollywood, and further afield. Two of the industry's most important software providers are located in Canada, Montreal's Softimage and Toronto's Alias/Wavefront. In Las Vegas and around the world, Canada's enormously successful Cirque du Soleil positions itself not merely as a circus company, but as a global entertainment corporation. Always eager to cross formal boundaries, Cirque's recent achievements not only include its second permanent Las Vegas installation, *O* (which grosses $2 million each week [see Bart 1999]). They also include, in crucial addition, alliances with global theme parks (Disney World), and with giant screen innovators such as Imax. Imax, in turn, is a Canadian company, and is in the midst of an ambitious expansion designed to make its theaters viable venues for a wide variety of twenty-first-century Hollywood product (Imax 2000).

This is not to suggest that Canadian cultural producers are poised to stage a continental coup. While Canadians will always look south to seek their fortunes, both the size of the U.S. market and the strength of American investment capital more or less ensure that Canadians—both companies and individuals—will continue to serve as America's junior partners. American entertainment capital will likewise continue to look north for inexpensive production opportunities and for reliable supplies of niche programming. But Canada's status as Hollywood's favorite new partner is not guaranteed in the long run. American television networks are on the perpetual lookout for new product bargains (e.g., the formats for both *Survivor* and *Who Wants to Be a Millionaire?* originate in Britain; and *Big Brother* is from the Netherlands). And American producers will go elsewhere for the right price and the right crews (e.g., *Gladiator* was shot in Malta, Morocco, Italy, England, Canada, and the United States). In fact, there is evidence that the MPAA is actively pursuing new production horizons. In February 2000, MPAA representatives met with Mexican government officials and outlined a list of thirteen "specific suggestions" to make Mexico more attractive to American producers. The proposals were modeled after Canada's system of subsidies and credits (Robb 2000a). So nothing is assured. New technologies, new sites of production, new genres, and new players all instantiate the myriad features that together constitute our current understanding of the term "globalization." And like continentalization, globalization is a patchwork process whose outcomes remain hard to elucidate in full, save two certainties. There is, first, the certainty of continued American dominance over the global media/entertainment sector. The second is that most people making their living in the entertainment industry will continue to be buffeted by changing production conditions. This is as true for film and television workers in southern California as it is for their counterparts in Canada, Europe, Australia, and elsewhere. It is the money, the actors, and the studios that go global; those who "just make a living" in the film and television industry continue to do just that. The anxieties prevalent in southern California today reflect a rift between those who still think of Hollywood as an American film and television business, and those who now properly understand it as a global entertainment industry. The anxieties prevalent in Canada continue to reflect both the vicissitudes of a national sector that has always grappled with the industry's international character, and Canada's near century-long experience of an open border with a sometimes less-than-comprehending continental partner.

NOTES

We would like to thank Aurora Wallace, John Lang, and Amy Baldwin for their contributions to this article. Also, unless otherwise stated, all dollar amounts are in U.S. currency.

1. The first rally was held on April 18 at Johnny Carson Park in Burbank. For information on the rallies, see <http://www.ftac.nct> [last accessed: 15 February 2001].

2. This breakdown of revenue streams is for feature films only. It does not include income from licensed merchandise or other media products, such as sound recordings and published material, which together can sometimes generate greater revenues than the direct sale and rental of the film property.

3. Negative costs are the sum total of all costs, including development and postproduction, prior to marketing and distribution. Please note that these figures refer only to those films produced or distributed by MPAA member companies. Over the last decade, MPAA firms distributed, on average, roughly 45 percent of all films released. Generally speaking, films released by nonmembers of the MPAA have lower budgets and lower associated marketing costs.

4. For useful overviews of the business of Hollywood see, inter alia, Balio (1985), Bordwell et al. (1985), Schatz (1996), and Wasko (1994).

5. Wasko (1998, 179) references IATSE figures, which show that nonunion projects might account for as much as 70 percent of total production.

6. In the summer of 2000, SAG, along with the American Federation of Television and Radio Artists (AFTRA), found itself in a prolonged strike for fair compensation for commercial work distributed via digital channels on television and in cyberspace (among other things) (Armbrust 2000a, 2000b).

7. Studio Canal is itself a Vivendi subsidiary.

8. In 1999, New York experienced its first drop in total production expenditures in six years, down by a little more than 10 percent to $839.4 million on 209 productions (Dawn 2000, 9). As a result, Thomas O'Donnell, the secretary treasurer for the Theatrical Teamsters Local 817 in New York, has indicated that his union is prepared to

make some concessions to keep producers from going abroad. "If you're looking for breaks, and you're shooting your whole movie here as opposed to shooting in Toronto, you're going to get some breaks on work rules" (12).

9. These figures need to be placed in the context of a nearly decade-long expansion in film and television employment, perhaps as high as ten thousand new positions annually (Kotkin 1999). The data also revealed that union workers got two-thirds more work in the industry in 1999 than they did in 1990 (Robb 2000b). A key employment indicator, however, the Motion Picture Industry Health Plan, showed a 3 percent dip in employment for behind-the-scenes workers in 1999.

10. For the record, the Monitor report only indicates the total value of lost production due to runaways at $2.8 billion. It does not provide a figure for Canada's share of the total. The $2.2 billion figure, which is now often cited in industry and press reports, is probably a reflection of the report's claim that 81 percent of all economic runaways end up in Canada.

11. The DGC derived this figure from an annual economic profile of the Canadian film and television industry prepared by PricewaterhouseCoopers, with the assistance of the Cultural Industries Branch of the Department of Canadian Heritage. The data form the basis of a report issued by the CFTPA and L'Association des Producteurs de Films et de Télévision du Québec. The most recent of these reports (CFTPA 2000) provides an even clearer picture of foreign involvement in the Canadian industry.

12. The MPAA's most recent report on production activity in California concludes that total expenditures came to $27.5 billion in 1996 (MPAA 1998). It is not altogether clear whether the pornography business is included in this figure. According to the *Los Angeles Times*, the porn industry is thriving in the Los Angeles basin, with production up by 25 percent in 1999 and total revenues climbing to over $4 billion (Gettleman 1999).

13. The Canadian Audio-Visual Certification Office (CAVCO) reports that U.S. companies received 94 of the 101 applications granted to foreign companies for the federal government's Production Services Tax Credit in 1998–1999 (CAVCO 2000, 13).

14. A third type of production involving foreign partners in Canada, treaty coproductions, lies outside this chapter's investigative remit. It warrants mentioning nonetheless that treaty coproductions nearly doubled in number in 1999 to the tune of an aggregate budget of $823 million Canadian. Canada benefits from coproduction treaties with over forty countries. Ninety-five percent of Canada's treaty coproductions to date have been with European partners, with France, the United Kingdom, and Germany being the top three coproducers (CFTPA 2000, 31–32).

15. It is not surprising then that roughly 250 animators and cartoonists of IATSE Local 839, the Motion Picture Screen Cartoonists, held a rally on April 13, 2000, outside KCET, the Los Angeles affiliate of PBS, to protest the "out-sourcing" of children's television production to companies such as Cinar and Nelvana (see Finnigan 2000).

16. The company's name reflects the merger of Alliance Communications and Atlantis Communications, completed in September 1998.

17. If the studio backlots have stood in for virtually every city and town in the world, the nearby countryside has likewise represented rural life abroad—sometimes with great care, sometimes with something less than that. As Mike Myers observes in *The Spy Who Shagged Me* (1999), "Isn't it *amazing* how the English countryside looks *nothing* like the hills of Southern California?"

18. In the fall of 1999, Cinar was accused of falsely crediting Canadians for scripts written by Americans in order to qualify projects for Canadian certification. One of the individuals involved, whose name appeared on 115 productions, and who earned royalties of $650,000, belonged to the sister of Micheline Charest, one of Cinar's cofounders. In March 2000, Charest and husband Ronald Weinberg resigned amid revelations that they transferred more than $100 million to a Bahamas investment fund without the board's approval. The company's books are in shambles (see Brooke 2000; Craig 2000; Marotte 2000). It could be that these events constitute an isolated case of corporate chicanery. However, in July 2000, Revenue Quebec announced that perhaps as many as one hundred film and television companies have deliberately or accidentally misrepresented their labor and production costs in government filings. It is unclear how much, of any, of the $97 million Canadian in 1999 Quebec tax credits were misappropriated (Kelly 2000). If there is a lesson to be drawn from these revelations, it is that despite the general increase in production activity that Canadian companies are enjoying, they nevertheless continue to depend heavily on government subsidies and tax credits in order to stay afloat.

19. For example, Quebec, British Columbia, and Ontario all match the federal government's 11 percent refundable tax credit, while Manitoba offers a 35 percent rebate on approved labor expenditures up to a maximum of 22.5 percent of total eligible production costs. Quebec has a special credit for special effects and computer-generated-image related costs incurred in Quebec. For a full rundown of provincial supports see "Provincial Funding Sources" (2000).

20. See for example, questions volleyed by committee members during the testimony of Ambassador Charlene Barshefsky, the U.S. trade representative, in U.S. House Appropriations Committee (2000). Readers interested in an overview of international trade law should consult Trebilcock and Howse (1995). For discussions of the application of international trade law to the cultural industries see Magder (1998, 1999), and Acheson and Maule (1999).

21. What is more, some Republican members of Congress expressed concern that the tax incentives might bolster the fortunes of the adult film industry, despite assurances that the tax credit would only be available to films that cleared a ratings board or received a broadcast or cable license.

22. Animation master class sponsored by the Canadian Consulate General, New York, January 25, 1999. Also see Sand (1994), Stalter and Johnson (1996), and Burston (2000).

REFERENCES

Acheson, Keith, and Christopher Maule. 1999. *Much Ado about Culture: North American Trade Disputes.* Ann Arbor: University of Michigan Press.
Alliance Atlantis. 2000. *1999 Annual Report.* Toronto: Alliance Atlantis Communications.
Armbrust, Roger. 2000a. "In Chicago, Actors' Strike Ain't Toddlin'," *Backstage,* 23 June, 3, 47.
———. 2000b. "SAG Strike Head: It's the Internet, Stupid." *Backstage,* 21 July, 1, 48.
Balio, Tino, ed. 1985. *The American Film Industry.* 2nd ed. Madison: University of Wisconsin Press.

Bart, Peter. 1999. "Quebecois Make Showbiz Waves in Las Vegas." *Daily Variety*, 15
    March, 18.
——. 2000. "Too Lean, Too Mean?" *Variety*, 26 June–9 July, 4–70.
Bates, James. 1999. "'Bring Hollywood Home' Echoes All the Way to Canada." *Los
    Angeles Times*, 27 August, A1.
Berton, Pierre. 1975. *Hollywood's Canada: The Americanization of Our National
    Image*. Toronto: McClelland and Stewart.
Boliek, Brooks. 1999. "'Film Production Act' in a Cameo on Capitol Hill." *Hollywood
    Reporter*, 15 July.
——. 2000. "Gore Runs with Runaway Issue." *Hollywood Reporter*, 26–28 May.
Bordwell, David, et al. 1985. *The Classical Hollywood Cinema*. New York: Columbia
    University Press.
Brooke, James. 2000. "A Make-Believe World, On Screen and Off." *New York Times*,
    16 April, B7.
Burston, Jonathan. 2000. "Spectacle, Synergy, and Megamusicals: The Global-
    Industrialisation of the Live-Entertainment Economy." In *Media Organisations
    in Society*, ed. James Curran. London: Arnold.
CA Trade and Commerce Agency. 2000. "Governor Davis' Film California First Fund
    Approved." Press release, 30 June. <http://www.commerce.ca.gov/latest/press/
    pr962413182.html> [last accessed: 15 February 2001].
Canadian Audio-Visual Certification Office. 2000. *Activity Report, 1998–9*.
    <http://www.pch.gc.ca/culture/cult_ind/cavco-bcpac/english.htm> [last accessed:
    15 February 2001].
Canadian Film and Television Production Association. 2000. *The Canadian Film and
    Television Industry: Profile 2000*. Coproduced with L'Association des Producteurs
    de Films et de Télévision du Québec and PricewaterhouseCoopers.
    <http://www.cftpa.ca> [last accessed: 13 September 2000].
Canadian Television Fund. 1999. *1998/9: Activity Report*. <http://www.
    canadiantelevisionfund.ca> [last accessed: 13 September 2000].
Cassidy, John. 1998. "The Comeback." *New Yorker*, 23 February–2 March, 122–127.
Christopherson, Susan. 1996. "Flexibility and Integration in Industrial Relations: The
    Exceptional Case of the U.S. Media Entertainment Industries." In *Under the Stars:
    Essays on Labor Relations in the Arts and Entertainment*, ed. Lois Gray and Ronald
    Seeber. Ithaca, N.Y.: ILR Press/Cornell University Press.
Cinar. 2000. "First Ever Arthur Primetime Special to Premiere Winter 2000 on PBS."
    Press release, 1 February. <http://www.cinar.ca/news-e/010200-e.htm> [last ac-
    cessed: 1 March 2000].
Craig, Susan. 2000. "Scandal Rocks Cinar." *Globe and Mail*, 7 March.
Dawn, Randee. 2000. "There's No Place Like Home." *Hollywood Reporter* (New York
    Special Issue) (June).
De Govia, Jack. 1999. "Speech to FTAC Rally, 8/15/99." <http://www.ftac.net/rally_
    speech_81599.html> [last accessed: 15 September 1999].
Dillon, Mark. 2000. "Tattersall Goes (American) Psycho." *Playback*, 1 May, 27.
Directors Guild of America and Screen Actors Guild. 1999. "DGA/SAG Commissioned
    Study Shows Total Economic Impact of U.S. Economic Runaway Production
    Reached $10.3 Billion in 1998." News release, 25 June. <http://www.sag.org/
    runaway/monitorfinal.html> [last accessed: 20 July 1999].
Directors Guild of Canada. 1999. "U.S. Study on 'Runaway' Productions Grossly Ex-
    aggerated." Press release, 9 July.

Dorland, Michael, ed. 1996. *The Cultural Industries in Canada*. Toronto: Lorimer.

———. 1998. *So Close to the State/s: The Emergence of Canada's Feature Film Industry*. Toronto: University of Toronto Press.

Duke, Paul, and Liza Foreman. 2000. "Kopelsons Mine Intertainment Coin." *Daily Variety*, 9 June, 1, 37.

Eller, Claudia, and James Bates. 2000. "Tiny Entertainment Companies Join Forces to Survive." *Los Angeles Times*, 6 June, C1.

Ernst and Young. 2000. *A Review of the Monitor Group Report on the Economic Multiplier for the U.S. Film and Television Production Spending*. Toronto: Director's Guild of Canada.

Film and Television Action Committee. 1999. "Rubber Stamp Campaign." <http://www.ftac.net/rubberstamp> [last accessed: 1 December 1999].

Finnigan, David. 2000. "Animosity: Runaway Art." *Hollywood Reporter*, 14–16 April.

Gettleman, Jeffrey. 1999. "L.A. Economy's Dirty Secret: Porn Is Thriving." *Los Angeles Times*, 1 September, A1.

———. 2000. "Trying to Keep the Movies from Moving." *Los Angeles Times*, 20 January, B1.

Gray, Lois, and Ronald Seeber. 1996. "Looking Ahead." In *Under the Stars: Essays on Labor Relations in the Arts and Entertainment*, ed. Lois Gray and Ronald Seeber. Ithaca, N.Y.: ILR Press/Cornell University Press.

Guback, Thomas. 1969. *The International Film Industry*. Bloomington: Indiana University Press.

Hamill, Dennis. 2000. "Canada Is Stealing Our Bacon." *Daily News*, 21 May.

Hirschberg, 2000. "The Samaha Formula for Hollywood Success." *New York Times Magazine*, 14 May.

Imax. 2000. *1999 Annual Report*. Toronto: Imax Corporation.

Internet Movie Database. <http://www.imdb.com> [last accessed: 15 February 2001].

James, Alison. 2000. "Ovitz Joins Foreign Legion." *Daily Variety*, 7 July, 1, 23.

Kelly, Brendan. 2000. "Quebec Finds Credit Abuse." *Daily Variety*, 14 July, 1, 22.

Kotkin, Joel. 1999. "Runaway Productions Pose Challenge for Hollywood." *Los Angeles Times*, 25 April, M1.

Kyser, Jack. 1998. "An Economist's Perspective." In *State of the Industry: The Economic Impact of the Entertainment Industry on California*. <http://www.mpaa.org/useconomicreview> [last accessed: 15 February 2001].

Lyons, Charles. 2000. "Passion for Slashin." *Variety*, 26 June–9 July, 1, 69.

Madigan, Nick. 1999a. "Canuck Helmers Defending Turf." *Daily Variety*, 12 July, 1, 49.

———. 1999b. "Prod'n Incentives Eyed." *Daily Variety*, 25 August.

Magder, Ted. 1993. *Canada's Hollywood: The Canadian State and Feature Films*. Toronto: University of Toronto Press.

———. 1996. "Film and Video Production." In *The Cultural Industries in Canada*, ed. Michael Dorland. Toronto: Lorimer.

———. 1998 *Franchising the Candy Store: Split-Run Magazines and a New International Regime for Trade in Culture*. Occasional Paper No. 34, *Canadian-American Public Policy*. Orono: University of Maine.

———. 1999. "Going Global." *Canadian Forum* (August).

Marotte, Betrand. 2000. "Cinar Founders Caught in Spotlight." *Globe and Mail*, 7 March.

Mazurkewich, K. 1995. "The Great Canadian Cartoon Conspiracy." *Take One*, no. 7 (Winter): 4–11.

Monitor Company. 1999. *U.S. Runaway Film and Television Production Study Report*. Los Angeles: Directors Guild of America and Screen Actors Guild.

Motion Picture Association of America. 1998. *State of the Industry: The Economic Impact of the Entertainment Industry on California*. <http://www.mpaa.org/useconomicreview> [last accessed: 15 February 2001].

———. 2000. "1999 Economic Review." <http://www.mpaa.org/useconomicreview> [last accessed: 15 February 2001].

Nelvana. 1999. "Nelvana Announces U.S. $40 Million Multi-Year Agreement with PBS to Produce Six Book-Based Series for First Ever Saturday Morning Kids' Block." Press release, <http://www.newswire.ca/releases/August1999/03/c0142.html> [last accessed: 31 August 1999].

"Playback Takes a Look Back at '99." 1999. *Playback*, 17 December, B2.

Pollack, Andrew. 1999. "Hollywood Jobs Lost to Cheap (and Chilly) Climes." *New York Times*, 10 May, 1, 19.

"Provincial Funding Sources." 2000. *Playback*, 6 March.

Provost, Gary. 1994. *High-Stakes: Inside the New Las Vegas*. New York: Truman Tally/Dutton.

Robb, David. 1999. "Hollywood Produces Biggest Demonstration." *Hollywood Reporter*, 16 August.

———. 2000a. "Incentives in Mexico Sought." *Hollywood Reporter*, 24–26 March.

———. 2000b. "Report: Film, TV Jobs Down Only 3% in '99." *Hollywood Reporter*, 5 January.

———. 2000c. "Runaway Foe Joining the Canadian Club." *Hollywood Reporter*, 2 February.

Sand, Katherine. 1994. "Enter the Digital Actor." *Journal of the British Actors' Equity Association* (October).

Schatz, Thomas. 1996. *The Genius of the System: Hollywood and Filmmaking in the Studio Era*. New York: Holt.

Shea, Jack. 1999. "Speech to the FTAC Rally on August 15." <http://www.hollywoodreporter.com/inwords/speeches/JackShea.asp> [last accessed: 31 August 1999].

Stalter, K., and T. Johnson. 1996. "H'wood Cyber Dweebs Are Raising the Dead." *Variety*, 4–10 November.

Standard and Poor's. 2000. *Industry Surveys: Movies and Home Entertainment*, 11 May.

Tillson, Tamsen. 2000. "Sharing the Wealth." *Variety*, 3–9 April.

Trebilcock, Michael, and Robert Howse. 1995. *The Regulation of International Trade*. New York: Routledge.

U.S. House Appropriations Committee. 2000. *Hearings of the Commerce, Justice, State, and Judiciary Subcommittee of the House Appropriations Committee*. 5 April.

Warren, Jodie, and Ian Edwards. 2000. "Market Roars As LGE Buys Trimark." *Playback*, 12 June, 18.

Wasko, Janet. 1994. *Hollywood in the Information Age*. Austin: University of Texas Press.

———. 1998. "Challenges to Hollywood's Labor Force in the 1990s." In *Global Productions: Labor in the Making of the "Information Society,"* ed. Gerald Sussman and John Lent. Cresskill, N.J.: Hampton.

Weingartner, Allen. 1999. Interview by Jonathan Burston. Los Angeles, 5 March.

Weinraub, Bernard, and Geraldine Fabrikant. 1999. "Studios Yell 'Cut!' As Costs Spiral for Filmmaking." *New York Times*, 13 June.

10

Upmarket Continentalism: Major League Sport, Promotional Culture, and Corporate Integration

Richard Gruneau and David Whitson

In March 1997, the Disney Corporation opened its Wide World of Sports Complex, a two-hundred-acre facility designed to host both professional and amateur events, including the Entertainment and Sports Programming Network (ESPN) X Games trials and the Atlanta Braves spring training, both of which were televised on either ESPN or ESPN2, the all-sports cable networks that Disney owns. The sports complex has since been host to other events, such as the Nike Air-it-out Championship and women's professional beach volleyball, both televised on the American Broadcasting Corporation (ABC) network, also part of the Disney media stable. Disney's interest in sports, including its ownership of the National Hockey League's (NHL) Anaheim Mighty Ducks, illustrates a broader trend that has seen large media conglomerates buying up sports "properties" of various types.

Time-Warner/Turner Sport's ownership of *Sports Illustrated*, along with the Atlanta Braves in major league baseball, and the Atlanta Hawks in the National Basketball Association (NBA), or the News Corporation/Fox Network ownership of Fox Sports Net, and the Los Angeles Dodgers (along with minority stakes in the New York Knicks and New York Rangers), are other notable examples of the integration of sports into the international leisure and cultural industries. These industries now include advertising, films and video products, popular music, and of course radio, television, computer games, and the Internet. They also include the tourism and holiday property industries, where investments in theater complexes and themed shopping districts are remaking urban landscapes around the world, and where sports such as skiing and golf are likewise gentrifying rural landscapes; and the fast food and beverage industries, where major corporate brand names such as McDonald's and Molson's have made themselves ubiquitous features of the rhythms of leisure, both at home and on vacation. In addition, the leisure and

235

cultural industries are now closely linked with various leisure equipment manufacturers: notably sports equipment and leisure wear, and the booming industry in personal audiovisual equipment and personal computers.

Since the mid-1970s, all of these industries have actively pursued the development of new kinds of cultural commodities. They have also sought to develop transnational markets for these commodities, made possible as a result of new information technologies and the growth of highly mobile business and professional elites. This stage in the development of the leisure and cultural industries has featured an increasingly sophisticated appreciation of market segmentation and customization; a relentless push by industry for deregulation and for the privatization of (formerly) public services; and the erosion of national restrictions on the mobility of capital. In the dynamic and deregulated business environments of end-of-the-century capitalism, national and transnational business mergers—often across diverse sectors of economic life—have conferred enormous advantages to corporate giants with the means to achieve a global market presence.

One highly visible dimension of this corporate-driven reorganization of leisure and cultural industries is the strategic construction of what might be called "transnational hierarchies" of consumption. In particular, there has been extensive promotion of so-called world-class entertainment products and events. This promotion has not only tended to marginalize many regional providers and independents, it has also had a visible impact on urban public policies, as local and regional governments across North America have competed to attract major league sports teams and other forms of world-class entertainment. In this competition, the largest and most affluent urban and suburban centers have a clear competitive advantage, the effects of which can be seen in regional cities across North America, where major league sports teams have departed (often leaving empty facilities in their wake), or remain in business only with ongoing public subsidies that absorb money from social programs. A related issue—similar to public subsidies to shopping malls that bring in national "big box" retailers—is that the subsidized expansion of nationally branded sports entertainment may take interest away from local institutions and businesses. Unchecked, such tendencies challenge the survival of regional cultures across North America, and of national cultural traditions in Canada and, to a lesser extent, Mexico.

In this chapter we outline a brief political-economic history of the emergence of major league sports in North America with particular reference to the various tendencies that have worked toward corporate and cultural integration on a continental and, indeed, global scale. But we also want to examine some of the limits of these tendencies and to discuss the emergence of new forms of opposition to them. Our analysis begins with a consideration of the early formation of major league sports in North America, first as corporate entities, and then as key elements in the developing national popular cultures of the United States and Canada.

MONOPOLIES, MEDIA, AND THE MAKING OF THE NORTH AMERICAN "MAJOR LEAGUES"

Organized sport in North America has its roots in the late eighteenth and early nineteenth centuries in a wide range of local folk games, masculine physical contests, and gaming activities practiced at fairs, picnics, taverns, social clubs, and community outings. As the United States and Canada became more industrial and urban societies throughout the nineteenth century, sport became progressively more commercialized. Commercial sport developed first in the form of periodical challenge matches, prize fights, games, and races staged by local clubs, individual promoters, and businesses (such as taverns) in communities across the continent. These early events generally attracted male audiences and were often surrounded by a considerable degree of gambling and drinking. The venues for these events depended upon what facilities were available in the community and often on whether or not the event was likely to be disrupted by the police. Depending on the sport, the organizers, and the nature of the venue, money may or may not have been collected at the gate.

From the late nineteenth century through the first two decades of the twentieth century, the commercialization of sport in North America gradually accelerated and became more systematic. Promoters organized regularly scheduled events on weekends, catering to the emergent rhythms of paid work and leisure in industrial towns and cities, and the weakening of religious prohibitions against fun on Sundays. In addition, many athletes began to receive payment for their services, and a large number of professional and semiprofessional events, teams, and leagues—in sports such as baseball, boxing, lacrosse, and hockey—had started up across the continent. The sporadic commercialism of an earlier era was giving way to a more formally commodified sport, involving paid labor by contracted athletes and the production and marketing of spectator sports as quasi-industrial entertainment products (cf., Gruneau and Whitson 1993, chapters 2 and 3).

In this mode, spectator sports gradually became one of the most commercially promising forms of popular culture in early-twentieth-century U.S. and Canadian cities, not least because they organized and celebrated skills and passions that had long been familiar features of male recreation. Early spectator sports also played to intercommunity rivalries, as club teams and athletes representing different ethnic, religious, and occupational communities competed against one another. As intercity travel became easier, of course, rivalries between cities became one of the characteristic subtexts of professional team sports. Like other areas of popular culture (e.g., music) the early commercialization of sports offered Canadians and Americans more professional and packaged versions of practices with which they had historically entertained themselves. But, it would lead to a culture of leisure that was less and less controlled by local participants, and more influenced by growing networks of promoters, sporting goods manufacturers, and facility owners. Commercialization would also lead to strengthening popular identifications with the market as the most innovative and reliable supplier of top-quality sporting entertainment.

With the development of professional leagues and regularly scheduled professional games, the relationship of sports teams and players to their home communities began to alter. The earliest competitive sports teams in North America were local recreational or amateur teams whose performances became closely linked to community pride. As long as teams were made up of local players, it was a credible part of popular mythology that a team's play said something about its home community and the qualities of its people. But, the growing quest to field winning teams in a market society opened the door to the hiring of professional "representatives" even if they came from outside the community. As this occurred, the older sense of community solidarity in which citizens supported the athletic efforts of their friends and neighbors was supplanted by a relationship more like that between a local business and its loyal customers, while the experience of civic pride was rearticulated in the more commercial language of civic boosterism. In this new commercial relationship, professional sports teams (the older term "club," with its residual connotations of membership, continued to be widely used) fulfilled their commitments to their supporters by fielding the best players local money could assemble. However, appeals for fan support continued to invoke the language of civic duty, the subtext here being that a community's ability to support a winning team was a marker of its collective dynamism and wealth (cf., Gruneau and Whitson 1993, 56–72).

Between the 1890s and the 1920s, professional teams and leagues in several sports were formed in resource towns, farming communities, and industrial cities across the United States and Canada. Most of them lasted only a few years before going out of business. One reason was that the professional teams in this era were organized in significantly different ways, and played in communities that had substantially different resources. In Canada, for example, the earliest professional hockey teams emerged out of amateur clubs, while others were controlled by rink owners, and still others by former players and affluent local entrepreneurs. Local athletic facility owners and event promoters, along with lumber, mining, and construction tycoons, were attracted to sports ownership as an opportunity to participate in a form of public culture that was well suited to their entrepreneurial energies and ambitions. These early local entrepreneurs were typically motivated by a powerful desire to bring winning teams to their home communities, as well as to make money. But few of these teams made much money: they played in small arenas, and unrestricted competition for players (within and between a number of regional leagues) soon led to wild escalations in player salaries. As a result, many teams folded, often after only one or two seasons (Gruneau and Whitson 1993, 86–92).

It soon became clear to a few forward-looking promoters and owners that the best way to solve the instability and unprofitability of the developing sports industry was to create effective monopolies whose members would honor one another's contracts, restrict access to the business, and work (more or less) collectively to establish their league in the best markets and drive competing leagues out of business. The gradual consolidation of these monopolies through the first three decades of the twentieth century reflected many of the same economic pressures and policies that were centralizing corporate power in the major industrial centers in the North American continent.

The case of professional hockey provides a useful illustration. In the years before World War I, good professional or semiprofessional hockey was played in Atlantic and western Canada, as well as in western Ontario, northern Michigan, and in several cities in New York, Pennsylvania, and Massachusetts. However, by the early 1920s most professional leagues in these regions had either disappeared or were decimated by the rise of the metropolitan-based NHL, formed initially in 1917. The problem was that the uneven development of regional economies across North America during the first three decades of the twentieth century was effectively undermining the ability of peripheral industrial centers to finance arenas large enough to compete with those being built in core industrial centers such as Toronto and Montreal in Canada, or New York, Detroit, Chicago, and Boston in the United States. During the mid-1920s, investors in the largest northern U.S. industrial cities began to see hockey's potential as a new entertainment product for the fast-growing urban middle classes which was a lucrative complement to boxing and other indoor sporting events. These investors aggressively pursued NHL franchises, driving up the value of the franchises and of players' contracts. Faced with competition from teams playing in arenas with unprecedented seating capacities for these times (fifteen thousand to twenty thousand), even the most competitive of the regional professional hockey leagues eventually folded, thereby ensuring that the best hockey would be played in U.S. and Canadian big-city markets (cf., Gruneau and Whitson 1993, 92–103).

Roughly similar patterns of development characterized the growth of baseball and football in the United States. While the timing and rate of commercial development in the two sports differed, in each instance teams sprung up in many small manufacturing centers as well as in the major cities, and both sports saw a series of regional leagues whose claims to superior status were seldom clear cut. Good players moved regularly to teams prepared to offer them more money, while owners were equally quick to move their teams in search of larger markets. Eventually, the most prosperous big-city clubs in each sport united in one league, and built league-wide agreements designed to guarantee exclusive access to the best markets, to share in certain league-wide revenues, and to control players' recruitment, mobility, and salaries (see Quirk and Fort 1992; Ingham, Howell, and Schilperoort

1988, 428–435). As effective monopolies, these leagues could also guarantee their member clubs exclusive "rights" to operate in these big-city markets. There was continued competition from a variety of regional amateur and minor professional leagues, but the facility owners in the major cities were eventually able to buy the best players, and to construct themselves as "big league" in the public mind. *This pattern of cartelization, stable monopoly as national institution, and the incorporation of potential competitors through mergers and/or expansions has characterized the development of every "major league" sport in North America.*

We want to highlight two points from this brief overview of the emergence of early major league sports in North America. First, while "official" or journalistic histories of major league sports typically celebrate key "builders" of the sport (e.g., in hockey, the Patrick brothers), a historical political economy of major league formation offers us a somewhat different view. From this perspective, although there are certainly examples of early owners whose commitment to "the game," *and* to their city and country, were undoubtedly genuine—hockey's Conn Smythe comes to mind—the consolidation of self-designated "major leagues" in the United States and Canada was primarily governed by owners' desires to promote the profitability of their individual and collective businesses. More importantly, the very idea of a major league sport itself is revealed as an essentially *promotional* construction—that is, a description whose credibility depends upon a single league gaining and maintaining a monopoly position in its sport, and controlling player talent, franchise placement, and the organization of sporting contests. At the same time, status as a major league sport has also depended upon a league gaining a presence in the biggest and most important cities, and on media coverage that has made that league—its games, its playoff and pennant races, and its "star" personalities—into an object of popular attention, not just locally, but across North America.

This breadth of attention raises a second point; that is, while the early development of both commercial and amateur sports in North America was locally and regionally based, there were important national and binational forces that shaped competition virtually from the outset. For example, transborder railway routes meant that it was often easier and cheaper for athletes and teams in southern Ontario, Quebec, and British Columbia to travel south into the United States for competition than to go east or west to play other Canadian teams. Furthermore, the development of circuit professionalism and the need for matchmaking and scheduling venues promoted the development of national and binational networks of information and commerce. At the same time, newly formed national sporting associations in both Canada and the United States in the late nineteenth century worked (not always successfully) to harmonize rules to enable and to regulate interregional and cross-border competition. Sporting goods manufacturers in the late nineteenth century also had an interest in standardizing rules and equipment, thereby developing national markets for "regulation" balls, sticks, golf clubs, and so on; and manufacturers such as Spalding worked with the sports governing bodies to disseminate rule books and to establish "official" status for brand-name equipment in a series of sports (cf., Hardy 1990).

Finally, growing North American interest in high-level sports was greatly enabled by telegraphy, and by the expansion of advertiser-supported newspapers in Canada and the United States. Early popular dailies gave ample and partisan coverage to local teams, but the sports pages were also able to play to a more general enthusiasm for sports among male readers by printing summaries provided by news wire services (e.g., the Associated Press) of important national and international competitions (cf., Gruneau and Whitson 1993; McChesney 1989). Most large North American dailies had developed separate sports sections by the early 1900s and as the century progressed the sports pages gave extensive coverage to sporting events of all kinds and to new star athletes such as Babe Ruth, Joe Louis, Red Grange, and the Conacher brothers. Through the extensive coverage they received in the daily press, championships in the most prominent leagues increasingly came to be defined as "national" events, and sports heroes became national, even international figures (cf., McChesney 1989, 56–58). Not unlike the business sections of major newspapers, the early sports pages presented their subjects as grand spectacle, complete with swashbuckling heroes. The star-centered approach that became a standard feature of sports journalism invested leading athletes with heroic, almost mythic qualities. In addition, early sports coverage spoke to readers as supporters of the home team, inviting identifications with the "city as a whole" before this way of thinking was commonplace. However, simply by relating local standards to those elsewhere, and keeping readers abreast of national and international results, sport's coverage in the press offered readers a sense of membership in the wider "world of sport" (cf., Rutherford 1978, 60–61; Gruneau and Whitson 1993, 83–85).

The advent of radio extended the decisive role played by popular daily newspapers in the construction of events such as the World Series, the Rose Bowl, the Kentucky Derby, and the Stanley Cup finals as national—even North American—events. Radio's decisive contribution lay in its ability to allow people across large spans of geographical space to follow major sporting events in real time. By the early 1920s, rising industrial incomes and active promotion by national advertising agencies—themselves new phenomena—had begun to create national markets for a growing number of prominent brands in U.S. consumer products (cf., Leiss, Kline, and Jhally 1990, 91–111, 124–155). The formation of national commercial radio networks in the United States in the late 1920s solidified this trend by establishing the unprecedented phenomenon of nationwide media audiences. The almost instant popularity of radio broadcasts of sporting events convinced advertisers that sports were among the best advertising vehicles for the promotion of national brand names, especially in consumer products targeted at male wage earners (Jhally 1984). With this in mind, large companies such as General Motors, Gillette, and Imperial Oil soon became regular sponsors on broadcasts that helped to elevate major sporting events such as the World Series and the Rose Bowl—along with their sponsoring corporations—to the status of U.S. national institutions. In Canada, Canadian Broadcasting Corporation (CBC) radio coverage of *Hockey Night in Canada*, from the 1930s through the early 1950s, had an even more pervasive cultural reach, making NHL hockey into a Saturday-night Canadian ritual, and raising interest in the game to the level of a national passion.[1]

An additional effect of these developments in both countries was to increase popular attention to all major league sports and to push professional sports to the forefront of an increasingly continental popular culture. Historians John Herd Thompson and Allen Seager (1985, 186–190) have pointed out that Canadian media in the interwar years were quick to cater to the interest their audiences showed in American popular culture, including major league sports. Over successive generations, as Paul Rutherford comments, "especially in the cities, Canadians became wedded to the idea that a continuous supply of American entertainment and sports was their birthright" (1993, 265). Just as new consumer-product brand names like Coke and Radio Corporation of America (RCA) sought to make themselves synonymous with the new pleasures that were part of North American progress and prosperity, so too did the major professional sports leagues create their places in a U.S.–based North American popular culture that was increasingly both binational and commercial.

POSTWAR CAPITALISM AND THE CHANGING NORTH AMERICAN SPORTS INDUSTRY

The examples noted earlier underline how the creation of national markets, and the emergence of dominant national "players"—in advertising, media, and consumer products, as well as in specific entertainment industries—all contributed to the making of a North American popular culture that prominently featured major league sports. Technological innovations in communications, and the creation of commercial broadcasting networks driven by advertising, together created unprecedented possibilities for mass producing sports audiences. Baseball's National and American leagues, followed later by the NHL, staked the earliest claims to be the sporting equivalent to other nationally branded products, and both consolidated these claims between the 1930s and 1950s. In the years immediately after World War II, the National Football League (NFL) also effectively consolidated its major league status, followed by the NBA. All of these self-designated major leagues flourished in the largest North American manufacturing and financial centers and most teams played out of landmark urban facilities that were built during the interwar years. With their venues paid for, and with low labor costs derived from effective control over player recruitment and movement, along with new revenues from the sale of television rights, major league franchises in the 1950s and 1960s were typically profitable. Most teams also had loyal fans and were viewed as civic fixtures. Still, as early as the late 1950s, there were important signs of change, beginning with the moves of the major league baseball Giants and Dodgers from New York to California.

These moves drew strong criticism from people who still believed strongly in the established notion of "representative" ties between local teams and their fans. It soon became evident, though, that local fan support was no longer enough on its own to keep a team in its "home" community, even in the most prosperous industrial cities. It was also clear that the demand for major league sports in new markets could not be fully satisfied by the transfer of existing teams, thus creating strong pressures for expansions into cities that were not then part of the major leagues. Much of this demand was arising in response to subtle changes in the U.S. economy: in particular, postwar shifts of wealth and population away from the older industrial centers of the Northeast and Great Lakes to the American West and South. By the 1960s, booming oil and gas wealth, aerospace industries, finance, and tourism were all contributing to growth in Dallas and Houston, Denver, Seattle, and Atlanta, as well as, of course, California. As these regions began to boom, their affluent populations constituted obvious new markets for professional sports, and there were wealthy local entrepreneurs anxious to buy and move existing teams or secure new franchises.

Despite major league baseball's movement into the Southwest, other established major leagues were initially cautious about expansion. In this context, a new American Football League (AFL) found an ample supply of cities anxious to host franchises. Likewise, despite modest NHL and NBA expansion in the late 1960s, rival professional hockey and basketball leagues sprung up in cities overlooked in these expansions. These rival leagues produced brief but costly bidding wars, leading within a few years, in each case, to the original league absorbing the strongest franchises from the rival group into a renewed major league monopoly. For the established major league teams, the combined effects of expansion and the absorption of successful teams from rival leagues brought in immediate revenues (in the form of franchise fees), while reestablishing monopolies and cornering new markets for television advertising.

The major league expansions of the 1960s and 1970s can be usefully viewed as exercises in revenue creation through franchising. Just like the fast food business, franchising in sports involves selling the rights to offer a national brand-name product (e.g., NHL hockey or NFL football) in a given market area. Indeed, expansion in major league sports in the 1960s and early 1970s coincided historically with the unprecedented growth of franchising in other businesses such as muffler shops, travel agencies, and of course fast food restaurants. This led to the eclipse of many kinds of independently operated local businesses, at the hands of nationally promoted, brand-name goods and services. Expansion in major league sports was thus entirely consistent with postwar developments in commerce that contributed to standardizing consumer opportunities *and* to eroding regional differences.

While franchising itself brought in significant revenues, the longer-term objective for all major league sports in the 1960s and 1970s was to secure and retain television contracts with the major American networks. Through the 1950s and early 1960s, it had become self-evident that television was dramatically increasing the numbers of people who were actively or casually interested in professional sports. Television technologies allowed audiences to see things they often missed in the arena, while commentary sought both to explain play and to make it more exciting than it often was. Television also brought athletes' faces into living rooms—it helped to "personalize" major league sports—and this played no small role in turning professional athletes (and broadcasters such as Howard Cosell) into celebrities. The effects of this were to make sports television of interest to new audiences beyond the core of already knowledgeable male fans, and to make the major leagues more widely watched and talked about than ever before.[2]

At the same time, large weekend audiences of viewers with a very predictable demographic composition—still mostly men—inflated the value of advertising revenues, fueling an upward spiral in what the networks were willing to pay for exclusive rights to televise major league games. The major leagues developed formulae for splitting national television revenues among member teams, and these revenues led to rises in profits for most teams. In response, players began to struggle to increase their own share of team revenues by mounting court challenges to the restrictive labor practices of the major leagues, hiring agents, and strengthening their collective bargaining positions through increasingly militant player associations. Some team owners' desires to sign "marquee players" who could help sell teams in new markets also served to raise player salaries to new heights.

Television was not, of course, directly responsible for all of these developments, but it played an integral part in the changing dynamics of the postwar professional sports business. Especially notable was the way television accelerated a delocalizing dynamic whose effects would be felt in several ways. At one level, this simply refers to the further popularization of major metropolitan teams at the expense of local loyalties, and the creation of continent-wide followings for teams such as the Dallas Cowboys or Chicago Bulls. At a more important level, though, what television did was to open up the market for sports entertainment by bringing new sports options to viewers in regions where these sports were not historically a major part of local culture. Television became the ultimate medium for the pursuit of continental audiences by all the major league sports, and those that used television most effectively—for example, the NFL and, later, the NBA—would vastly increase the followings for their sports and all the products associated with them. In general, television became a catalyst for an intensified competition *among sports* for market share, a competition for hearts and minds in which promotional savvy and resources would be very important, and regional traditions no guarantee of continued fan loyalty, especially among the young.

By the 1980s, it was becoming evident that North American sports leagues unable to increase their continental profile risked losing their regional fan base to more actively promoted rivals. The case of the Canadian Football League (CFL) provides an apt illustration. During the late 1940s, the Western Interprovincial Rugby Football League and the (Eastern) Interprovincial Rugby Football League—regional precursors to the CFL—existed as two of several regional professional or semiprofessional football leagues in North America, led by the NFL. Moreover, even though the rules differed slightly from U.S. football, the Canadian leagues—especially in the west—had benefited from access to a large pool of itinerant U.S. players and coaches (cf., Cosentino 1995). And, at a time when the U.S. networks were experimenting heavily with programming, the Ontario- and Quebec-based interprovincial leagues briefly had a U.S. television contract with the National Broadcasting Corporation (NBC) in 1954.

Through the 1950s and 1960s, the eastern and western football leagues consolidated into one league, the CFL, and drew large (by Canadian standards) radio and television audiences for CBC broadcasts of the league's annual Grey Cup championship game. The licensing of a new private television network in Canada (CTV) in the early 1960s broke the CBC's broadcast monopoly of CFL coverage and drove up the value of the league's television rights. In 1980, the league signed a lucrative three-year Canadian television deal with Carling-O'Keefe breweries, and then followed with an another three year deal, this time for the (then) remarkable sum of $33 million (CD). Coupled with record attendance across the league, the size of this television contract suggested to many fans that the league had a bright future as major league sporting entertainment in Canada. The federal government had even acted to protect the league's status as a national Canadian cultural institution by acting in the mid-1970s to block the placement of a new U.S. World Football League franchise (a briefly lived rival to the NFL) in Toronto.[3]

The CFL's flagship franchise was the Toronto Argonauts, and following the arrival of major league baseball in the city and the construction of the Sky Dome in the late 1980s, the Argonauts gained access to a much-hyped major league venue. Lured by the prospect of a professional football team playing in a new world-class stadium, the Argonauts were purchased in 1988 by a new "big-league" owner, Harry Ornest, who also owned the St. Louis Blues. Three years later, Ornest sold the team to his NHL colleague, Los Angeles Kings owner Bruce McNall, who in turn brought Canadian hockey legend Wayne Gretzky and comedian John Candy into the ownership group. In a blitz of publicity, the Argonauts signed U.S. college superstar Rocket Ismail and went on to win the Grey Cup. McNall sold the Toronto press on the idea that the CFL—with more good teams and marquee players—could effectively sell its product in the U.S. cable television market. Despite a downturn in real estate prices that had chilled some of the boomtown mentality that swept Toronto during the 1980s, the successes of the Toronto Blue Jays and the new-look Argonauts, and even the apparent success of the Sky Dome itself, all seemed to reinforce the image of Toronto as a world-class city on the international entertainment stage (Kidd 1995).

However, illusions about the CFL as any kind of competitor in the world of major league sporting entertainment were short-lived. While Toronto might find the investment and sponsorship base to compete for marquee players with NFL teams, this was always an absurd proposition in cities such as Winnipeg, Regina, Hamilton, and Edmonton. Throughout the late 1980s, the market value of the league's Canadian television rights fell as teams across the league struggled with diminishing fan interest and inflated payrolls. On an average weekly basis, network and cable audiences for NFL football in Canada showed that more and more Canadians were actively following the American game. Canadians still enjoyed CFL football, but they also understood clearly that the "major league" NFL represented the pinnacle of the game. Moreover, despite McNall's hype about lucrative American cable television revenues, the CFL was never able to catch on as a valuable commodity in the U.S. market. In the end, McNall abandoned the Argonauts even before his own fortunes collapsed, and the team's brief taste of Hollywood ownership finally ended with Candy's tragic death. Still, the idea of entering the U.S. sports entertainment marketplace as a solution to the CFL's problems stayed alive, leading to a brief and ill-fated CFL expansion into a number of U.S. cities from 1993–1995.

The assumption that major league status—and major league profits and salaries—required a larger presence in U.S. popular culture was also central to the NHL's expansion strategy from the 1970s to the 1990s. In contrast to the CFL, the NHL had been the major league in its sport for more than half a century and, in addition to its rock-solid Canadian fan base, the NHL maintained a strong following in the major northern U.S. cities that had had teams since the 1920s. Still, American interest in the NHL was historically confined to these regions, with almost no presence in other parts of the country. Postwar NHL expansions have been designed, for the most part, to build interest in hockey in the growing U.S. population centers of the South and the West, and to develop the kind of continent-wide fan base that would lead to national television contracts like those enjoyed by the NFL and the NBA.

However, the NHL's pursuit of audiences in the Sunbelt has been accompanied by growing instability among the league's Canadian franchises, especially those in smaller cities. Several of these franchises owed their existence to the formation of the rival World Hockey Association (WHA) in the early 1970s. The WHA placed franchises in several smaller Canadian cities where hockey interest was high, hoping that strong support at the gate would ensure their success. However, escalating payrolls and undercapitalized franchises, along with stiff NHL opposition and the failure to secure anything more than modest television revenues, prevented the WHA from competing successfully with its more established rival for more than a few years. In 1979, the league folded and the NHL absorbed the most financially stable WHA franchises—Winnipeg, Edmonton, and Quebec, along with Hartford in the United States—thereby reestablishing its monopoly over major league hockey. Calgary would join the NHL a year later as a result of the purchase and transfer of the struggling Atlanta Flames.

All of these cities were small markets by major league standards, which factor in the size and spending power of regional television audiences and increasingly include evaluations of the number of corporate head offices in any region. However, all these Canadian cities were hockey hotbeds, and with salaries at 1980s levels their arenas were large enough, and the communities affluent enough, to support major league hockey very well. By the late 1980s, both Edmonton and Calgary had won Stanley Cups, and often played to sellout crowds. Despite such successes, though, the idea of NHL franchises in small Canadian cities was viewed by many U.S. owners as a step back from the league's efforts to sell the game to a wider U.S. audience. That is why a strong Canadian bid to move the St. Louis Blues to Saskatoon in the late 1980s—a city even less known to U.S. fans than Calgary or Edmonton—stood no chance of approval (cf., Gruneau and Whitson 1993, 224–234, Dryden and McGregor 1989, chapter 1).

By the early 1990s, it became evident that every Canadian NHL franchise was threatened by the escalation in players' salaries. Average NHL salaries tripled between 1989 and 1994, from $180,000 to over $500,000, and they doubled again over the ensuing five years. Whereas Edmonton and Calgary were able to win Stanley Cups in the 1980s with total player budgets of less than $4 million, today many NHL teams spend upwards of $30 million, and some, such as the New York Rangers, spend more than $50 million. The Rangers' mediocre record in recent years illustrates that money alone cannot ensure success; however, anything near this level of spending is simply beyond the means of most Canadian teams, where (outside Toronto) potential revenues are markedly smaller. This disadvantage has been exacerbated as the value of the Canadian dollar dropped steadily through the 1990s and players across the league were demanding and receiving payment in U.S. funds. Finally, U.S. teams also paid lower taxes than Canadian teams and many U.S. NHL teams in the 1990s were able to improve their economic position by moving into new, often publicly subsidized arenas (cf., McKay 1998, 28–37).

The first Canadian NHL team to sell in this volatile climate was the Quebec Nordiques, who were relocated to Denver in the summer of 1995 and promptly won the Stanley Cup the following spring in their first season as the

Colorado Avalanche. Those same 1996 playoffs also saw the last games of the Winnipeg Jets, despite several years of attempts by Jets fans and civic boosters to secure sufficient public funds to underwrite the team's losses and to finance construction of a new arena. In the summer of 1996, the Jets' new owner moved the franchise to Phoenix to play in the America West Arena, which is also home to the Phoenix Suns. Then, in 1998, it was the Edmonton Oilers who appeared on the verge of being sold, only to be rescued at the last minute by a consortium of local investors. The Oilers' example was followed in 1999 by the Ottawa Senators' threat to move, unless all three levels of government in Canada reduced the team's tax bills. Even the storied Montreal Canadiens, historically the NHL's most successful franchise, have recently been moved to complain that their municipal property taxes of close to $10 million Canadian annually are more than the total in such taxes paid by all the U.S.–based NHL teams, and that the club's deteriorating financial position is reflected in a diminishing competitiveness on the ice.[4] Underlining the point, Molson's Breweries, longtime team owners, sold the Canadiens to U.S. interests in January 2001, though the team is expected to remain in Montreal.

Throughout all of this, the NHL has continued to show little will to make the kind of changes, such as substantial revenue sharing, that might stabilize the future of its Canadian franchises. The league did institute a modest plan in the 1990s to help "small-market" Canadian teams offset the weak position of the Canadian dollar. However, the NHL's major strategy for helping its Canadian franchises has been to lobby various levels of government for increased public assistance or reduced taxes to struggling Canadian teams. Meanwhile, on top of the structural difficulties faced by all Canadian NHL franchises, even the more stable NHL teams in Toronto and Vancouver have had to fight harder for their share of the urban entertainment dollar, in the face of new competition that has arisen with the recent expansion of the NBA into these cities.

NEW FORMS OF CORPORATE AND CONTINENTAL INTEGRATION IN THE 1990s

It is important to recognize how large a role public money has played over the past twenty-five years in bringing major league sports franchises not only to "small market" Canadian cities, but to many U.S. centers as well. In 1950, the Cleveland Indians baseball team was the only major league franchise in North America that played in a publicly owned facility (Shropshire 1995, 1). However, since the 1960s, although private investors have paid the franchise fees, by far the majority of expansion teams in the North American major leagues have been given publicly financed facilities to play in, thus socializing one of their major costs.

Illustrations of these subsidies are legion. In Canada in the 1970s, public money built Northlands Coliseum and Commonwealth Stadium in Edmonton, the Saddledome in Calgary, and, of course, the debt-ridden Olympic Stadium in Montreal. In the 1980s, public borrowing built the Toronto Sky Dome, while in the mid-1990s, funds from a federal government "infrastructure" program underwrote major renovations—mostly to add new luxury boxes—to both Northlands and the Saddledome. In the United States, the level of public subsidy to professional sports facilities has been even more pronounced. Every one of the more than forty U.S. expansion teams and relocated franchises in the North American major leagues between the early 1960s and late 1980s drew on some sort of public investment or subsidy, ranging from interest-free loans, zoning concessions, and subsidized rents, to outright financing through general obligation bonds (Shropshire 1995; Noll and Zimbalist 1997). And, in the 1990s, there has been an even more intense round of subsidized stadium and arena construction. For example, between 1990 and 1996 alone, more than thirty professional sports venues were built in North America—mostly in U.S. cities—at a total cost of $4 billion, and it has been projected that another forty major league "sports palaces" will be constructed by 2003, at an additional total investment of $7 billion (Laing 1996, 23).

Not all of this construction has been publicly financed, however. In Canada, private-sector funding has built new hockey arenas in Vancouver, Montreal, and Toronto, and, in the United States, the private sector has either built or contributed significantly to new facilities such as Boston's Fleet Center, the Kiel Center in St. Louis, and the Bradley Center in Milwaukee. Still, the bulk of funding for new sports facilities in the United States—in Baltimore, Cleveland, Nashville, Arlington (Texas), Denver, and Seattle, to name only a few striking examples—has continued to come from the public sector; and often the levels of public subsidy are spectacular.[5] For example, when the Los Angeles Rams NFL franchise negotiated to move to St. Louis in 1995 the state of Missouri, the city of St. Louis, and the local county willingly incurred a $262 million debt to provide the Rams with a new seventy-thousand-seat stadium, the Trans World Dome. The city also sold "personal seat licenses" to fans and the $70 million in proceeds from these licenses was then kicked back to the Rams to defray moving costs and build a $10 million practice facility. In addition, the Rams were able to lock in a very favorable annual rent for the next thirty years, while retaining rights to the revenues generated by concessions, "naming" fees paid by the stadium sponsor, and the major portion of any revenues generated by additional stadium advertising. Commentators have tallied the total cost to St. Louis taxpayers as approximately $700 million; all of this at a time of financial austerity in city budgets across the United States (Laing 1996, 24).

That cities are willing to pay such amounts to attract or keep sports franchises needs to be understood in the context of the erosion of traditional industries in many regions of North America, greater mobility of capital, and the search for new kinds of urban economic activity. In addition, with the globalization of markets and audiences for popular entertainment, and given the desires of civic boosters to attract educated "information" workers, the value of being on the circuits of world-class sports events and concerts is widely perceived to have risen. These features of the development of Western capitalism since the 1970s have combined to produce what British geographer David Harvey (1987) calls "the entrepreneurial city," in which civic (and regional) authorities feel pressured to offer infrastructure and other incentives to attract new businesses—or just to keep existing ones. Growing and declining cities alike now "compete" aggressively for every kind of investment and the jobs that come with it. They have long done so for manufacturing, of course; but with manufacturing jobs declining in many centers, civic leaders now campaign intensely for information-processing and telecommunications functions; new businesses in advertising and design; new shopping complexes, entertainment centers, and tourist venues; and other "consumption-biased" forms of investment (cf., Zukin 1991). The latter of these underscore the growing role of leisure and entertainment in the North American urban economy, and the perceived importance of the sorts of infrastructure (sports venues, concert halls, and theme parks) that can sustain a city's national and global visibility.

These dynamics in the 1990s have given owners of major league sports franchises in North America unprecedented leverage in their push for subsidized renovations, or the construction of brand new facilities. It is particularly striking that owners' demands have often had nothing to do with the physical inadequacy of their existing venues. Many of the sports stadiums and arenas that were vacated, extensively renovated, or demolished in the 1990s were less than twenty years old and in good condition. The issue here is more a matter of "economic obsolescence" in a volatile time of limited supply and high demand. In this context, economist Robert Baade has suggested that: "The shelf-life on sports facilities seems to be ever-compressing as teams force local authorities and municipalities to build them new venues so that every conceivable source of revenue they can identify can be engineered into the new structure" (quoted in Laing 1996, 24).

For owners, this means, first and foremost, being able to assume control over revenues generated from the facility from sponsorship deals, such as leasing the name of the stadium, as well as from other events, including concerts and trade shows. Owners have also wanted new facilities that are "wired" to take advantage of digital media technologies, and designed to optimize revenues by commodifying the spaces in the venue more intensely: for instance by selling advertising on rink boards, dasher boards, and high-tech electronic scoreboards. Using space effectively for revenue production also means increasing revenues through more concessions, higher value–added concessions (wine and premium ice cream, as well as more expensive beer and hot dogs), and restaurants. Most of all, though, it refers to premium seating—club seats and luxury boxes—which means moving the game upmarket and pursuing affluent "audiences" rather than a broad base of traditional fans. This movement of stadia "upmarket" offers distinct advantages to large metropolitan-based teams (in relation to smaller regional cities) because it is the size and wealth of the local corporate sector that governs how many boxes can be sold and at what prices.

None of this is entirely new. We have already noted, for example, how urban arenas for NHL hockey in the 1920s were built to attract middle-class fans instead of blue-collar "crowds." Similarly, "company tickets" have long constituted an important portion of the season subscriptions in virtually all major league venues. However, today's luxury suites and sky boxes are of a different order: they simply bring in much more revenue than any previous form of seating in major league sports venues. This is particularly important because revenue from luxury boxes does not have to be shared with other teams in the league. All the major leagues have agreements of different types that require individual franchise owners to share television revenues and, in some instances, gate receipts;[6] so there is a strong incentive—especially in times of escalating salaries—to maximize revenues that do not have to be shared. This accounts for the current frenzy for new facilities with abundant luxury boxes as well as new opportunities for sponsorship and concession revenues. Owners who have been able to secure such new facilities have seen the overall value of their franchises soar (Ozanian et al. 1995, 42–56).

In addition to revenues generated through new sports facilities, the major leagues have also sought to expand revenues from the licensing and promotion of merchandise bearing "official" team or league insignia. Team caps and jerseys were a small source of additional profit for major league teams until the 1980s, when the NBA and the NFL showed that a more aggressive approach to the licensing of insignia for reproduction, and the promotion of team apparel as fashion items, could yield an enormous return (e.g., $3 billion per year for the NFL alone in the mid-1990s) (Tadeschi 1999). As this occurred, major league team logos and colors became a greater part of the familiar repertoire of popular symbols and meanings in North America, especially among teens. Merchandise sales leveled off for all the major leagues in the late 1990s, but the possibilities for new retailing and merchandising initiatives (on a global scale) through the Internet have led to an explosion of new partnerships and ventures between teams, athletes, and various Internet providers: examples include the recent strategic partnership between Athlete Direct and Time-Warner/America On-line (AOL) to host Web pages for star athletes, including chat rooms, fan club material, and opportunities to purchase merchandise; and the earlier creation of a Web-based "sports center"—hosted by San Francisco Forty-niner quarterback Steve Young—at imall.com, a prominent virtual retailer. Furthermore, all the major leagues have their own presence on the

Web supplying statistics, team histories, and information, along with links to sites that engage in selling merchandise.

These examples only reflect the tip of the digital iceberg when it comes to the creation of new revenue streams through strategic partnerships and corporate integration in major league sports. By 1997, more than twenty million homes in the United States had computers with Internet access, in addition to another 25.8 million computers owned by businesses (Schiller 1999, 106). In addition, a high percentage of the owners and users of these computers were affluent and male—prime targets for sports marketers. Moreover, "hit counters" on the growing numbers of specialty sport sites in the United States through the 1990s were revealing that Internet surfers had a seemingly insatiable interest in sports information of all types. For example, the NFL's official website received 360,000 hits on each of the two days of the league's college draft in 1998 (130). That kind of interest is why CBS made an estimated $100 million investment in its own website, sportsline.com, in the late 1990s, and why ESPN has invested heavily in its own site, sportzone.com.

If the Internet appears to hold the promise of a new merchandising and advertising bonanza for the North American major leagues, it is also clear that it will not do this on its own, nor will the Internet displace the importance of television in the foreseeable future. For most of the last thirty years large network television contracts have been a source of dependable and increasing revenue for the North American major leagues. Major television contracts will continue to be big revenue suppliers to the major leagues for the next several years, but more as a result of complex multiple-broadcaster deals than single network projects. For example, the NFL's current eight-year, $17.6 billion television contract (expiring in 2005) is split between Disney (ESPN and ABC), Fox, and CBS. Similarly, the NBA's four-year, $2.64 billion contract (expiring in 2002) is divided between Time-Warner/Turner Sports and NBC; and major league baseball's five-year, $1.7 billion contract that expired in 2000 involved ESPN, Fox, Fox/Liberty, and NBC (Strauss 1998, 16).

The growth of these large multiple-broadcaster deals is a result of several factors. For one thing, the domination of television by major national broadcasters has been eroded around the world in the last two decades by deregulation, and by the growth of cable and satellite providers who put together "networks"—and hence, audiences—in very different ways. This expansion of subscription television has been promoted in some countries (e.g., Britain and Australia) by the fact that pay television operators (e.g., BskyB and Foxtel) have been able to offer subscribers exclusive access to the most popular "national" sports (football and rugby, respectively). At the same time, in North America, the spread of subscription television has spawned the phenomenon of around-the-clock specialty sports channels (e.g., ESPN in the United States, The Sports Network in Canada, along with even more specialized channels dedicated to particular sports such as golf and automobile racing). Subscription television has opened up new revenue possibilities for individual teams (selling packages of games to regional cable operators if league rules allow it), as well as for the major leagues as a whole, who have benefited from a competition between cable and satellite television operators and older networks for the sale of broadcast rights.

All of this has fragmented television audiences, attracting advertisers who have an interest in the predictable composition of specialty market segments. By 1998, the four main network broadcasters commanded less than 60 percent of the prime time U.S. television audience, while cable channels and other new media increased their market share (Schiller 1999, 136). Sports specialty channels have been among the most successful of these channels, evidenced by the fact that Disney's ESPN became more profitable in 1995–1996 than Disney's "other" network, ABC. Of course, advertisers still have an interest in the large audiences for traditional network programming; which is why advertising revenues in the late 1990s for the major networks continued to grow, and why the networks have fought hard to keep their share of major league sports audiences. However, the most striking area of advertiser-driven growth in the late 1990s has been in the audience segmenting cable television networks (137).

Rights fees for major league sports have continued to escalate during this reorganization of the television market because sports audiences tend to be predictable and saleable and because sports television still costs less to produce than prime time drama or comedy. More importantly, because monopoly providers continue to restrict the supply of major league sports—as well as of major international sporting events such as the Olympics and World Cup—the global demand for *the best* sports "properties" shows no sign of abating. This burgeoning global market holds huge potential dividends for advertisers. That is why, by the mid-1990s, Disney's ESPN was televising sports on a twenty-four-hour basis in 21 languages and in more than 165 countries. ESPN has been especially important for Disney, because it has given the company access to a market that has long eluded it: young, comparatively affluent men around the world.

Disney's plan for transnational sports television is not so much based on the idea of selling North American sports abroad as it is on tailoring broadcasts and advertising to local markets. Thus, ESPN has aggressively pursued broadcast rights for soccer in Latin America, table tennis in Asia, and cricket in India (Herman and McChesney 1997, 83). Like Disney, NBC has also used sports to build its international businesses. NBC's Superchannel broadcasts sports in Europe, and NBC Asia airs events as diverse as golf, volleyball, and U.S. college football. Still, the leader in the globalization of sports broadcasting has been Rupert Murdoch's News Corp. In the early 1990s, Murdoch's ownership of the rights to broadcast Premier League soccer and NFL football were important factors in the profitability of BskyB in England and the Fox Network in the United States. Since then, Murdoch has acquired full or part interest in nineteen of twenty-three regional sports networks in the United States, and, in 1996, Fox Sports and Tele-Communications Incorporated established a joint venture to create a global sports network designed to compete internationally with ESPN (Herman and McChesney 1997, 76–79; Geer 1997, 52–53).

It is not at all clear at this point exactly how the sports television marketplace will evolve over the next decade. Commentators in recent years have suggested that the values of sports television rights and, indeed, of major league franchises themselves, are highly inflated, and that falling ratings in several sports, along with notable levels of fan disaffection with high player salaries and high ticket prices, provide warning signs of an impending crash. What this argument overlooks, though, is the extent to which the escalation in sports television rights is now being driven by a global competition for market share of upmarket audiences, in a media environment where the lines between the production and distribution of media content have blurred beyond recognition. This argument also overlooks the immense scale of civic investment in sports in the United States and Canada—also driven by new forms of market competition—that has seen billions of dollars of public funds pumped into the major leagues. Perhaps the only thing that can be said with assurance is that traditional broadcasters in the future will continue to play a smaller role in sports in their own right, as they become integrated into larger media conglomerates. As part of such combines, broadcasters will cross-market to and support the providers of more specialized and customized information services such as cable, satellite, and the Internet. Still, there is little indication at this point that the economic value of major league franchises and media rights will collapse anytime soon.

What also seems likely is that the trends that we have been describing will continue to favor those leagues and teams around the world (in the absence of effective revenue sharing agreements) that can deliver the most valuable audiences to advertisers. Across western Europe, for example, the growth of subscription television, integrated into huge conglomerates such as News Corp. and Vivendi/Canal Plus, has led to exploratory talk of a European "super league" in which the big metropolitan clubs in the major soccer countries would no longer share television revenues with their more-regionally based rivals. Like the major leagues in North America, the formation of one dominant European super league would dramatically increase the economic value of the franchises within it, likely pricing them out of the market for local ownership in all but a handful of cities, and strengthening the tendency toward ownership by media-based corporations.

This latter tendency is even more evident in the North American major leagues, where cross-ownership and cross-marketing to continental and global audiences have become the order of the day. By cross-ownership we mean the ownership of sports teams by corporations that also have substantial interests in related leisure and media businesses such as beer, films and videos, leisure and sports wear, theme parks, television, and high-tech industries such as software design. Cross-ownership, of course, simply extends in a strategic direction an already established tendency toward corporate ownership in sports, as opposed to individuals or small groups of local investors. This is not to say that individual or local ownership has disappeared from major league sports in North America; you can see both models represented in the ownership of the smaller Canadian NHL teams (in Ottawa, Calgary, and Edmonton), as well as some of the smaller U.S. cities in the NBA and in Major League Baseball (MLB). Still, owners of large corporations have obvious competitive advantages, including access to capital, increased lobbying power with local governments, more developed and geographically diversified marketing programs, and the ability to cross-market professional teams with other members of the corporate family.

One of the most traditional patterns of cross-ownership in the North American sports industry involved the ownership of teams by breweries, whose beer sales were promoted by their association with the team (e.g., Busch in St. Louis, Coors in Denver, and Molson's in Montreal). Other early patterns of cross-ownership saw sports teams purchased by local media outlets, where the media provided regular exposure for the team, and the team provided impetus for fans to either purchase papers, listen to the radio, or watch television. As long as teams did not run at a loss, and visibly helped to sell advertising or to build sales of a related product, this simple synergy usually worked reasonably well. Since the mid-1980s, though, in the wake of widespread deregulation of the media industries in North America, and the advent of new digital technologies, large-scale entertainment conglomerates have tried to extend and develop such "synergies" in more sophisticated ways. To do this the traditional providers of media content began to search for partners across the broad range of production, promotion, and distribution, and large media companies felt a need to get even larger in order to compete effectively in the global arena. As this occurred, sports teams suddenly became important in ways beyond their ability to sell a single product or to promote advertising in local markets, and beyond the narrowly drawn issues of a team's record of profit and loss.

This was the context in which big international media players such as Disney, News Corp., Time-Warner, Blockbuster Video, and Viacom began in the late 1980s and 1990s to acquire greater holdings in sports, including the ownership of a large number of major league teams. Sports not only provided valuable content for the network and cable operations run by these companies, they also promised a wealth of new promotional possibilities. The most commonly cited example is Disney's cross-marketing of theme parks, movies, cable television, and merchandise with its major league teams in hockey and baseball (Mighty Ducks of Anaheim in the NHL and Anaheim Angels in MLB). However, other more recent examples of synergy—especially between sports and the so-called high-tech industries—are even more revealing. For instance, in an early move to enlarge its Internet audience, Microsoft Corporation struck strategic alliances with more than two dozen media partners (including Time-Warner and Disney) to "showcase their online offerings via packages of entertainment, business, news, sports, and lifestyle channels" (Schiller 1999, 103). The recent mergers between AOL and Time-Warner, and Seagram with French media leaders Vivendi/Canal Plus, promise similar synergies, where "entertainment properties" of different types will be used for broader promotional purposes.

These examples of the involvement of major international corporations emphasize the new global reach both of North American major league sports and of the media that promote them. Today, like large media corporations more generally, most of the U.S.–based major leagues are considering how to expand globally, if only because growth in North American markets now seems to have leveled off. Indeed, the NFL's recent $17 billion television contract only makes sense if it is seen as a global promotional venture rather than something limited to the U.S. domestic market. The challenge for Fox, CBS, and ESPN—the partners in the deal most likely to broadcast NFL games outside the United States—will be to try to increase global audiences for the NFL and its merchandise. The interest generated in the NBA (and Nike) by the "Dream Team" in Barcelona also prefigured the enormous potential—not fully realized, perhaps, since the retirement of Michael Jordan—for merchandising North American sports insignia clothing in Europe and elsewhere. Likewise, Fédération Internationale de Football Association, instead of abandoning its efforts to "go global" in the wake of the relative failure of World Cup '96 in the United States, has simply switched the focus of its effort, for now, to the burgeoning markets of East Asia. Today, all the major professional sports seek to demonstrate to transnational advertisers that they can attract global audiences in the manner achieved so far in sports only by the Olympic Games.

These transnational growth strategies in sports take to a global stage the "expansion" and search for wider markets that has characterized the growth of the sports entertainment and consumer goods industries in North America for almost a century. What is new today is that the search for expanded sports markets is not being pursued by the sports leagues alone; rather, North American major league sports have become strategically incorporated—through the sale of media, merchandising, and sponsorship rights, and through outright ownership—into the broader corporate agendas of transnational media conglomerates. Here, the goal is first and foremost to pursue global market segments whose members have significant disposable incomes and to bring these potential consumers more directly into the orbit of luxury capitalism. In other words, the quest is for global "class" audiences more than for global "mass" audiences (cf., Schiller 1999, 135). But even among the global masses, for those industries whose goods can be sold cheaply enough to find their way into the "youthful economies of South African townships and Latin American barrios—cigarettes, soft drinks, cassettes—the potential profits are prodigious" (Dyer-Witheford 1999, 136). In the competition to market goods to both of these types of global audience, North American major league sports have clearly become more visible and popular internationally—for instance, as strategic partners in the promotion of North American brand-name soft drinks to the world's masses, but also, on their own terms, as markers of cosmopolitanism for global upmarket consumers. This growing international visibility and popularity poses some of the same challenges to traditional regional and national sporting practices in other parts of the world as those that occurred *within* North America during the formation of the major leagues.

LIMITS, LOCAL VARIATIONS, AND RESPONSES TO GLOBALIZATION

This is not to say that the increased global availability and popularity of North American major league sports as a consumer choice will necessarily have the effect of *fully* colonizing the world's other regional and national sporting cultures. On the contrary, even within the countries of the Americas themselves there is little today to suggest that regional and national sports will be completely eclipsed by growing hemispheric audiences for the NBA, the NFL, the NHL, or even Major League Baseball (the only one of the major league sports that Latin Americans play professionally, and the only one that includes players from Hispanic countries). There is, to be sure, an undeniable sense in which older correspondences between culture and place within North America have been steadily undercut by franchising and by the creation of continental markets for cultural products of different types, along with other consumer goods. Cities such as Seattle and Atlanta (as well as Toronto) are much more similar in what might be called their "public culture" than they used to be in the 1950s, and the franchising of major league sports has played no small role in this, as has (on a much larger scale) the franchising of many other kinds of national brand names (e.g., McDonald's, the Gap, and Wal-Mart). Extending this line of argument, as Mexico and other countries to the south become urban and industrial consumer societies in a fuller sense, and as trade agreements open up their markets (and their media) to more global franchises and brand names, they too will become "North Americanized" in many of the same ways that Canada has, with Dallas Cowboys jerseys as familiar in Managua and Manzanillo as they are in Moncton. Still, the growing international media visibility of major league sports, and the hemispheric spread of insignia merchandise, only tell part of the story. For example, Mexico City has seen decent turnouts for a couple of preseason NFL exhibitions, and Mexicans who are cable subscribers often watch American sports on channels from Dallas, Los Angeles, and Denver. Nonetheless, the *regular* interest that most Mexicans take in American sports—something very different from the novelty of an exhibition match—remains much less than the interest they take in their own soccer leagues, or indeed in the Mexican professional baseball league. Local sports, in other words, and local rivalries, still hold considerably more interest (almost everywhere outside the United States) than NFL matches between, say, Indianapolis and Tennessee, even if such matches involve some of the best football players in the world (cf., Leifer 1996). By the same token, while there are, to be sure, audiences for NFL-style football in cities such as London, Amsterdam, and Barcelona, interest in the European-based World Football League has not taken off as its sponsors (and the NFL) had hoped. Similarly, the NHL has gained little or nothing, in the way of regular income, from playing exhibitions in Europe and Japan (or from its ill-starred participation in the Nagano Olympics). Even in Canada, despite good audience ratings for the NFL, and shaky NHL franchises, older national traditions continue to show a stubborn durability. Thus, the CFL has found renewed success in the late 1990s as a more modest, nationally based, and second-tier professional league, and the franchise values of Canadian minor hockey league teams have escalated as more and more Canadians have been priced out of the NHL market.

Viewed in a global perspective, recent events suggest that the sports industry optimism of the early 1990s—when all the North American major leagues planned expansions in the belief that good marketing could sell "any sport, anywhere"—was exaggerated. North American sports in Europe and Japan have been modestly successful in attracting mobile and affluent young men who appear to want to signify their identifications with global consumer culture by participating in "cosmopolitan" forms of sporting consumption. However, while this *kind* of audience is attractive from a marketing standpoint, the sizes of audiences for North American major league sports in Europe and Japan do not suggest any overwhelming cultural or economic breakthrough. Even within North America itself, the expansions of the NHL into the American Sunbelt and of the NBA into Canada are by no means an unqualified success.

In many respects, these recent league expansions in major league hockey and basketball are not unlike the spread of sushi and cappuccino bars into upscale malls around North America. The range of consumer and lifestyle options is expanded for those who can afford them. But, the resulting signifiers of taste and fashion arguably have more to do with gentrification, boutique capitalism, and with marketing images of "difference" and novelty, than with any widespread changes in the habits and interests of ordinary people, let alone enduring changes in regional or national cultures (cf., Zukin 1991). It is certainly true that the NBA's movement into Canada has stimulated increased interest in basketball in Toronto and Vancouver, and that playoff hockey in Miami a few years ago prompted pickup hockey games in Latino districts of that city. However, it is not at all clear, at this point, how deeply rooted and enduring these interests are, or how likely they would be to survive numerous years of losing seasons or a franchise move away from the cities in question. More importantly, in the absence of strong local traditions of fan support, the economic successes of the franchises themselves have become overly dependent upon the fragile loyalty of the local business and professional classes.

All of this suggests that the broadscale incorporation of North American major league sports into national cultures around the world is likely to be much more uneven than many commentators have predicted (or feared). What is more profound in its effects on the sporting cultures of other countries is the international export of North American–style business structures and practices in sports. Outside of North America, the business of sports has widely been understood as something more than a purely commercial enterprise. Professional sports clubs and leagues in countries as varied as England, Germany, Spain, Australia, and Brazil have certainly pursued profits, but in these countries a strictly market-oriented approach to sports—with its tendency toward profit-maximizing cartels, franchises in the best markets, and featuring a relentless pursuit of national and continental audiences—has been counterbalanced by the force of local and national traditions, coupled with a sense that sports teams are community institutions.

By the late 1980s, though, it was becoming clear that the structures of professional sports outside of North America were being pressured from the same combination of commercial challenges and opportunities (many of them associated with the changes in public media regulation and new media technology that we have outlined earlier) that were transforming nearly every other form of capitalist enterprise around the world. That is why, over the past decade in several European countries and Australia, professional teams have folded or moved to other more financially attractive communities; club teams have been converted to joint-stock companies and shares floated on the stock markets; teams have been bought up by large media interests; and traditional competitions (notably, soccer's European Cup) have become transformed so as to maximize continental television audiences.

These changes dramatize the extent to which the owners of prominent sports teams in more and more countries—along with the global promoters of world-class sporting events—have now widely embraced the long-standing premise of the U.S.-based entertainment industries: that cultural products are commodities that can be capitalized and marketed according to the same principles that govern the conduct of other businesses (cf., Whitson 1998, 58–59). Recent changes in the structures and conduct of the sports business outside of North America also represent the spreading influence of transnational advertisers and corporate media interests into numerous economies and cultures, and the global spread of the tendency for media conglomerates to buy up sports teams and events, transforming them from civic and national sports "institutions" into heavily promoted international media "properties."

Even here, there are important economic limits to how far the globalization of North American business norms and practices can proceed. Most notably, the successful global diffusion of world-class sports as an upmarket consumer choice depends upon there being significant populations who have the disposable incomes to afford them. That is at least part of the reason why the continentalist tendencies of U.S.–based major league sports show little indication at this point of being broadly extended into Latin America. Despite the "modernizations" that have been forced upon many Latin American economies over recent decades, and despite rises in living standards for those in white-collar employment, no Latin American economy today has a middle-class large and affluent enough to pay the ticket prices—or to attract the kind of advertising dollars—that North American major league sports franchises require in order to pay current major league salaries. This explains, of course, why baseball players from Mexico, Venezuela, and the Dominican Republic have historically gone to play in the United States whenever they could. Similarly, now that European soccer salaries have risen to the same heady levels as U.S. sports salaries—as a result of the more intensive commodification of the game outlined earlier—even Brazilian soccer (widely regarded as producing many of the best players in the world) has become an "export industry," developing talent for the Spanish and Italian leagues while the home league sinks into mediocrity (Galeano 1998, 206–209). Brazilian clubs still play to large crowds, as do clubs in Mexico and other Latin American countries. However, professional team sports in these countries is still priced as working-class entertainment, players are paid accordingly, and there are not the kind of corporate and middle-class audiences to support moving sports upmarket, as has effectively happened in North America and, more recently, in Europe.

This is not to say that Mexico and other Latin American countries lack a culturally cosmopolitan middle class. These are, especially in the larger societies, countries with sophisticated urban cultures and substantial numbers of well-educated professionals and public servants. Recent trade agreements, and the neoliberal agenda pursued by the International Monetary Fund at the urging of Mexican and other Latin American governments, have also supported the growth of small and prosperous entrepreneurial classes in many parts of Latin America, alongside more traditional big landowners and industrialists. However, these policies have also done little to resolve long-standing rural and urban poverty; they have exacerbated class divisions and tensions; and, in many areas, have increased the numbers of displaced, underemployed, and unemployed people (cf., Cleaver 1990). Even among employed professional and white-collar populations, typical salaries in Latin America cannot support the lifestyles that people in such occupations might enjoy in Canada or the United States. And, if many middle-class fans are now priced out of the professional sports spectator market in Canadian cities such as Vancouver or Edmonton, it is difficult to see how Mexico City or Caracas could support northern major league sports, with its world-class salaries.

That western Europe and North America can and do support these things has made them magnets for players from all around the world (especially from eastern Europe and other "developing" countries) in their respective sports. However, this can be seen as a marker, of sorts, of the chasm that still separates the affluent "North" from the rest of the world, and the kinds of conspicuous consumption that North American standards of living can permit.

In the optimistic hyperbole that so often announces the arrival of the "global village," there is often the suggestion, as marketing guru Theodore Levitt once put it, that "as people gain access to global information, so they develop global needs and demand global commodities, thereby becoming global citizens" (quoted in Robins 1991, 28). In this kind of discourse, and in the promotional culture that it exemplifies, identity becomes less a matter of geographical or social location—let alone the political solidarities that potentially followed from identifications based in place—and more a construct of consumer sovereignty and of product preferences and lifestyle choices. This celebration of new, upmarket consumer opportunities—and of people's identities and even rights as consumers—has emerged as one of the central legitimating elements in the post–Cold War triumphalism of global capitalism, often serving as an answer, of sorts, to those who question the global spread of neoliberal economic policies, the underfunding of public institutions, and the polarization in wealth that is increasingly visible in many so-called world-class cities (Sassen 1996). As Robert Reich (1992, 20–25) has argued, this discourse suggests a diminishing commitment to the welfare of individual nations among the world's market elites, so long as the facilities and products *they* use and consume—the airports, convention centers, research parks, and (we would add) leisure and consumption goods and spaces—are both world class and secure.

Over the past decade, the North American major leagues, along with their strategic partners in advertising and large media conglomerates, have played the siren songs of global market citizenship and global investment in world-class products and facilities effectively—to justify massive public subsidies and tax concessions, command huge fees for media rights, and promote themselves to new audiences, both within North America and abroad. But, one unintended consequence of the unfettered commercialism associated with all of this has been to undermine much of the legitimacy of the claims once made by professional sports teams that they are truly civic or national institutions. Today, almost everywhere that world-class sports are produced and sold, fans are forced to confront the fact that "they" do not own or control their teams: Murdoch does, and Disney, AOL, or some other ownership group whose commitment to profit maximization in continental and global markets is likely to be greater than its commitment to the local or national community.

The disaffection (and, sometimes, despair) that typically accompanies this realization has recently provided a basis in North America for a healthy public skepticism about the major leagues' claims of making a significant contribution to local economies, and about the value of public subsidies to attract and keep major league teams in any given city. Indeed, despite their spectacular successes through the 1990s, prosubsidy forces in the United States now appear to be having a somewhat more difficult time, and have lost public referenda in several communities. Meanwhile, in Canada, a federal government proposal in the spring of 2000 to provide tax relief and public support to NHL teams had to be withdrawn three days later after a firestorm of public protest across the country (cf., Whitson, Harvey, and Lavoie 2001). And, in England public opposition to global corporate ownership in sports was dramatically evident in the high-profile campaign mounted by Manchester United fans to block the sale of "their" team to Murdoch's News Corp. None of this amounts to any sustained resistance to current tendencies in the political economy of major league sports. However, it does suggest a growing public awareness of the extent to which sports today have lost much of their former anchorage in place—in addition to their previous institutional distinctiveness—as they have become more tightly integrated into the global leisure and cultural industries.

NOTES

Unless noted otherwise, all dollar amounts are in U.S. currency.

1. The significance of the CBC in Canada was intensified by the regulated character of Canadian broadcasting. For a more developed analysis, see Rutherford (1990) and Gruneau and Whitson (1993, 103–106).

2. Useful histories of the early relationships between television and sports in North America include Johnson (1971), Powers (1984), and Rader (1984). More concise discussions are found in Eastman and Meyer (1989, 97–119) and Bellamy (1989, 120–133).

3. Much of the information in this discussion of the CFL comes from a series of interviews conducted by Rick Gruneau in May and June 1983 with the late Jake Gaudar, the former CFL commissioner.

4. For a commentary on this and later attempts by the NHL to get reductions in teams' "public cost," see Whitson, Harvey, and Lavoie (2001).

5. For additional material on the sports stadium subsidy debate, see Euchner (1992), Rosentraub (1997), and Noll and Zimbalist (1997).

6. National television revenues, for example, tend to be shared by teams in all the major leagues, whereas only the NFL has tried to develop formulae for sharing revenues generated by local media. The NFL and Major League Baseball also have agreements governing the sharing of gate receipts between home and visiting teams, but this is not the case in the NBA and NHL. See Shropshire (1995, 10).

REFERENCES

Bellamy, Edward. 1989. "Professional Sports Organizations: Media Strategies." In *Media, Sports, and Society*, ed. Lawrence Wenner. Newbury Park, Calif.: Sage.

Cleaver, Harry. 1990. "Close the IMF, Abolish Debt, and End Development." *Capital and Class* 39:17–50.

Cosentino, Frank. 1995. *A Passing Game: A History of the CFL*. Winnipeg: Bain and Cox.

Dryden, Ken, and Roy McGregor. 1989. *Home Game*. Toronto: McClelland and Stewart.

Dyer-Witheford, Nick. 1999. *Cyber-Marx: Cycles and Circuits of Struggle in High Technology Capitalism*. Urbana: University of Illinois Press.

Eastman, Susan Tyler, and Timothy P. Meyer. 1989. "Sports Programming: Scheduling, Costs, and Competition." In *Media, Sports, and Society*, ed. Lawrence Wenner. Newbury Park, Calif.: Sage.

Euchner, Charles. 1992. *Playing the Field: Why Sports Teams Move and Cities Fight to Keep Them*. Baltimore, Md.: Johns Hopkins University Press.

Galeano, Edwardo. 1998. *Soccer in Sun and Shadow*, trans. Mark Fried. London: Verso.

Geer, John. 1997. "Fox's Law: Rights Fees Can Only Go Up." *Financial World*, 17 June, 52–53.

Gruneau, Richard, and David Whitson. 1993. *Hockey Night in Canada: Sport, Identities, and Cultural Politics*. Toronto: Garamond.

Hardy, Steven. 1990. "Adopted by All the Leading Clubs: Sporting Goods and the Shaping of Leisure, 1890–1900." In *For Fun and Profit: The Transformation of Leisure into Consumption*, ed. Richard Butsch. Philadelphia: Temple University Press.

Harvey, David. 1987. "Flexible Accumulation through Urbanization: Reflections on Postmodernism and the American City." *Antipode*, no. 19:3.

Herman, Edward, and Robert McChesney. 1997. *The Global Media: The New Missionaries of Corporate Capitalism*. London: Cassell.

Ingham, Alan, Jeremy Howell, and Todd Schilperoort. 1988. "Professional Sports and Community: A Review and Exegesis." *Exercise and Sports Science Reviews:* 427–465.

Jhally, Sut. 1984. "The Spectacle of Accumulation: Material and Cultural Factors in the Evolution of the Sports/Media Complex." *Insurgent Sociologist*, no. 12:3.

Johnson, William O. 1971. *Super Spectator and the Electric Lilliputians*. Boston: Little, Brown.

Kidd, Bruce. 1995. "Toronto's Sky Dome: The World's Greatest Entertainment Centre." In *The Stadium and the City*, ed. John Bale and Olof Moen. Keele: Keele University Press.

Laing, Jonathan. 1996. "Foul Play." *Barron's*, 19 August.

Leifer, Mark. 1996. *Making the Majors*. Cambridge, Mass.: Harvard University Press.

Leiss, William, Stephen Kline, and Sut Jhally. 1990. *Social Communication in Advertising*. 2nd ed. Scarborough: Nelson.

McChesney, Robert. 1989. "Media Made Sport: A History of Sports Coverage in the United States." In *Media, Sports, and Society*, ed. Lawrence Wenner. Newbury Park, Calif.: Sage.

McKay, Shona. 1998. "Can We Afford to Play Our Own Game?" *Financial Post* (February).

Noll, Roger, and Andrew Zimbalist, eds. 1997. *Sports, Jobs, and Taxes: The Economic Impact of Sports Teams and Stadiums*. Washington, D.C.: The Brookings Institution.

Ozanian, Michael, with Tushar Atre, Ronald Fink, Jennifer Reingold, John Kimmelman, Andrew Osterland, and Jeff Sklar. 1995. "Suite Deals: Why New Stadiums

Are Shaking Up the Pecking Order of Sports Franchises." *Financial World,* 9 May, 42, 56.

Powers, Ron. 1984. *Supertube: The Rise of Television Sports.* New York: Coward and McCann.

Quirk, James, and Rodney Fort. 1992. *Pay Dirt: The Business of Professional Team Sports.* Princeton, N.J.: Princeton University Press.

Rader, Benjamin J. 1984. *In Its Own Image: How Television Has Transformed Sports.* New York: The Free Press.

Reich, Robert. 1992. *The Work of Nations.* New York: Vintage.

Robins, Kevin. 1991. "Tradition and Translation: National Culture in Its Global Context." In *Enterprise and Heritage: Crosscurrents of National Culture,* ed. John Corner and Sylvia Harvey. London: Routledge.

Rosentraub, Mark. 1997. *Major League Losers: The Real Cost of Sport and Who's Paying For It.* New York: HarperCollins.

Rutherford, Paul. 1978. *The Making of the Canadian Media.* Toronto: McGraw Hill–Ryerson.

———. 1990. *When Television Was Young: Primetime Canada, 1952–1967.* Toronto: University of Toronto Press.

———. 1993. "Made in America: The Problem of Mass Culture in Canada." In *The Beaver Bites Back? American Popular Culture in Canada,* ed. D. Flaherty and F. Manning. Montreal: McGill-Queen's University Press.

Sassen, Saskia. 1996. "Whose City Is It? Globalization and the Formation of New Claims." *Public Culture* 8:205–223.

Schiller, Dan. 1999. *Digital Capitalism: Networking the Global Market System.* Cambridge: Massachusetts Institute of Technology Press.

Shropshire, Kenneth. 1995. *The Sports Franchise Game.* Philadelphia: University of Pennsylvania Press.

Strauss, Lawrence. 1998. "Does Money Tilt the Playing Field? When Sports Coverage Becomes Marketing." *Columbia Journalism Review* (September–October): 16–17.

Tadeschi, Bob. 1999. "Sports Leagues Hope Athletic Feats Spark Impulse Buys." *New York Times,* 5 July.

Thompson, John Herd, and Allen Seager. 1985. *Canada 1922–1939: Decades of Discord.* Toronto: McClelland and Stewart.

Whitson, David. 1998. "Circuits of Promotion: Media, Marketing, and the Globalization of Sport." In *MediaSport,* ed. Lawrence A. Wenner. London: Routledge.

Whitson, David, Jean Harvey, and Marc Lavoie. 2001. "The Mills Report, the Manley Subsidy Proposals, and the Business of Major League Sport." *Public Administration,* in press.

Zukin, Sharon. 1991. *Landscapes of Power: From Detroit to Disneyland.* Berkeley: University of California Press.

11

Multimedia Policy for Canada and the United States: Industrial Development as Public Interest

Vanda Rideout and Andrew Reddick

The continentalization of communications policies and practices in North America is generally considered to be part of a broader global trend of market integration and domestic policy liberalization. A decade ago, the Canada–U.S. Free Trade Agreement (CUSFTA) helped pave the way for domestic policies of liberalization, deregulation, and internationalization. These were justified by arguments of economic efficiencies, increased opportunities, and reduced prices for consumers. The North American Free Trade Agreement (NAFTA) increased industrial development for global trade by including trade in telecommunications services. More recently, these arguments have been replaced by new ones, such as the need to be one of the leaders in the information society and knowledge economy so as not to be left behind in the information age. Digitization and a combination of different forms of media increasingly ease the dissemination of these services through various telecommunications networks to create what is perceived as an inevitable seamlessness of cross-border communications that ostensibly defies control or regulation. However, while the technical means of packaging and delivering media content may be new, the content itself largely is not. As such, the choice by governments to selectively not regulate new media and the Internet benefits certain industrial and political interests, at the expense of the public, especially as citizens and as consumers.

This raises a number of questions, explored in this chapter, about new media policy frameworks in Canada and the United States. The chapter considers whether there is a continental new media policy, how domestic new media policies may differ from previous media policy, and whether there has been a "break" with traditional regulatory approaches. In addition, it examines the tensions between the regulation of traditional media and the ostensible lack of regulation of new media. Finally, it considers the implications of the new on-line marketplace for citizens particularly to meet the need for a diversity of information resources.

New media policy in Canada and the United States is composed of five major elements: the new media policy framework within the North American and international free trade regimes; national competitive advantage and industrial policy; corporate market strategies; myths about multimedia; and changes in domestic communication policies and practices. These have created three major contradictions that are common to both countries. First, instead of providing a new consumer panacea, higher costs and poorer quality media for citizens have resulted through a redefinition of the public interest from that of broad economic, social, and cultural equity to an eroded and narrowed economistic concept. Second, contrary to their promarket ideology, both national governments, as part of industry support policies, introduce some of the limitations of the free market by providing massive content development subsidies for certain types of new media. Finally, as opposed to the creation of vibrant competitive markets, both domestically and internationally, new media is becoming an icon as much for the integration and conglomeration of communications companies as it is for the integration of communications content.

WHAT IS SO NEW ABOUT NEW MEDIA?
TRADITIONAL AND NEW MEDIA

New media has become one of those terms that is widely used, though poorly defined. To start, we feel it is useful to sketch out how we have thought of new media for the purposes of this chapter.

Traditional or old media, as it is sometimes called, consists of audio, print, visual, or music content. Products include compact discs–read-only memory (CD-ROMs), video tapes, films, and programs that are distributed electronically via radio or television broadcasting networks, cable television, or satellite networks. Print media, such as newspapers, books, and magazines, also fit into the traditional media category. The print media have experimented with a wide range of technologies to improve product delivery through computers, television broadcasting, satellite, CD-ROM, and the telephone networks. The first common element of this older media is that they are usually made by one producer and are aimed at a wide or mass audience. Furthermore, there is no interactivity other than audience consumption.

New media services, which may also be referred to as multimedia, incorporate computer software programming, formatting, and networking technologies. The convergence of these technologies permits the digitization of text, graphics, data, audio, still visual, full-moving video, and animation distributed and delivered for exhibition to personal computers, television sets, or other technologies by using the Internet delivery system. The range of new media products include video games, CD-ROMs, entertainment, news, e-mail, on-line paging services, faxing, e-commerce, Internet Protocol telephony, as well as services delivered over the World Wide Web and the Internet. The distinguishing features of new media are its use of digitization, interconnected networks, and interactivity. Individual interactivity permits one-on-one (producer–end user) media content that can be tailor-made and received when the end user chooses.

While the previous examples clearly are "new media," they still form a minority of media products and services. Moreover, what appears to be meant by new media by many observers encompasses a range of traditional media products and services. New media seems to have as much to do with pack aging as it does with content or how it is delivered.

For others such as Pierre Lévy (1997), what is new about new media is the creation of a new and more complex knowledge relation.[1] This new relationship is made possible by global networks, such as the Web, that in Lévy's view are dynamic, fluid, and open (191). The similar postmodern position of Mark Poster maintains that society has moved from a first to a second media age (1995, 24–26). The new media age is distinguished by people who communicate by computer, thereby forming a new set of human/machine relations and establishing new kinds of electronic meeting places on the Internet. The integration of telephone, radio, film, television, and the computer produces reconfigured words, sounds, and images to form multimedia content.

Is this combination of technology and content new, or is it more the deep ening and extension of a new form of distribution? Skeptics point out that film was the first to combine media such as text, images, and sound to produce multimedia (Monaco 2000, 534). What digitization accomplishes is that it codes and compresses sounds, images, and data for media and communications systems. The major advantage of digitization can be seen in the new delivery systems and the rise of networks such as the Internet and databases. An argument can be made then that new media has less to do with the combination of these media than it does with digitizing images and sounds. Critics such as Kevin Robins and Frank Webster note that new media is more ambiguous and problematic than proponents claim, while at the same time digitization increases control over discrete media and networks (1999, 228). Others, such as Vincent Mosco, explain that cyberspace is not new but a restructuring, reshaping, and extension of communications "created over the history of communication technology and accelerating with the telegraph, telephone and broadcasting technologies" (1999, 42). Perhaps the best way of describing how we are treating new media is that it is *multi*media—that is, a combination of media to which has been applied the latest technological developments of media content manipulation and new delivery systems, such as the Internet, but without government regulation in the public interest. But we should add that it is content that is not easily captured or subjected to the traditional forms of regulation, though many of its components may be (e.g., broadcasting). This does not mean it cannot be regulated, but that it would have to be regulated in a different way. Concurrently, new media is still very much influenced, regulated, and governed by trade agreements as well as government industrial and cultural development policies and programs. It is also regulated by the decisions of companies. Some of these rules are embedded in computer code (operating instructions) determining what functions are or are not possible. Other rules, such as what content is developed, are decided by managers. Together, these are different forms of regulation for multimedia and the Internet.

NORTH AMERICAN TRADE AGREEMENTS AND MULTIMEDIA POLICY

NAFTA and CUSFTA provide conditions for strategic alliances that integrate countries into different degrees of economic globalization. These continental trade deals work alongside specific global institutions such as the World Trade Organization (WTO), the World Bank, the International Monetary Fund (IMF), as well as institutionalized planning organizations such as the Group of Eight (G8) and the Organization for Economic Cooperation and Development (OECD). Essentially, these institutions help manage global economic relations and negotiate the terms of international development and underdevelopment.

Both CUSFTA and NAFTA are significant documents that affect communications and multimedia policies in Canada, the United States, and Mexico. Both agreements advance a de facto new constitution for North America, one that institutionalizes the power of markets and multinational firms over the public sphere (Warnock 1988). Moreover, both agreements add additional communications policy layers to domestic communications policy restructuring. What is particularly important about CUSFTA is that it is the first trade document to extend free trade beyond goods to *services* and *investments*. Section 1408 of CUSFTA is key for multimedia because it opens free trade in enhanced and value-added services such as computerized data, audio, video, and information services.

Included in NAFTA is a commitment to liberalization that applies to the federal levels of government as well as provinces and states. This liberalization extends to any restricting policies, licensing requirements, and nondiscriminating measures (Canada 1992, article 1208). When NAFTA's most-favored-nation clause is applied to multimedia firms such as American Telephone and Telegraph (AT&T), American On-Line (AOL)/Time-Warner, Rogers Communication, or Bell Canada Enterprises (BCE), both the United States and Canada must treat them as equals, as if they were all domestic firms. An entire chapter in NAFTA (chapter 13) is devoted to telecommunications issues such as enhanced and value-added services. Enhanced services are significant for multimedia products and services because they employ computer-stored or -restructured processing applications, including formatting, content, codes, and even the protocols of transmitted information with telecommunications (article 1310). Another area that impacts multimedia is intellectual property (chapter 17). Although the protection and enforcement of intellectual property is guaranteed for copyright, sound recording, trademarks, and encrypted programs delivered by satellite, NAFTA states that they are not to be used as barriers to trade. Cross-border access to use public telecommunications networks and services is also guaranteed for private corporate networks. Finally, NAFTA creates a free-flowing data and information zone so that businesses can move information freely throughout the region.

Internationalization of communications effectively places limits on the scope of domestic regulators and public interest policy. The telecommunications and intellectual property provisions in NAFTA and the WTO not only serve as vehicles to promote liberalization, deregulation, and internationalization, despite opposition, but also establish a nontransparent trade regime for multinational firms and global services users. These trade agreements, essentially the result of undemocratic processes, are documents that make business rights and commerce the primary criteria for setting social and public policy. Of less importance are the democratic rights of citizens in any country to retain a public service mandate and social policies through distinctive national treatment (Rideout and Mosco 1997, 99).

INTERNATIONAL MULTIMEDIA POLICY

In 1995, the WTO replaced its predecessor the General Agreement on Tariffs and Trade (GATT), thereby making trade policies broader in scope. With an eye on trade in services, the WTO incorporated the General Agreement on Trade in Services (GATS). WTO/GATS goes further than the service sections in NAFTA and CUSFTA by targeting the areas of communications, cultural, and computer services. Communications services include postal, telecommunications, and audiovisual; cultural services covers entertainment, news agencies, libraries, archives, and museums; and computer services entails consulting, computer hardware installation, software implementation, and data processing (WTO 1998b). The WTO, OECD, and the governments in Canada and the United States consider multimedia to be very important because of its impact on the North American economy and on the gross domestic product (GDP).

For example, in 1992 one part of Canada's multimedia industries, the book and periodical publishing and newspaper sectors, contributed $4 billion Canadian to the GDP. Publishing accounted for 12,900 full-time jobs and 1,600 part-time jobs. The film and video industry, another part of multimedia, with main activity in production, laboratory, and postproduction services, distribution, and exhibition, contributed $824 million to the GDP, providing 17,900 full- and part-time jobs and work for 7,800 freelancers. As of 1994, 42 percent of broadcasting industry revenues were generated by cable television services, including pay television and specialty services, and 58 percent from traditional off-air radio and television. In total, the broadcasting industries' contribution was 0.4 percent of the total GDP. By 1994, the broadcasting industry had eliminated four thousand jobs, bringing the number of full-time jobs down to forty-six thousand. The computer services industry, another component of multimedia, consists of software product development and professional and processing services. The industry contributed 0.9 percent of the GDP to the total economy. More importantly, the computer services industry's rate of growth is 7 percent compared to the whole economy average of 5 percent, and the broadcasting industry fared significantly worse than the whole economy with an increase of only 2 percent. By 1994, employment in the computer services industry in Canada increased by twenty-six thousand to provide ninety-nine thousand jobs (OECD 1998, 8).

The dominance of media by the United States, both continentally and internationally, is evidenced in a number of the multimedia industries. Clearly, the United States is the largest producer of audiovisual content with the largest share of the world music market at 30.5 percent. In the European Community countries of Germany, the United Kingdom, and France, U.S. companies had a 20.9 percent share compared to Canada at 2.8 percent. The United States also ranks first in terms of the gross box office revenues that are generated domestically at $5 billion. In addition, the median market share of U.S. films in Europe is 74 percent.[2] According to the Motion Picture Association of America, the total number of jobs the U.S. motion picture industry (production, distribution, videotape sector, and theaters) had created over the 1985–1995 period was 270,000. Added to the Hollywood film industry is the 29 percent of the industry comprised of independents, generating another $8.3 billion in revenues and 36 percent of the employees of the film industry. Video sales alone accounted for 49 percent of Hollywood's worldwide revenues. In 1997, information technology–producing industries added 350,000 jobs. By 1994, the broadly defined multimedia industries were estimated to contribute 5.72 percent of GDP or $385.2 billion and almost six million jobs or 4.8 percent of the total American workforce (OECD 1998, 10, 18, 19–20).

The more immediate concern of the WTO is the still heavy regulation of audiovisual services by most countries. Regulatory mechanisms include broadcasting legislation, ownership restrictions, domestic production subsidies, and domestic content rules. In order to overcome what it perceives to be rigid regulatory obstructions, the WTO recommends extending competition, liberalization, and deregulation to multimedia and audiovisual services so as to move away from cultural exemptions in trade agreements, as well as other protectionist cultural policies (WTO 1998a, 6).

Other multimedia policy concerns for the WTO include global e-commerce. As previously discussed, the WTO's broad policy support includes a competitive e-commerce environment that provides open market access for the free flow of information through the Internet, with the least intrusive means of regulation (WTO 1998b, 65). Acceptable Internet content regulation for the WTO includes self-regulation that may involve software with filters and information tracking, or producer codes of conduct. Regulation by governments, however, is considered passé, meaning that frontline regulatory practices should not be continued (38). In essence, the North American and international neoliberal multimedia policies repeat the choruses from the same song sheet over and over again.

COMPETITIVE ADVANTAGE AND INDUSTRIAL STRATEGY

Industry players and international trade institutions such as the WTO and the OECD view media content as a new growth industry. These international organizations reflect the values and goals of their member states, particularly the more economically dominant countries within them. As opposed to a diversity of values and goals, mediated into a consensus by international organizations, the commonality of goals among leading industrial countries (e.g., the European Community, the United States, Canada, Australia, and so on) has meant that the articulation of an economic-centric policy approach has been achieved with relative ease, though the implementation of this in both developed and developing countries has been more problematic. What these players and institutions want to ensure is that regulatory structures, communications and media policies, and trade restrictions do not creep into the so-called multimedia environment.

The view advocated by business and these global institutions is that multimedia content needs to develop in a competitive and liberalized environment. Unlike traditional forms of media, the emergence of the Internet and much of multimedia in structural formats not easily contained by existing broadcasting and telecommunications policy frameworks, permit what can be best described as a laissez-faire free-for-all involving product development, and increasing market share and control. Not unlike the gold rushes of mining ventures of the past, to date, in this development stage, industry urges government not to attempt to regulate multimedia content or the Internet (Canadian Radio-Television and Telecommunications Commission [CRTC] 1999a; Oxman 1999). How tenuous this antiregulatory stance is will become clear once market shares and market power have been established and pressures by media companies for the need to protect capital investment with public regulation increase.

CORPORATE MARKET STRATEGIES

On the one hand, the multimedia marketplace, particularly in the context of the Internet, can be characterized as a wide open opportunity where any individual or company can compete and provide a diverse array of new forms of content to any other participant. This is often the view of regulators, industry, and other Web promoters. This may be descriptively useful in that there are over a billion Web pages on the Internet. Many are operated by businesses, and there is a burgeoning market for CDs, games, and other media in multimedia format, plus easy access for people who wish to hawk their wares or opinions on-line. However, this is a substantively weak understanding because it ignores certain realities. These include: no one knows who else is on the Web, or how to easily find them; consumers prefer to deal with known, established organizations; services with value for consumers are those that aggregate a number of products and services, with ease of access; and individuals are drawn to services that possess significant assurances of security, privacy, and other quality service components (Ekos Research Associates 1998). Most of these attributes are outside the abilities of that sea of individual content and service providers so readily heralded by the Web-democrats and promoters. But these are well within the resources of those companies that already have some degree of market power and dominance in communications. In addition, the emerging structure of the North American media market is taking form where a handful of integrated media companies dominate at the top of each domestic market, and some of these again dominate globally, for example, AOL/Time-Warner, Disney Corporation, Microsoft Corporation, BCE, and Rogers. A large number of smaller content and service providers supply content for these market leaders, or cater to smaller niche segments. But there is no equality or democracy of market presence, power, or dominance between individuals providing content and established companies in the emerging market hierarchy.

At the level of infrastructure and technology, U.S. and Canadian communications companies are making their wares available on an increasingly integrated web of technologies, including digital wireless telephone and data; cellular services; multipoint microwave distribution systems; satellite services; and digital terrestrial networks. Using this converged technological platform, companies are providing, either separately or in various types of integrated packages, the full scope of services including telephony, data, broadcasting, Internet, and related services. With this structuring, companies are able to operate seamlessly on a continental basis.

Furthermore, the majority of companies are not taking big risks in the development of new services, with the exception of the infrastructural costs of the development of Internet protocols within their networks. In fact, much of the new content offerings tend to be existing products or services that have already proven themselves using other technologies (e.g., business telephone services and broadcasting) or in other consumer market formats, such as newspapers, reference materials, educational content, music, and home shopping. Requiring considerable expense and investment, something that again lessens the ability for many individual Web users to dethrone industry leaders like AOL and Microsoft, the products from other formats are repackaged in electronic format in an attempt to re-create these markets as multimedia (on-line or on-disc) (Reddick 1999).

While there are many more means or channels of distribution, whether using the Internet, digital television channels, and so on, any multimedia product or service beyond simple text production such as filmed entertainment is still very costly. When these different types of content are combined, higher costs are added to the various stages of production and distribution. These production, distribution, and marketing conditions mean that not only will the content creation and distribution process remain a hierarchical one, as with other media, but it will also similarly require the support of companies or organizations with substantial resources and market access and presence. As previously discussed, the various media forms are already dominated domestically and internationally by a handful of companies. Multimedia, rather than creating a wholly different marketplace and structure, is just being added to the mix of product lines, such as film, music, print, cable television, and so on. As part of a broad trend, these other content and cultural products and services have been, by and large, produced and distributed by monopolists or oligopolists for decades, even though there have been differences or variations at the domestic levels in Canada and the United States. What is somewhat different is that whereas particular firms may have dominated one or a few parts of the communications sector, now, with corporate, technical, and content convergence, a handful of firms are dominating the whole communications marketplace. Where new capital (e g , dot com companies) has achieved some success in the marketplace, it has quickly merged with traditional media businesses, as in the case of AOL/Time-Warner. The plethora of niche players either play the role of content "piece workers" for the dominant companies, are added to the corporate stables through takeovers, or disappear or languish at the margins of the market (OECD 1998, 5; McChesney 1999, 16–17).

With this continental industrial integration, there is also a common social class dimension to this market strategy that has been aggravated by the shift in communications policy to commercialization and competition. As economic strategy, no longer tempered by public interest objectives, such as universality in telephony and broadcasting, the best market segments from which to recoup the high costs of new product and services development are those of business and professional and upper-income consumers. The strategy of most Canadian and U.S. media companies is to target these business and consumer segments. Added to this are any public institutions that, through heavy public subsidy such as the U.S. e-rate for libraries and schools, offer some further opportunity of increasing profitability. The high-end consumer segment, comprising the more wealthy and technically advanced communications households, tends to be an early adopter of a wider array of new technologies. This segment also has the greatest disposable income for content services. This form of economic stratification means that access problems for many individuals are created for both new products and services and existing ones. Canadian and U.S. citizens risk being excluded if they lack sufficient income to afford the services or live in low-income urban or rural areas where it is not profitable for companies to provide service. Beyond access, the same holds true for content. As opposed to the creation of a diversity of content to meet all needs, both commercial and noncommercial content, the multimedia market structure means that the most profitable content receives preference in financing and development. Moreover, the type of content developed is more likely to meet the tastes and needs of elite consumers than those of more moderate means and interests, and who have yet to become mainstream multimedia and Internet users (Reddick 1999, 93–94).

There is an emerging problem at the continental level that extends from market relations carried over from the shift from monopoly to competitive domestic markets. This problem is that neither the strategies of companies, nor the emerging market structure are likely to change to meet the broader set of public-interest economic, social, and cultural goals unless government intervenes—a practice currently anathema to those dominating the industry. Such intervention would have to provide innovative methods, measures, or changes that address a range of issues at the domestic and continental levels, such as how the multimedia industry is financed, how content is created and packaged, how prices are set, how the marketplaces are structured, and the terms for the consumption of multimedia products and services. The irony here is that the Internet, generally considered to be at the core of the multimedia industry, was designed and initially operated as a dispersed or distributed network, one that was open and ostensibly democratic in permitting a diversity of views, content, and the conditions to allow some equality of access. However, without public intervention, these very same attributes will accelerate a controlled, concentrated market structure.

A NORTH AMERICAN COMMUNICATIONS NEOLIBERAL POLICY REGIME AND THE UNREGULATION OF THE INTERNET

Throughout the past three decades, the governments of Canada and the United States have succeeded in restructuring communications policy. In essence, both governments have implemented a neoliberal communications and media policy regime. Regime processes include liberalization, commercialization, privatization, and internationalization (Mosco and Rideout 1997,

168). This has meant that both the American and Canadian governments have introduced private-sector competition in broadcasting and telecommunications, thereby expanding the number of participants in the market who offer more communications services and delivery systems. Both communications regulators, the U.S. Federal Communications Commission (FCC) and the CRTC, have overturned previous cross-ownership rules in telecommunications, broadcasting, cable television, and the print industries. Central to the emerging continental market model, commercialization, which applies to both public- and private-sector organizations, replaces public interest regulation that emphasized affordability and universality with market regulation. Often referred to as deregulation, market regulation rules provide little to no public performance regulation and nebulous self-regulation. At the same time, new regulation is largely concerned with the establishment and maintenance of a level playing field for competitors, such as network interconnection, mergers, market behavior, and so on. According to the regulators, public interest objectives are achieved because the array of competitors who offer communications services and alternative distribution systems help consumers through increased product and pricing choices.

The emphasis on competition and commercial concerns over public service aspects of communications policy was undertaken by a series of governments in both countries as they introduced new telecommunications legislation reflecting the overt ideology of the market economy. Canada implemented the Telecommunications Act (1993) followed by the United States in 1996.

The United States' open, unregulated, and competitive policy approach to products and services was affirmed with multimedia and other computer-based communications services and applications in the early 1970s with the FCC's first inquiry on the role of computer applications on the telephone network (Horwitz 1989; Schiller 1982). Seeking innovation, development, and market growth, the FCC chose not to regulate data services. Since that time, the information technology industry in the United States has grown to where it now accounts for one-third of overall economic growth. The goal then, as now, was to create conditions for U.S. international leadership in the computer and communications fields (Kennard 1999).

The market regulation approach was institutionalized as policy and law for multimedia with the U.S. Telecommunications Act (1996). The main purpose of the act was to rewrite the rules and framework for the telecommunications and broadcasting markets so that firms operating in one area of communications could expand into other sectors and product lines—for example, phone companies into cable television service. The act also removed many of the regulations adopted over the years to limit or control market behavior. Beyond the rewriting of the rules for traditional communications services, the act left decision making about investments, development, and market structuring of multimedia completely in the hands of companies

(Schiller 1999, 1–24). Traditional public-interest rules were considerably weakened, with the most significant remaining efforts involving universality of basic telephone service, and the introduction of subsidies for Internet connectivity to such public institutions as schools, libraries, and community access centers (McChesney 1999, 74, 128).

Throughout the development of policy around the 1996 Telecommunications Act and related initiatives, there was little public consultation or participation in the decision-making process, leaving much of the decision making to be influenced by industry. Beyond the lack of opportunity to participate, many public interest groups were not overly concerned about the general market approach with communications policy, naively believing that their interests would be better served by the market alone, rather than with public oversight of the market by government (McChesney 1999, 130). One of the most important acts of the U.S. government that exemplifies the ideology underlying communications policy was the privatization of the Internet backbone in the mid-1990s. Developed with public funding and made available as an open network system, the handing over of this key infrastructure with no limits on commercialization or privatization relegated the public interest a minor role in the future development of the Internet.

Circumstances have been little different in Canada. Several sections in the 1993 Telecommunications Act speak to social and cultural policy objectives. However, these have largely been subjugated by another section (7 f) that dictates that preference in regulation should be given to a competitive market approach. Notwithstanding that there is nothing in the act that would give priority to one objective over another, the CRTC has emphasized this section and paid little attention to the others. Moreover, there is no evidence that the CRTC even has a good grasp of what social and cultural needs of Canadians are in the context of multimedia and the act. In fact, multimedia generally falls into a gray area between Canada's broadcasting and telecommunications acts. Multimedia is not considered by the federal government or the CRTC as traditional broadcasting fare. This, coupled with a desire to avoid hampering its development, largely at the pleading of industry, has led the CRTC to exempt multimedia from regulation—whether market behavior or public interest regulation. This policy position opens the door to further continental integration of the Canadian and U.S. multimedia markets. In Canada, public interest groups were split on the best regulatory approach to multimedia. Some, still wedded to the libertarian attributes of the earlier Internet, wanted no regulation and blithely assumed that corporate control would be impossible. Others, identifying growing market control and corporate dominance of multimedia and the Internet, not unlike that which exists in other areas of communications, called for public interest regulation to balance corporate and citizen interests (CRTC 1999a, 14).

FCC Report on Internet Unregulation

Offering only a passing comment on the importance of the role of government funding—primarily through the U.S. military, the National Science Foundation, and later universities—in the creation and early development and use of the Internet, the FCC propagates the view that the Internet's development and growth have largely been the result of market forces. The relatively recent growth of commercial services and e-commerce, and the role and importance of public institutions and public information as the primary form of content—circumstances comparable to Canada—have largely been ignored in this revisionist history. This interpretation of history is linked by the FCC to its practice since the first computer-data inquiry of 1966 of not regulating computer-based services. The FCC's goal during this period was to ensure that the marketplace, not regulation, allowed innovation and experimentation to flourish as this applied to computer and data services. The FCC refers to this policy approach as a tradition of "unregulation" (Kennard 1999).

The "FCC and the Unregulation of the Internet," however, does usefully explain the policy history and path of deregulation of telecommunications, spectrum, and computer applications. In the area of telecommunications, the FCC deregulated the equipment market allowing users to connect their own equipment to networks. A deregulated and flexible licensing policy was also established for spectrum services (i.e., wireless voice and data) that was driven by the goal of encouraging innovative uses of wireless data services and creating more competition in the marketplace. The computer inquiry proceedings established a competitive market approach for the development, marketing, and use of computer-data products and services over networks. Moreover, the FCC also exempted new or enhanced service providers from regulation, particularly for access charges normally paid by interexchange carriers. The absence of these costs as intended was to maintain the lowest price possible for dial-up Internet services, thereby encouraging widespread use by businesses and the public (Oxman 1999). Many of these same goals and themes were advocated by the United States during the free trade negotiations and were included in the final chapters of both NAFTA and CUSFTA. Bolstering market integration, the Canadian government has adopted many of the same policy changes in telecommunications.

However, during this period, like the CRTC in Canada, the FCC also maintained regulatory control over telecommunications networks. While there was deregulation of pricing and interconnection, there has been continuing regulation to ensure that communications networks are available on a universal basis and are affordable for the majority of the population. The series of subsidies in telephony have been augmented by some subsidies for computer-Internet connectivity, largely involving the wiring up of schools, libraries, and community access centers with the so-called e-rate. So while on the one hand the FCC had taken an "unregulation" approach to some products and services, contrary to its claims, it had very much taken a regulatory approach and used market behavior rules to guide the general shape and form of the current communications industry. The FCC has taken the position that as the steward of the communications public interest in communications, its role is to ensure that all communications businesses have a fair opportunity to compete. However, American citizens who may be harmed by these market players are not afforded a similar fair opportunity (Oxman 1999, 25). Interestingly, the FCC now argues not for the deregulation of traditional services as they are increasingly carried on the new data networks, but for the use of regulation when any signs of anticompetitive market behavior arise. As evidenced in the AT&T and Microsoft antitrust proceedings, a particular silence in this position is that much of the regulation of traditional services not only involved competitive issues, but also other objectives relating to social needs (1999).

The Canadian New Media Report

Prior to the multimedia hearing, the CRTC and the Departments of Heritage and Industry commissioned a study on mechanisms to promote the development and distribution of Canadian multimedia content and services (Wall Communications 1998). What the report points out is that any mechanisms selected to support the creation or distribution of multimedia content need to be balanced with Canada's international obligations. What this means in Canada's case is that any action the government takes toward the country's culture must be both appropriate and necessary in light of the growing integration of world trade. Consequently, the mechanisms chosen regarding multimedia policy must take into consideration whether they are likely to violate any provisions of trade agreements to which Canada is a signatory.

Domestic regulatory and policy considerations can be traced to the CRTC convergence report in which one of the key questions raised was: Will new and emerging services contribute to the objectives of the 1991 Broadcasting Act? This raised a concern involving the degree to which the broadcasting legislation may affect or capture multimedia. If, for example, the services provided by multimedia suppliers meet the definition of broadcasting under the act, multimedia suppliers falling under the legislation would have to either be licensed or formally exempted. Until the CRTC examined the extent to which multimedia activities fell under the act, as well as clarification of the role of the CRTC with respect to multimedia, new industry players feared that they would be operating in an environment of uncertainty (Rideout 1998).

The CRTC's *Report on New Media* (1999a) clears up any uncertainty surrounding multimedia, the broadcasting and telecommunications acts, and the role of the commission. Françoise Bertrand, the chairperson of the CRTC, explained, "our message is clear, [w]e are not regulating any portion of the

Internet" (CRTC 1999b, 2). The rationale the CRTC used for not regulating the Internet included not wanting to put the industry at a competitive disadvantage in the global marketplace and to ensure the growth of multimedia services. According to the CRTC, market forces provide Canadian presence on the Internet, and are supported by a strong demand for Canadian multimedia content. Business participants' statistics show that Canadian websites make up 5 percent of all Internet websites. French-language content, however, only makes up 5 percent of total Internet content (CRTC 1999a).

Broadcasting-related issues in the multimedia debate included the Internet and public space and the exclusion of Internet content (multimedia) from broadcasting definitions. Concerning the first issue, the CRTC explained that the Internet is not a "public place" as identified in broadcasting legislation. The CRTC reasoned that programs are not transmitted to cyberspace but through it. The second issue was dealt with in an exemption order for broadcasting services delivered over the Internet to include alphanumeric text, customizable content, and video game programming. The report concurred with the views of industry that the distinguishing features of multimedia are neutral and technological including the use of digitization, interactivity, and interconnected networks (CRTC 1999a, 5–11). In 1998, the CRTC dealt with telecommunications issues by approving tariffs and interconnection rules in which cable and telephone companies could provide higher-speed access to their Internet telecommunications facilities and to Internet service providers (ISPs). Essentially, the report delivers an industrial development policy approach to multimedia services rather than policy in the civic/cultural public interest.

MYTH AND MULTIMEDIA

While there has been much new content produced with the Internet and multimedia, perhaps one of the greatest successes has been the production of myths. Of the many that abound about the Internet or the information highway, two are particularly relevant for multimedia. One involves the benefits of a market-only approach, the second that there is actually a free market approach to content and culture.

The theory of the market approach to networks and content services, as opposed to the traditional equity or universality approach, is that networks and services are developed and made available where capital investment is recoverable and revenues are sufficient to maintain them. This ensures that economic resources are used to their maximum efficiency. Competitive markets, free of distorting public interference, induce firms to increase efficiency, introduce technical innovations, and reduce their costs. The most efficient and innovative firms become the market winners, and individuals, as consumers, benefit from the choice of products available and lower prices.

   In the United States, and more recently in Canada, the unregulated, free
market is pitched as the most rational, fair, and democratic system for producers and consumers. Distortions from government regulation and public
policy are removed or lessened. The expected results are that a vibrant competitive Internet and multimedia economy will be open to both producers or
consumers. As with Canada, government justification for this policy shift also
includes the need to develop new technologies and help domestic companies compete in the international marketplace (Reddick 1999, 86; McChesney 1999, 137).
   However, the structure and practices of the multimedia industries in both
countries suggest that reality is different from the myth. As opposed to vibrant competition, there is instead greater concentration of ownership and
control of networks and content. The power of dominant firms in communications subsectors has been extended to the whole sector. And while there
has been a short-term flurry of new entrants and competition, success and
profitability for any company over the long term, given the immense investments necessary to participate in the market and to gain and hold market
share, means that a major goal has to be the elimination of as much competition as possible. As noted by Robert McChesney (1999, 137), if the market
myth was real, then why have not the companies dominating the communications sector fallen apart and been unseated by these changes? In practice,
we see greater emphasis on market position and profitability, which is determined largely by audience size, advertising revenue, and exportable products (such as multimedia, broadcasting, or telecommunications services) to
increase revenues and expand in the lucrative international marketplace
(Mosco and Reddick 1997, 24).
   Moreover, governments in both countries have provided major subsidies
to help create these "market" approach networks and services. In the United
States, for example, perhaps the largest corporate subsidies in history continue to be awarded under the veil of national security and defense spending, some of which support the development of multimedia. For example, in
terms of Internet and related communications industry support, over 85 percent of the research and development costs in the electronics industry have
been supported by the government (McChesney 1999, 142). Through the
1996 Telecommunications Act, public subsidies have also been created to facilitate public access, such as the e-rate initiative. Providing subsidies for Internet connectivity to libraries, schools, and community access centers, these
monies invariably support the investments and development initiatives of
the dominant communications companies. In Canada, the Community Access Program, SchoolNet, and LibraryNet programs perform similar functions. While on the one hand there is an equity aspect to the initiatives because they do afford low-income and other disadvantaged citizens with
access, on the other hand the rationale underlying these efforts is also as
much about creating or extending the consumer market for commercial mul-

timedia products and services. These examples belie the claims that the market is either able to provide affordable service and useful content to these segments of the public, or to roll out infrastructure and services without massive public subsidy.

Perhaps one of the most outrageous myths involves content development. While there are some similarities between Canada and the United States in that both support content, Canada's cultural policy approach is overtly and purposely designed to prevent or lessen continental integration in this area. There are two aspects to the myths involving content development. The United States, in attacking the domestic content development and protection policies and initiatives of Canada and other countries, has long advanced the view that all forms of such content support are major distortions that undermine the normal operation of the marketplace. Canada, for example, has been recently threatened with a trade war over culture by the United States, because as trade lawyer James Blanchard puts it, Canada sees culture as a nonmarket social resource important to national and individual interests and betterment, whereas the United States sees content and multimedia as "products of a wealthy, entertainment industry in search of a worldwide free market" (quoted in Kenna 1999). In this view, culture and content are simply commodities like any other and should not be the subject of special protection or public support. In practice, however, we find that the level of in digenous multimedia content and cultural support development in the United States dwarfs the protective efforts of Canada and most other countries. However, unlike Canada, much of the support in the United States is not done through telecommunications and broadcasting policy avenues. In fact, the existence and levels of support for content development in both countries is a continuation of long-standing policies in other areas of media—whether film, print, or music—in the support of the development of indigenous commercial and noncommercial information products.

A 1999 study completed by CICITT Incorporated found that while the U.S. industry is dominant in the world as the developer, producer, supplier, and exporter of multimedia, these efforts have been largely promoted by the U.S. government. Support includes providing "massive funding and support through a variety of industrial programs, including research and development, public projects and programs at both the state and federal levels, and through its multi–billion dollar defense and aerospace programs" (1999, 58–59). Content development is also supported through procurement by state and federal governments, and the transportation, education, and health sectors. The report goes on to note that "few if any other countries can afford to take this approach which should not be mistaken for a laissez-faire approach to multimedia technology and content" (59). The three largest government agencies involved in the support of multimedia content in the areas of education, arts, heritage, and culture are: the National Endowment for the Arts (e.g., $94 million in support in 1997), the National Endowment for the

Humanities (e.g., several hundred million dollars in support since the 1970s, including $12 million for education and access and $30.5 million for cultural content development in 1999), and the U.S. Department of Education (e.g., $132 million in Challenge Grants, $50 million in school content support for literacy and the underserved, and $75 million in teacher assistance with new technologies in 1999). Other initiatives, many of which include private-sector partnerships or support, also involve the National Aeronautics and Space Administration, the National Science Foundation, the Department of Energy, the Department of Defense, the Defense Advanced Research Projects Agency, the National Library of Medicine, the Library of Congress, and the Smithsonian Institution (63).

The second aspect of this content myth, and an interesting contradiction, is that Canadian policy support for multimedia content largely focuses on the development of commercial content by private companies as opposed to public noncommercial content. This is a shift away from a more balanced tradition and reflects the closer integration of values and practices in content production, at least in industrial content development, on a continental basis. As such, with the exception of some smaller initiatives, Canadian content policy support has largely been driven by that very American ideal of industrial policy as public interest. The Department of Canadian Heritage established a separate funding mechanism for multimedia. The Multimedia Fund is part of the federal government's "Connecting Canadians" agenda. Commencing in 1998–1999, government funding of $30 million Canadian over a five-year period is provided. The fund, which is administered by Telefilm Canada, assists with the development, production, distribution, and marketing of Canadian cultural multimedia products in both French and English (Canada 1998). Interest-free repayable contributions are provided for this new cultural industry in order to increase production and improve distribution of Canadian educational or entertainment cultural content. Multimedia enterprises will have access to an interest-free advance of up to 50 percent of their development budget to a maximum of $75,000. An interest-free, fully repayable loan will be available for up to 50 percent of the production budget, to a maximum of $250,000. Additionally, an interest-free fully repayable loan is also available for up to 50 percent of a company's marketing budget, to a maximum of $150,000. A third of the funds are to be allocated to French-language products, and incentives will be offered for projects delivered in both English and French (Rideout 1998, 22–23).

What qualifies as multimedia services is digital technology that allows graphics, live video, animation, text, fixed images, audio, and data to be delivered simultaneously to a computer screen, enabling users to interact with the content. Examples of multimedia content include long-distance learning products, virtual tours of heritage sites, and interactive games for children, among others. These services may be delivered on CD-ROM, through the Internet, or via a personal computer and cable television. Eligibility was expanded to small- and medium-sized businesses with less than two hundred full-time employees and earnings of less than $12 million annually.

The Department of Canadian Heritage has also established a new directorate that, in part, is responsible for multimedia development. The main purpose of the directorate is to provide a policy framework for the development of content, though largely in support of electronic commerce and cultural industries development. However, support had not been developed for citizenship and other forms of noncommercial multimedia content (Public Interest Advocacy Centre/Canadian Library Association 1999).

Other funds that help finance multimedia content include the Bell Multimedia Fund, and before that the former Stentor Fund. Recent programs by Industry Canada have been targeted toward Canadian multimedia content in the entertainment and educational genres. Support for Canadian multimedia content and to nurture the multimedia industry has also been provided by such government departments as Human Resources Development Canada, the Department of Foreign Affairs and International Trade, and Industry Canada. These departments share in the government's "Connecting All Canadians" agenda, announced in the 1998 budget. This agenda has six areas of emphasis for national leadership in multimedia that are intended to ensure that, among other things, all Canadians will have access to multimedia, that the country will be a leader in electronic commerce, and that Canadian content will occupy a place of prominence on the Internet (Rideout 1999).

As part of resistance against full continental and international integration, the Canadian government, concerned with the effect that the WTO's policy recommendations will have on culture including audiovisual services, has recommended that a Coalition for Cultural Diversity (CCD) be established that would allow countries to maintain their domestic cultural polices, but without compromising access to foreign markets (*Canadian Communications Reports* 1999). Just how successful the CCD will be depends on whether there is enough support from other countries. The United States is not supportive of this initiative. Certainly, the OECD's position on content touts the liberalization line. The OECD and the United States have endorsed the development of the Global Information Infrastructure (GII) stating that it will provide more equitable access to all media and content resources.[3] What is really at issue here is the new markets that the digital communications networks promise in which content is viewed as a new growth industry (OECD 1998).

In both Canada and the United States, there is, however, considerable demand by the public and public interest group organizations for a great diversity of community, citizenship, and cultural information resources, especially noncommercial content. While the commercial multimedia companies produce content of value for people as consumers (e.g., entertainment, news, and so on), the public values and demands as much, if not more, socially relevant information (Ekos Research Associates 1998, 2000). In Canada, a broad range of public institutions, community organizations, and cultural groups have been actively involved in the development of this socio-cultural content. However, this has been done with little direct support from government or industry. What help does exist pales in comparison to the support provided by government for the development of commercial content. Moreover, support for this type of content in Canada is a fraction of that provided by the U.S. government for noncommercial cultural and social content (Reddick 1998).

In the United States, while there are numerous programs (discussed earlier) that support certain types of public content, there is also widespread demand for more efforts in this area to meet the broader information needs of the public. The educational, civic, community, and other groups interested in using digital communications to extend their efforts in the multimedia arena often lack the skills and resources to achieve these goals. For example, Connecticut Public Broadcasting Incorporated is spearheading an initiative to form alliances with social groups to ensure that multimedia content is available that meets individuals' lifelong learning, civic citizenship, health, artistic, and cultural life needs (Connecticut Public Broadcasting 2000). This aims to meet the challenge that the Children's Partnership describes as "severe gaps in Internet content meeting the needs of low income and immigrant groups, despite their increasing use of the Internet" (Children's Partnership 2000). Even the presidential Public Interest Advisory Committee's recommendations on public interest obligations for digital television and programming identified diversity of content as a major problem. Though only writing on the digital television aspect of multimedia, problems with other formats were also identified. The committee's recommendations called for the creation of noncommercial digital channels for education purposes and the expansion of public interest obligations through regulation (Sommerset-Ward 1999). The National Telecommunications and Information Administration (NTIA) has similarly raised concerns about the lack of a true diversity of content in the digital age. In a letter submission to an FCC review of broadcast ownership rules, the NTIA called for constitutional protection for diversity of information and views in an attempt to convince the FCC to apply, in both spirit and practice, the public interest obligations of the U.S. Telecommunications Act section 202 (h), as opposed to relying lamely on competition as a surrogate for this. Public interest groups in Canada have similarly found their national regulator, the CRTC, to either not understand social and cultural needs and diversity, or simply take comfort in ignorance and ideology, rather than make the effort required for insight, balance, and fairness (Irving 1999).

In many respects, the elites in both the U.S. and Canadian governments, also largely proponents of the reliance on a competitive market approach, have, to date, not fully grasped or understood the importance and attraction of diverse public sociocultural information resources for the public, whether in multimedia or traditional formats. While there is no shortage of information on CDs or the Internet, there is a shortage of relevant, quality, and diverse information resources to meet the various segments of the public's full range of economic, social, cultural, and citizenship needs (Reddick, Boucher, and Groseilliers 2000, 56–57).

CONCLUSION

While some multimedia is new and has been created in a form that is unique to CD-ROMs or the Internet, as of yet the majority of the content combined into a multimedia format and distribution is content that has been produced in other traditional formats, such as film, print, music, and so on. Much of this content has been, historically and currently, regulated by national governments and supported through various fiscal and program initiatives. The purposes underlying such regulation and other support include industrial, social, cultural, and political policy objectives. Contrary to the objective of creating an integrated continental market, these cultural and content policy objectives in both the United States and Canada are primarily geared to domestic industrial development and, in the case of Canada, complemented with attempts to preserve indigenous cultural integrity. The combination of these policy objectives with varying degrees of emphasis comprised what has been considered to be public interest policy and regulation.

The similarity of the United States and Canada adopting complementary or a continental nonregulation or selective application of regulation approach to multimedia and the Internet has two major implications. First, redefining traditional media as part of multimedia or extending the umbrella of multimedia to cover traditional media, creates pressures to extend the exemptions for companies from social and cultural obligations afforded multimedia. Second, the competitive market and national economic development goals for multimedia by government, without the concurrent application of social and cultural policy objectives (through regulation or other forms of support), redefine and narrow the conception and practice of public interest to that of industrial development that is primarily geared to export. Moreover, pressures by industry and international trade regimes to extend this reregulatory framework to traditional forms of media would mean that the public interest, traditionally incorporating the sum balance of economic, social, and cultural objectives, would similarly be redefined as industrial policy, and the citizen's stakes in this would be reduced to that of shoppers choosing among products and services. This would further economic integration of Canada and the United States at a continental level, and result in the erosion of regulations, programs, and other forms of support that ensured that some equitable balance existed between the needs of business and citizens.

The issue is not whether multimedia and the Internet can or cannot be regulated. In point of fact, both are extensively regulated now and this will

likely increase in the future. For example, the CRTC has established a policy on third-party ISP interconnection on cable systems to facilitate competition and consumer choice of existing and new services. As of the first
part of 2001, the FCC was still dithering on this issue. The CRTC also ex-
empts other nonprogramming content. Multimedia is also subject to existing offensive content, hate, libel, and copyright laws. Consumer protection
laws also have some application to such new services or transactions involving these services and content. In Canada, the federal government
passed a new privacy law in the spring of 2000 that provided some regulation of the use of personal information for transactions involving the Internet, e-commerce, and multimedia.

The concepts of regulation and policy have many different meanings for
different interests. Often, the term "regulation" is considered at a generalized all-encompassing level, rather than with specificity. As such, "all or
nothing" perspectives are adopted whether or not there is a role for regulation. Markets do not, however, emerge naturally on their own. They are
created by government and its agencies that set the frameworks and rules
of the road and provide incentives; by companies that make decisions and
investments that privilege certain structures, practices, and products/ser-
vices over others; and by consumers who, depending upon financial circumstances and need, purchase products in the market. In addition to
commercial, market-based products, there are also numerous public
goods or nonmarket products and services that people require to satisfy
other needs, such as sociocultural and civic activities and interests. The
provision of these also requires a public governance role in the establishment of frameworks, rules, and investment relating to the development,
distribution, and access to these products and services. However, an un-
resolved tension now exists between those efforts to further integrate the
economic and industrial aspects of communications at a continental level,
and the need to continue older forms of domestic regulation and to
achieve economic, social, and cultural objectives.

Multimedia does not stand alone from our broadcasting and telecommunications networks and services, but is a component of these. In many ways, at
the heart of the debate on whether there will be some need for regulatory
oversight, now or in several years' time, and what form that should take, if required, is the historical difference between those who perceive and use communications networks and services as commercial, private economic undertakings, and those who perceive and use them for economic participation, as
well as for essential social and other noneconomic undertakings. So, on the
one hand, there is an argument for economic efficiency and industrial policy,
and on the other, there is the argument for equity, access, and social policy.

Broadly speaking, government or public regulation in both countries,
though to different degrees, has traditionally been undertaken as a means for
achieving a balance in these industrial, cultural, social, and political policy

objectives. Regulation is also seen as a tool in both countries, when necessary, to rationalize the economy or economic activity in a sector, such as in response to monopolies, market power by incumbents, and so on, and safeguarding the public interest. Industries that have been subject to some form of regulation, and different degrees of regulation at different junctures, include communications, transportation, financial services, and energy. What is common to these and the social decision to apply some form of ongoing public oversight through regulation is that these are infrastructural or essential services that underlie all economic and many social activities. The rationale for regulation, then, is that these are infrastructures necessary for access by all under reasonable terms in order to participate in society. Robert Horwitz has called these infrastructures "connective institutions" that are "channels for trade and discourse which bind together a community, society or nation" (1989, 7, 9, 14). Where communications differs from other utilities and commodities is that, in addition to playing a fundamental role in facilitating economic activities and participation, communications has a central role in the circulation of information and is a means for democratic communication and participation.

Another form of regulation is market decision making. Investment decisions relating to network and product design, infrastructure deployment, content, and services by companies will largely form multimedia and the related communications marketplace over the next several years. Some of the most dominant of these companies are based in the United States and already have a firm command of the continental marketplace. Is such market decision making—undertaken without some framework or level of supervision afforded by the Canadian and U.S. governments and their regulatory agencies, the CRTC and the FCC—sufficient to meet the diverse needs of the public and the objectives of each nation's communications laws? Based on the logic of the market, and historical example (e.g., the development of radio and television), the answer is no.[4]

Increased government regulation in both countries of multimedia and the Internet will be accomplished through the efforts of both industry and public interest groups. The types of regulation likely to be sought by industry (and in some instances already being advocated) include copyright protection, protection of financial investments, offensive content, security of transactions, protection and recourse against hackers and those creating computer viruses, and ongoing tax exemptions, among others. For example, in September 1999, the Global Business Dialog on Electronic Commerce released a set of proposals to regulate the Internet to make it easier for companies to conduct business in cyberspace (Boudette 1999). The challenge for public interest groups for better regulation is greater than for industry given the current industrial development bias of policy.

There are, however, many different ways that governments can regulate. Traditional regulatory tools can still be relevant, though how they are applied may need to vary. If some of these traditional mechanisms are considered to be unwieldy or ineffective, there are other options, some of which have been created by multimedia technology. For example, Lawrence Lessig argues that because computer code (that which runs, shapes, designs, and operates multimedia and the Internet) can be programmed to any purpose, it can also be written to ensure public interest objectives (1999, 20). This of course requires awareness and will on the part of policymakers, and new regulatory approaches to extend national policy frameworks and objectives to this end. This raises the issue of the yet unaddressed need for greater collaboration between Canadian and U.S. regulatory agencies and government policy departments. This is necessary to explore and develop ways to effectively deal with and regulate market behavior on a continental, in addition to a solely domestic, basis. Required contributions by companies for indigenous content development, Web portal design, cataloging Web information, and many other possibilities can easily be accomplished through existing, traditional regulatory tools—all that is missing is will on the part of governments. These types of initiatives are critical to balance economic and industrial policy objectives and market interests with those of social and cultural policy and the interests and needs of citizens.

There are a few differences between Canada and the United States in the treatment of multimedia as a cultural or commodity product that appear to go against continental integration. By and large, however, multimedia policy treatment in both countries to advance industrial development, to not regulate the Internet, and to exclude public interest multimedia content helps further continental integration.

NOTES

Unless otherwise noted, all dollar amounts are in U.S. currency.

1. According to Lévy, new information and communications technologies have the potential to expand and enhance human cognition (1997, 90).

2. Selected countries include Belgium, Denmark, Finland, France, Germany, Greece, Ireland, Italy, Luxembourg, the Netherlands, Norway, Portugal, Spain, Sweden, Switzerland, and the United Kingdom.

3. GII principles include the encouragement of private-sector investment, the promotion of competition, open access to telecommunications networks for information providers and users, and flexible regulatory environments that keep pace with technology and market change (OECD 1998).

4. While substantively different in terms of content, from an industrial and structural perspective, early radio was as "open" as the Internet in its infancy. The broadcast model, as opposed to a continuation of a fully interactive open model for radio, was greatly facilitated by licensing through regulation, a reliance on advertising for revenues, among other factors. See McChesney (1994) and Vipond (1989).

REFERENCES

Boudette, Neal. 1999. "Business Unveils Scheme to Regulate Internet." *Financial Post*, 13 September, C10.

Canada. 1988. *The Canada–US Free Trade Agreement*. Ottawa: Minister of Supply and Services Canada.

———. 1992. *North American Free Trade Agreement*. Ottawa: Minister of Supply and Services Canada.

———. 1998. "Copps Launches Multimedia Fund." Canadian Heritage News Release, Ottawa, 8 June.

———. 1999. *Canada and the Future of the World Trade Organization*. Government Response to the Report of the Standing Committee on Foreign Affairs and International Trade. Ottawa: Minister of Public Works and Government Services Canada.

Canadian Communications Reports. 1999. 24 November, vol. 25, no. 18.

Canadian Radio-Television and Telecommunications Commission. 1999a. *Report on New Media*. Ottawa: Supply and Services. <http://www.crtc.gc.ca> [last accessed. 16 February 2001].

———. 1999b. "CRTC Won't Regulate the Internet." *News Release*, 17 May, 2.

Children's Partnership. 2000. "The Digital Divide's New Frontier." 23 March. <http://www.childrenspartnership.org/pub/ibw-income/index/html> [last accessed: 1 April 2000].

CICITT Inc. 1999. "Development and Access to Multimedia Content: An International Comparison of Policies, Programs, and Practices." A Report to Canadian Heritage and Industry Canada (July).

Connecticut Public Broadcasting Incorporated. 2000. "The Mapping the Assets (MTA) Plan." <http://www.mappingtheassets.org> [last accessed: 15 January 2001].

Ekos Research Associates. 1998. *The Information Highway and the Canadian Communications Household*. Ottawa: Ekos Research Associates.

———. 2000. *Rethinking the Information Highway: Privacy, Access, and the Shifting Marketplace*. Ottawa: Ekos Research Associates.

Horwitz, Robert. 1989. *The Irony of Regulatory Reform*. Oxford: Oxford University Press.

Industry Canada. 2000. "John Manley Announces the Awarding of Multipoint Communication." *Connecting Canadians*, 24 March. <http://www.connect.ge.ca/en/ne/1510-e.htm> [last accessed: 16 February 2001].

Irving, L. 1999. Letter to FCC MM Docket no. 91-221 and MM Docket no. 98-35 NTIA. 12 February.

Kenna, Kathleen. 1999. "Work Out Cultural Deal or Face Trade War, U.S. Warns Canada." *Toronto Star*, 21 November. <http://www.thestar.ca/> [last accessed: 1 April 2000].

Kennard, W. 1999. "The Unregulation of the Internet: Laying a Competitive Course for the Future." Speech to the Federal Communications Bar, San Francisco, 20 July <http://www.fcc.gov/speeches/kennard/spwek924.html> [last accessed: 11 February 2001].

Lessig, Lawrence. 1999. *Code and Other Laws of Cyberspace*. New York: Basic.

Lévy, Pierre. 1997. *Cyberculture*. Paris: Editions Odile Jacob.

McChesney, Robert. 1994. *Telecommunications, Mass Media, and Democracy, 1928–1935*. New York: Oxford University Press.

———. 1999. *Rich Media, Poor Democracy: Communication Politics in Dubious Times.* Urbana: University of Illinois Press.

Monaco, James. 2000. *How to Read a Film: Movies, Media, Multimedia.* 3rd ed. New York: Oxford University Press.

Mosco, Vincent. 1999. "Place Matters: Citizenship and the New Computer Technopolis." In *The Communications Revolution at Work,* ed. R. Boyce. Montreal: McGill-Queen's University Press.

Mosco, Vincent, and Andrew Reddick. 1997. "Political Economy, Communication, and Policy." In *Democratizing Communication?* ed. M. Bailie and D. Winseck. Cresskill, N.J.: Hampton.

Mosco, Vincent, and Vanda Rideout. 1997. "Media Policy in North America." In *International Media Research: A Critical Survey,* ed. J. Corner, P. Schlesinger, and R. Silverstone. New York: Routledge.

Organization for Economic Cooperation and Development. 1998. "Content as a New Growth Industry." Directorate for Science, Technology, and Industry. OSTI/ICCP/IG (96) 6/ Final. Paris: Organization for Economic Cooperation and Development, 1–25 May.

Oxman, Jason. 1999. "The FCC and the Unregulation of the Internet." Office of Plans and Policy, Working Paper No. 31. Washington, D.C.: Federal Communications Commission.

Poster, Mark. 1995. *The Second Media Age.* Cambridge: Polity.

Public Interest Advocacy Centre and Action Réseau Consommateur. 1998. "Submission of the Public Interest Advocacy Centre and Action Réseau Consommateur to Telecom Public Notice CRTC 98-20-1 and Broadcasting Public Notice CRTC 1998-82-1 New Media—Call for Comments." Ottawa: Public Interest Advocacy Centre.

Public Interest Advocacy Centre/Canadian Library Association. 1999. Minutes of PIAC/CLA key stakeholder meeting. Ottawa, 3 March.

Reddick, Andrew. 1998. *Community Networks and Access Initiatives in Canada.* Ottawa: Public Interest Advocacy Canada.

———. 1999. "Access and the Information Highway." In *The Communications Revolution at Work: The Social, Economic, and Political Impacts of Technological Change,* ed. R. Boyce. Montreal: McGill-Queen's University Press.

Reddick, Andrew, Christian Boucher, and Manon Groseilliers. 2000. *The Dual Digital Divide: The Information Highway in Canada.* Ottawa: Public Interest Advocacy Centre (with funding from Human Resources Development Canada and Industry Canada).

Rideout, Vanda. 1998. "Broadcasting Policy Review for Community Access Initiatives: Limitations and Advantages." Prepared for Industry Canada's Information Highway Applications Branch, Ottawa (July).

———. 1999. "Connecting Canadians—In Whose Interests?" Paper prepared for the Canadian Communication Association Conference for the Canadian Social Sciences and Humanities Congress, Sherbrooke, Quebec, May.

Rideout, Vanda, and Vincent Mosco. 1997. "Communication Policy in the United States." In *Democratizing Communication? Comparative Perspectives on Information and Power,* ed. M. Bailie and D. Winseck. Cresskill, N.J.: Hampton.

Robins, Kevin, and Frank Webster. 1999. *Times of the Technoculture.* New York: Routledge.

Schiller, Dan. 1982. *Telematics and Government.* Norwood, N.J.: Ablex.

———. 1999. *Digital Capitalism: Networking the Global Market System.* Cambridge: Massachusetts Institute of Technology Press.

Sommerset-Ward, Richard. 1999. "Public Interest Obligations in Broadcasting: International Comparisons." Benton Foundation. *The Digital Divide Beat* 1 (5) (16 April).

Streeter, Thomas. 1996. *Selling the Air: A Critique of the Policy of Commercial Broadcasting in the United States.* Chicago: University of Chicago Press.

Vipond, Mary. 1989. *The Mass Media in Canada.* Toronto: Lorimer.

Wall Communications. 1998. "Study on Mechanisms to Promote Development and Distribution of Canadian Multimedia and Other New Media Content and Services." Ottawa: Canadian Heritage and Canadian Radio-Television and Telecommunication Commission, 31 March.

Warnock, John W. 1988. *Free Trade and the New Right Agenda.* Vancouver: New Star Books.

World Trade Organization. 1995. *Trading into the Future.* Geneva: World Trade Organization.

———. 1998a. "Audiovisual Services." S/C/W/40 98-2437 (June): 1–19.

———. 1998b. *Electronic Commerce and the Role of the WTO.* Geneva: World Trade Organization

Index

About the Contributors

Jonathan Burston is an assistant professor at the department of culture and communication at New York University. The recent holder of a Social Sciences and Humanities Research Council (Canada) Postdoctoral Fellowship, he previously held Fulbright and Commonwealth Scholarships. Burston's most recent publication, "Spectacle, Synergy, and Megamusicals: The Global-Industrialisation of the Live-Entertainment Economy," is found in *Media Organisations in Society* (2000). His book on the same topic is forthcoming. Burston's current research is on Siliwood, Las Vegas, multimedia convergence, and the coming era of digitally produced "synthespianism."

Richard B. Du Boff is a professor of economics emeritus at Bryn Mawr College. He has also taught at the Institute of Social Studies (The Hague) and had fellowships from the National Science Foundation and National Endowment for the Humanities. His articles have appeared in a number of journals, and he is currently working on "global capital" as a new stage of accumulation, as well as revising his *Accumulation and Power: An Economic History of the United States* (1989).

Richard Gruneau is a professor of communication at Simon Fraser University in Burnaby, British Columbia. He received his masters in sociology from the University of Calgary, and his doctorate in sociology from the University of Massachusetts. Professor Gruneau has written or coauthored three books and edited or coedited four other books on communication, popular culture, sport, and the media.

Ted Magder is the director of communication studies and an associate professor of media ecology at New York University (NYU). He is the author of

Canada's Hollywood: Feature Films and the Canadian State (1993) and *Franchising the Candy Store: Split-Run Magazines and a New International Regime for Trade in Culture* (1998). Magder has also published numerous articles on the political economy of the cultural industries and the international trade in media products. Born in Toronto, Magder was the director of the mass communication programme at York University from 1987 to 1996. He coteaches a NYU–University of Amsterdam summer abroad course on media globalization. In 1991, Magder won the Distinguished Teacher of the Year Award in the Faculty of Arts at York University. In 1986 Magder was a postdoctoral fellow at the University of Westminster's Centre for Communication and Information Studies in London.

Catherine McKercher is an associate professor in the School of Journalism and Communication at Carleton University in Ottawa, Canada. She has worked as a wire service and newspaper reporter and editor in Canada and the United States and is coauthor of *The Canadian Reporter* (1998). She is currently working on a book about labor union convergence in the North American media.

Vincent Mosco is a professor of communication, sociology, and political economy at Carleton University. He received his doctorate in sociology from Harvard University. Professor Mosco is the author of four books and editor or coeditor of seven books on telecommunications, mass media, computers, and information technology. His most recent book is *The Political Economy of Communication: Rethinking and Renewal* (1996). Professor Mosco is a member of the editorial boards of academic journals in the United States, Canada, and England. He has held research positions and served as a consultant to governments, universities, corporations, and trade unions in North America, Asia, and Africa. Professor Mosco is currently working on a Canadian government-funded research grant to address the rise of postindustrial high-technology districts and is completing a book on mythologies of cyberspace.

Mari Castañeda Paredes is an assistant professor in the department of communication at the University of Massachusetts at Amherst. Her areas of interest include the political economy of communication, media, and public policy, telecommunications history, and new media activism.

Andrew Paxman is a graduate student at the University of California at Berkeley. For eight years he was a journalist in Latin America, chiefly Mexico City, spending five of those years as the regional correspondent for *Variety*. With journalist Claudia Fernández, he is coauthor of *El Tigre: Emilio Azcárraga y su imperio Televisa (Grijalbo)* (2000), a biography of the late media mogul Emilio Azcárraga Milmo, which became an instant bestseller following its publication.

Andrew Reddick is a policy and government relations consultant based in Canada. He specializes in the political economy of public policy and regulation primarily in communications, but also in matters relating to transportation, financial services, and privacy. He has authored and coauthored a number of reports, articles, and book chapters on communications and other policy issues. Recent publications include: *The Dual Digital Divide: The Information Highway in Canada* (2000) and "Access and the Information Highway" in *The Communications Revolution at Work* (1999).

Vanda Rideout is an assistant professor of sociology at the University of New Brunswick. She has published research on telecommunications policy and the social impacts of new media in Canada.

Enrique E. Sánchez-Ruiz is a professor in the department of social communication at the University of Guadalajara. He received his doctorate in education and international development from Stanford University in 1984. He is the author of ten books on various aspects of communication, culture, film, and development. He has served as the president of the Mexican Association of Communication Research and the president of the Latin American Association of Communication Researchers.

Alex M. Saragoza received his doctorate from the University of California at San Diego and teaches history in the department of ethnic studies at the University of California at Berkeley, where he has also served as the chair of the Center for Latin American Studies and as the codirector of the Berkeley-Stanford Federal Resource Center on Latin American Studies. A specialist in modern Mexican history, he is currently working on a book-length study of Mexican tourism, focusing on the development of Acapulco in the post–World War II era. He is the author of *The Monterrey Elite and the Mexican State, 1880–1940* (1989) and a forthcoming study, *The State and the Media in Mexico: The Origins of Televisa*.

Dan Schiller is a professor of library and information science, communications, and media studies at the University of Illinois at Urbana-Champaign. He received his doctorate in communication from the Annenberg School of Communication at the University of Pennsylvania. Professor Schiller has also held academic appointments at Temple University, the University of California at Los Angeles, and the University of California at San Diego. He is the author of four books on the history of the press, the history of communications studies, and the political economy of telecommunications and new information technologies, the most recent being *Digital Capitalism* (1999). He has served on the editorial boards of scholarly journals in the United States, England, and Spain, and as an adviser to government agencies and universities in the United States and abroad. He is a continuing contributor to *Le Monde Diplomatique*.

Gerald Sussman is a professor of urban studies and communications at Portland State University. He is the author of *Communication, Technology, and Politics in the Information Age* (1997) and coeditor of *Global Productions: Labor in the Making of the "Information Society"* (1998) and *Transnational Communications: Wiring the Third World* (1991).

Lora E. Taub received her doctorate in communication from the University of California at San Diego. Her dissertation, *Enterprising Drama: The Rise of Commercial Theater in Early Modern London*, laid both the theoretical and historical basis for her subsequent work on cultural commodification and new media technologies. Having completed fieldwork for an ethnographic study of technology practices in an elementary school in São Paulo, Brazil, she is now assistant professor of communication at Muhlenberg College.

David Whitson is a professor of Canadian studies at the University of Alberta. He writes regularly on sport, popular culture, tourism, and cities; and has coauthored *Hockey Night in Canada: Sport, Identities, and Cultural Politics* (with Richard Gruneau) (1993)and *The Game Planners: Transforming Canada's Sport System* (with Don Macintosh) (1990).